THE GOVERNOR GENERAL'S HORSE GUARDS:

SECOND TO NONE

The motto of The Governor General's Horse Guards is

NULLI SECUNDUS,

which translates from Latin as

SECOND TO NONE.

*The concept embodied in this motto eloquently expresses the
ethos of the Regiment, to strive always for the highest standards
and best quality, and reflects the relentless determination of its
members, past, present and future, to do their best.*

The third Standard of The Governor General's Horse Guards, presented in October 1994. (GGHG Archives)

BATTLE HONOURS

North West Canada 1885

South Africa 1900

Mount Sorrel, Somme 1916, Flers-Courcelette, Ancre Heights, **Arras 1917, '18, Vimy 1917, Hill 70, Ypres 1917, Passchendaele, Amiens,** Scarpe 1918, Hindenburg Line, Canal du Nord, **Cambrai 1918,** Valenciennes, Sambre, France and Flanders 1915-18

Liri Valley, Melfa Crossing, Gothic Line, Lamone Crossing, Misano Ridge, Fosso Munio, Italy 1944-1945, Ijsselmeer, North West Europe 1945

BATTLE HONOURS SHOWN IN BOLD TYPE WERE SELECTED TO BE
EMBLAZONED ON THE REGIMENTAL STANDARD

THE GOVERNOR GENERAL'S HORSE GUARDS

Second to None

John Marteinson

with

Scott Duncan

Maps and drawings by
Christopher Johnson

Published for
THE GOVERNOR GENERAL'S
HORSE GUARDS FOUNDATION

by
ROBIN BRASS STUDIO
Toronto

Published and distributed for
The Governor General's Horse Guards Foundation
137 Hall Street, Richmond Hill, Ontario L4C 4N9, Canada
by
Robin Brass Studio Inc.
10 Blantyre Avenue, Toronto, Ontario M1N 2R4, Canada
Fax: 416-698-2120 / www.rbstudiobooks.com

Printed and bound in Canada by Friesens, Altona, Manitoba

National Library of Canada Cataloguing in Publication

Marteinson, J. K. (John Kristjan), 1939-
    The Governor General's Horse Guards : second to none /
John Marteinson with Scott Duncan.

Includes bibliographical references and index.
ISBN 1-896941-28-1

1. Canada. Canadian Army. Governor General's Horse Guards –
History. I. Duncan, Scott (Scott M.) II. Title.

UA602.G682M37 2002   358'.18'0971   C2002-903404-3

THE GOVERNOR GENERAL'S HORSE GUARDS, which has inherited the history and traditions of many antecedent units, along with those of its British Allied Regiments The Blues and Royals and The 1st The Queen's Dragoon Guards, has the proud distinction of having the longest continuous service of any regiment in the Canadian Army. Button's Troop, organized in 1810 as part of the 1st York Regiment of Militia, was the first cavalry formed in Canada. Denison's Troop, formed in 1822 and granted the title the Governor General's Body Guard in 1866, was acknowledged in the 19th century to be the finest body of volunteer cavalry in the country. The Mississauga Horse, dating from 1904, was a dashing sister Toronto cavalry unit with whom the Body Guard was amalgamated in 1936.

The 4th Canadian Mounted Rifles, raised for service in the First World War by both the Body Guard and the Mississauga Horse, was one of the truly élite units of the Canadian Corps on the Western Front between 1916 and 1918, and is now officially perpetuated by the Horse Guards. Over the whole of its long existence, citizen soldiers of this Regimental family have served Crown, Empire, Commonwealth and country with pride, dedication and devotion. They have demonstrated their loyalty and readiness to serve the causes of justice and freedom on many occasions over nearly two centuries – the War of 1812, the rebellions of 1837 and 1885, the South African War, the First and Second World Wars, Korea and far-flung peacekeeping missions. I also note this Regiment's long tradition of providing guards and escorts to members of the Royal Family and Vice-Regal representatives. The history of The Governor General's Horse Guards should indeed be an inspiration to all Canadians who value worthy ideals, pride in past accomplishments and aspiration to excellence.

In this my Jubilee year, as Colonel-in-Chief of The Governor General's Horse Guards, I welcome this new history of the Regiment.

ELIZABETH R.

RIDEAU HALL

THE GOVERNOR GENERAL'S HORSE GUARDS is the oldest and most distinguished continuing regiment in Canada, both in the militia and regular Canadian Forces. The Horse Guards have always loyally escorted Governors, Governors General, Lieutenant Governors and members of the Royal Family.

The Governor General's Horse Guards: Second to None highlights the accomplishments of civilians who, to this day, commit to serve Canada in times of conflict and fulfill ceremonial roles with pomp and dignity. The individual and collective availability of the Horse Guards, their courage and willingness to train in times of peace and fight in times of war are inspiring. Canadians can be proud of their military excellence.

Although the regiment's early history is based around the early British settlers in the Toronto area, it has always been reflective of the growing multicultural mosaic of our country. It is this typical Canadian openness that has helped the Horse Guards create great alliances and amalgamate successfully with other regiments, while keeping its noble identity.

I am very grateful to The Governor General's Horse Guards Foundation for supporting this publication and for promoting the heroic deeds of those who served and still serve in its ranks. This book is a most valuable addition to our military history.

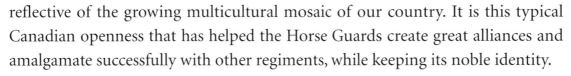

Adrienne Clarkson
Governor General of Canada
Colonel of the Guards Regiments

HEADQUARTERS HOUSEHOLD CAVALRY
HORSE GUARDS, WHITEHALL

This message comes to you with the best wishes of all serving Blues and Royals on the occasion of the publication of this regimental history during our Queen's Golden Jubilee year. The Blues and Royals are rightly proud of their alliance with The Governor General's Horse Guards.

Since 1992 the Blues and Royals have made up both the armoured reconnaissance regiment in Windsor and the mounted regiment in London in equal parts with our sister regiment, The Life Guards. Nevertheless, we continue to maintain our tradition and separate identities as urged to do so by Her Majesty on the occasion of our last Presentation of Standards in 1993.

Since the earliest days, at the Battle of Queenston Heights through the Boer War, the two World Wars and Korea to the present day, your distinguished history has been frequently illustrated by gallantry, tenacity of purpose and operational effectiveness. These attributes have truly marked The Governor General's Horse Guards as second to none.

On behalf of all serving Blues and Royals, in my capacity as Commander Household Cavalry, and also as Silverstick in Waiting and one of your Honorary Trustees, I send best wishes and hope that the next 192 years may prove as distinguished as the last.

H.P.D. Massey
Colonel
Commander Household Cavalry

1st The Queen's Dragoon Guards

Our long-standing affiliation with The Governor General's Horse Guards is a source of great pride and affection to 1st The Queen's Dragoon Guards. Both our Regiments are the result of amalgamations, in our case 1st King's Dragoon Guards and the Queen's Bays (2nd Dragoon Guards) in 1959, both having been formed over 300 years ago and both individually affiliated to the Horse Guards. All three Regiments fought alongside each other in Italy.

As Governor General Roland Michener said in his address on the occasion in 1967 of the Presentation by him of a new Standard to The GGHG, the Standard is a strong piece of cloth, made up of individually weak strands of silk. He likened each strand of the woof to the lives of those who have served, and the warp to the lives of those serving. The QDG like to feel that some of those strands are the past and present members of your affiliated Regiment.

We have many times enjoyed exchange visits between individuals, and we are proud to have two QDGs as Honorary Trustees of The GGHG; we look forward each year to your article in our Regimental Journal, which keeps us up to date with your doings. May this important affiliation long continue, and go from strength to strength.

Colonel J.I. Pocock MBE
Honorary Colonel

Lieutenant Colonel G.T. Baldwin
Commanding Officer

The Royal Canadian Dragoons have a long history directly entwined with that of the Governor General's Body Guard and, later, The Governor General's Horse Guards. Indeed, in the early years of Dragoons' history and our beginnings with the Canadian Cavalry Corps School we share many common roots with the already-established Body Guard. Our first commanding officer, J.F. Turnbull, led our contingent that accompanied Denison's Body Guard to Touchwood Hills during the Northwest Campaign in 1885. Since that time our Regiments have shared the bonds of tradition and a similar, if not a common, history. Soldiers from the Body Guard served with the Dragoons during the Boer War and proved their gallantry and valour on the field of battle. Perhaps the most notable of those soldiers was Capt H.Z.C. Cockburn who, alongside two Dragoons, was awarded the Victoria Cross for his actions at the Battle of Leliefontein on 7 November 1900. The Dragoon's First World War battle honours – Somme, Flers-Courcellette, Hindenburg Line, Cambrai, and France and Flanders – are shared with the 4th CMR. Similarly, in our respective armoured reconnaissance roles during the Second World War, we share the battle honours Liri Valley, Gothic Line, Lamone Crossing, Misano Ridge, and Italy 1944-45. Both Regiments transferred to North West Europe in 1945 for the Liberation of Holland and the end of the war.

In the years following the war, the close relationship continues. For today's soldiers of The Royal Canadian Dragoons our affiliation with The GGHG is one of mutual benefit. Dragoons were augmented by Horse Guard soldiers during operational tours in Kosovo, and are still being augmented by them for tours in Bosnia. The Horse Guards are able to conduct first class operational training at the Dragoon home station in Petawawa. We are frequently operating indistinguishable one from the other – Regular and Reserve, Dragoon and Horse Guard.

Our close affiliation has garnered a mutual respect and genuine camaraderie between the soldiers of our units. The RCD hold The GGHG in high esteem, and respect and value the opportunity to maintain our affiliations. The Governor General's Horse Guards has a long and distinguished record of service. Its Regimental history is a credit to all Horse Guards and Dragoons past, present, and future, will join with others and profit from this important historical book.

J.K. Dangerfield
Lieutenant-General (Retired)
Colonel of the Regiment

D.J. Milner
Lieutenant-Colonel
Commanding Officer

Contents

LIST OF MAPS

Introduction

There is a mystique, a magic, a fundamental ethos in a Regiment that captures the mind, the heart, the very soul of all who have the privilege and honour to serve in it.

For a Regiment is a living entity, made up of generations of men and women who have served in its ranks. It is a military family linked by close bonds of friendship, comradeship, respect and trust that have grown out of the shared experience of service in a common cause. It is a family with soul and spirit that values honour and dedication above all. It is a family with common ideals and valued traditions that have developed throughout its existence. It is a family with a proud past – a history of devoted service in war and peace, in adversity and good times. The Governor General's Horse Guards is such a regiment. This book is intended to ensure members and friends understand the history and traditions that confirm our right to the Regimental motto *Nulli Secundus* – Second to None.

The origins of the Regiment begin with the leadership of two very determined men: John Button, a Loyalist, and George Taylor Denison, both of whom saw the need for mounted men to assist in the defence of our new country – Canada. The cavalry troops they raised were all-volunteer – rare at the time – and they set a fine standard for all subsequent generations of Horse Guards.

During the War of 1812-1814, Button's troop of dragoons was on active duty throughout the conflict, and many members were involved in the fighting at Fort George and at Fort Detroit alongside the Niagara Light Dragoons. Several of the men who later formed Denison's Troop helped defend the colony in the famous battle of Queenston Heights in 1812 and later during the American attack on the town of York in 1813. Our Regimental heritage thus dates back to the very beginnings of the Militia in Ontario.

In December 1837, Button's Troop joined with Denison's York Dragoons to assist in putting down the rebellion in Upper Canada, and were kept on active duty for the better part of sixteen months chasing down rebels throughout the southern part of the province. Their effectiveness in defending the colony was rewarded with the distinction of being titled the Queen's Light Dragoons.

The Regiment's long established tradition of guarding and escorting Vice Royalty had its beginnings in 1838, when the Denison and Button Troops joined forces to provide a mounted escort to Lord Durham, the Governor of Canada. Over the years, continuing to the present time, the Regiment mounted escorts for every Governor General and almost every Lieutenant Governor of Ontario. The Regiment's first Royal Escort was provided for the Prince of Wales in 1860, and then for the Duke and Duchess of Cornwall and York in 1901. During the Royal Visit of Their Majesties King George VI and Queen Elizabeth in 1939, the Horse Guards was honoured to escort the reigning sovereign for the first time. Since then, escorts have been provided for Her Majesty Queen Elizabeth II on three occasions, 1959, 1973 and 1984, and for Queen Elizabeth, the Queen Mother in 1962 and 1979.

While the Button and Denison troops had worked together in operations in both 1812 and 1837, they were first formally joined together in 1853 when the 1st Regiment York Light Dragoons was created. This lasted until 1865, when the Button Troop was placed in a separate York County cavalry squadron. Twenty-four years later, the Button (Markham) Troop formally became part of the Governor General's Body Guard, and their heritage again firmly came to our Regimental family.

During the Fenian Raids of June 1866, the newly renamed Governor General's Body Guard was the only cavalry called out to help repulse a Fenian 'army' that had crossed into Canada near Fort Erie. While the unit was called out too late to be involved in the infamous battle at Ridgeway where the

Canadian Militia suffered an ignominious defeat, it rushed on to seal the frontier at Fort Erie against further incursions.

The commanding officer of the Body Guard, Lieutenant Colonel George Taylor Denison III, was undoubtedly the first Canadian military intellectual. After studying the employment of cavalry during the US Civil War, he wrote a book entitled *Modern Cavalry,* in which he argued that cavalry of the future could only be successful if they were employed as mounted riflemen. Later, in 1877, he wrote *A History of Cavalry,* still one of the best histories of the mounted arm ever published. His writings were widely acclaimed, especially in Germany and Russia, and his ideas on mounted rifles were eventually adopted by most Western armies. Another member of the Denison family, and a former commanding officer, Lieutenant Colonel Frederick Denison, commanded the Canadian Nile Voyageurs in Egypt in 1884, the first occasion when Canadian Militiamen were deployed overseas.

By the time of the North-West Rebellion in 1885, the Body Guard had earned a reputation as being the finest cavalry in the country. The unit was the only major body of trained cavalry deployed to the North West Territories, but once there it was inappropriately used to guard the line of supply instead of the mounted rifles job it was best prepared to do. The Regiment's first battle honour – 'North West Canada 1885' – was awarded for this service.

The Boer War in 1899 provided the occasion for the first major Canadian overseas military expedition. The Governor General's Body Guard contributed 43 officers and men to the Canadian contingents between 1899 and 1902. The Regiment's first Victoria Cross was won at the Battle of Leliefontein in November 1900 by Captain H.Z.C. Cockburn, who was then serving with the Royal Canadian Dragoons. The Regiment was awarded the battle honour 'South Africa 1900' for its substantial contributions.

When the First World War broke out in August 1914, the Minister of Militia chose not to mobilize any of the existing Militia units. Instead, he created literally hundreds of 'numbered' battalions. Many members of the Body Guard joined the 3rd (Toronto) Battalion, but in November 1914 the 4th Canadian Mounted Rifles was formed primarily from squadrons provided by both the Body Guard and the Mississauga Horse. The 4th CMR was converted to infantry in late 1915, and in the front-line trenches in France it quickly earned a reputation as being an élite unit within the Canadian Corps. A second Victoria Cross was won for the Regiment by Private Tommy Holmes at Passchendaele in October 1917. Members of the 4th CMR were awarded a host of decorations for bravery: nine Distinguished Service Orders, 39 Military Crosses, 37 Distinguished Conduct Medals and 98 Military Medals. While the 4th CMR did not bear our Regiment's name, its members originated with us, and the Horse Guards officially perpetuate its gallant actions. Their distinguished history belongs to us, as do their battle honours: 'Mount Sorrel', 'Somme 1916', 'Flers-Courcelette', 'Ancre Heights', 'Arras 1917, 1918', 'Vimy 1917', 'Hill 70', 'Ypres 1917', 'Passchendaele', 'Amiens', 'Scarpe 1918', 'Hindenburg Line', 'Canal du Nord', 'Cambrai 1918', 'Valenciennes', 'Sambre', and 'France and Flanders 1915-18'.

The Mississauga Horse, a dashing Toronto cavalry regiment dating from 1904, and the historic Governor General's Body Guard were amalgamated in 1936 to become The Governor General's Horse Guards.

Shortly after the outbreak of the Second World War, the Regiment was mobilized as a motorcycle regiment but was converted in 1941 to a tank unit of the 5th Canadian Armoured Division. When the structure of Canada's armoured divisions was altered in England in 1943, because of its acknowledged high standards of operational capability the Horse Guards was selected to become the division's armoured reconnaissance regiment. The unit fought with distinction in all of the division's major actions during the Italian campaign in 1944-45 – the Liri Valley battles, the breaking of the Gothic Line and the difficult advance along the Adriatic coast. In 1945, the Regiment was redeployed to North-West Europe with the rest of First Canadian Corps, and it fought its last battles of the war in the liberation of the Netherlands. During the war years, The Governor General's Horse Guards served with the same high distinction demonstrated throughout its existence, and its members were rewarded with six Distinguished Service Orders, two Military Crosses, one Distinguished Conduct Medal, eight Military Medals and one British Empire Medal. Its battle honours include: 'Liri Valley', 'Melfa Crossing', 'Gothic Line', 'Lamone Crossing', 'Misano Ridge', 'Fosso Munio', 'Italy 1944-45' and 'Ijsselmeer'.

In the post-war era, members have continued to serve loyally through times of prosperity and adversity, in both armour and reconnaissance roles, preserving the high standards and distinct traditions that the Regiment has built over its long existence in the Canadian Militia. In 1951, the Horse Guards recruited 223 men for service in Korea, the largest number provided by any Militia unit in the country. Today, as the senior armoured regiment in the Militia, we are one of the most demographically representative of all units of Canada's modern-day army: our members come from many different backgrounds, races, religions. And our soldiers continue to serve

Queen and country well beyond our borders on UN peace-keeping operations and NATO peace support missions.

Peacetime service has always been marked by a lack of good equipment and a shortage of funds. That has never deterred members of this Regiment, now or in the past, and has undoubtedly contributed to a unit characteristic of improvisation – doing the best one can with what little is available. There are also other notable Regimental characteristics: good leadership; ingenuity; a determination to get the job done well; self sacrifice – giving of time well beyond the call of duty; accomplishing the impossible or near impossible; showing great pride in serving honourably. The Regiment has always been known for doing all that with great flair – drilling smartly in colourful distinctive uniforms, keeping our cavalry heritage to the fore in important ceremonial events with the Cavalry Squadron, and through our Regimental Band, and our Cadets. And the support and guidance of The Governor General's Horse Guards Association, the Regimental Trustees and The Governor General's Horse Guards Foundation adds great encouragement and strength.

The Regiment, and its family, is a unique and treasured entity. It is a sacred trust to be nurtured, improved, cared for, and loved. It is to be passed by each generation to following generations in better condition than it was found, placing an enormous onus on those currently serving. This, indeed, has been the tradition of The Governor General's Horse Guards for almost two centuries. Our history and heritage are thus passed to our successors for their constant care and affection.

The Governor General's Horse Guards, Canada's Senior Militia Regiment, embodies the concepts of the citizen soldier and service to country. This book is our record and testimony, and will contribute to a better understanding of our remarkable past, and it establishes the long standing foundation on which the Regiment will build in the future.

Nulli Secundus – Second to None

Colonel H.N.R. Jackman, OC, KStJ, CD, O Ont
Honorary Colonel

Lieutenant Colonel Peter W. Hunter, CD
Honorary Lieutenant Colonel

Acknowledgements

The production of a regimental history is inevitably a team effort, and a great many Horse Guards have made important contributions to this book, for which the authors are most grateful. The Regimental Trustees' History Committee has provided advice and encouragement throughout the project, and we thank especially Colonel Peter Hunter, Lieutenant Colonels John Burns, Jeffrey Dorfman and David Friesen and Major Eric Taylor for their tireless efforts in reading successive versions of the manuscript. A number of veterans also made valuable comments on the Second World War chapters, including Lieutenant Colonels Allan Burton, Douglas Crashley, Charles Baker and Captains Bud Wass and Bob Murray. Captain Jim Davis provided significant help with the post-war chapter. Many members of the Regiment loaned photographs from their personal collections.

Dr. Steve Harris and Major Michael McNorgan of the Directorate of History and Heritage read all or parts of the manuscript. The maps and vehicle drawings which add so significantly to the book were drawn by Chris Johnson. David Batten photographed the Cockburn Victoria Cross and South Africa medal generously loaned by Upper Canada College. Greg Baynes scanned the portraits of commanding officers and RSMs. Major Lew Grimshaw loaned a number of the badges illustrated. Our thanks to all.

John Marteinson
Scott Duncan

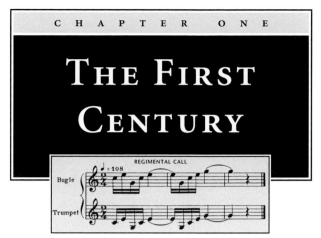

CHAPTER ONE

THE FIRST CENTURY

One of our nation's most distinguished military historians once characterized Canadians as "an unmilitary people". While that description may contain more than just a shred of truth, especially when seen against the background of public indifference towards the military in recent years, it has never applied to the many generations who have served loyally in the military family now known as The Governor General's Horse Guards.

The Horse Guards' long and distinguished story has its roots among the early pioneer settlers of Upper Canada. Many who came to the shores of Lake Ontario in the last decades of the 18th century were United Empire Loyalists who had steadfastly supported the Crown during the American Revolutionary War. Some had served in militia units alongside the British Army in the unsuccessful struggle against the rebels, and all had had their property in the American colonies confiscated when the British conceded independence. The Loyalists brought with them a justifiable concern that the safety and security of their families and homes were still threatened by the new republic to the south. And they also brought the ancient British concept that all able-bodied men had a duty to take up arms to defend their homeland in times of crisis.

By 1791 the population of the area had grown sufficiently that a new province called Upper Canada was created. The first lieutenant governor arrived in 1792: John Graves Simcoe,

a former colonel of the Queen's Rangers, which had fought in the Revolutionary War, and which included a cavalry component. Simcoe had the massive task of organizing an effective administration for the new colony, but from the outset he was also greatly concerned about its defences.

Simcoe brought the matter of provincial defence to the second sitting of the Legislative Assembly of Upper Canada on 31 March 1793, and the first Militia Act was passed. The citizen army that was thus created was based on the model of the British militia of the day. The act established universal liability for service by males between 16 and 50, and every man was required to provide his own firearm. Simcoe also convinced authorities in Britain to re-create his old regiment, the Queen's Rangers, as a full-time unit. The Rangers were to have two important roles: they were to serve as a nucleus for the defence of the colony, and they were to spend two days a week building roads and bridges and clearing land.

Under the terms of the act, each county was to have its own regiment of infantry. Within these county regiments each company had to be paraded and inspected by its captain at least twice a year. Militiamen were not paid, and there were fines for absence from the semi-annual parades. Because of a heightened threat of invasion from the United States in 1794, the upper age limit for the Militia was raised to 60, and the first regular battalion, the Royal Canadian Volunteer Regiment, was recruited in the province.

There was no provision for cavalry in the original Militia Act, even though Simcoe had indeed recognized the need for it: he had originally asked that two troops be included in the Queen's Rangers. There were, after all, long distances to be traversed, and horses were the main means of transportation along the very primitive roads between the settlements. But cavalry, with its need for horses, saddles, bridles and swords, was much more expensive for citizens to raise and maintain than infantry, and it was thought that in any case the heavily wooded countryside made the employment of mounted troops difficult.

In February 1796 Simcoe had the town of York (today Toronto) designated as the temporary capital of the province, and over the next two years the settlement grew rapidly as land was cleared for homes, farms and places of business. In 1798 the first Militia unit was raised in York County, and among its officers were Lieutenant John Denison, formerly of the British militia, who had come to Canada in 1792, and Lieutenant John Button.

By late 1801 the threat of an imminent American invasion had lessened, in large part because of an armistice between the British and French, and the two regular corps, the Queen's Rangers and the Royal Canadian Volunteers, were disbanded in 1802. The defence of the province was thus left largely in the hands of the relatively small and ill-equipped militia and a single regiment of British regulars.

But the tenuous peace in Europe did not last very long, for by mid-1803 Britain and France were again at war. Moreover, relations between the United States and Britain became increasingly hostile. After the U.S. purchase of Louisiana from the French in December 1803, the Americans intensified their expansion into the territory south of the Great Lakes, but ran into considerable opposition from Indian tribes, who looked to the British for support. Many Americans came to think that elimination of British rule in the Canadian provinces would put a stop to the Indians' resistance to white settlement, and increasingly there were calls for military action against Upper and Lower Canada. At the same time, Royal Navy enforcement of an embargo on ships entering European ports controlled by Napoleon further angered the United States. Because of the growing tension, and with only a few regular British troops available to defend British North America, it was obvious that some effort had to be made to strengthen the Militia.

To improve the general quality of the Militia in Upper Canada, a new Militia Act was passed in 1808. In a measure to enhance readiness for an emergency, the Act called for one annual muster of each company, and not less than two nor more than four 'call outs' for arms inspection and rudimentary training. And, for the history of a cavalry regiment, it contained a very important clause which authorized the formation of troops of cavalry in the regimental districts.

BUTTON'S TROOP OF CAVALRY

The first request to form a troop of cavalry under the terms of the 1808 Act came in 1810 from a 38-year-old gentleman farmer in Markham Township, John Button, who was then serving as a Lieutenant in the 1st York Regiment of Militia. It is recorded that a rash of disloyal speeches and acts by men who favoured joining the United States prompted Button's action, and the support of well-to-do farmers in the Markham district who had good riding horses made the proposition a practical one. Button received permission from Lieutenant Colonel William Graham, commanding officer of the 1st York Regiment, to form a troop of dragoons from among the 'yeomen' of Markham Township. This troop was initially designated 11th Company, 1st York Regiment of Militia. It was the first Militia cavalry ever organized in Upper Canada.

Within the troop, the men had to provide their own horses, saddles and bridles, as well as their own clothing, but in 1812 the government supplied sabres and pistols. A local history notes that "previously appointed constables [from Markham Township] were all members of that troop". Among those original members of Button's Troop were Quartermaster George Playter, Senior Sergeant Joshua Clarkson, Sergeant Christopher Hiltz, Privates Peter Pelkie, Henry Pringle, Nicholas Hagerman and John Van Horn. The officers and senior non-commissioned officers no doubt wore the uniform of the York Regiment of Militia, described in Chambers' 1902 history of the Governor General's Body Guard as "red coats with wide black breast lappels and broad tail flaps; high collars, tight sleeves and large cuffs; on the head a black hat, the ordinary high-crowned civilian hat, with a cylindrical feather some eighteen inches inserted at the top … at the left side … scarlet at the base, white above."

While a continuous link to the cavalry troop formed by Major Button in 1810 cannot be verified from the available records, The Governor General's Horse Guards regards the Button Troop as its earliest ancestor.

THE WAR OF 1812

From 1809 to early 1812 the threat of invasion from the United States became very real and many influential American politicians openly urged the annexation of the Canadian provinces, by military action if necessary. Major General Isaac

MAJOR JOHN BUTTON

John Button became a prominent and much respected citizen in Markham, and a leading light in the Militia of Upper Canada. He was born in New London, Connecticut, in 1772 and came to Upper Canada in 1798. There is some evidence that he spent his first two years there with Butler's Rangers in the Niagara area. His application for a land grant in Markham Township was approved in 1801, and Button soon became a prosperous farmer in Markham Township.

He served in the 1st York Regiment of Militia as a lieutenant, and in 1810 he obtained permission from the commanding officer to form a troop of dragoons within that regiment, the first cavalry unit raised in Upper Canada. Button was promoted captain by Isaac Brock in July 1812. He and his dragoons were on active duty throughout the War of 1812, carrying despatches between Fort George, York and Kingston. When in 1821

Major John Button, commander of Button's Troop 1810 to 1831. (Markham Museum)

the York Militia was reorganized to reflect the growing population, the Button troop became part of the 1st North York Regiment. Button was promoted major on 29 October 1831, retroactive to 12 November 1828 by Lieutenant Governor Sir John Colborne. He commanded the Markham Troop until October 1831, when his eldest son, Francis, succeeded him.

John Button was one of the magistrates of York County (who in those days served as local administrators, controlling public expenditures, appointing constables and other local officials, granting licences, etc.), being appointed to that position in 1833. He was known to be a Tory and an ardent opponent of the Reformer William Lyon Mackenzie, who was a member of the Legislative Assembly for the district.

John Button founded a dynasty that for many years was influential in the cavalry in Upper Canada. He died in 1861 at the age of 89.

Brock, sent to Upper Canada in 1810 as commander-in-chief to improve the defences of the colony, faced a daunting task. There were only about 1,200 British regulars scattered in small garrisons throughout the province, and even though there were another five British battalions in Lower Canada (Québec) they were all needed there. The 11,000-strong Militia was poorly armed, and in any case had virtually no training. On top of this, the Legislature was not inclined to authorize more money to be spent on defence. The situation grew even worse with the election of a large number of so-called War Hawks to the United States Congress in November 1811, which enabled these men to put great pressure on the U.S. government to oust the British from Canada. It seemed that war was now inevitable.

In response to this growing risk, Brock, then also acting administrator of Upper Canada, in March 1812 persuaded the Legislature to pass an amended Militia Act. A key provision of this act was the requirement to create two volunteer companies, termed flank companies, in each Militia regiment, consisting of "not more than one third of the strength". These flank companies were required to train for six days each

month, although without pay or allowances. Despite the lack of monetary incentive, volunteers flocked to join the flank companies that were quickly formed by almost all regiments, and because of the training they received in the three months before the war began they were able to provide the bulk of the Militia force for the subsequent defence of the Detroit and Niagara frontiers. Among the members of the flank companies formed by the 3rd York Regiment of Militia was Lieutenant George Taylor Denison.

Brock also understood the need for fast-moving mounted troops in the most threatened part of the colony, and the first independent cavalry unit in the province, officially named the 1st Troop of Lincoln Cavalry but usually called the Niagara Light Dragoons, was formed on 1 May 1812 in Niagara. This troop was placed under the command of a Revolutionary War cavalry veteran of the Queen's Rangers, Major Thomas Merritt, great-grandfather of Lieutenant Colonel William Hamilton Merritt of the Body Guard. Thomas Merritt's son, William Hamilton Merritt, was initially a lieutenant in the troop, but after March 1813, when the troop was reconstituted, he served as commander with the rank of captain. The

Officer of the York Regiment of Militia. **This was the original uniform worn by the officers of Button's Troop in Markham when it was part of the 1st York Regiment. Painting by G. Embleton (Directorate of History and Heritage)**

troop, which had a strength of 58 other ranks, was formed as a regular Provincial corps for the duration of the war and was not a Militia unit.

On 18 June 1812 the United States formally declared war on Britain, although it was not until 25 June that anyone in Upper Canada learned this, and American troops were slowly deployed into the frontier areas at Detroit and Niagara. The first Americans to invade Canadian soil came across the Detroit River on 11 July, and until they withdrew a month later they simply occupied a small area of land opposite Fort Detroit, in the area that is now Windsor.

On 27 July, Captain John Button, along with other Militia officers, was invited to dine with General Brock to discuss plans for the defence of the colony. One of the results of this dinner was that Button's troop was called out on active service as the 1st York Troop of Horse of the Volunteer Corps, with four sergeants, one trumpeter and 34 privates. A few days later part of the Niagara Light Dragoons, under Lieutenant Merritt, was detailed to maintain communications between Burlington and Amherstburg, around the flank of the invaders, and 15 members of Button's troop were attached to them for this task. A manuscript history of the 2nd Dragoons states that their operations "ranged over a wide area between Burford and Port Talbot, scouting, guiding, carrying despatches, and capturing enemy spies and scouts".

To deal with the invasion on the Detroit frontier, Brock in the meantime assembled a small force of British regulars and Militia and sailed from Port Dover to Amherstburg on 8 August. A 10-man section of Button's troop, under a sergeant, was part of this column. On arriving in Amherstburg, Brock met the great Shawnee Indian chief, Tecumseh, who had brought a group of about 600 warriors. This ad-hoc force then marched on Fort Detroit. After a day of bombardment, Brock's troops formed up on 16 August for an assault on the fort, but the thoroughly demoralized American commander surrendered his garrison without a fight. Morale soared in Upper Canada when the population heard of this victory, and a large proportion now became convinced that the province could indeed be defended. And almost as important as this moral victory was the large cache of arms captured from the Americans: 35 cannon, 2,500 muskets, 500 rifles and a large stock of ammunition. The weapons went a long way toward arming the Militia effectively for the battles which were to come.

As soon as Fort Detroit had been secured, Brock rushed to Niagara, where he knew the Americans were assembling a large force on their side of the Niagara River. He distributed the captured American weapons and organized as effective a defence as was possible with his force of about 1,000 British regulars and 600 Militia and Indians. The expected attack finally came very early in the morning on 13 October 1812 when the Americans ferried an invasion force across the Niagara River at the village of Queenston.

As the American boats approached the base of the steep escarpment, they were fired on by a battery of guns on the heights, and by troops of the British 49th Regiment and a flank company of the 2nd York Regiment. Brock, who was awakened at Fort George by the sounds of battle, rushed to Queenston, ordering Militia units along the way to follow. Just as he arrived at the battery a group of American troops

Trooper of the Canadian Light Dragoons, depicting the uniform worn during the War of 1812 by members of Button's Troop who served with Merritt's Niagara Light Dragoons. Painting by G.A. Embleton. (Directorate of History and Heritage)

reached the top of the cliff, and a hail of musket fire drove Brock and the artillerymen down the hill. Brock proceeded to muster all available troops in Queenston and as the first light of dawn broke he led them, sword in hand, in a charge up the slope. Then, having advanced to only 50 metres from the American position, Brock was mortally wounded by a musket ball in the chest. A second charge organized by Brock's aide de camp also failed, and the British and Canadian troops retreated. The Americans held the commanding heights, and the British commander-in-chief was dead. This action might have been an even greater disaster for Canada had it not been for a small group of Indian warriors which continued throughout the morning and early afternoon to skirmish with the Americans in the woods on Queenston Heights.

The Americans showed little inclination to exploit their success, despite eventually having well over a thousand men across the river. And when General Roger Sheaffe, who took command after Brock was killed, mounted a counter-attack in late afternoon with about 900 regulars together with companies from the York and Lincoln Militia and a number of Mohawks, the Americans simply crumbled, and most surrendered. The battle of Queenston Heights ended as a clear British/Canadian victory, and it was the last major attempt by the Americans to invade Canada in 1812.

There is a small Regimental involvement in the victory at Queenston Heights: Lieutenant Aaron Silverthorn, who a few years later was one of

British General Service Medal. Three members of Button's Troop were awarded this medal with the 'Detroit' bar.

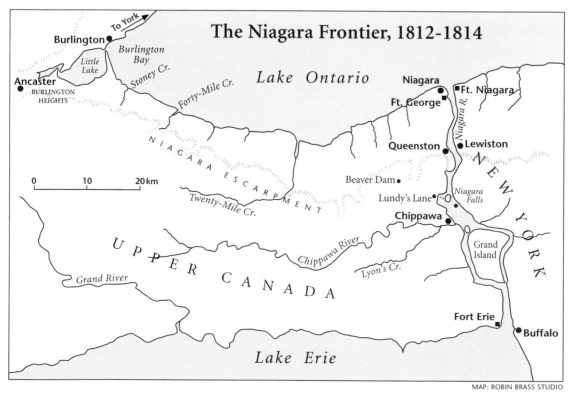

The Niagara Frontier, 1812-1814

the original officers in Denison's Troop, was present at the battle with a flank company of the 2nd York Regiment, and Trumpeter Aneas Bell was at General Brock's side when he fell. A few kilometres away, Button's Troop, the only Militia cavalry on active service at the time, was among the units brought to reinforce the garrison at Fort George. From then until after the end of hostilities, elements of Button's troop served continuously, carrying despatches between the capital at York and the field headquarters at Fort George (or for a brief time at Burlington), and between York and the garrison at Kingston.

1813 proved to be the most difficult period of the war for the people of Upper Canada. That year the Americans focused their attention on what they termed the central theatre of operations – the Niagara peninsula and Lake Ontario. Their first major operation was an amphibious raid directed against the provincial capital at York.

Shortly before dawn on 27 April a force of about 1700 American regulars landed four kilometres west of the town. The invaders quickly overcame the few Indians opposing the landing, and the American troops rapidly moved eastward toward the town. Valiant attempts were made by companies of the British 8th Regiment and the Royal Newfoundland Regiment to stop the Americans, but the enemy's superior strength overcame all opposition. When the cannon at the Western Battery was accidentally blown up around noon, General Sheaffe decided that further efforts to hold York were pointless. He simply gave up the fight, and ordered the British regulars to withdraw toward Kingston. Sheaffe paused briefly at the eastern edge of town to give instructions to Colonel Chewett, commanding officer of the 3rd York Regiment, to negotiate a surrender as best he could.

In the meantime, a group of men of the York Militia, led by Lieutenant George Denison, had been carrying out instructions to set fire to a new ship, the *Isaac Brock,* then under construction, and to burn a frigate, the *Duke of Gloucester,* which was undergoing repairs. Denison's men succeeded in burning the *Isaac Brock,* but they were not so successful with their other task, as Chambers noted in the 1902 Regimental history:

> The naval officer in charge of the frigate refused to have the torch applied, and while Lieutenant Denison was engaged in a heated discussion over the point, the frigate was captured with all on board of her, and Mr. Denison was a prisoner for six months until exchanged.

Another Militia party did, however, succeed in blowing up the main magazine on the lakeshore. The tremendous explosion rocked the whole town, and falling debris killed and injured a number on both sides, including the American general Zebulon Pike. While the Americans were thus deprived of some of their expected booty, they clearly had won the day. Under terms of the surrender negotiated by Colonel Chewett, all members of the Militia at York became prisoners-of-war, among them Captain John Button, but most were paroled the same day and sent home. The Americans remained in York until 2 May, and by the time they abandoned the town, York had been thoroughly looted and vandalized.

The Americans launched a second invasion of the Niagara peninsula on 25 May with over 4,000 soldiers, and this time they quickly overpowered the British and the Canadian Militia defenders. The British regulars and Militia retreated to Beaver Dam (Thorold), where General Vincent strangely gave orders to the Militia to return to their homes. The British regulars then pulled back all the way to Burlington, the main supply depot in the southern part of Upper Canada, leaving the pursuing Americans in control of the whole of the Niagara frontier. To many the situation was grave; it appeared that the British were about to abandon Upper Canada. But a bold night attack by the 8th and 49th Regiments at

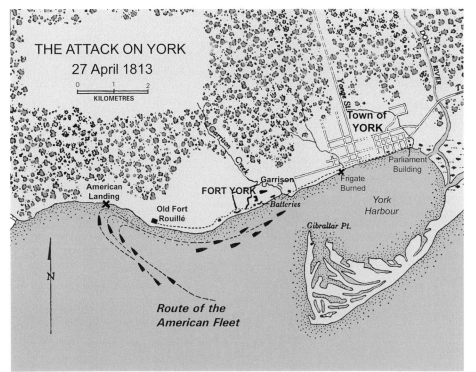

THE ATTACK ON YORK
27 April 1813

0   1   2
KILOMETRES

Town of YORK

American Landing

FORT YORK

Old Fort Rouillé

Garrison Creek

Batteries

Frigate Burned

Parliament Building

York Harbour

Gibraltar Pt.

N

Route of the American Fleet

The partially completed Provincial Marine vessel *Isaac Brock* in York harbour, burned by Lieutenant George Denison and his men on 27 April 1813 to prevent its capture by the American invaders. (Toronto Reference Library)

Stoney Creek on 6 June routed the Americans, and they hastily retreated to Fort George.

The Americans retained control of the area around Fort George until December, but their activities were severely constrained by a perimeter of outposts manned by Indians and British regulars. At this time the enemy organized a cavalry troop manned by renegade Upper Canadians and led by two former members of the Legislative Assembly, Joseph Wilcox and Benajah Mallory. This band of mounted traitors knew the territory well, and they spied for the Americans and conducted hit-and-run terror raids throughout the Niagara region and along the northern shore of Lake Erie. The job of countering this terrorist unit was given to Captain William Hamilton Merritt's Troop of Niagara Provincial Light Dragoons, and it was their main task for much of the remainder of the year.

[Merritt's Troop] … followed up the irregulars with persistent perseverance, literally dogging their steps, capturing many of them, and bringing them to trial and the halter. Captain Merritt's men entered with such zest into the discharge of their function of heading off Wilcox's men that at last the latter dared not venture out of the American lines.

After July 1813 the military situation in the Niagara peninsula became a stalemate. But on the Detroit front the situation

for the British/Canadian force had rapidly deteriorated after the failure of several raids on American forts and the erosion of Indian support that resulted. Fearful of an American offensive which he believed he could not hold with his force of only about 900 men, General Henry Procter, the British commander, decided to abandon the western territory and retreated in a highly disorganized manner along the Thames River in the direction of Burlington. The Americans, however, followed closely and caught up with Procter's force at Moraviantown on 5 October. A 10-minute battle turned into a disastrous defeat for the British/Canadian force in which the only display of good leadership came from Chief Tecumseh, and he unfortunately was killed during the fighting. Once again the Americans appeared to be on the verge of capturing Upper Canada, but they had in fact outrun their supplies, and hastily retreated to Detroit. In Lower Canada there was better news: both American attacks – at Chateauguay in October and at Crysler's Farm in November – were defeated.

Once Lieutenant George Denison was released from captivity in the autumn of 1813 the Army headquarters in York decided to capitalize on his boldness and innate initiative, and he was often employed on 'special service'. Chambers' history of the Body Guard notes that "he had a great deal of riding to do" carrying important communications between York, Kingston, Burlington and posts on the Niagara frontier. At one time in late October 1813 he was sent to Kingston to bring up to York a flotilla of *bateaux*, small open boats, loaded with supplies. In later years he told how it was necessary for the bateaux to creep along the shore to avoid capture by the American fleet then controlling Lake Ontario, and of a narrow escape – hiding the bateaux in the mouth of a small stream – when American war vessels approached. On another occasion in mid-July 1814, during the last American invasion of the Niagara frontier, he was

sent with a large sum of money, about $40,000 [in gold coins], from York around to the army headquarters in the Niagara frontier. He was approaching St. David's when a dragoon came galloping towards him at full speed. When he came near he said: "Are you the officer from York with a large sum of money?" Not knowing his object, [Denison] at first denied it, when the man said: "St. David's is captured, the enemy are coming this way and I have been sent to warn him to go back to York." Two more dragoons came in sight, chased by a party of the enemy's cavalry. [Denison] turned and galloped away, and was chased several miles, escaping with great difficulty.

There was little fighting other than periodic raids during the first six months of 1814 as both sides made preparations for what all knew was the final stage of the war. Napoleon had been defeated in the battle of Paris on 31 March, and the British acted quickly to send another 14 regiments to Canada, although few of these actually saw service in Upper Canada. While the British and Americans had begun to talk about peace negotiations, both continued to prepare for further fighting. Seeking to better their military position, the Americans again invaded the Niagara frontier on 3 July 1814. The battles at Chippawa on 5 July and at Lundy's Lane on 25 July were among the bloodiest of the war, but neither were decisive. A British attempt to capture Fort Erie on 14/15 August was a costly failure, and even more troops were lost when the Americans sallied out to attack on 17 September just as the

British and Canadians were preparing to pull back to Fort George. Eventually the Americans decided to withdraw to winter quarters on their own side of the Niagara River, and the last of the invaders withdrew from Upper Canada on 5 November. The war officially came to an end on Christmas Eve 1814 with the signing of the Treaty of Ghent, which simply restored all pre-war territory. In thirty months of war neither side had gained anything at all, but Canadians generally believed they had won a great victory since they had successfully repulsed a series of American invasions.

The apparently successful outcome of the war no doubt served to raise the self-esteem of the Canadian Militia as a whole, although it did very little in the long run to persuade the Legislative Assembly to spend more money on defence or otherwise improve the overall quality of the Militia. For the cavalry arm, however, the wartime exploits of the Niagara Light Dragoons and the one British regular cavalry regiment, the 19th Light Dragoons, repeatedly proved the utility of mounted men in a variety of roles in the defence of Upper Canada. While the primary tasks of the cavalry had been scouting and reconnaissance, service as couriers and armed escort for supply columns, on several occasions they very effectively participated in punitive raids on American settlements, mounted attacks on piquets and outposts, and served as flank and rear guards in a number of engagements. And while there had been only some 186 men in the Militia cavalry in both Upper and Lower Canada during the course of the war, including Button's troop, the relative effectiveness of that small number undoubtedly had an important effect on decisions to increase the number of volunteer cavalry units in the Militia in the years following the war.

The Button troop was not taken off active service until the summer of 1815. While records of its activities in this period are scanty, it is known that the Troop continued to serve as a component of the 1st York Regiment of Militia in the years following the end of hostilities, even though the arms issued during the war were withdrawn in 1816. This was a difficult period for the Militia, as the public lost interest in military affairs once peace was restored, and defence had a very low priority with the Provincial administration. It is likely that the Button troop mustered with the 1st York Regiment on the required one day each year. John Button's eldest son, Francis, who had served as a private during the war years, was commissioned as a cornet in the troop in July 1818. Militia Lists for 1820 and 1822 show John Button as captain, William Marr as lieutenant, and Francis Button as cornet. Records of the period show that Button continually pressed the Adjutant Gen-

Officer and Dragoon, 19th Light Dragoons in full dress, 1814. Painting by Charles Stadden. (Parks Canada)

The uniform worn by Button's Troop ca. 1818, thought to have been worn by the Niagara Light Dragoons during the War of 1812, and later acquired from Ordnance surplus. (GGHG Archives)

eral's department for the reissue of arms appropriate to the cavalry, but without results.

Button's troop was present on parade with the York Militia on 23 April 1823 when the colours of the wartime Volunteer Incorporated Battalion, emblazoned with the battle honour 'Niagara', were presented at York to "the Militia of Upper Canada". The York Militia had been designated to receive these colours on behalf of all who had served during the War of 1812.

A history of Markham Township describes the uniform worn at this time by Button's troop as "blue jackets and bear skin helmets, purchased at members' expense", and suggests that these were "of out-dated pattern purchased through auction sales of surplus and obsolete equipment and stores that were held from time to time at depots throughout the province". It is probable these were the uniforms that had been worn by the provincial dragoons, Merritt's Niagara Light Dragoons, during the war. As Button's men were occasionally attached to the Niagara Light Dragoons, it is also possible this same uniform may have been worn by the troop during the war years.

DENISON'S TROOP

Despite the government's clear lack of concern, there appears to have been something of a revival of interest in the Militia among elements of the population in the early 1820s, most evidently demonstrated by the growing number of volunteer sub-units – cavalry troops and rifle companies – that were formed and attached to the county infantry regiments. In December 1821, for example, a volunteer troop of cavalry was created in the 1st Lincoln Regiment at Niagara, perhaps reflecting the Niagara Light Dragoons that originated in the same regiment. And in 1822 an amended Militia Act was passed which renewed the 1808 authorization to form cavalry troops.

In August 1822, Colonel Chewett, commanding officer of the 1st West York Regiment, asked Captain George T. Denison, then commanding a company in the unit, to form a cavalry troop for the regiment. Captain Denison was known to be a "particularly good horseman", and he set about this task with characteristic energy and enthusiasm. He selected Aaron Silverthorn, a farmer living near York, as his lieutenant, and Charles Richardson, a barrister, as cornet.

No time appears to have been lost in procuring the men and setting to work. Drills were started and an organization completed and maintained in spite of repeated discouragement. The officers and men went to great expense to provide themselves with uniforms, and they were promised from time to time that swords and pistols would be issued to them. But they got nothing but the promises.

Chambers' history of the Regiment says that "the character of the troop as one of light dragoons was a foregone conclusion", and the title York Dragoons was used from a very early stage.

The earliest uniform of the troop was chosen by Captain Denison. He discovered that a former tailor of the 13th Light Dragoons had recently

The uniform of the 13th Dragoons, adopted by Denison's Troop in 1822 and worn, with some modifications, until 1837. (GGHG Archives)

LIEUTENANT COLONEL GEORGE TAYLOR DENISON I

George Taylor Denison I was born in Yorkshire, England, on 29 December 1783, and he came to Canada with his parents in 1792. The Denison family settled in York in 1796, and George's father, John Denison, was one of the first officers appointed when the Militia of Upper Canada was created.

George Taylor Denison was commissioned from the rank of sergeant in the 3rd York Regiment prior to the outbreak of the War of 1812, and he saw service on the Detroit and Niagara frontiers after the American invasion. He was present in York when the Americans captured the town on 27 April 1813 and was in command of a party of militiamen which burned the Provincial warship, the *Isaac Brock*, to prevent its capture by the Americans. He was taken prisoner that day and held for six months before being released. Denison was thereafter employed on "special service", often carrying important messages for the commander-in-chief. Following the war he continued to serve in the Militia, and in 1822 was a company commander in the 1st West York Regiment.

Captain George Denison formed the York Dragoons in August 1822, at the request of the commanding officer of the 1st West York Regiment, and for many years played a prominent role in the establishment of the principle of voluntary service in the Militia in Canada. Then a major, he took an important part in putting down the Rebellion at York in 1837, and the York Dragoons were kept on active service under his command until the end of July 1838, having been granted the honorary title of the Queen's Light Dragoons for their effective service.

Denison was a prominent landowner, and for many years he served as a magistrate in Toronto. For a time he was an alderman on the Toronto City Council representing St. Patrick's ward. In Au-

Lieutenant Colonel George Taylor Denison I wearing the original uniform of Denison's Troop. (GGHG Archives)

gust 1838 he was promoted to the rank of lieutenant colonel and given command of the 1st West York Regiment of Militia. In 1846 he was appointed to command the 4th Battalion Toronto Militia. He died in December 1853 and was buried with full military honours.

A Tarleton helmet, of the type worn in the 1820s and early 1830s by both Button's and Denison's Troops. This headdress had been issued to regiments of the British Light Dragoons in the late 1770s, and was considered obsolete by the British by 1803. It was, however, common to have old war stocks passed on to the Militia years after decommissioning by the British regulars.

immigrated to York and set up shop, and he was skilled in producing uniforms of that regiment's design. It thus came to be that Denison's troop would be uniformed in the pattern of the 13th Light Dragoons:

a blue coatee, with buff facings over the breast, thickly laced with silver for the officers, and laced also on the sleeves and back. The shako was of bear skin, of helmet shape, but with a plume of red and white feathers standing erect up the side. The overalls had a double white stripe down the outside. A girdle or sash was also worn.

This uniform was worn by Denison's troop until 1837.

Despite the brief interlude of popular enthusiasm, the remainder of the 1820s and the early 1830s were not good times for the Militia of Upper Canada. The population of the colony was growing steadily, and the newcomers were concerned mainly with establishing their new homesteads. It appears that the only Militia to drill and carry out training on a regular basis in this period were the Button and Denison Troops, and they were certainly the only Militia units in which everyone wore a uniform. While the infantry regiments continued to exist on paper, the annual muster on King George III's birthday, 4 June, was their only activity. An early history of Toronto describes one of these annual military "training" days in the early 1820s:

> The costumes of the men may have been various, the fire arms only partially distributed, and those that were to be had not of the brightest hue, not of the most scientific make, the lines may not always have been perfectly straight, nor their constituents well matched in height…. Nevertheless, as a military spectacle, these gatherings and manoeuvres on the grassy bank … were always anticipated with pleasure and contemplated with satisfaction…. And then, in addition to the local cavalry corps [Denison's Troop], there were the clattering scabbards, the blue jackets and bear-skin helmets of Captain Button's Dragoons, from Markham and Whitechurch.

The Militia continued its progressive decline in the late 1820s, in part because the colonial administration believed that defence was the responsibility of the British government and simply would not spend money on arms or equipment. Both Denison and Button continued to badger provincial Militia authorities for the issue of swords and saddlery, but nothing was issued to either troop until some years later. Paradoxically, this neglect of the Militia came at the very time that civil discontent among segments of the population in both Upper and Lower Canada was becoming a serious internal problem.

Button's troop nonetheless continued to thrive, if only because of John Button's strength of character and vigour. In 1831 he was promoted major, and his son, Francis, who had been commissioned in July 1818 was promoted captain, both retroactive to April 1828. While records are somewhat vague, it appears that Francis Button took over the command of the Markham troop from his father in October 1831.

THE REBELLION OF 1837-38

While the rebellions that took place in Upper and Lower Canada in 1837 and 1838 had differing causes, the popular discontent did have a common grievance against relatively

undemocratic colonial administrations, and the rebel leaders in Toronto and Montreal did attempt to coordinate their efforts.

In Upper Canada the Reform Party, led by journalist William Lyon Mackenzie, had as its goal the elimination of the autocratic power then wielded by a group of prosperous families termed 'The Family Compact'. It is certainly true that real authority in the province was at that time exercised by members of old, established families who held all key administrative appointments in both the province and the city of Toronto. It is equally true that the Legislative Assembly was weak. When the Reform Party failed to overturn the Tories in the general election of 1836, they began to plot a coup d'état to achieve independence from British rule. In some areas the population was seriously divided in its loyalties, and it became

Contemporary drawing of the Battle of Montgomery's Farm, showing a few of the loyalist volunteers and mounted men of the York Dragoons. (GGHG Archives)

common knowledge that groups of rebels had organized and armed themselves, often with locally forged pikes. In Markham Township, for example, it was known that two former members of Button's troop were associated with the rebels. But even though Lieutenant Governor Sir Francis Bond Head had many times been warned of the risks, he adamantly refused to take any but the most modest of steps to prepare for an armed uprising.

The Militia of Upper Canada, poorly equipped and entirely untrained, was ill prepared to play an effective role in putting down a rebellion. In June 1837 Anna Jamieson wrote this account of the annual muster of the Militia at Erindale:

A few men, well mounted and dressed as lancers in uniforms which were, however, anything but uniform, flourished backwards on the green sward...; themselves and their horses equally wild, disorderly, spirited, undisciplined; but this was perfection compared to the infantry. Here there was no uniformity attempted of dress, of appearance, of movement; a few had coats, others jackets; a greater number had neither coats nor jackets, but appeared in their shirt sleeves, white or checked, clean or dirty, in edifying variety. Some wore hats, others caps, others their own shaggy heads of hair. Some had firelocks, some had old

swords suspended in their belts or stuck in waistbands, but a greater number shouldered sticks or umbrellas.... The parade ended in a drunken bout and a riot ... but it was all taken so very lightly....

Rebellion broke out first in Lower Canada in mid-November 1837, and on 23 November the *Patriotes* inflicted a serious defeat on a column of British regulars at St. Denis. The British, however, captured St. Charles two days later, and the last rebel stronghold was taken on 14 December.

Mackenzie's followers were encouraged by the rebel success at St. Denis, and hundreds flocked to his cause. By 5 December nearly 800 men had gathered at Montgomery's Tavern on Yonge Street, just north of what is now Eglinton Avenue, although many were without weapons. That night a party of them started to march south down Yonge Street in an attempt to take the city by surprise. Near Yonge and Dundas their advance guard met a 20-man picket placed by Sheriff Jarvis. "What ensued was pure comedy; each side discharged their muskets and turned and fled in great precipitation in opposite directions."

At this obviously dangerous time there were only two trained militia bodies in Toronto: a volunteer rifle company of about 70 young men that had been formed about a year earlier by Colonel James Fitzgibbon, and the York Dragoons under Major George Denison. These volunteer companies immediately offered to serve with the 1st Regiment West York Militia. The regiment's order book in the Toronto Public Library lists the officers of the dragoon troop – Major G.T. Denison, Captain Thomas Denison, Lieutenants R.L. Denison and George B. Rideout, Ensigns G.T. Denison II, William J. Coates, and Edwin C. Fisher. This small force was soon supplemented when Captain Francis Button rode into Toronto with 20 men from Markham, "uniformed in the clothing of Capt Button's old troop", and volunteered to serve with the York Dragoons under Denison "to form a squadron". Then over the next day thousands of loyal militiamen from the surrounding area were warned of the rebellion and set out for Toronto to help defend the colony.

During the morning of 7 December Colonel Fitzgibbon set about arming and organizing the hundreds of loyal men who had flocked to City Hall. He initially placed Major Denison in command at Fort York, west of the town, with part of the York Dragoons manning the defences. About mid-morning Fitzgibbon led the main body of his makeshift force north along Yonge Street toward Montgomery's Tavern, spurred on by the marching music of two bands and cheered by enthusiastic crowds along the road. Three troops of cavalry, including part of the York Dragoons, accompanied Fitzgibbon's column.

A much-depleted group of rebels had positioned themselves at Gallows Hill, just south of what is now St. Clair Avenue, and the 1,500-man militia column reached the rebel position at about one o'clock. The ensuing battle was short and sharp, and the rebels broke and fled. Some cavalry were employed in "the fruitless chase after W.L. Mackenzie, and one detachment of forty mounted men was despatched from Montgomery's to destroy Gibson's house and farm buildings four miles further on."

The ignominious defeat of Mackenzie's rebels did not, however, put an end to the threat, and the York Dragoons were kept on full-time service for much of the next sixteen months. During this time the unit was paid by the British government as regular cavalry – sergeants 7 shillings 1 pence per day, corporals 6 shillings 5 pence, and privates 6 shillings – and members were supplied with accoutrements and flintlock carbines and 1821-pattern light cavalry sabres.

Because the York Dragoons were not adequately equipped for operations in cold weather, winter uniforms were issued from British stocks:

good serviceable blue cloaks with buff collars, which completely covered both men and horses. The tall collars on the cloaks, together with a fur cap, covered entirely the back of the head and neck, and nearly the whole of the face. The hats were of a peculiar construction, made of a sort of imitation dog skin. They looked as if made of an oblong piece of fur, doubled in the centre, and stitched up on each side, with a bag of red cloth with tassel on one side, somewhat like the present busby bag.

Some members of the York Dragoons, including Ensign George Taylor Denison II, were part of a column of about 500 men sent from Toronto on 9 December under Colonel Allan MacNabb to put down a rebel force in the London area. This force reached Scotland Village on 14 December, but the rebels there had already dispersed. MacNabb's force then marched to Chippawa, where Mackenzie and a few supporters had occupied Navy Island, above Niagara Falls, and established what they called a "Provisional Government of the State of Canada".

There were several raids by American 'Hunters' across the Niagara frontier over the course of 1838. Chambers' history

Painting depicting an officer of the Queen's Light Dragoons in 1837, a Montreal regiment that bore the same name as the Denison Troop. The uniforms of the two units were very similar except for the elaborate braid on the front of the Toronto unit's tunic. (Courtesy of René Chartrand)

relates: "There were so many centres of trouble, and they changed so rapidly, that the two rebellion years imposed a great deal of duty upon the mounted corps – patrol, despatch, and escort duties appear to have been particularly frequent."

THE QUEEN'S LIGHT DRAGOONS

An unpublished history of cavalry units in southern Ontario by Ernest Green commented on the employment of cavalry in this period:

> The work of the cavalry was an outstanding feature of military operations during the rebellion. The mounted men were ubiquitous and their services were essential to operations in such a great and sparsely-settled country, traversed by only the crudest roads and lacking any other means of communication. They were among the first troops in the field at every alarm and always the last to be relieved from duty. They patrolled the province from its eastern to its western extremities and to the northern fringes of settlement; their despatch riders covered thousands of miles of roads and trails.

The efficiency of the York Dragoons was certainly noted by the Provincial military authorities, for the unit was granted the honorary distinction of being titled the Queen's Light Dragoons.

The value of the cavalry arm in Upper Canada had been proven conclusively, and by the end of the rebellion many of the county regiments had created attached troops of cavalry. But perhaps the most telling acknowledgement of the need for mobile troops was the British Army's move of two regular cavalry regiments to Canada in 1838.

It was during this period of active duty that the Troop's original 13th Dragoons-pattern uniform was simplified. The buff plastron (shield-like facing) on the breast of the jacket was removed, and the lace or braid was put directly on the garment. The Tarleton helmet was replaced with a handsome Regency-style bell-top shako with a white plume, on which was mounted a shako plate in the form of a Maltese cross surmounted by a crown. In the centre of the shako plate was the royal cypher 'VR' surrounded by an annulus bearing the title Queen's Light Dragoons. A few years later a new shako plate was adopted: the royal coat of arms with a scroll above reading 'Queen's Light Dragoons' and one below reading 'Toronto'.

By the spring of 1838 rebel activity had been greatly reduced and the Dragoons' tasks were centred on the area around Toronto. There was also time for ceremonial. On 9 April 1838 the Regiment's long tradition of providing guards and travelling escorts to governors and lieutenant governors had its beginning when the Queen's Light Dragoons provided an escort to Sir George Arthur, Lieutenant Governor of Upper Canada. Then, on 23 and 24 May the troop participated in the first parade in the province in honour of the young Queen Victoria's birthday. During July patrols were deployed regularly, day and night, along the main routes into the capital, and on 18 July the Denison and Button troops joined forces to provide an escort to Governor General Lord Durham. Finally, on 31 July 1838 the unit was stood down from active service.

In early August 1838 Major George Denison I was promoted lieutenant colonel to take command of the parent unit, the 1st West York Regiment. His son, Lieutenant Richard L. Denison, was then promoted captain to take command of the Queen's Light Dragoons.

The rebels were, however, still active, and members barely had time to resume their civilian lives when on 31 October 1838 the Queen's Light Dragoons were again placed on active service for despatch, patrol and other garrison duties. The despatch duty consisted of carrying messages along a 200-kilometre stretch of road between Cobourg and Oakville for a period of a month at a time, alternating on orderly duties at the headquarters in Toronto with the cavalry troop of the 3rd York Regiment.

The stationing of a regular British cavalry regiment in Upper Canada provided an excellent opportunity for the colonial troops to learn from the professionals and thus improve their capability to conduct mounted operations. In December 1838 a cavalry school was organized at Fort George in Niagara by a squadron of the King's Dragoon Guards to give instruction in cavalry drill and in 'interior economy' of a regiment. Each troop of cavalry and volunteer dragoons in Toronto, Hamilton and Niagara Districts were required to provide one officer, a sergeant, a corporal and a private, with their horses, to attend the school for two or three weeks. Thus began a long tradition of regimental training at Niagara Camp. This school also marked the earliest links between the unit and the King's Dragoon Guards, which were formally affiliated as Allied regiments in 1930. By the spring of 1839 all remaining threats of rebellion had been quelled, and the Queen's Light Dragoons were finally relieved from active service on St. George's Day, 23 April 1839. Button's troop returned to Markham as an independent entity.

One of the notable legacies of the rebellion was passage of a new Militia Act in 1839, reflecting a heightened awareness by the government of the importance of having the capability of defending the colony. Among the Act's important provisions was a clause that allowed the lieutenant governor to create cavalry units separate from the territorial Militia regiments, to which all cavalry troops had until then been connected. This brief burst of enthusiasm for a more effective Militia did not, however, have much real effect, as the whole of the Militia in Upper Canada had again begun to descend into one of the dead periods when there was little government support or money for defence.

When the Queen's Light Dragoons were stood down from active service in April 1839, the troop was required to turn in all of the uniforms, arms and accoutrements that had been issued, since they belonged to the British Army. The consequence of this was that the Queen's Light Dragoons were now 'naked'. To overcome this problem, the officers of the troop immediately bought enough swords and sword belts to loan to the NCOs and men, and they also began to buy shakos, jackets, pouches and belts, also for loan. "Thus for years, the whole troop equipment belonged to the officers … a unique experience in the Upper Canada militia."

Despite a continuing perception of threat from the ever-expanding United States, the 1840s were lean years for the Militia. The union of the two provinces in 1840 did create a single militia for the whole of Canada, but that did not translate into greater interest in military affairs or more funding. Throughout the decade the Queen's Light Dragoons continued to parade voluntarily, without pay, a number of times each year, and for several years the Troop was the only unit of the Militia in York that met for training on a regular basis. But its members certainly got no official encouragement, and even less from the majority of the population. Captain Frederick C. Denison's *Historical Record*, published in 1876, contains a passage that indicates the difficulties of serving in the troop at that time:

Even the people of the town discouraged volunteering…. When men appeared in uniform they were laughed at for being soldier-mad. The result was that rather than show themselves on the streets they sought a quiet place to drill, where they would be left undisturbed. Men who would do this were true patriots.

Lieutenant Colonel Richard L. Denison, second commanding officer of Denison's Troop, 1838 to 1848. (GGHG Archives)

In the spring of 1843 the troop was called upon to provide a mounted escort for Sir Charles Metcalfe, the new Lieutenant Governor of Canada West, meeting him as he arrived on the outskirts of Toronto and accompanying him into the city. By 1843, with the appointment of Robert Denison as cornet, all of the officers in the troop were brothers. It would appear that the troop had some difficulty in attracting officers from outside the Denison family, in part at least because the officers had to bear the expense of providing the uniforms and kit of the men.

In 1846 the Denison troop was reorganized and its name was changed to 1st Toronto Independent Troop of Cavalry. Captain Richard Denison left to take a major's position in the 4th Battalion of Toronto Sedentary Militia, which was commanded by his father, Lieutenant Colonel George Denison I. Captain George Denison II was appointed to command the troop.

Few records exist of Button's troop in this period, and some historians have suggested that it was dormant for a time in the 1840s. A history of the town of Markham, however, illustrates a letter from the adjutant of the 1st Battalion York Militia dated 9 June 1848 addressed to "Captain Francis Button, Commanding the Cavalry – 12th Battalion, No. 1 York Militia", informing him of the annual muster for his troop. It is thus most probable that the troop continued to exist over this whole period, parading only on the required one day each year.

If the 1840s had been lean years indeed, the 1850s began more auspiciously. Denison's troop provided a 28-man mounted escort and guard to Governor General Lord Elgin in May 1850 at the opening of Parliament. This was a practical necessity rather than pure ceremonial, as the governor general had been threatened with violence during his visit to Toronto. From that time, on every occasion of the opening or proroguing of Parliament by Lord Elgin, a mounted escort was found by the troop.

The unit was first raised to regimental status in March 1853 when the 1st Regiment York Light Dragoons was formed, the first occasion when the Denison and the Button troops were formally linked. The new regiment was to have four troops: 1st Troop was the Denison troop, 2nd Troop was the Markham troop under Captain William Marr Button, 3rd Troop, from Oak Ridges, was raised by Lieutenant Colonel N.T. McLeod. A

Tunic of the Queen's Light Dragoons and York Light Dragoons, worn from 1838 until the 1850s, now in the Canadian War Museum. The tunic is missing its gold lace epaulettes. (Courtesy of René Chartrand)

Commission scroll issued to Cornet Robert Denison in 1846, later a commanding officer of the Denison Troop. (GGHG Archives)

4th Troop was to have been raised by Lieutenant Colonel J.S. Dennis but this was never done. George Taylor Denison II was promoted lieutenant colonel to command the regiment, and Captain Robert B. Denison was placed in command of 1st Troop. In September 1854 George Taylor Denison III was gazetted cornet in 1st Troop.

The launching of a major British and French operation against Russia in the Crimea in the summer of 1854, even though thousands of kilometres distance from Canada, was to have a significant and lasting effect on the organization of the Canadian Militia. The British government decided to withdraw most of the British garrison in Canada to sustain the war effort in Crimea, and the colonial government was made to understand clearly that it would now have to take responsibility for its own defences. The result was a thorough restructuring of the militia by means of the Militia Act of 1855.

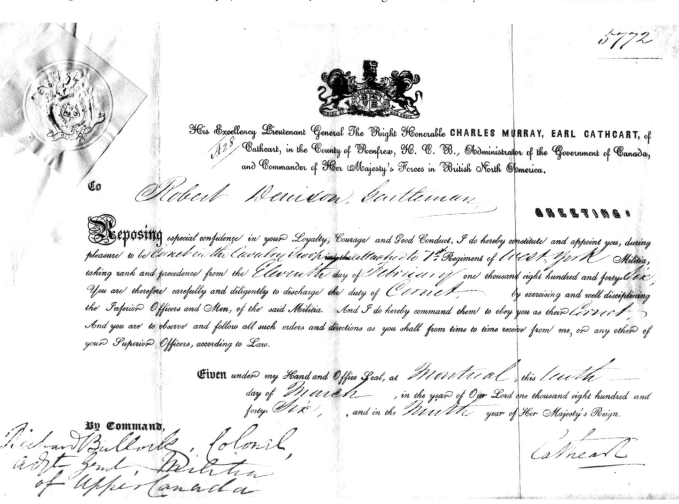

Shako worn by the Queen's Light Dragoons, ca 1840, this one with the Royal coat of arms shako plate. The white feather plume is missing. (GGHG Archives)

THE MILITIA ACT OF 1855

The key provisions of the new Militia Act were the creation of two classes of militia in Canada, active and sedentary. The Active Militia was to consist of volunteer units, thus in effect bringing an end to universal enlistment of all men, although the provision lingered on in legal theory until 1950. The Active Militia was initially not to exceed 5,000 men. Within this number, 583 cavalrymen were authorized in Canada West (Ontario), distributed in 11 troops. Each troop was authorized 55 all ranks: a captain, a lieutenant, a cornet, three sergeants, three corporals, one trumpeter and 45 privates. Officers and men were required to provide their own uniforms and saddlery, but both men and horses were to be paid for ten training days per year. The government accepted its responsibility to provide swords and pistols.

The 1st and 2nd Troops of Volunteer Militia Cavalry of the County of York were officially formed, by authority of a General Order dated 27 December 1855, as part of the 1st York

Light Dragoons, which thus became the first volunteer cavalry unit raised under the provisions of the new Act. 1st Troop was the Denison troop which continued to wear the 1837-pattern uniform, and the 2nd was the Oak Ridges Troop. The old 2nd Troop, the Button troop, was initially put into the sedentary militia, but after protests from its members it was reactivated as the Markham Troop of Volunteer Militia Cavalry on 17 July 1856 under the command of Captain William Button. In early 1858, the Yorkville Troop of Cavalry, formed only a year earlier as the 4th Troop of the York Light Dragoons, was disbanded and its members transferred to the Oak Ridges Troop.

The newly re-created York Dragoons immediately got to work. During the winter of 1855-56 "… a considerable amount of hard drilling was done". The Regiment was on parade for Queen Victoria's birthday celebrations on 24 May 1856 and on 9 June participated in the first annual drill under the new law, when swords and belts, pouches and Colt revolvers were issued. At this time the government provided storerooms for the Regiment's arms and equipment on Queen

Lieutenant Colonel George Taylor Denison II, commanding officer of the Denison Troop, 1848 to 1850, and commanding officer of the 1st Regiment York Light Dragoons 1853 to 1865. (GGHG Archives)

Street near Bathurst. A week later Sir Edmund Head, the Governor General, inspected the Regiment's two troops and pronounced "his entire satisfaction at their appearance and efficiency".

In November 1856 Captain R.B. Denison gave up command of 1st Troop to organize an artillery battery, which created a problem of command succession. The senior subaltern was George Taylor Denison III who was only 17, and considered far too young. But no other officer was willing to assume leadership of the troop, so Denison was given temporary command on 15 January 1857, as a lieutenant, with the promise of being confirmed on the condition that he recruit the troop to full strength (50 men). Denison, a very strong-willed and stubborn young man, soon succeeded in doing precisely that, and he did a most creditable job in command of the escort to Sir Edmund Head at the opening of Parliament in February 1857. He was promoted captain on 22 April, still 17 years old!

1st Troop's young commander soon had another test of his mettle. In August 1858 he had again to organize a mounted escort to the Governor General for the opening of Parliament.

Captain Francis Button, commanding officer of Button's Troop 1831 to 1853. (Markham Museum)

This time, however, serious violence was expected because of public unrest, and Denison was told to provide as large an escort as possible. Before the parade he reported that he was up all night, with his sergeant major, Orlando Dunn, visiting all his men personally to ensure that they would appear. The journey to the Parliament Buildings turned out to be uneventful, but there was trouble on the return journey, with booing, hissing and shouting at the Governor General. One of the troopers struck a man making offensive gestures, which put an end to the demonstrations.

The Militia cavalry confronted an early example of bureaucratic failure to appreciate the need for a balanced all-arms force when in 1859 the government prepared a new Militia Act which would have abolished the cavalry arm entirely. Senior officers were, however, able to bring enough pressure that the cavalry was saved, but the cost was reduced numbers and reduced pay. The strength of the troops was reduced from 50 to 30 men, and the number of authorized days of paid training was reduced from ten days to six. (At this time a trooper's pay was $1.00 per day, decimal currency having been introduced in Canada in 1858.) Other annoying restrictions were applied: all unit training had to be done on six consecutive days in June, rather than being spread over the whole year, even though the men would not be paid until December. The frustrations of Militia service appear not to have changed much over the past century.

Lieutenant Colonel Robert B. Denison, officer commanding 1st Troop of the 1st Regiment York Light Dragoons (The Denison Troop), 1850 to 1856. (GGHG Archives)

The visit of HRH The Prince of Wales, later King Edward VII, in August 1860 brought the Regiment's first involvement in a royal tour. Both the Denison troop and the Oak Ridges troop of the York Light Dragoons were detailed to provide escorts for the Prince during his stay in Toronto, and they also took part in a Royal Review held at Queen's Park.

Colt Navy revolver (.36 cal.) of the type issued to the Denison Troop in 1856.

In *Soldiering in Canada*, published in 1900, Colonel George Denison III wrote that the Royal visit

caused the expenditure of a great deal of money by the officers and men of the corps. We had no saddles or bridles furnished us, and each man had to furnish his own. So they all had ordinary hunting saddles, and the ordinary light riding bridles. To give an appearance of uniformity we had head stalls or front pieces made with a broad white band across the front and two pieces of leather crossed with bosses, and they had loops by which they could be put in front of any ordinary bridles. This at a little distance gave the appearance of uniformity. To cover the saddles we had sheepskin covers made, dyed a dark blue and edged with a scalloped border of white cloth. These being fastened over the saddles with surcingles, gave them a uniform appearance.

Newspaper reports of the day commented that the cavalry was "very soldierlike in their uniforms of blue and silver", and the Prince of Wales, on leaving, praised the work of the cavalry escort very warmly. Improvisation has clearly always played a part in getting a job done well in the Regiment.

The outbreak of civil war between the United States and the Confederate States in April 1861 once again strained relations between Britain and America, and by extension reinforced the threat that Canadians perceived from their southern neighbour. Public interest in defence rose once again, and the immediate effect on the Canadian Militia was a great increase in the number of volunteer units. A government commission recommended that the strength of the active Militia be increased to 50,000, including 27 troops of cavalry, but that was rejected by Parliament as too expensive. Nonetheless, in 1863 the strength of the Active Militia was raised from 5,000 to 35,000, and many Canadian regiments trace

Captain George Taylor Denison III, who took command of the Denison Troop of the York Light Dragoons in 1857. This photo is believed to date from 1859 or 1860. Note the Sabretache of the York Dragoons. (Ontario Archives 5.560)

their origin to this time. The effect on the York Light Dragoons was that the authorized strength of each of the two troops was increased from 30 to 60 all ranks, 56 men and NCOs, three officers and a surgeon. At this same time the unit was moved to quarters in Block House No. 1 at Old Fort York, which was to be home to the Regiment for more than 40 years.

The American Civil War, often termed the first modern war, involved massive armies and battles on a scale never before seen, and it involved a host of new technological innovations which changed the nature of battle. One of the first to recognize the magnitude of the military revolution was George Taylor Denison III, who had carefully watched the course of the war, "trying to learn as many new lessons as possible from the practical working of new conditions caused by rifled fire-arms, revolvers, telegraphs, railways, etc." Denison's studies resulted in the publication of his book *Modern Cavalry* in 1868.

The Civil War had a number of long-lasting effects in Canada. One of these was that the British recognized the futility of any attempt to defend Canada and let it be known very clearly that the responsibility for defence "must rest … mainly and principally on Canada itself". This, together with well-founded rumours of raids by militant Irish-American, led politicians in Canada and the Maritime provinces to think in terms of political union as an essential precondition for defending British North America. The Charlottetown Conference in September 1864 began the process which led to Confederation three years later.

In the meanwhile, the greater public interest in defence was to have a decided effect on the structure of the York Light Dragoons, but it did not bring about much change in the generally poor quality of equipment supplied by the government. On 23 October 1865 the Denison troop was inspected by the Adjutant-General commanding the Militia, Colonel Patrick MacDougall. Every officer and man – 60 in all – was on parade, and the troop showed that it was well drilled. Major Denison took the opportunity to ask two things: that he be allowed to form a second troop, and that the troop be provided with proper cavalry saddles. About a month later the troop did receive 35 Hussar saddles, not enough to go around, but protests fell on deaf ears. It would be years before more were supplied.

The growth of the cavalry did, however, affect the unit's organization. On 22 December 1865 the Oak Ridges and Markham troops were officially organized as The 1st Squadron of Volunteer Light Cavalry of the County of York. This brought to an end the regimental status of the York Light Dragoons, and Denison's Troop was once again an independent entity.

THE GOVERNOR GENERAL'S BODY GUARD

April 1866 was a significant time in the history of the Regiment, for on the 27th of that month the Governor General approved the unit's official name as the Governor General's Body Guard of Upper Canada.

The origin of the name that the Regiment would bear for the next 70 years can be traced to a request made by its officers in 1861 for recognition of the special relationship that had developed since the practice of providing escorts to the Queen's representative had begun in 1838. Nothing came of that request, and there was great consternation when the officers of the troop read in the official gazette of 13 April 1866 that the

designation "Governor General's Body Guard" had been awarded to a newly formed unit, the Royal Guides from Montreal. Major Denison made an immediate personal protest to members of the cabinet in Ottawa, reminding them that the unit was the oldest troop in Canada with a continuous existence. Justice was done quickly, at least in part: the Montreal unit was to be the Governor General's Body Guard of *Lower* Canada, and Denison's troop would be the Governor General's Body Guard of *Upper* Canada. The provincial distinction would soon become irrelevant, as only a few years later the Montreal unit simply disappeared.

FENIAN RAIDS OF 1866

The demobilization of hundreds of thousands of battle-hardened soldiers in the United States in 1865 resulted in a fresh threat to Canada's survival, a surge in the strength of a fanatical group of Irish-Americans called the Fenian Brotherhood and their para-military arm, the Irish Republican Army. The Fenians held to the strange notion that if the British could be expelled from British North America and held hostage, their dream of an independent Ireland would somehow be helped. The Fenians openly stockpiled arms and recruited and trained men, and their grandiose plans for raids and incursions into Canada and the Maritime provinces were well known.

The Fenians continued to plot, and reports of an imminent invasion of the Niagara peninsula by a large Fenian force were received on 29 May 1866. Orders to call out 400 Toronto militiamen were issued on 31 May, and the Queen's Own Rifles deployed to Port Colborne during the afternoon of 1 June, just after word was received that a Fenian 'army' had crossed into Canada near Fort Erie.

Major Denison was alerted belatedly shortly after noon on 1 June by Major General Napier, who commanded the British forces in Upper Canada. Orders were received at about 1500 hours to turn out the Body Guard and leave for the frontier early the following morning. Denison at once alerted his officers and sent out the corporals

Drawing of Old Fort York ca. 1860, home to the York Light Dragoons and the Governor General's Body Guard from 1863 to 1902. (Toronto Historical Board)

and sergeants to bring the men and their horses to a rendezvous at the Exhibition Grounds. By daybreak the troop had been assembled and soon afterward moved to the docks to embark on the steamer, *City of Toronto*.

The boat sailed at 0800 hours, arriving at Port Dalhousie about 1100, where news was heard about fighting at Ridgeway. Here Denison had a train made up to take the Body Guard to Port Robinson, the nearest point on the railway to Chippawa. At Port Robinson the troop detrained, the men and horses were fed, and the Body Guard then marched to Chippawa. Once there, Denison was advised to wait until evening to join Colonel Peacocke's force – some 1,700 men, including three companies of the British 47th Regiment of Foot, two companies of the British 16th Regiment, the 10th Royal Grenadiers, and the Lincoln Militia – which was assembling at New Germany. In any case, many of the horses, after the hard riding of the previous night, needed to have their shoes looked after. Oats were purchased, and the men fed their horses on the roadside or on the sidewalks. Some men lay on the grass to snatch a few minutes' sleep, as they had had none the previous night; others were busy at the blacksmith's shop having their swords sharpened.

Later that afternoon the Body Guard rode from Chippawa to New Germany. They arrived shortly after 1700 hours, just as Colonel Peacocke's force had begun to move toward Stevensville, where they were to join together with Colonel Booker's force of about 850 men that had initially been sent to Port Colborne. The Body Guard were immediately sent forward as an advance guard. In his book, *Soldiering in Canada*, Major Denison recalled:

> we marched some two or three hours, the pace of my force being regulated by the rate at which the infantry of the main body could march. ... I began to chafe almost at once at not being able to push on. I felt that there was no reason why I should not go on until I struck the enemy's pickets, for I knew I could easily fall back if overmatched.

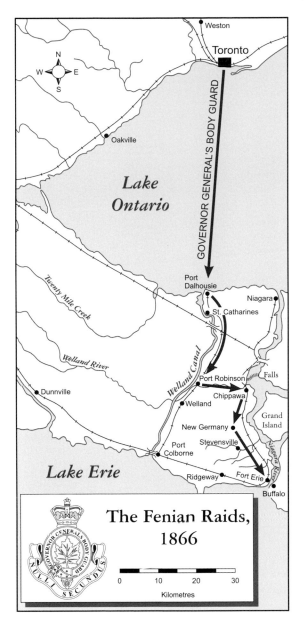

The Fenian Raids, 1866

After the column had marched for about 15 kilometres, just as daylight was fading the leading horsemen spotted some men on the road, at a point where marshy woods closed in on both sides. Denison went forward and deployed a reconnaissance patrol of four men. In the dusk they saw one man, who quickly disappeared into the woods. The patrol continued for about 150 metres, but in the darkness could not confirm the enemy's presence. Colonel Peacocke then deployed two companies of the 16th Regiment to search the bush, but the woods were so dense and the ground so wet and soft, that they could not proceed in the darkness. Peacocke also confronted with a destroyed bridge just beyond, chose to halt until daylight. The Fenian picket that had been spotted got away to Fort Erie, where they reported that they had been driven in by British cavalry.

It was an uncomfortable night for the troops; all that the men of the Body Guard had to eat was a single hardtack biscuit that Major Denison had issued while crossing the lake. Denison was appalled at the lack of administrative preparation, commenting in *Soldiering in Canada*:

> The want of organization or preparation, in view of the long threatenings, seems almost incredible. I had to take my corps on a campaign without the carbines I had asked for, but with revolvers for which we had only some four or five ten-year-old paper cartridges for each. We did not know whether they would go off or not. We had no haversacks, no water-bottles, no nose-bags.... We had no canteens, no knives or forks, or cooking utensils of any kind....

We had no clothes except those on our backs.... We had no tents and no blankets.

Meanwhile, Booker's force had moved by train to Ridgeway, where Booker learned from locals that the Fenians were in the vicinity. The Fenians by then were in position on Limestone Ridge, about two kilometres north of the village of Ridgeway. Booker, without any cavalry for reconnaissance, pushed on to his appointed rendezvous at Stevensville. As it marched onward, this force literally stumbled upon the Fenian position, and a battle ensued.

The surprised Canadian militiamen fought bravely in the early stages of the action,

Drawing of a night camp during the 1866 operations against the Fenians. (NAC C 48845)

but when several Fenians appeared on horseback someone cried out "cavalry", and Booker gave the orders to prepare to receive a cavalry charge. The Queen's Own Rifles square, however, just gave the Fenians a concentrated target, and many men were hit. When Booker ordered a withdrawal there was great confusion; the Militia line crumbled, and men ran to the rear, giving the Fenians what amounted to a victory. The Fenians then scuttled back to Fort Erie, where another short fight occurred with a small group of militiamen who had gone to Fort Erie on a tugboat.

It had been a near disaster. George Stanley, in his book *Canada's Soldiers: The Military History of an Unmilitary People,* made the following criticism:

The original order calling out the militia did not include any cavalry units, and Lieutenant-Colonel Denison, who commanded the Governor General's Body Guard, was obliged to beg General Napier to issue instructions for the mobilization of his unit. It was therefore … not until the following day that Denison was able to join Peacocke. Thus both Peacocke and Booker were dependent upon civilian observation for military information. The importance of horsemen is apparent from the effect which the few

mounted Fenians had upon the infantry: it was the threat of a cavalry attack at Limestone Ridge which turned victory into defeat for the Canadian forces.

News of the defeats at Ridgeway and Fort Erie reached Peacocke in his bivouac just before dawn on 3 June, and he ordered the Body Guard to ride toward Fort Erie to report on the situation. Before the troop set out a supply column finally arrived, and the men of the Body Guard had their first meal since leaving Toronto:

Just before daybreak the wagons came up from the rear with some beef and hard-tack. The beef was given to us in small chunks. We made fires of the rail fences, and, sticking the small pieces of meat on slivers of wood, we cooked them over the fire by toasting them…. We went to the brook near by to get a drink.

In his *History of the Fenian Raids* Major Denison described what followed:

Recalling some of the scouts, we then proceeded on the gallop up the river towards Fort Erie, being informed by the people we met that a number of the Fenians were still there. On coming in sight of the village, we saw men dodging in every direction, but when we got up [about 0600 hours] nearly all were hidden or gone; muskets, bayonets and belts were scattered along the road, where men had dropped them in their flight. A few prisoners were taken by us, and the wounded were placed under a guard. ... After placing guards over the prisoners and the arms ... the men and horses were billeted in the taverns, as both were nearly used up by about forty hours' almost continuous exertions.

An hour later Colonel Garnet Wolseley arrived in Fort Erie, followed by a column commanded by Colonel Lowrey of the 47th Regiment. Colonel Peacocke arrived in due course with his column, and the following day the whole force camped on the high ground in the rear of the village. The Body Guard put out pickets at the upper and lower ferry. Again, there was a lot of discomfort for the men during the first few days: the unit still had no tents, and had to borrow some from the British gunners. The messing was for some time very crude, but on 4 June a trainload of supplies ar-

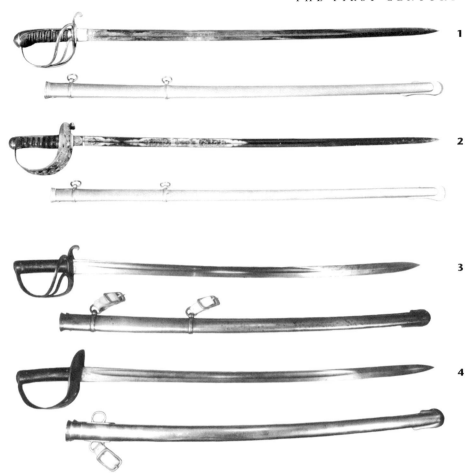

Officers' swords: 1. 1821 pattern light cavalry sabre carried by Governor General's Body Guard officers from 1837 to 1912. 2. 1896 pattern cavalry sabre, Mississauga Horse.

Governor General Body Guards troopers' swords: 3. 1853 pattern cavalry troopers sword issued in 1855. 4. 1890 pattern cavalry troopers sword which replaced the 1853 pattern. (GGHG Archives)

rived for the volunteers, sent by the inhabitants of Toronto. The Body Guard remained at Fort Erie for three weeks, doing outpost and patrol duties. "We had a campfire in the middle of our camp every evening, and the men not on duty gathered around it, singing songs and telling anecdotes and enjoying themselves."

The men got the name of 'Denison's Guerillas', partly, I think, from the fact that I had got them all supplied with jack-boots in which their trousers were tucked.... As no mounted men wore these in the army at that time, and those we had were the common lumbermen's boots, they looked very rough and ready, and gave the men an irregular appearance, but they were very serviceable and useful.

By mid-month, relative calm had been restored in the frontier area. When the St. Catharines' cavalry were deployed to Ridgeway, the Body Guard established a post halfway between Fort Erie and Ridgeway to maintain communications with Port Colborne. On 20 June the whole force was ordered to go home.

To counter the continuing threats of further Fenian incursions, a training camp was set up at Thorold, under Colonel Wolseley. In addition to some British regulars, there were three or four militia battalions, and the Body Guard remained there between 14 August and 5 October, reinforced briefly by the Cobourg cavalry. During this time the unit established posts at Chippawa, under Sergeant Major Dunn, and at Black Creek, Fort Erie and Ridgeway, and from these sites patrolled the length of the Niagara River every night. For the effectiveness of this work the unit received plaudits from Wolseley. The Body Guard was relieved of duty on 6 October and returned home to Toronto. During this time Major Denison was promoted brevet lieutenant colonel.

The Body Guard carried out its annual training at a camp on Garrison Common in early June 1867, the last as a part of the Militia of the Province of Canada. Much of the training centred around preparation for the Confederation Day parade, and there was also some satisfaction that the unit was issued with Spencer repeating carbines which would make the troop more effective than it had been during the Fenian raid.

CONFEDERATION

Confederation Day, 1 July 1867, was marked in Toronto, as in most other major centres in the new Dominion, with an elaborate military review. The Body Guard, along with the other Toronto units, the Queen's Own Rifles and the 10th Royal Grenadiers, and the remaining British units, the 13th Hussars, a battery of the Royal Artillery, and the 17th Regiment of Foot, all paraded in full dress uniforms, led by bands playing stirring marches and appropriate patriotic music. It was a fitting way to mark the birth of the new nation.

But Confederation brought no immediate change for the Militia in the Canadian provinces, for the existing provincial militia acts continued in force until the Dominion Parliament could produce a Bill which applied to the whole country. In the meantime units simply carried on as they had in the past.

Early in October 1867, twenty members of the Body Guard attended a cavalry school organized by Colonel Jenyns, the commanding officer of the13th Hussars, the British regular cavalry regiment based at the New Fort (Stanley Barracks). This school proved to be a magnificent opportunity to learn cavalry drills and manoeuvres from professional soldiers, and it resulted in a marked improvement in the training that the unit was able to organize for itself.

The first Dominion Militia Act was passed in Parliament on 22 May 1868, and in most respects provided continuity with established practice and law. The principle of universal liability for military service was upheld: the reserve militia was to consist of all able-bodied male British subjects between 18 and 60 in case of a levée en masse. The active militia was to consist

Canada General Service Medal with 'Fenian Raid 1866' bar, as awarded to members of the Governor General's Body Guard who participated in the operations.

of the volunteer militia, the regular militia, and the marine militia, all of which, in any case, were comprised of volunteers.

The Volunteer Militia would contain all volunteer units serving at the time the Act was proclaimed, thus giving continuity with existing provincial corps. The Act did, however, require that each commanding officer had to muster his unit within three months to explain the Act, administer an oath of allegiance to each officer and man, and have every member sign a muster roll. The new law provided for annual paid drills for 40,000 officers and men for not less than 8 nor more than 16 days, with the number of allowable training days being regulated by the annual parliamentary money vote. Nine military districts were created: one in Nova Scotia, one in New Brunswick, three in Quebec and four in Ontario. These were sub-divided into 22 brigade areas, and then into regimental districts, which for the most part conformed to the boundaries of federal electoral ridings. This last provision gave rise to many problems in subsequent years, as senior appointments within Militia units came to be seen as falling within the purview of the dominant political party's patronage.

MODERN CAVALRY

The detailed study that Lieutenant Colonel George Taylor Denison III had made of the employment of cavalry during the American Civil War was finally revealed to the world with the publication of his book *Modern Cavalry* in London in the summer of 1868. This book was to have a very significant effect on the organization and employment of cavalry for many years, not only in Canada but also in the major armies on the European continent.

Technological change was at that time beginning to have a notable effect on the employment of all armies on the field of battle. As would happen on numerous occasions over the next fifty years, the value of cavalry was being seriously questioned, mainly because of the widespread introduction of rifled firearms and cannon, all with greater accuracy, longer range and much improved rates of fire than earlier weapons. These weapons, simply put, were able to annihilate any traditional charge of heavy cavalry. The whole nature of warfare was undergoing a revolution.

Denison's purpose in writing *Modern Cavalry* was to demonstrate that cavalry was still *the* pivotal arm, *the* essential mobile element on the modern battlefield, but only if there were a major change in the way that mounted men were employed. Basing his views mainly on the successful employment of cavalry in the Confederate Army, Denison believed that cavalrymen of the future would have to be employed as mounted riflemen, trained as infantry, but still retaining the instincts and mobility of cavalry. Mounted rifles, in his view, could combine speed of movement with the ability to concentrate dismounted firepower when and where it was needed, both in the offence and defence. Mounted riflemen, he argued, would be capable of performing all of the usual tasks given to light cavalry – raiding, scouting, covering a retreat, pursuing an enemy or guarding the flanks of a main force – but they would also be able to fight dismounted as infantry whenever the tactical situation required it, and because of this they could be used to hold ground, which cavalry could not do.

Denison also argued that it was far more difficult to achieve a high level of proficiency with cavalry armed with swords or lances than it was with mounted riflemen, and he maintained that all volunteer militia cavalry should be mounted rifles. He did not, however, rule out the retention of heavy cavalry, but suggested that they could be employed in their traditional offensive role – the charge – only when conditions were especially favourable.

Denison's ideas were roundly condemned by the British as those of an upstart colonial, but they were well received by the Germans and Russians, and the book was translated into several languages within the next few years. It would take several decades before Denison's concepts were widely accepted in Canada, but it is interesting to note that the Canadian cavalry deployed to South Africa in the Boer War at the turn of the century were all mounted rifles units, and that the Canadian Cavalry Brigade in the First World War was almost always employed as mounted rifles.

A member of the band of the Governor General's Body Guard, ca. 1879. (GGHG Archives)

On 18 August 1868, shortly after his return from launching *Modern Cavalry* in Britain, Lieutenant Colonel George Taylor Denison III abruptly resigned his commission and command of the Governor General's Body Guard. He had been led to believe he would be appointed Deputy Adjutant General of Militia if he dropped his legal claim to retain ownership of a former Confederate vessel, the *Georgian*, and he was outraged when Minister of Militia Sir George Etienne Cartier rudely informed him that he would never get the appointment. Denison vowed that he could not continue to serve while Cartier remained as Minister. On the departure of George Taylor Denison III, Edwin P. Denison was promoted captain and given command of the Body Guard. At this time Cornet Frederick C. Denison was promoted lieutenant, and Sergeant Major Orlando Dunn was gazetted cornet.

This drawing of mounted rifles troops was used as an illustration in George Taylor Denison III's book, *Modern Cavalry*, published in 1868. The uniforms bear a striking resemblance to those worn a few years later by the Body Guard. (GGHG Archives)

Captain Edwin P. Denison, commander of the Denison Troop 1868 to 1872. The Maltese Cross badge on the shako is the original badge used by the Queen's Light Dragoons in 1838. (GGHG Archives)

In early October 1868 the Body Guard, along with the Oak Ridges, Markham, Burford, St. Catharines and Grimsby troops of cavalry paraded under the commanding officer of the 13th Hussars for eight days of instruction on the Garrison Common in Toronto, the first brigade camp for cavalry in the new Dominion. Throughout this period the members of the Body Guard were judged to be the cleanest and best turned-out at every guard inspection. The final day of the camp was unexpectedly much more exciting that had been intended. As the culmination of the week of training there was a demonstration of a cavalry charge, aimed in the direction of packed spectator stands. The horses, however, appeared to think that the demonstration was a race, and each exerted itself to win. The riders fortunately managed to veer off to the flanks just in time to miss hitting the spectators, many of whom it appears had already abandoned the stands in great haste.

The new Governor General of Canada, Lord Lisgar, paid his first official visit to Toronto on 2 June 1869, and the Body Guard was proud to provide a mounted escort under Lieutenant Frederick Denison on that occasion. Then in October 1869 a travelling escort was found for the visit of HRH Prince Arthur, later The Duke of Connaught, who had come to Canada to serve a one-year tour of duty with the Royal Engineers in Montreal.

The quality of cavalry training in the Militia suffered a setback in the autumn of 1869 because of the impending withdrawal of the British garrison. The 13th Hussars were soon to return to England, and the commanding officer reluctantly notified the Adjutant General that because he was about to sell the regiment's horses the annual cavalry school in Toronto could no longer be continued.

That same autumn the new Dominion was forced to confront the beginning of its first significant internal challenge. After years of negotiation, the Hudson's Bay Company agreed to relinquish its vast holdings in the North West and have the territory incorporated into Canada. There had been, however, no consultation with the people of the Red River settlement. The Métis in particular were concerned that their semi-nomadic way of life would be disrupted by an influx of white settlers, and they established a provisional government led by Louis Riel. Riel barred the entry of the newly appointed lieutenant governor, and set in train a convoluted political crisis that was not settled until the next spring.

The Prime Minister stopped the transfer of Rupert's Land to Canada as soon as he heard of the 'rebellion', and insisted that the British send a military force to put it down. A Red River expedition, consisting of two composite battalions under Colonel Garnet Wolseley, was thus despatched in May 1870, even though negotiations were being carried on with Riel's provisional administration. The expeditionary force arrived at Fort Garry in August 1870, after a gruelling trek through the waterways and portages of northern Ontario, only to find that Riel and his henchmen had fled. Manitoba was admitted to Confederation on 15 July 1870. This strange episode had little direct effect on the Body Guard, as the only member of the unit involved was Lieutenant Frederick C. Denison, who served as Colonel Wolseley's aide-de-camp.

The Fenians again threatened Canada's external security in the late spring of 1870, and in late May two brief Fenian incursions were quickly repulsed. During this time of tension the Body Guard was held in readiness, but the unit's services were not required as the trouble was confined to the Quebec border. During the summer of 1870 all British regular troops were withdrawn from Ontario, and those who remained in other parts of the country were returned to Britain in 1871. The defence of the Dominion was now entirely in the hands of the Canadian Militia.

A major change in the pattern of the uniform of the Governor General's Body Guard was made in 1871, as a result of a Militia-wide study of uniform styles the previous year. The Body Guard chose to adopt a uniform patterned after that worn by the 6th Dragoon Guards: blue tunics with white facings, and German silver helmets with white horsehair plumes. Standing Orders published in 1910 by Colonel William Hamilton Merritt described the uniform:

> The officers' tunic is of blue cloth, edged all round, including top and bottom of the collar, with round-back silver cord, with three-quarter inch lace all round for field officers, but round the top only for captains and lieutenants; the cuffs pointed with one and one-half inch lace round the top, and figured braiding extending to eleven inches from the bottom of the cuffs for field officers, with an Austrian knot of round-back silver cord, and a tracing of braid in the form of eyes, eight inches deep for captains, and with a similar knot, and a tracing of plain braid, seven and a half inches deep for lieutenants…. Shoulder straps similar to Household Cavalry, lined with blue. Badges of rank in gold.

The uniform for NCOs and men was of the same pattern if somewhat less elaborate, the edging being white cord rather than silver. The officers imported the helmets from England, and sold them at cost to the men.

In the autumn of 1871 the Body Guard confronted a very serious threat to its existence. The district staff, in the manner of staff officers of all ages, concocted a plan to bring conformity to the organization of cavalry units. They wanted to create two similarly organized cavalry regiments out of all of the troops and squadrons in Ontario, with the Body Guard forming part of the second regiment. This would have brought an end to the unit's place as the senior cavalry unit in the country, and the officers sent a petition to Governor General Lord Lisgar asking that he intervene. Lord Lisgar responded as had been hoped: he decreed that the precedence of the Governor General's Body Guard would not be changed.

Captain E.P. Denison retired as commanding officer on 1 March 1872, and Frederick C. Denison was promoted captain and placed in command. Cornet Orlando Dunn was promoted lieutenant, and Clarence A. Denison was appointed cornet.

A change in the organization of the cavalry in Ontario did, however, occur, and it affected the Markham troop. In May 1872 the 2nd Regiment of Cavalry was officially formed, with headquarters at Oak Ridges, and seven troops, including the Markham troop. Brevet Lieutenant Colonel William Button was appointed as a squadron commander in the new regiment.

Training was certainly not neglected in these years, for in June of both 1871 and 1872 the Body Guard participated in brigade-level camps at Niagara-on-the-Lake for 16 days of intensive training. In 1872 the Body Guard provided the largest troop, and it was attached to 2nd Cavalry Regiment. That year the unit was issued with Snider carbines, and in the final major exercise of the camp, the Body Guard formed the advance guard of the attacking force, and distinguished itself by capturing a complete infantry company.

Lord Dufferin made his first visit to Toronto as Governor General in October 1872, and the Body Guard furnished numerous escorts during his stay in the city. At a grand ball given by His Excellency, the men of the unit also formed a guard line to the entrance hall.

Annual drills in 1873 and 1874 were conducted at the Old Fort in Toronto. In July 1874, Lord Dufferin again visited Toronto, and the Body Guard once again formed a Vice Regal escort. An attempt was made in 1874 to increase the establishment of the Body Guard from a troop to a squadron of two troops. Lieutenant Dunn actually organized a second troop, which was paraded, but the new organization was never officially sanctioned because the Adjutant General who had authorized this was sacked before the General Order was published. The increase to squadron strength had to wait for two years.

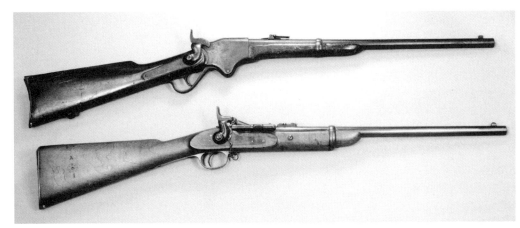

Top: The .50 calibre Spencer carbine, issued to the Body Guard in 1867. Bottom: Snider carbine (.577 calibre), issued to the unit in 1872. (Royal Canadian Military Institute)

The annual training camp in June 1875 took place at Holland Landing, along with the Markham troop (Captain Elliot) and the Oak Ridges troop (Captain McConnell). The Body Guard took advantage of the camp's location to practice its long-range march discipline: the unit rode from Toronto to Richmond Hill, and thence to Holland Landing, a distance of 63 kilometres, in 15 hours.

On 5 May 1876 a Militia General Order was published authorizing the increase of the Body Guard to squadron strength, with two troops. 'A' Troop remained under the command of Captain Frederick C. Denison, and 'B' Troop was formed under Captain Orlando Dunn, a position he held for 20 years. At this time Lieutenant-Colonel George Taylor Denison III was appointed commanding officer for the second time, after an eight-year absence from the unit. He returned to the Militia at his own request, so that he would be eligible to compete in the Russian Czar's competition for "the best work on cavalry and military operations on horseback in all ages and countries". Lieutenant Clarence Denison was appointed

Detail of the 1871 Body Guard officers' tunic, as modified in 1880. Note that badges of rank in 1880 were moved from the collar to braided shoulder boards. This uniform was patterned after the uniform of the British 6th Dragoon Guards. (GGHG Archives)

Lieutenant Colonel Frederick Denison, CMG, commanding officer of the Denison Troop (as a captain) 1872 to 1876. He later raised and commanded the Canadian Nile Voyageurs in Egypt in 1884-85. (GGHG Archives)

adjutant. Funding for Militia training was considerably reduced in 1876, and until 1884 annual training camps were conducted at Stanley Barracks – sometimes called the New Fort – in Toronto, rather than at Niagara.

The regimental badge that was used for the next seventy years with only minor variations was adopted formally in 1876: a maple leaf within a garter bearing the corps designation, surmounted by the Imperial crown, and with the motto Nulli Secundus beneath.

The Body Guard band was formed in 1877. For a number of years it dressed in the Regiment's dragoon-style uniform, but for a time in the 1890s it adopted the elaborate braided uniform of the British 13th Hussars.

In September 1877 Lieutenant-Colonel G.T. Denison III was notified that he had won first prize in the Czar of Russia's competition for the best history of cavalry, and he received a purse of 5,000 roubles. *A History of Cavalry* was published in London later that autumn. The book is undoubtedly the very best history of the development and employment of cavalry written until relatively recently. The contents cover the earliest use of cavalry under Cyrus the Great through to the Franco-German War in 1870, and the concluding section reiterates the arguments made in *Modern Cavalry* for the adoption of mounted rifle tactics if cavalry of the future was to retain its preeminent place on the battlefield. Few in the Canadian Militia, unfortunately, ever read the book, but it was highly regarded in Russia and Germany and was used as a standard text in the German General Staff Academy.

The first visit to Toronto of the new Governor General, the Marquis of Lorne, and his wife, HRH The Princess Louise, took place on 5 September 1879. So as to be available for all ceremonial occasions, the Body Guard went into camp for three weeks on the Garrison Common, along with the Markham and Oak Ridges troops and the Toronto Field Battery, and over this time provided mounted escorts to Their Excellencies on many occasions during their stay. On 9 September a grand military review was held for the Governor General, with many units participating, including 'A' Battery of the Royal Canadian Horse Artillery, the Port Hope and Peterborough cavalry troops, and seven battalions of infantry.

In addition to conducting its training, the Body Guard in this period had developed a busy social life, with an annual ball organized by the NCOs and men every January, socials,

The Helmet plate badge adopted by the Governor General's Body Guard in 1876, 11 cm high and 9 cm wide. Two versions are known, one with piercing around the central maple leaf as shown here, the other with a solid brass backing behind the leaf. (GGHG Archives)

dinners and church parades. Whenever the occasion required, the unit provided mounted escorts for the Lieutenant Governor or Governor General, such as in October 1883 when Captain Orlando Dunn commanded a travelling escort for the first visit of the newly appointed Governor General, the Marquis of Lansdowne.

A major step in the development of cavalry in Canada took place on 21 December 1883, when the first troop of permanent cavalry, known as the Cavalry School Corps, later named the Royal Canadian Dragoons (RCD), was formed at Québec. The purpose of this school was to provide instruction to Militia cavalry units across the country, and thus improve the standard of training and operational capability. There was no doubt that such a school was very much needed: it had been 13 years since the last British cavalry regiment had left Canada, and it had become obvious that the quality of training in the Militia cavalry had slipped badly over that time. The Body Guard contributed one of its promising young officers, Lieutenant E.T.H. Heward, to the new Permanent Force.

Dominion Day in 1884 was marked by a large military parade in Toronto to celebrate the 50th anniversary of the city's incorporation. Chambers' history of the Regiment notes that once again, "the Body Guard made a splendid showing".

(Left) A sabretache worn by officers of the Governor General's Body Guard, ca. 1880. Other similar Regimental sabretaches had a navy blue background. (GGHG Archives)

(Right) German silver Albert-pattern dragoon helmets with a white plume were acquired in England in 1871. (GGHG Archives)

The Governor General's Body Guard mounted escort provided during the 1879 visit to Toronto by the Governor General, The Marquis of Lorne, and his wife, Her Royal Highness The Princess Louise. (GGHG Archives)

In late August 1884, Major Frederick Denison, then on the list of retired officers, received an unexpected telegram from the Governor General, which forwarded a message from Sir Garnet Wolseley, with whom he had served in the Red River Expedition in 1870. Wolseley explained that he was then preparing a campaign to relieve Khartoum in the Sudan, and he needed skilled boatmen to ferry troops and supplies over the cataracts and fast-flowing rapids on the Upper Nile. He recalled how just that sort of thing had been done in moving his Red River force through northern Ontario, and he asked if Frederick Denison would raise and command a body of *voyageurs* for service on the Nile. Denison felt obliged to accept, and sailed on 14 September with his contingent of 380 boatmen, having just been promoted brevet lieutenant colonel.

The Nile *Voyageurs* carried out their arduous job with all the skill and tenacity Wolseley had anticipated, largely because of the devotion to duty of Colonel Denison, and at the end of February 1885 they began to make their way back to Canada. Denison returned to Canada in May, and he was made a Companion of the Order of St. Michael and St. George for his services to the Empire.

THE NORTH-WEST REBELLION, 1885

In the years that followed the annexation of the North West Territories in 1870, the sway of the Dominion government was gradually solidified as more and more white settlers arrived to till homesteads, and the North West Mounted Police established outposts to enforce Dominion law and order. But the original inhabitants of the territory, the Indians and Métis, had grown increasingly unhappy. Indian bands were confined to reservations, where Indian Agents tried, unsuccessfully, to make farmers out of men who had been proud, nomadic hunters, and where near starvation and dependency on food handouts was the result. The large number of Métis, especially in Saskatchewan Territory, never did have their land claims or other grievances satisfied. By 1884 discontent was rampant, and in June a delegation of Métis invited Louis Riel to return from his exile in Montana to lead them.

Riel's agitation was initially peaceful, aimed at building consensus among the Métis, Indians and white settlers for a petition to Ottawa. But the government paid no attention, and in March 1885 Riel formed a provisional government with Batoche as its capital. The first battle of the rebellion took place on 27 March at Duck Lake, when the Mounted Police and a small party of volunteers from Prince Albert were defeated when they tried to recapture a storehouse of supplies and ammunition. On learning of the fighting, the government, fearful of a general uprising of the Indians and Métis, decided quickly to call out the active Militia to put down the rebellion. Major General Frederick Middleton, a regular British officer, was sent to the West to assess the situation while a force was assembled. The news spread quickly and was greeted with enormous public enthusiasm: an expeditionary force of some 5,000 men was to be raised from across the country. In Toronto, the Queen's Own Rifles and the 10th Royal Grenadiers received orders on Friday, 27 March to mobilize 250 men each, and by the following Monday they had boarded trains bound for the West.

Authority to call out the Governor General's Body Guard was given by the staff on 30 March, but it was not received by Colonel Denison until nearly 1800 hours on 1 April. As the Body Guard band was then at its usual weekly practice, the bandsmen were sent out to bring in the sergeants for a brief-

The Canadian Voyageurs, recruited by Sir Garnet Wolseley to ferry troops and supplies up the Nile River to Khartoum in the Sudan, were commanded by a Body Guard officer, Lieutenant Colonel Frederick Denison. (NAC C2878)

ing, and a notice was sent to the local newspapers calling out the men.

On 2 April the unit paraded at its armoury, the blockhouse at Fort York, and saddles were issued. Because Colonel Frederick Denison was still in Egypt, the adjutant, Captain Clarence Denison, was given command of 'A' Troop, and Lieutenant W.H. Merritt was made acting adjutant. Mr. Charles Mair, who had been one of Riel's prisoners at Fort Garry in 1870, was appointed quartermaster, and he made arrangements to receive the Body Guard's allotment of equipment for the operation. Colonel Denison was less than enthusiastic about what was issued from the Militia stores:

It was worse than supplied to the men who went to Ridgeway, and God knows that was bad enough!… We had been issued blankets that had been condemned, in most of which there were holes. I insisted on an extra supply, and obtained three for each man, and as the holes were not all opposite one another, they were of some use….

Orders to entrain were not received until 1930 hours on Monday, 6 April, and it took another few hours of final prepa-

rations before the unit could be marched to the station. The horses were loaded on the train at 2300 hours, and two and a half hours later the train pulled out with 80 officers and men and 74 horses.

Getting to the North West was certainly going to be at least half the battle. Four lengthy gaps still existed in northern Ontario in the yet uncompleted Canadian Pacific Railway line, and the men and horses would have to march between the sections of track. To add to the difficulties, spring had not yet arrived in the Ontario northland, and temperatures at night still dropped to minus 25 degrees. What the men might confront at the end of each section of track no doubt caused some worry, for in some places snow drifts along the railway were as high as the top of the coaches.

At noon on Thursday, 9 April the train reached the end of the most easterly section of the CPR line near Dog Lake, where the ground was still covered in more than a metre of snow. Here the Body Guard had to unload for a march of 64 kilometres to the next finished section of the railway, where another train was waiting. To get the horses off the train, a ramp had to be constructed of railway ties, not an altogether easy task in the deep snow. To complicate matters, the ties were icy, and blankets had to be laid over the slippery wood to give the horses a sure footing as they were led down the steep ramp.

Once the horses were offloaded they had to be fed and watered, and then saddled, while the stores and equipment had to be loaded onto a convoy of large sleighs. After about three hours the difficult march began. In places where the railway roadbed had already been constructed the going was fairly easy, and many parts of the trail were already well packed by the troops that had travelled over the route during the previous two days. But there were also many sections of rough, treacherous trails through the bush. Many a horse fell, and many a sled dumped its cargo as it slid into metre-deep potholes. It wasn't until well after nightfall when the Body Guard reached the construction camp at Magpie Lake, where there were a couple of tents and a few log shelters where the horses were stabled to give them some protection from the bitter cold. There was, however, no place for the men to sleep, "so after eating supper shortly after midnight, they tried to snatch a little sleep as best they could, most of them lying down under blankets in the sleighs."

At dawn on 10 April the Body Guard set out on the remaining 25-kilometre march to the second section of completed track. Here, at what the preceding contingents had termed 'Camp Desolation', the men and horses were again fed, and the "tedious process of loading the horses on cars was again gone through…" The train available here was very rudimentary: the cars were simply open flatcars on which sides and seats had been hastily cobbled together from rough boards. About noon the train started out on the 190-kilometre ride to Port Monroe, on the shore of Lake Superior, where the track again ended. It wasn't until 16 hours later that a thoroughly chilled group of men and horses arrived.

At daybreak on 11 April the horses were unloaded and fed, after which the men were given breakfast, and the Body Guard then started out on what would be the "hardest experience of the campaign", across the first part of the second gap, 58 kilometres to a camp at Jackfish Bay. Nearly 50 kilometres of this distance was across the ice of Lake Superior. About 20 kilometres out on the ice the sleighs with the baggage and dismounted men left the main column to head for an inlet known as McKellar's Bay, where they picked up a short piece of track to take them to Jackfish Bay. But, to avoid yet another loading and unloading of the horses, the mounted column proceeded straight across the ice.

At the point where the column divided, the corps stopped for its mid-day meal. As there was a biting wind blowing, the horses were drawn up in a line facing the south. They were fed from the nose-bags, while the men stood in the shelter of the horses, and, with a lump of corned beef in one hand and a piece of bread in the other, ate their dinners. Water drawn through a hole cut in the ice furnished

Sketch by Captain R.W. Rutherford shows troops and horses detraining on 9 April 1885 at Dog Lake, the first gap in the still incomplete CPR, during the arduous voyage to the West through the northern Ontario wilderness. (Glenbow Museum)

After a 64-kilometre march from the railhead at Dog Lake, the Body Guard reached 'Camp Desolation' on 10 April 1885, where the unit loaded the horses and men on open flatcars for the next stage of the rail journey. This drawing from the *Canadian Illustrated War News* shows the 10th Royal Grenadiers from Toronto who had preceded the Body Guard by a few days. (NAC C6748)

(Below) *The Governor General's Body Guard Crossing the Ice on Lake Superior, 11 April 1885.* Painting by A.H. Hider, depicting the 60-kilometre march across the frozen vastness of the lake. The brown tone of the background is not the original colour, but rather the unfortunate effects of acid deterioration caused by corrugated cardboard that held the painting in its frame. (Governor General's Horse Guards Officers' Mess)

drink for both men and horses. The worst part of the march was to follow.

Until the column divided, the track along the ice was packed and clearly marked by the sleighs which for some days had been plying between these points;

but when we left the track to go some twenty miles across a vast prairie or desert of ice, with snow in drifts everywhere, there was no track and we had to pick our way.... The snow … had been blown by the wind, so that in some places there would be glare ice, and in others snow, from a quarter of an inch to perhaps a foot or even more in depth.... As we marched on the glare ice, the horses, without their hind shoes, slipped about and travelled with difficulty. When the snow was deep (and the deeper it was, the more certain the result), the horses' hoofs would go through the snow to the crust ice, and through it down two or three inches to the solid ice below that. When the snow was deep the horses were almost mired … their hoofs catching and tripping them in the crust ice.

All the while the wind from the north kept getting stronger, snow began to fall, and the temperature fell to nearly minus 20 degrees.

We kept marching and pushing on as fast as we could, but did not reach Jackfish Bay, then a small contractors' camp of tents and a few buildings, until about 8 p.m., just at dusk. The weather being intensely cold, no efforts were spared to try and find shelter for the horses, and they were stored away in all sorts of places, twelve being stored in a root house, and many in tents.

The men spent the night in an empty warehouse, which seemed a great luxury.

The Body Guard remained at Jackfish Bay until 13 April because there was no transport to continue. That morning it was bright, clear and cold, and at 0830 hours the unit began its march across the ice to a place called Winston's, the railhead for the next section of track, which was reached by mid-afternoon. Here there was a train of flat cars, and the whole process of building ramps and platforms of ties had to be done again before loading the horses. This train took the unit another 80 kilometres to Nipigon, the start of the last gap in the railway track, and here too the time-consuming building of an unloading platform had to be repeated. About nightfall the Body

Guard started its last march, again across ice, to Red Rock. Colonel Denison had been told that it was only about five kilometres to Red Rock, and to follow the track across to a light on the other side of the lake. The march proved to be a very long five kilometres: the light on the other side just didn't get any brighter for several hours. Finally, just before midnight the column reached Red Rock, a distance of well over 15 kilometres, and they found that the light had been a large beacon fire.

At Red Rock the men again went through the now very tedious procedure of constructing a loading ramp for the horses before the train could leave. The Body Guard finally arrived in Winnipeg at 0100 hours on 15 April, exactly eight days after leaving Toronto and having travelled a little over 2,500 kilometres.

When Colonel Denison arrived in Winnipeg he expected that orders from General Middleton would be waiting for him, but there were none. The Body Guard unloaded the horses and stores, and the local staff told the unit to camp on a nearby piece of flat ground that the men soon named 'Mud Flats'. Here there was a long shed that gave good shelter for the horses, but the troops had to make do with bell tents.

We pitched our tents in the snow, scraping the snow out of the interior so that the floor of the tent was composed of a thick, clammy, greasy clay.... We ordered a quantity of hay, and put that on the ground to prevent our sinking in the mud, and putting oil sheets over the hay, we were able to lie down without getting actually wet.

The Body Guard waited in these cold and damp conditions for the next week, during which time the squadron exchanged their Snider carbines for the new military issue Winchester 45-75 calibre carbine which was also used by the North West Mounted Police. While in Winnipeg the men read sensationalist press reports coming out of the North West that the situation in Saskatchewan was far from good. According to these reports Riel supposedly had between 1500 and 2000 men with him at Batoche, and that large numbers of Indians and Métis were assembled near Battleford and Fort Pitt. They also speculated that Indians in the Touchwood Hills between Fort Qu'Appelle and Humboldt were likely to harass the troops as they marched toward Batoche.

General Middleton's plan for the campaign had been leaked to the press and was widely reported in the newspapers: he intended to establish his main operational base at Clarke's Crossing, just north of Saskatoon on the South Saskatchewan

The log-cabin telegraph station at Humboldt, which served as the Body Guard headquarters during the North-West Rebellion. (NAC C753)

A group of Body Guard men outside their bell tent at Fort Denison in Humboldt. Note that most of the men are wearing a short tunic called a stable jacket, issued just prior to deploying to the West, while the man standing at the left is wearing the standard Body Guard tunic with the Austrian knot at the cuff. (NAC C751)

River, and from there he would advance against Riel's forces at Batoche. One column, which he would lead himself, would march across the prairie from Qu'Appelle, on the CPR line, with Boulton's Horse, French's Scouts, two artillery batteries, half the Infantry School Corps (RCR), the 10th Royal Grenadiers, and the 90th Winnipeg Rifles. A second column, led by Colonel W.D. Otter, with 'B' Battery, half the Infantry School Corps, the Queen's Own Rifles, the Ottawa Sharpshooters (later the Governor General's Foot Guards), and the Midland Battalion, would proceed further along the CPR line to Swift Current, and then march north to the South Saskatchewan River where they would board a steam boat that would carry them eastward along the river to Clarke's Crossing. Middleton was forced to modify this latter part of his plan when he learned of the massacre that had taken place at Frog Lake,

when he instructed Colonel Otter to move cross country directly to relieve the besieged stockade at Battleford. A third, smaller column, led by General Strange, would move against Big Bear from Edmonton, eventually joining up with Middleton at Fort Pitt.

It wasn't until late in the evening on 22 April that Colonel Denison finally got orders to move. The Body Guard was to move "at once", along with the Cavalry School Corps and the Winnipeg Troop of Cavalry. The unit left Winnipeg by rail on the morning of 23 April, arriving at Qu'Appelle station the next afternoon. After loading the waiting supply wagons, the Body Guard moved off across the prairie, and reached Fort Qu'Appelle, 27 kilometres further on, by dusk. There Denison heard news of the battle of Fish Creek which had been fought that day: Middleton's column had been ambushed by a Métis

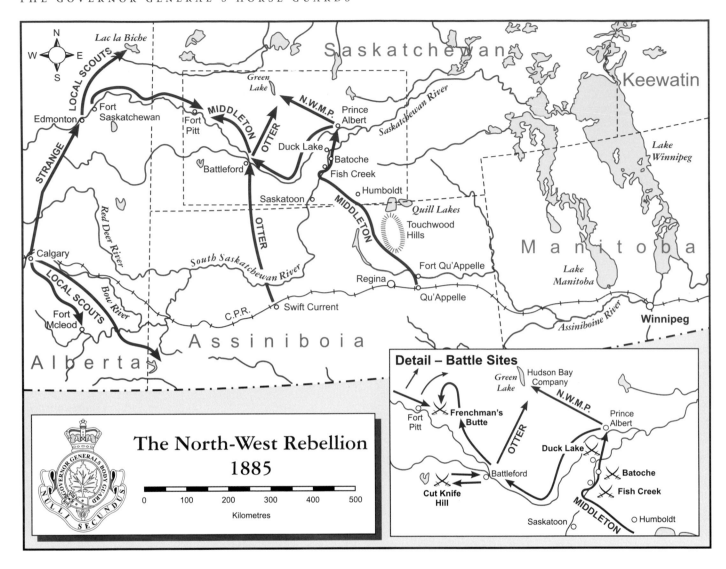

The North-West Rebellion 1885

Detail – Battle Sites

force and had been forced to withdraw after suffering heavy casualties.

By this time the one essential weakness in Middleton's campaign plan was becoming glaringly apparent, both to the commander and to the public. All his ammunition, food, forage and supplies, even firewood, had to be transported to the front from the CPR rail line at Qu'Appelle, roughly some 320 kilometres, and this essential line of communications was unprotected over most of that distance. On 22 April a "leading Toronto paper published a letter from its correspondent at the front, an ex-cadet of the Royal Military College, in which the weakness was laid bare…":

Our rear is unprotected, and we are not certain that, if anything should happen to us, the Indians at Touchwood Hills would not attack our transport and cut off our supplies…. No arrangements have been made … to even guard our

transport service, and, as you know, we are surrounded by Riel's scouts on all sides, and no doubt he is perfectly aware of our numbers.

Around midnight on Sunday, 26 April Denison got orders to march at once to Humboldt, 200 kilometres away, which was becoming a key way-station in the line of communications. There was great difficulty in assembling the horse-drawn transport wagons, but the Body Guard set out the next day. They reached Humboldt, which consisted of a single log house which doubled as the telegraph station, on the night of 1/2 May. There Denison had a telegram from Middleton instructing him to remain there and await further orders.

At Humboldt, Denison found a large stockpile of food and supplies, growing larger every day, all piled in the open. Lacking other operational instructions, and being a thoroughly practical soldier who understood first hand the importance of

food and equipment, he decided that these supplies "were in an absolutely indefensible position", and that if they were to be guarded they would have to be moved. Out in the open prairie about 600 metres from the telegraph station, Denison found two knolls with a depression between them that could be used as a protected location. Here he put into practice his ideas about cavalry having to be mounted rifles: the cavalrymen were set to work digging rifle pits on the two knolls, which over the next days were expanded into connected and mutually supporting defensive works. "The stores, which were accumulating every day, were brought over and piled in a V-shaped pile, the point outward, so that each face could be enfiladed by the fire from the two works." The unit encampment at Humboldt came to be known to the soldiers as Fort Denison.

Colonel Denison was nonetheless acutely aware that guarding stores well in the rear was not the proper role for the most highly trained cavalry unit of the Canadian Militia: "As I saw my horses in the little valley eating hay that cost about $600 a ton to transport, for the grass had not yet begun to grow … I could not help smiling at the absurdity of the whole business. General Middleton, I am satisfied … did not want me up there at all, so he left me on the prairie guarding stores with cavalry." Colonel George Stanley, in his monumental work on the rebellion, *The Birth of Western Canada*, noted:

Trained in the theory of the impregnable British square he [Middleton] relied entirely upon infantry, thus forfeiting the advantage of mobility in a country which lent itself to rapid movement. His cavalry were stationed in the rear to

Another of Trooper Kershaw's sketches from *The Canadian Pictorial & Illustrated War News*, showing here the arrival of a despatch rider at Fort Denison. (GGHG Archives)

protect the line of communications when they should have been at the front. Moreover, when cavalry were finally summoned to the front they were ordered there in inverse order of training! For mounted troops Middleton relied solely upon local corps, such as French's Scouts and Boulton's Scouts … in preference to the Governor General's Body Guard – a well-trained cavalry corps under command of Colonel G.T. Denison, one of the foremost cavalry officers of this time…. Had it not been for the fact that Riel overruled Dumont's plan to take advantage of the superior mobility of the Métis, Middleton's lack of horse might have proved an expensive blunder.

On 2 May the Militia suffered yet another setback, the defeat of Otter's force by Chief Poundmaker at Cut Knife Hill, near Battleford.

In part because of the Body Guard's location at the telegraph station nearest to the area of operations, Colonel Denison found that, in addition to protecting supply lines to the front, he and his men had an important role in maintaining communications to Middleton's field headquarters. "Despatches kept pouring in from all points, from General Strange, from Winnipeg, from Battleford, from Qu'Appelle, Swift Current, etc., all demanding attention from the General." Despatch riders were sent out each day, but it took nearly two days to get messages to Middleton's headquarters south of Batoche and get a reply back to Humboldt. Trooper Scholfield, one of the first of the despatch riders sent out on this mission, was shot at during his return journey, and his horse wounded. He was the only member of the Body Guard to come under fire during the Rebellion, and the only one to get the 'Saskatchewan' bar to the North West Canada medal.

Denison found that in many instances telegrams to General Middleton needed immediate replies, and he took it upon himself to act as a senior staff officer:

If it was advisable to give a reply at once, I would write it at the bottom of the message … [always beginning] 'An answer from the General cannot be had for two days. You had better not wait. You had better do, etc., etc.', and I would give directions. These would go to the General … and he would see exactly what I had done. I wrote to the General … and said I would continue in this course unless he told me not to do so.

General Middleton wrote back a few days later thanking Denison for his work.

Both to ensure the security of his post and to maintain the operational effectiveness of his troops, as soon as the unit was settled in Denison began to deploy daily mounted patrols to watch over the approaches to Humboldt. Some patrolled the supply route through the Touchwood Hills to give some protection to the wagon convoys, while others were sent to cover the trails to the north and northwest.

Early on the morning of 10 May one of the patrols spotted two riders approaching from the north, and doing as they had been instructed, they split and circled widely so as to be able to surround the riders when they were intercepted. On being questioned, the riders turned out to be Lord Melgund, Middleton's chief of staff (who, as the Earl of Minto, would return as Governor General), and his British aide. Melgund wanted to see Colonel Denison, so was escorted into the Body Guard camp. Denison was most surprised to see the Chief of Staff so far from the front, especially as he was aware that a battle at Batoche had already begun the day before. Melgund wrote several despatches, no doubt detailing Middleton's initial setback at Batoche, which were transmitted to Ottawa over the telegraph line by Sergeant Harry Wilson, who was an expert telegraph operator, an early example of the exceptional skills brought to the Militia by its citizen soldiers. Melgund and his assistant, with fresh horses, then set off for Qu'Appelle. Denison thought it strange that the Chief of Staff was departing for the east but surmised that it was to "get regulars from Halifax" to prepare for a British rescue mission.

Soon after Melgund's departure, Colonel Denison received instructions from Middleton to move the York and Simcoe Battalion to Humboldt as a reinforcement, and to ship forward as much of the stock of supplies as he could arrange. He managed to round up 54 wagons and teams over the next day and get them loaded with thousands of pounds of supplies of every kind, hay, oats, hardtack, salt pork, tea and sugar. This convoy started early on 12 May, with an escort of 35 men under Captain Clarence Denison, who wrote in his diary on 14 May as the convoy was approaching Batoche: "The escort had very hard work, the flanking patrols having to be frequently relieved, the country being very much broken, with very many bluffs."

Near Batoche the lead patrol met two Body Guard troopers who were returning to Fort Denison after having carried messages to Middleton's headquarters. They were able to tell Captain Denison about the victorious outcome of the battle of Batoche two days earlier, when the Midland Battalion and the

A somewhat fanciful contemporary sketch depicting Lieutenant William Hamilton Merritt's party pursuing Chief White Cap's band. In reality, after Merritt's troop tracked them down White Cap and his people surrendered without a struggle. (GGHG Archives)

10th Royal Grenadiers had rushed the Métis positions and driven them out. The riders also carried new instructions for Captain Denison's convoy of supplies: they were now to proceed to Clarke's Crossing where Middleton had moved his headquarters earlier on the 14th. The convoy altered its course to move to Clarke's Crossing along a trail following the South Saskatchewan River, but soon halted for the night.

The next morning a hasty visit was made into the village of Batoche so that the men could see the now-famous place, and a short while later, before Lieutenant Merritt's rear guard had left Batoche, Louis Riel gave himself up nearby. The Rebellion was at an end, even though there were still several bands of hostile Indians that had to be pacified.

In the early afternoon of 18 May Troopers McNab and Simms, while out on a daily patrol to the north of Humboldt, spotted a small group of Indians coming toward the high hill where they had established an observation post. They concealed themselves and managed to capture one man, who turned out to be a brother of the Sioux chief, White Cap. (It was mainly Sioux from White Cap's band who had defended so valiantly at Fish Creek two weeks earlier.) During an interrogation back at Fort Denison it was found that White Cap and his band were trying to escape to the United States.

Colonel Denison ordered Lieutenant Merritt to take 25 men and a local interpreter to try to capture White Cap and his people; his instructions were that there was to be no fighting if it could be avoided and that he should attempt to negotiate a surrender. On being told of the peaceful intentions of Merritt's mission, White Cap's brother agreed to help find his tribesmen. The search took nearly two days. The Indians were most adept at covering their tracks, and had it not been for the old Sioux's great skill in following what seemed an invisible trail it would have proven impossible. Finally, as the sun was getting low on their second day out they came across White Cap's camp. White Cap's brother and the interpreter were sent into the camp with a flag of truce, and they found that the Indians were prepared to give up peacefully.

Merritt and his men went into the camp and were treated hospitably. They were given the use of a tepee, as it had begun to rain, and they were fed bear steaks by their so-called captives – the only food the Indians had. The next morning, the 19th, White Cap and his chief braves solemnly smoked a peace pipe with Lieutenants Merritt and Fleming, and afterwards the Chief presented the pipe to Lieutenant Merritt. The Body Guard detachment and 22 of White Cap's band then began a hundred-kilometre trek back to Humboldt. The Sioux remained at Humboldt for over a month before being released, and during that time it was noted that "their behaviour was everything that could be desired".

Three examples of the Regimental badge with the Victorian crown. The bronze cap badge was the first to be worn, probably on wedge caps introduced in 1885. It is believed that the gilt version is an officers' badge dating from the late 1880s. The third badge, of notably lower quality, is thought to have been produced in Toronto in the early 1900s. (GGHG Archives)

After 20 May when the York and Simcoe Battalion arrived at Fort Denison, the Body Guard was used mainly to escort ammunition convoys, and there was plenty of time for recreation and sports. Perhaps as a reward for their good service, the men of the unit received an issue of new cork helmets to carry home.

The North West Rebellion came to an official end on 2 July, after Middleton had pursued the remaining rebel Indians to Battleford and Fort Pitt and Poundmaker had surrendered. The Body Guard began their homeward journey on horseback on 9 July, arriving at Qu'Appelle on 13 July to wait for a train to Winnipeg. In *Soldiering in Canada,* Colonel Denison told a story about how well trained the unit's horses had become while in the West:

> While at Humboldt we used to let our horses pasture on the prairie around us, and after a few days they learned the call for 'feed', and would trot in to the picket lines when the trumpet sounded. We always brought them in that way. At Qu'Appelle during the day, the horses had been given one feed of oats on the picket lines and had been turned out to pasture. There were only two or three men in camp, so I thought I would try the call for 'feed' on the horses and see if they would come in to the new quarters. The call was sounded, and the horses, who were scattered for a mile away, turned towards camp and trotted in to their places on the lines….

Once in Winnipeg, the Body Guard handed in their Winchester carbines and retrieved their old Snider carbines from Ordnance stores there. The

The North-West Canada Medal, awarded to all members of the Body Guard who served with the unit in the North-West Territories during the rebellion.

journey from Winnipeg to Toronto began on the afternoon of 16 July, and was "slow and hazardous" because the rail line was still not quite finished, even though track had been hastily laid across all of the gaps that had caused so many difficulties on the outward trip. "It was imperfectly ballasted, curves had not been adjusted, and bridges, trestles, etc., were at several points of a most flimsy character", especially east of Port Arthur. Near Jackfish Bay there was a near disaster: first, three cars jumped the track, one of them tipping on its side. The men and horses from these cars were crowded into others. Then, only three kilometres further on the lead car tipped over just as it had crossed over a very high curved trestle. Had the accident happened only moments before the whole train would have been dragged off the trestle and into the water 30 metres below. The men and horses in the overturned car had to be got out through the roof, and then marched along the track into Jackfish Bay, where, fortunately, more cars were available.

The Body Guard reached Toronto on 23 July at 0600 hours, after seven days aboard the train. They detrained at the Queen's Wharf and marched to the nearby Exhibition Grounds, where they were greeted by the mayor. The unit then participated in a parade in the afternoon to welcome the whole of the Toronto contingent. The next morning, after a brief inspection by the Deputy Adjutant General, the men were dismissed and sent to their homes. The final ceremony marking the Body Guard's service during the Rebellion took place eleven months later when North West Canada medals were presented to members of the Governor General's Body Guard by the wife of the Lieutenant Governor at Queen's Park on 24 May 1886.

Thirty-four years passed after the Rebellion before the Regiment was awarded its first battle honour – **North West Canada 1885** – by General Order 69/19 on 2 September 1919.

PEACETIME SOLDIERING

The Body Guard rapidly adjusted to the pace of peacetime soldiering after its return from Western Canada, but undoubtedly with a greater sense of pride and self-worth. This was true in most Militia units, for the operation in the North West was the first that had ever been conducted by Canadians on their own, even though the commander of the force had been British. In 1886, and for the next five years, a week-long annual training camp was held at the Exhibition Grounds in Toronto, and selected officers and men periodically attended Royal Schools at the Cavalry Corps School in Québec to obtain certificates of qualification. The active calendar of social activities was also resumed. A gala ball, replete with lavish decorations, was organized by the NCOs and men at the Horticultural Pavilion in January 1886, and many civic dignitaries and senior officers of the garrison were present. This was repeated in January 1887. The officers organized mess dinners in the fall and winter, and the Sergeant's Mess and the Men's Canteen organized socials, smokers and sports events. Despite Colonel Denison's dislike of fraternization between the ranks, the unit had become the 'family' around which many members' social life revolved.

The spring of 1889 is remembered as a particularly important time in the history of the Regiment. In early May the Markham and Oak Ridges troops were detached from the 2nd Regiment of Cavalry and returned to the Governor General's Body Guard as 'C' and 'D' Troops after having been separated

The orderly room tent during a Body Guard exercise at Well's Hill, ca 1893. Note the three quite distinct uniforms: the 1871-pattern tunic worn by the trumpeter on the left and the seated sergeant, the frock coat worn by the NCO second from the left, and the new-style patrol jacket worn by the officer on the right. Also note the pith helmet and the wedge caps, both new at this time. (GGHG Archives)

for 17 years. On the 17th, the Body Guard was formally given the status of a regiment of four troops by a Militia General Order, and it was also designated a 'city corps', which allowed it to train annually.

At the end of May 1889, Major and Brevet Lieutenant Colonel George Taylor Denison was promoted to the substantive rank of lieutenant colonel and confirmed as commanding officer of the Regiment. Captain and Brevet Lieutenant Colonel Frederick C. Denison was promoted substantive major, and

The Regiment's field kitchen during a summer camp in the 1890s, some of the four wagons issued in 1889. (GGHG Archives)

A.H. Hider made this drawing depicting the Body Guard at the gallop during a training camp in 1896. (GGHG Archives)

Lieutenant William Hamilton Merritt was promoted captain. The Regiment's establishment was fixed at 23 officers, 203 NCOs and men, 205 horses and 4 wagons. "During the succeeding year the regiment in its new form was put upon a thoroughly sound and efficient footing."

The Regiment had yet another occasion to serve the Royal Family on 30 May 1890, when the Body Guard provided an escort of three officers and 35 men on the occasion of the visit of HRH The Duke of Connaught, a future Governor General. And in October 1893 the Regiment formed a travelling escort for the Earl of Aberdeen on the occasion of his first visit to Toronto as Governor General.

In the early 1890s the Regiment continued to hold an annual training camp every June. In June 1892 the unit conducted an eight-day route march to Hamilton, in 1893 a regimental camp was held at Wells Hill and in 1894 at Mimico. The exception to this practice was in 1895, when, because of a Department of Militia budget crisis over the purchase of Lee-Enfield rifles, there was no training by any Militia unit. The move of the Royal Canadian Dragoons from Québec to Stanley Barracks in 1893 undoubtedly benefited the Body

Lieutenant Colonel Orlando Dunn, acting commanding officer of the Governor General's Body Guard in 1893, retired in 1897 after 44 years of continuous service with the unit. (GGHG Archives)

LIEUTENANT COLONEL GEORGE TAYLOR DENISON III

George Taylor Denison III was born in Toronto on 31 August 1839, the eldest son of Colonel G.T. Denison II. He was educated at Upper Canada College and studied law at the University of Toronto.

Young George Denison III was commissioned Cornet in the family-raised and supported volunteer cavalry unit, Denison's Troop, on his 16th birthday. Less than two years later he was placed in provisional command of the Troop at the age of 17 years with the rank of lieutenant, and having proved his mettle was promoted to the rank of captain in April 1857. With an absence of only eight years, he remained in command of the Governor General's Body Guard until June 1898.

Lieutenant Colonel Denison led his unit in action in the Fenian Raids of 1866 and in the North West Rebellion in 1885. He was one of Canada's first truly intellectual soldiers and an avid student of both military history and tactics. He followed the events of the American Civil War very closely, and he was among the first to recognize that the revolution in weapons technology and the employment of massive armies in the field had changed the whole nature of warfare. In particular he studied the employment of cavalry, and concluded that if cavalry was to remain the dominant arm on the battlefield

Lieutenant Colonel George Taylor Denison III, commanding officer of the Governor General's Body Guard from 1876 to 1898, and prior to that commanding officer of the Denison Troop from 1856 to 1868. In February 1899 he was made the first Honorary Lieutenant Colonel of the Regiment, a post he held until his death in 1925.

of the future it would have to be organized and trained as mounted rifles. His book, *Modern Cavalry*, was published in England in 1868 and his ideas gained wide acceptance in Germany and Russia. Later, in 1877, he published *A History of Cavalry*, which won first prize in a competition sponsored by the Czar of Russia. This work for many years was recognized as the best cavalry history in any language.

Colonel Denison was also a political activist although he never sought elected office outside of the city of Toronto. Holding strong anti-American views, he was a known supporter of the Confederacy during the American Civil War and was several times accused of harbouring Confederate spies. He ran into difficulty with the government after the war when he was involved in purchasing a vessel, the *Georgian*, which many believed the Confederacy had intended to outfit as a privateer. In 1868 he co-founded an organization known as Canada First, a stridently nationalistic movement committed to fostering Canadian nationalism within the context of strong links to the Empire.

In 1877 he accepted an appointment as senior police magistrate in Toronto, a position he held until 1920. George Taylor Denison died on 6 June 1925. He is remembered as one of the most capable and colourful of the Militia officers of his day.

Guard, as professional cavalry instructors were then always near at hand, and the Dragoons served as a model for the Militia troopers to emulate.

The Regiment's official name was amended on 13 July 1895 to Governor General's Body Guard, when the words "for Ontario" were formally deleted from the title. This simply recognized the long-standing if unofficial custom within the unit and the Militia as a whole, for the Body Guard "for Lower Canada" had ceased to exist many years before.

In 1896 the Regiment was issued the new Lee-Enfield .303 calibre magazine-fed carbines and 1890-pattern cavalry

swords. Training camps were continued in 1896, 1897 and 1898 at Toronto Junction. In addition, the Regiment held voluntary parades periodically, including one each year for the Toronto Brigade Thanksgiving field day. This annual sports meet was very popular with the troops, and the Body Guard proved to be especially capable in the riding and jumping competitions. Lieutenant George Peters was one of the Regiment's outstanding riders of this time and often took the largest number of prizes, his main competition coming from the RCD regulars.

Queen Victoria's Diamond Jubilee in May 1897 was a major event throughout the British Empire, and the celebrations in London were attended by military contingents from all parts of her realm. The Body Guard contributed one officer and four NCOs to the Canadian contingent sent to London: Captain Fleming, who was given the honour of being second-in-command of the Colonial Escort, Regimental Sergeant Major A.M. Stretton, Squadron Sergeant Major F. Flint, Squadron Sergeant Major A. Secord, and Lance Sergeant E.W. Hodgins. All members of the contingent were awarded the Queen's Diamond Jubilee Medal.

It was a truly sad day for the Body Guard when on 16 November 1897 Lieutenant Colonel Orlando Dunn retired after 44 years of continuous service. Colonel Dunn, who had been acting commanding officer in 1893 during the absence of Colonel George Taylor Denison III, was highly esteemed by all members of the unit, and at the time of his retirement he was the oldest officer in the active Militia.

The end of another era was marked when Lieutenant Colonel George Taylor Denison III retired from the Militia on 8 June 1898. Other than for an eight-year period (1868 to 1876), he had served since 1857 as commanding officer of the Regiment. At this time Lieutenant Colonel Clarence A. Denison was promoted and appointed to command. To fill the vacancies that were thus created, Captain William H. Merritt was promoted major, and Lieutenant H.Z.C. Cockburn was promoted captain. Less than a year later, on 1 February 1899, Colonel Denison was appointed as the first Honorary Lieutenant Colonel of the Governor General's Body Guard.

Lieutenant Colonel Clarence A. Denison, commanding officer 1898 to 1903. (GGHG Archives)

The annual training in 1899 was conducted at Niagara Camp for twelve days in June. This was the longest training concentration in many years, and it was also significant as the first occasion when the mounted units in southern Ontario were formed into a cavalry brigade for training as part of Colonel W.D. Otter's 2nd Division.

THE BOER WAR

What has come to be known as the Boer War in South Africa broke out on 11 October 1899 when Boer raiders crossed from their independent Orange Free State into the British territories of Natal and Cape Colony.

The actual causes of the war have always been somewhat obscure, one historian having written: "Nothing is more significant than that when the war broke out the nation [Britain] as a whole did not know what it was all about…." Undoubtedly the conflict had its roots in a long-standing antagonism between the Boers, the original Dutch Calvinist settlers, who wanted nothing more than to be left to their own devices, and British colonists who began to arrive after Britain took the Cape after the defeat of Napoleon. As the British population grew, the Boers trekked northward, eventually creating their own republics – Orange Free State and Transvaal. The first Anglo-Boer war was fought in 1880-81, and a British defeat at Majuba Hill gained the Boer republics a measure of quasi-independence. But the discovery of a major gold field in Transvaal in 1886 led to a massive influx of British miners and businessmen. The Boers feared their puritanical way of life was threatened by these easy-living foreigners, and among other restrictions denied them the right to vote. Beset by complaints from British residents, Britain tried to intimidate the Boers. But the Boers would not be bullied, and they struck first, naïvely thinking that they could then bargain from a position of strength.

But in Britain there was intense public clamour to go to war, to teach the rude Boers that they could not tread on the rights of British subjects. So another of 'Queen Victoria's Little Wars' in Africa was planned. The British really did not want large contingents from the Dominions, but they did ask for token commitments as an expression of Empire solidarity.

Prime Minister Wilfred Laurier believed, no doubt with some justice, that the problem was one of dubious British imperialism, and he was convinced Canada should play no role in the venture, but the same sort of martial ardour seen in Britain found expression in many parts of the country. Laurier soon found himself in a trap: on 3 October 1899 the British government sent a telegram "thanking Canada for the offer of

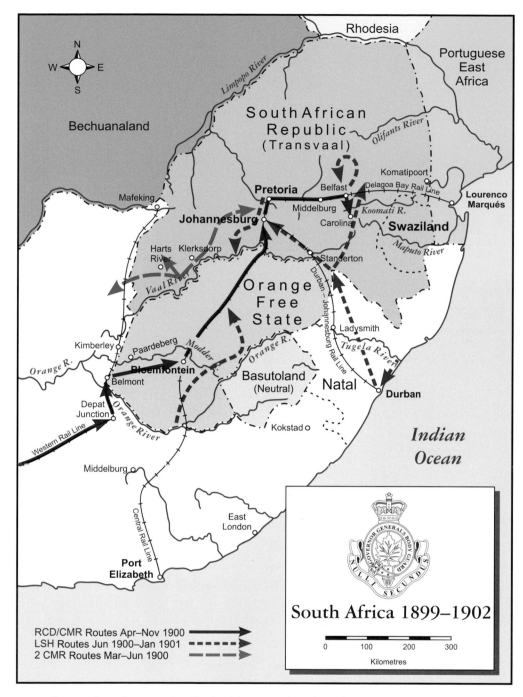

South Africa 1899–1902

RCD/CMR Routes Apr–Nov 1900
LSH Routes Jun 1900–Jan 1901
2 CMR Routes Mar–Jun 1900

0   100   200   300
Kilometres

sisted of five men. There was no difficulty filling the ranks, and a bare two weeks after being formed what came to be known as the First Contingent was en route to South Africa.

Shortly after the First Contingent had set sail from Québec City, public opinion forced the Prime Minster to offer more men, at least in part because the British Army meanwhile had suffered several costly defeats. This time the British wanted mounted men, as the main actions of the campaign had become chasing down parties of Boer horsemen. In late December 1899, therefore, instructions came to raise a Second Contingent of two battalions of Mounted Rifles and three batteries of horse artillery. At this same time, Major William Hamilton Merritt went out to South Africa on his own to serve as a squadron commander with a mounted unit known as Brabant's Horse.

The 1st Battalion Canadian Mounted Rifles, which was renamed Royal Canadian Dragoons after its arrival in South Africa, was recruited around a core of regulars from the RCD, with the majority of the men coming from the Militia cavalry units in central Canada. The 2nd Battalion, soon known simply as the Canadian Mounted Rifles, found the bulk of its officers and NCOs in the North West Mounted Police and recruited mainly in Western Canada. Both battalions were organized with two squadrons, each with four troops.

The Body Guard contributed 22 officers and men to the 1st CMR (RCD), a full ten percent of the Regiment's strength. As did many Militia officers, Captain H.Z.C. Cockburn accepted a reduction in rank to lieutenant and was assigned to command Second Troop in 'A' Squadron. Most of the NCOs and men from the Body Guard were posted to this troop.

troops", even though no such offer had been made. This telegram was immediately leaked to the press, and many Canadians now claimed that the nation's honour was at stake. Only days later, on 14 October 1899, Laurier announced that Canada would provide a thousand men to the Imperial cause.

The Canadian contingent was to be an infantry battalion, the 2nd Battalion, Royal Canadian Regiment, under the command of Lieutenant Colonel W.D. Otter. While the nucleus of this unit's officers and NCOs came from the RCR regulars, most of the men were recruited from Militia units across the country. The Body Guard's contribution to the 2nd RCR con-

The Royal Canadian Regiment, with whom a number of Body Guard members served during the Boer War, pauses during the march to Paardeberg. (NAC PA17037)

SERVICE WITH 2nd BATTALION, ROYAL CANADIAN REGIMENT

Members of the Regiment who served with the RCR had a very difficult year in South Africa, sometimes chasing mounted Boer commandos on foot, sometimes languishing on guard duty in isolated outposts. The unit was always beset by administrative and supply problems, which were compounded by rampaging enteric fever that reduced it to less than half strength by the time it returned to Canada in November 1900.

The major action fought by the RCR was the battle of Paardeberg in late February 1900, where a gallant charge by two companies of the RCR ended a ten-day siege and brought the surrender of the Boer general Piet Cronje. Two members of the Body Guard served with great distinction in this action. Sergeant E.W. Hodgins showed great leadership during the final charge on Cronje's Laager, and Trooper F.C. Page received a Mention in Despatches for selfless disregard for his own safety while carrying wounded men off the battlefield on 18 February 1900. Page was subsequently mortally wounded on 27 February, the final day of the battle at Cronje's Laager. He was the first member of the Body Guard to be killed in action.

WITH THE ROYAL CANADIAN DRAGOONS

It took a considerable amount of time to get the Second Contingent recruited and organized. The Royal Canadian Dragoons did not depart Halifax harbour until 21 February, their ship anchoring at Cape Town exactly a month later. After a two-week pause the RCD began a long and difficult march from Cape Town north into the war zone in the Orange Free State.

The unit's first encounter with the enemy took place on the Dewetsdorp road on 22 April 1900, when 'B' Squadron was ambushed by a party of Boers. Lieutenant D.D. Young, a member of the Body Guard who later joined the Permanent Force, was involved in this brief action. Here the Dragoons learned the first lessons about how practical mounted rifles tactics differed from cavalry theory in this rough, barren land: they would be far less vulnerable to Boer riflemen lying in ambush if they were well spread out when riding rather than closed up in cavalry style.

The Dragoons were attached to General Lord Roberts' column in May and early June, marching toward the Boer capital at Pretoria along the railway line from Bloemfontein. The unit was part of an ad hoc brigade, consisting of the CMR and a British mounted rifles unit, commanded by Brigadier General E.A.H. Alderson, whose association with Canadians would in 1914 gain him command of 1st Canadian Division. Their task was to provide an advance guard of scouts to prevent the main column from being ambushed.

The lead squadron had to check all the gullies and steep-sided, boulder covered hills called kopjes that could shelter an enemy force, and all farms were searched for able-bodied men and caches of weapons. Ambushes were an ever-present danger, but it was soon discovered that the Boers tended to open fire at long ranges and that they were not particularly good shots. It was, nonetheless, exhausting work under extremely harsh and uncomfortable conditions. The RCD historian, Brereton Greenhous, describes the life of the men during this advance:

bivouacs often seemed to be selected without any consideration for either human or animal comfort…. They were likely to be veiled in a fog of dust if not located in a marsh. Often cow dung was the only fuel to hand when men and horses would stumble into camp, late at night and utterly exhausted. After feeding, watering and picketing his animal, and swallowing his own meagre supper and the issue tot of rum, each trooper would wrap himself – fully clothed against the freezing night temperatures – in his mackinaw and blanket to catch what sleep he could. Conditions were harsh and the sickness rate appalling.

Throughout May the Boers conducted a clever delaying action to cover their withdrawal northward, and the Dragoons were involved in one battle after another with enemy rearguards. Finally, on 6 June the RCD entered Pretoria. The Dragoon historian quoted one of the men: "We were a rough looking crowd. Very few of us had shaved since leaving Cape Town. Our uniforms were disgraceful, riding breeches torn at the knees. A most dishevelled lot of conquerors…."

In late July Lord Roberts began an eastward advance on Belfast intended to eliminate the Boer forces in the hills of eastern Transvaal. The RCD were grouped with French's column on the south of the Pretoria to Belfast railway line, alternating between advance and flank guard duty and guarding the guns in the rear. By this time the Dragoons were down to about half strength because of sickness and disease. By late August the column had reached the outskirts of Belfast and camped. Here for the first time in the campaign the men had shelter, of a sort. Some tents had been issued, but many men built jerry-rigged hootchies out of corrugated iron sheets they had 'liberated' from Boer farms.

In these primitive quarters and totally unhygienic conditions, lice became a constant problem. Some of the men found monkeys as pets, and one enterprising trooper later wrote how he had trained his to pick lice out of the seams of his clothing.

The Boers by this time relied on the classic guerilla tactics of hit-and-run attacks and sabotage, and the British response was to form flying columns to harass and pursue the Boers around the vast tracts of rough, treeless veldt. The RCD were attached to General Smith-Dorrien's column at the beginning of November, and were employed as advance guards in a series of search-and-destroy missions in the countryside around Belmont which were intended to force the Boer guerillas to abandon the Komati River basin, in part by burning their farms and killing their animals. It was on one of these raids that the Dragoons fought their major action of the war.

THE BATTLE OF LELIEFONTEIN

In the foggy, pre-dawn darkness of 6 November 1900 a column of about 1,200 men started out from Belfast, the Dragoons in the advance guard. The RCD scouts had advanced only about seven kilometres when they came under fire from Boer sharpshooters who forced the column to deploy. A series of attacks by units in the main body gradually pushed the Boers back from one ridge line to the next, and by late morning the column had closed up to a strong defensive position that the Boers had established along the rocky Witkloof escarpment. Several costly frontal attacks failed to dislodge the Boer commando, so Smith-Dorrien decided to mount a flanking operation, using the RCD, two of the Royal Canadian Field Artillery's 12-pounder guns and two companies of infantry.

The RCD 'battle group' swung out cross-country to the south west shortly after 1400 hours, heading for Leliefontein farm, where it was thought they could threaten the Boer line of retreat without having to cross the Koomati River, and in this way perhaps induce the Boers to withdraw. It took the Dragoons and their gunners most of the day to work their way around the flank of the Boer position, and they burned several farm buildings as they inched forward. For much of the time they exchanged fire with guerilla groups, and several men were wounded. When darkness fell the Dragoons camped for the night near Leliefontein, while the Boers lit signal fires to call in reinforcements.

By the morning of 7 November the Boer commando had built up a force of some 300 men, with more on the way. General Smith-Dorrien, never having intended to engage in a pitched battle, decided that in the circumstances the wisest course of action was to call off the operation and return to Belfast. Knowing that the Boers would likely try to attack as he pulled back, he sent word to the Dragoons that they were to form a rear guard, with the RCFA's two 12-pounder guns, to protect the withdrawal of the main body and its slow-moving ox-drawn supply train. The Boers had in fact already planned to counterattack Smith-Dorrien's force, and they were quick to appreciate their advantage when they observed the first stages of the withdrawal.

Colonel François Lessard, the Dragoon commanding officer, gave orders to his three remaining troops to deploy in six 15-man sections, each about 500 metres apart, with the two field guns and Sergeant Holland's carriage-mounted Colt machine gun just behind the centre troop. As the Dragoons were taking up their positions at about 0900 hours, Boer commandos several kilometres away were seen beginning to advance, both on the left flank and from the front.

The Action at Leliefontein. **Painting by Peter Archer depicting the rearguard action which resulted in the award of three Victoria Crosses on 7 November 1900, including one to Captain Hampton Zane Churchill Cockburn of the Body Guard. (Courtesy The Royal Canadian Dragoons)**

By 1000 hours Boer horsemen had arrived at the forward edge of the Dragoon screen. But it was still too early for any thought of a withdrawal, as the transport column had not yet pulled back far enough to be safe. At about that time Lieutenant Cockburn's troop, on the extreme left, came under heavy attack. As soon as Colonel Lessard became aware of this he ordered the gunner commander, Lieutenant Morrison, to take one of his guns to help Cockburn. The gunners quickly limbered up and galloped a thousand metres eastward to Cockburn's position, which was still holding out when the gun arrived. Barely twelve shots had been fired at the advancing Boers, however, when Colonel Lessard arrived, shouting, "For God's sake, Morrison, save your gun!" Another large party of Boers were at that very moment coming in on the left rear, threatening to encircle the entire Dragoon position. As the gun was again limbered up and raced to the rear, Cockburn extended and dismounted his already depleted troop: the men knew it was their duty to ensure that the gun was not captured.

Lieutenant Morrison later recalled: "We had not gone fifty yards before the Mausers began to sing Hark from the tomb! … I turned in my saddle and saw the like of which I had not seen before in this war. Square across our rear a line of Boers a mile long was coming on at a gallop over the plain, firing from their horses." Nearby, Sergeant Holland had been providing covering fire with his Colt machine gun. But now the gun jammed, and Holland knew that he had no time to clear the jam before the Boers would be on top of him, so he dismounted the gun, grabbed a horse from one of Lieutenant Cockburn's horse holders and galloped to the rear.

Cockburn's troop was then overrun by the Boers. His horse was killed in the melée, and he was slightly wounded when his dead horse fell on him. There was no choice but to surrender.

The Boers continued to press their attack for another hour or so, and the Dragoon rearguard, along with the two guns, delayed as best they could, often engaging in a mounted melée while gradually closing in on the retreating main body of the force. Another member of the Body Guard, Lieutenant Elmsley, was wounded in this fighting. By this time the horses pulling the 12-pounders were so exhausted that they could barely move at a walking pace, and once again the Boers closed in on the guns. One last time the Dragoons had to come to their rescue: Lieutenant Turner, already wounded in the neck and arm, rushed in with about a dozen men, dismounted, and poured heavy fire into the Boer line. This small group held out long enough that the guns managed to reach the rearmost of the main body. Turner and a few men were able to escape just before being overrun, but a number of his troopers were captured.

The Boers finally gave up their attack in mid-afternoon when the remaining Dragoons were reinforced by about 60 men of the CMR, who had been guarding the flank of the main body. That same evening the Boers, having no facilities to hold prisoners, released all the Dragoons who had been captured that day. All the men, including Lieutenant Cockburn, remarked on how well they had been treated, and General Smith-Dorrien sent a letter to the Boer commander praising the humane treatment given to the prisoners.

While the entire operation ended in failure, the gallantry that had been shown by many Dragoons was quickly recognized. Smith-Dorien noted that the Dragoon action was "an event unprecedented in this war" and that he had "no praise too high for the devoted gallantry" that had been shown, and he made personal recommendations for a number of awards. In April 1901 three awards of the Victoria Cross were announced in the *London Gazette,* to Sergeant Holland, Lieutenant Turner, and the Body Guard's own Lieutenant Cockburn. This was the largest number of VCs ever awarded to a Canadian unit for a single action.

While the Dragoons took part in a few minor actions after

Major H.Z.C. Cockburn, VC (GGHG Archives)

The Victoria Cross and the Queen's South Africa Medal awarded to Captain H.Z.C. Cockburn. (Courtesy of Upper Canada College, photos by David Batten)

Leliefontein, their numbers were now so depleted that the unit was no longer effective. In any event, the twelve-month enlistment was coming to an end. The RCD departed South Africa on 12 December, and arrived in Halifax on 9 January 1901.

When Captain Cockburn returned to Toronto on 25 February 1901 he was met at the railway station by the whole Regiment and by the boys of his old school, Upper Canada College, in a welcome befitting a national hero. In recognition of his valiant service he was promoted brevet major on 17 May 1901 and confirmed in substantive rank in July. He subsequently served in the Regiment as a squadron commander until he moved to western Canada in 1905. He died in 1913.

SERVICE WITH THE 2nd CANADIAN MOUNTED RIFLES

In December 1900 both Colonel Denison and Major Merritt separately offered to raise and lead another CMR battalion for service in South Africa, sending their offers directly to the British government via Lord Strathcona. The British government expressed interest in both proposals, but seemed more favourable to Merritt's since he was a South Africa veteran, and had made detailed plans. In February 1901 the British sought the consent of the Canadian government. The Canadian authorities decided in March that all requests for recruitment in Canada had to be routed through Ottawa,

and Major Merritt's offer thus simply died. This initiative did, however, lead to a decision by the government to recruit an official Third Contingent for South Africa.

On 29 November 1901, Militia Orders announced the formation of the Third Contingent, which was to consist of a regiment of six squadrons of mounted men, each 143 strong.

Instructions were sent out to Militia units and to the NWMP to begin recruiting for the 2nd Battalion, Canadian Mounted Rifles. Lieutenant Colonel T.D.B. Evans, who had commanded the Canadian Mounted Rifles in South Africa in 1900, was named commanding officer. The Governor General's Body Guard contribution to the 2nd CMR consisted of Major W.H. Merritt who was to be second-in-command, Captain J.H. Elmsley, who had served with the Royal Canadian Dragoons in 1900, Sergeant Edwin Hodgins, who had served with the RCR, and thirteen men.

Three squadrons that had been recruited in Eastern Canada sailed from Halifax with 515 horses on 14 January 1902, under Major Merritt. The remaining three squadrons, including the members of the Body Guard, sailed two weeks later with Colonel Evans.

2nd CMR arrived in South Africa in mid-February, and concentrated at Newcastle for three weeks, testing horses and equipment. During this time there was a serious disagreement between Colonel Evans and Major Merritt. Merritt tended to see his part of the regiment as an independent command, and he made an approach to senior British officers to have the unit split in two. Evans, with some justice no doubt, believed this to be subversive. These unfortunate command rivalries were sorted out only when Major Merritt broke a leg, and being unfit for operations, was placed in charge of the unit's base camp at Klerksdorp, in western Transvaal. There "he performed

valuable service" for the remainder of the time the 2nd CMR was in South Africa.

At Klerksdorp the 2nd CMR joined Major General Walter Kitchener's 16,000-man division for a major operation intended to round up Boer guerillas who continued to attack convoys and lines of communications in western Transvaal. Its only major action during their five-month tour in South Africa took place near Harts River, some 30 kilometres from the western boundary of Transvaal, on 31 March 1902. At this time the unit was part of an 1,800-man column commanded by a Colonel Cookson, whose task was to locate the main Boer encampment. During the westward march of the column, 2nd CMR was split into three groups. Lieutenant Callaghan and the regiment's scouts were with the column's advance guard. Colonel Evans, with 'A', 'B' and 'C' Squadrons (the western Canadians), rode with the main body, and Major Cameron, with 'D', 'E' and 'F' Squadrons were assigned to escort the slow-moving supply and baggage convoy.

At around mid-morning on 31 March the advance party scouts sighted about 500 Boers a few kilometres ahead. As they continued forward, the scouts were ambushed and several men and horses were killed, but the Boers broke contact when Cookson's main body arrived. Cookson decided to camp briefly in the open in the valley of the Harts River to wait for the supply column to catch up. But the choice of the campsite could not have been more unfortunate, for on the ridge imme-

Troops of 2nd Canadian Mounted Rifles chasing down small bands of Boer guerillas in the final stages of the Boer war, February 1902. Major W.H. Merritt, Captain J.H. Elmsley and Sergeant Edwin Hodgins served with this unit.

Sergeant Major Edwin Hodgins, appointed Regimental Sergeant Major in 1903, carried out his duties in South Africa with 2nd CMR with great distinction, especially his gallant actions at Harts River for which he was mentioned in despatches. (GGHG Archives)

Harts River was, next to Paardeberg, Canada's costliest battle during the war in South Africa, with 13 killed and 40 wounded.

Other than the occasional crop-burning mission, the remainder of 2nd CMR's time in South Africa was uneventful. The Boers began negotiating a surrender in mid-April. 2nd CMR remained in Klerksdorp until mid-June, and at the end of the month the unit boarded the SS *Winifredian* for the voyage back to Canada.

A total of fifty members of the Body Guard served in South Africa during the Boer War, one of whom, Private F.C. Page, was killed in action and another six were wounded. In June 1933 the service of members of the Governor General's Body Guard during the war in South Africa was officially recognized. The Regiment was awarded its second battle honour: '**South Africa, 1900**'. For reasons that have never been adequately explained, the Regimental contribution to 2nd CMR in 1902 was never recognized in the same way.

MORE PEACETIME SOLDIERING

Public interest in military matters was undoubtedly awakened in Canada as a result of the Boer War and the success of the Yukon Field Force in preserving law and order during the gold rush in the Klondike, and this was nowhere more evident than in the periodic willingness of Parliament to allow several substantial increases in Militia appropriations during the first decade of the 20th century. More money for defence meant many things. For the Permanent Force it allowed reform and modernization that had been contemplated since before the Boer War to proceed, including the creation of proper service corps essential for the support of a field army. For the Militia, increased funding meant a gradual but steady growth in the number of both combat arms and service support units. It also allowed for larger unit establishments, and it brought a significant increase in the quality of training, since many more militiamen were able to attend summer training camps and provisional schools.

But for the Body Guard,

Regimental Sergeant Major Alexander Stretton, RSM of the Body Guard from 1892 to 1903. (GGHG Archives)

diately above was a 2,500-man commando of seasoned Boer fighters, and the ground in the immediate vicinity of the camp was indefensible. Just as the last of the supply wagons arrived at the camp the Boers attacked. Sharpshooters poured a withering fire onto the British and Canadian defenders, and seven times Boer horsemen charged. But under cover of two farm buildings and hastily dug pits, the camp held out despite taking heavy casualties. Eventually the Boers cut off the rearguard, the only troops that had remained well outside the encampment.

Professor Carman Miller's history of Canadian participation in the war states: "One of the most heroic Canadian actions of the battle occurred during the Boers' successful attack on the rearguard." Once they had given up their effort to capture the main encampment, the Boers turned their attention to the isolated rearguard, made up of Third and Fourth Troops of 'E' Squadron, who were mostly men from Toronto. Faced with a large number of Boer horsemen charging down on them, Lieutenant Carruthers and Sergeant Edwin Hodgins, a well-respected member of the Body Guard, ordered their men to dismount and face the attack. Miller's history continues: "With little cover except the long grass, the outcome was never in doubt. Nonetheless a ferocious and sustained battle ended only after the Canadians had exhausted their ammunition and seventeen men were dead or wounded." Colonel Evans later wrote that this action "was well worthy of the best traditions of Canada and the whole Empire." Carruthers and Hodgins were mentioned in despatches for their bravery, little enough recognition since what they had done at Harts River was precisely what had won the Victoria Cross for Lieutenants Turner and Cockburn just over a year earlier.

The Victorian Crown collar badge of the Governor General's Body Guard, introduced into wear ca. 1900. Also shown is the metal shoulder title brought into use about the same time. (GGHG Archives)

Tunic of the Body Guard uniform adopted ca 1890.

the years surrounding the turn of the century were not especially good, despite the opportunity of some of its members to serve in South Africa. The calibre of training in the Regiment during the 1890s had undoubtedly slipped quite significantly, no doubt in part because, except in 1899, the unit had been obliged to do its summer training in local camps rather than at Niagara. Reports on the annual inspection of the Regiment in Niagara Camp in 1901 and 1902 judged that the unit was "in a poor state of efficiency", and that the horses were "a very poor lot". And there were cryptic notations that certain of the officers appeared to be dissatisfied with the senior leadership.

FORMATION OF THE TORONTO MOUNTED RIFLES

The Militia cavalry of this period were, of course greatly influenced by the experience of the mounted rifles units in South Africa, and there was a growing sense in Ottawa that all cavalry in Canada ought to be reorganized as mounted rifles, as proposed by Colonel Denison years earlier. Undoubtedly these ideas influenced the decision to form a unit in April 1901 named the Toronto Mounted Rifles, with 'J' and 'K' Squadrons. Command of the new unit was given to a well-known Body Guard officer, Major George A. Peters. The four original troop leaders were Captain Hume Blake, Lieutenant D.L. McCarthy, Lieutenant John H. Moss, and Lieutenant John R. Meredith. The unit went to camp for the first time at Niagara in June 1901. As there was no room for the new unit in the University Avenue Armouries – the cavalry wing had not yet been built – quarters were found in an old stable off University Avenue.

The Body Guard also grew significantly in 1901. The regimental establishment was increased to four squadrons of 81 NCOs and men each, for a total authorized strength of 361 all ranks, and 324 horses. At this time 'C' Squadron was moved to Woodbridge and Brampton, and 'D' Squadron was located in Aurora. That May the rank of second lieutenant was abolished in the cavalry, with a corresponding increase in the number of lieutenants allowed.

Regimental training in the period 1901 to 1914 followed much the same pattern. Twelve days of field training were authorized each year, and in all but one year prior to the First World War this took place at the brigade camp at Niagara. The usual syllabus up to 1910 provided one day for 'marching in', three or four days for musketry training, five or six days for cavalry drill and tactics, and one day for 'marching out' – tearing down the tents, the return of stores, pay parade – and then departure of the units for home, by lake steamer for the Body Guard. After 1910 the time allocated for shooting was reduced, as units were expected to carry out much of their musketry work before arriving, and additional time was thus available for cavalry field training.

One of the perennial concerns of cavalry commanding officers of this time was accommodation for horses at Niagara Camp. Horses, most of which were at that time rented by the

A group of Body Guard NCOs strike a pose for the photographer at Niagara Camp, ca 1901. Note that two are wearing Khaki tunics which were permissible dress after the South African war. (GGHG Archives)

Regiment from local farmers, were usually simply tethered in the open in the horse lines, and if the weather was bad they suffered terribly. Each year some would become ill and die, and the Militia Department's standard payment for a dead horse, $200, was considered inadequate. As a consequence, those who owned good quality horses were reluctant to bring them to camp, and the quality of the horses the Regiment was able to get from farmers was deteriorating. This problem was to bedevil every cavalry unit training at Niagara for years to come, even though some horse shelters were built in 1905.

In mid-October 1901 the Duke and Duchess of Cornwall and York, later King George V and Queen Mary, made a Royal Visit to Toronto. This visit occasioned a mass review of the Militia in Ontario, with 11,000 men on parade, including the cavalry brigade. In preparation for this gala parade, three days of rehearsals with the other four cavalry regiments preceded the great day, and in the meanwhile the Body Guard provided a Royal Escort for the arrival of the Royal Couple on 10 October. As was their due, the Body Guard was positioned at the right of the line on the parade, but as it turned out to be a wet and thoroughly miserable day the soldiers did not remember the parade with any pleasure. One of the highlights of the Royal Visit was the presentation of South Africa decorations and medals by His Royal Highness, beginning with Major Cockburn's Victoria Cross. The Duke then presented a

sword of honour to Major Cockburn on behalf of the City of Toronto. On the departure of the Royal Couple, the Regiment was given the honour of escorting them to the railway station.

In June 1902 the Regiment provided eight sergeants to the Canadian Contingent sent to the coronation of King Edward VII. The coronation unfortunately had to be postponed because the King was seriously ill, so the whole of the Canadian party returned home. When King Edward recovered, the Coronation was rescheduled for August, and this time Sergeant F.D. Burkholder represented the Body Guard in the small military contingent sent by Canada. All received the King Edward VII Coronation Medal.

In the autumn of 1902 the Body Guard moved to new quarters in the University Avenue Armouries, giving up the Regimental home of some 40 years in the Block House at Fort York.

TORONTO LIGHT HORSE

The official beginning of the unit that was later to be named the Mississauga Horse took place on 1 April 1903: on this date the Toronto Light Horse was created by the formation of three squadrons and the amalgamation of 'J' and 'K' Squadrons of the Toronto Mounted Rifles, which had been authorized two years earlier. Major George A. Peters was named commanding officer of the TLH, and he was promoted lieutenant colonel in

A postcard of the Body Guard's Travelling Escort, shown outside the new Regimental home at the University Avenue Armouries. (GGHG Archives)

1904. In 1905 the Toronto Light Horse was officially increased to regimental status, and the name was changed to 9th Toronto Light Horse.

The creation of the Toronto Light Horse was not well received by many in the Governor General's Body Guard, and for some time relations between the two units were very cool, since they were competing for recruits and training facilities. A dispute over space in the crowded University Avenue Armouries was resolved only when the District Officer Commanding personally intervened to allocate one of the Body Guard's squadron rooms to the TLH.

The Toronto Light Horse developed very rapidly under the capable leadership of Lieutenant Colonel Peters. In the report on the annual inspection of the unit at Niagara Camp in 1903, Colonel Lessard, the Inspector of Cavalry, noted that the unit then had ten officers and 79 men, but as yet no qualified NCOs. Nonetheless the unit received high praise for its good standard of training and discipline. By the summer of 1904 the unit had grown to 18 officers and 202 men, and following the 1904 inspection Colonel Lessard reported that Peters was "a most excellent officer" and that the unit had "a very smart lot of non-commissioned officers", with all but two of the officers being rated as very good or excellent.

The uniform of the Toronto Light Horse was patterned after that of the British 5th Dragoon Guards: a scarlet tunic with myrtle-green facings, gold lace and brass buttons, and blue trousers with a broad cavalry-yellow stripe down the pant leg. The officers, using a bit of artistic licence, chose to wear a lancer-style gold and crimson waist girdle. The officers' brown leather cross belt carried a binocular case rather than the traditional cartouche pouch, while the men wore a brown leather rifle bandoleer. Riding boots and gauntlets were also in brown leather. The headdress was a white cork pith helmet with a myrtle-green pugaree, with the cap badge mounted at the front.

Lieutenant Colonel George Peters, commanding officer of the Toronto Light Horse 1903 to 1906. (GGHG Archives)

Regimental Sergeant Major H. Seddon, RSM of the Toronto Light Horse and then the Mississauga Horse 1905 to 1908. (GGHG Archives)

One of the changes in cavalry dress in the years following the Boer War was the adoption by many units of the Boer 'slouch hat', a wide brimmed khaki felt hat worn with the left side of the brim turned up and pinned, and with a pugaree in the unit's facing colour. The Body Guard dyed their hats dark blue, and wore a large version of the collar badge – a maple leaf surmounted by a crown – on the pinned up left side. The Body Guard used the pugaree as an intricate system of rank identification: other ranks wore a plain white pugaree, senior NCOs wore a blue and white herring-bone pattern, while officers had a blue and white diagonal stripe pattern. The Mississauga Horse wore a khaki hat with a myrtle green pugaree and a green ostrich feather behind the badge on the turned up brim, and this hat continued to be worn in the Regiment until in the 1930s. For summer camps, the Mississaugas later adopted a straw version of this hat, often called a 'cow's breakfast'. The slouch hat was smart looking and gave the men a rugged cavalier appearance.

At a change of command parade in July 1903, Lieutenant Colonel William Hamilton Merritt took over as commanding officer of the Body Guard from Colonel Clarence Denison. This brought to an end a continuous period of 82 years when members of the Denison family served in command of the unit.

The Body Guard showed a distinct improvement in training standards under Merritt's leadership, and morale picked up noticeably over the next several years. The Regiment was consistently rated as "good" at its annual inspection, although in 1907 the Inspector of Cavalry noted that "the rural squadrons [are] in better condition and better mounted than the city squadrons".

Earl Grey, the new Governor General, made his first visit to Toronto in late April 1905, and the Body Guard continued the now long-standing practice of providing an escort to the Vice Regal party on such occasions.

Colonel Merritt was already probably not held in the highest regard by Colonel William Otter, the District Officer Com-

The Body Guard's white metal slouch hat badge, adopted ca. 1902. This is a larger version of the collar badge adopted two years earlier. It was sometimes worn by NCOs above their chevrons. (GGHG Archives)

manding, but an event on the final day of the 1906 camp at Niagara would have done nothing to improve that situation, as Desmond Morton relates in his biography of Otter:

On the 19th [of June], Sir Frederick Borden [the Minister of Militia] arrived for his annual visit, assembling the more senior officers to describe the changes which were transforming the militia. Next day, there was the usual field day and a thousand cavalry were lined up by Lieutenant Colonel William Hamilton Merritt of the Body Guard to stage a spectacular charge. A combination of limited space and misjudgement sent one end of the galloping line hurtling toward Otter and his guest. The two men narrowly escaped being trampled under foot.

THE 9th MISSISSAUGA HORSE

That units have the occasional bad period has always been a fact of life in the Militia, and the quality of regimental leadership is no doubt one of the contributing factors. While the Body Guard was still undergoing a revival, 1906 was one of those unfortunate times for the Toronto Light Horse. Colonel Peters was on sick leave throughout 1905 and 1906, and the regiment suffered a decline during his absence. The District Officer Commanding decided that a reorganization of the unit was required, and in the autumn of 1906 'A' Squadron was moved to Barrie, 'B' Squadron was relocated to Eglinton and 'C' Squadron was located in Oakville, leaving only 'D' Squadron in Toronto. Major Vaux Chadwick was named acting commanding officer during this period of reorganization. As only part of the regiment was now based in Toronto, it was agreed that the regiment's name should be changed to reflect the new territorial limits. Following broad consultation it was decided to name the regiment for the Mississauga Indians, who had earlier occupied the territory now encompassed by the unit. The regimental designation was thus changed on 1 May 1907 to 9th Mississauga Horse. Chadwick was promoted lieutenant colonel and confirmed in command in November 1907.

The Tercentenary of Québec in July 1908 was celebrated as a major national festival, and a large military contingent from across the country gathered in Québec to participate in the pageant. Neither the Body Guard nor the Mississauga Horse was selected to be part of the Ontario representation because of funding limitations, but the Body Guard did provide a Royal Escort for the Prince of Wales when he visited Toronto after the Tercentenary events. In December 1908 command of the Body Guard passed to Lieutenant Colonel F.A. Fleming.

On 24 May 1909 the Body Guard provided the usual mounted escort for the Governor General, Earl Grey, when he visited Toronto for the 50th running of the King's Plate. The annual training camp in 1909 was conducted over a twelve-day period in late June at Lambton, a site near the Humber River that had recently been acquired by the government for new barracks. This year the Regiment had 205 all ranks in camp, with 177 horses, which unfortunately left sixteen officers and 106 of the men 'untrained' that year for lack of funds to take them to camp.

By 1909 the Mississauga Horse had regained the high level of competence shown in its early years under Colonel Peters. The regiment took 23 officers, 203 NCOs and men and 197 horses to camp at Niagara. This year emphasis was placed on mounted manoeuvres and reconnaissance operations rather than on drill, and the annual inspection report rated the unit "well above average".

Both of the Toronto cavalry regiments thrived in the period 1910 to 1914, and the antipathy of the early 1900s gave way to friendly rivalry. The Body Guard and Mississauga Horse held joint sports meets throughout this period, and began to form combined teams to compete with other units in the garrison. In all of these years both units took ever larger numbers to the annual camps at Niagara. Inspection reports for the most part noted continual improvement in manoeuvres and field duty, and regularly commented on the enthusiasm and hard work of all ranks. One thing that the two Toronto cavalry regiments had in common at this time was that the cavalry uniforms issued to the men were worn out and in deplorable condition. Inspecting officers at Niagara Camp thus always had something negative to include in their reports.

The summer camps always attracted high-ranking visitors, but the VIP visitor to the June 1910 camp was even more high-ranking than usual. Field Marshal Sir John French, Inspector-General of the Imperial Forces, came to observe the training at Niagara, and he seemed most pleased with the quality of the Militia cavalry trooper. In a lecture to the officers he stressed the mounted rifles concept: "the only proper role for cavalry in a country of the character of Eastern Canada. They should

Lieutenant Colonel William Hamilton Merritt, commanding officer of the Governor General's Body Guard 1903 to 1908. (GGHG Archives)

rely on the rifle rather than the sword for their power of offence." Another of Colonel Denison's converts.

The Royal Canadian Dragoons hosted a refresher course for field officers from every cavalry unit in Canada in May 1910. This was the first time officers from so many units had been given an opportunity to meet, and on the initiative of Colonels Merritt and Fleming of the Body Guard and Colonel Chadwick from the Mississauga Horse, the Canadian Cavalry Association was formed. For many years this association served as the collective voice of all cavalry and mounted rifles regiments in the country, and it continues to this day as the Royal Canadian Armoured Corps Association.

The Coronation of King George V on 22 June 1911 provided

(Left) The Weston Troop of the Governor General's Body Guard, June 1907. By this time the slouch hat was the primary field headdress of the unit. (Toronto Reference Library, T32072)

Regimental Sergeant Major George Smith, RSM of the Body Guard 1908 to 1914. (GGHG Archives)

Lieutenant Colonel F.A. Fleming, commanding officer of the Body Guard 1908 to 1913. (GGHG Archives)

Regimental Sergeant Major Edward Godfrey, RSM of the Mississauga Horse 1908 to 1911. (GGHG Archives)

an opportunity for Militia units to contribute to a 700-strong military contingent sent to London for the festivities. The Body Guard and the Mississauga Horse each sent three NCOs, who received the King George V Coronation Medal on a special parade in London on 30 June. On this occasion each Militia unit received three additional medals – one for the commanding officer, one for a warrant officer or NCO, and one for the senior trooper in the unit. This year the Mississauga Horse appointed their first Honorary Colonel, Colonel H.C. Cox.

In 1912, in addition to participation in the camp at Niagara, the Mississauga Horse, was selected to train as part of a composite cavalry brigade, with the 6th Hussars and 24th Grey's Horse, at the Army's large training area at Petawawa that had been acquired in 1905. This brigade camp proved of great practical

value to the regiment's effectiveness, in part because of the high calibre of tactical instruction provided by British cavalry officers who were brought in on exchange. Later in the year, one of the highlights of the winter social season was a gala ball hosted by the Mississauga Horse at the University Avenue Armouries.

Lieutenant Colonel Sanford F. Smith took over as commanding officer of the Body Guard in January 1913 on the

Men and horses of 'D' Squadron of the Mississauga Horse at camp in Niagara in 1907. (GGHG Archives)

death of Colonel Fleming. This year Colonel Merritt donated a handsome silver trophy to the Canadian Cavalry Association for annual award to the unit that demonstrated best horsemanship by a team of four officers. The competition was judged by the Inspector of Cavalry during his annual inspection of units at their summer training camps in 1913, and the Governor General's Body Guard was extremely proud to be the first winner of the trophy. In November 1913

Colonel H.C. Cox, Honorary Colonel of the Mississauga Horse 1911 to 1930. (GGHG Archives)

Regimental Sergeant Major S.A. Wynn, RSM of the Mississauga Horse 1911 to 1914. (GGHG Archives)

previous three years, most of the training focused on field manoeuvres, and the units had reason to be pleased with the degree of competence that was achieved. At the beginning of the camp new khaki uniforms were issued to replace once and for all the tattered old field uniforms, but, alas, the new uniforms were judged to be "of poor quality". This year the Body Guard was rated as the best regiment at Niagara.

Lieutenant Colonel H.D.L. Gordon was appointed commanding officer of the Mississauga Horse.

In the autumn of 1913 and the spring of 1914 both the Body Guard and the Mississauga Horse held weekly parades for drill and other basic training, and the Body Guard usually spent Saturday improving their musketry skills on the range at Long Branch. The 1st Cavalry Brigade camp at Niagara in June 1914 was one of the best attended in years, and both regiments paraded around 325 all ranks and nearly 300 horses. As in the

When the members of the Body Guard and the Mississauga Horse left Niagara Camp in late June, war clouds were already beginning to form over much of Europe, but as no one understood that this was soon to affect almost all of them, nothing interfered with their laughter and good spirits and remembrances of what fun they had experienced with their friends. They could hardly be expected to understand that the intensive training just completed would simply not be adequate to prepare them for the rigours and the horrors most would confront in the years ahead.

Mounted escort for Governor General Earl Grey at the 50th running of the King's Plate, May 1909. (GGHG Archives)

(Left) Troops of the Mississauga Horse relax during summer camp at Niagara, 1909. (Right) Body Guard NCOs break for tea, ca. 1910. Note the variety of dress: some are wearing tunics with a white collar and epaulette, others are in the less elaborate navy patrol dress; most are wearing slouch hats, but one staff sergeant has the new forage cap. (Both, GGHG Archives)

A Mississauga Horse squadron in the field, 1913. (GGHG Archives)

Badge of the 9th Mississauga Horse, worn during the period 1907 to 1914. The badge of the Toronto Light Horse was of identical design except that the top scroll read Toronto Light Horse. (GGHG Archives)

GGBG King's Crown Helmet plate and badge. After the coronation of King Edward VII, the design of the Regimental badge was altered to incorporate the Tudor Crown, but it appears that the new badge was not produced and worn until about 1911.

The Governor General's Body Guard at Camp Niagara, ca 1913. (GGHG Archives)

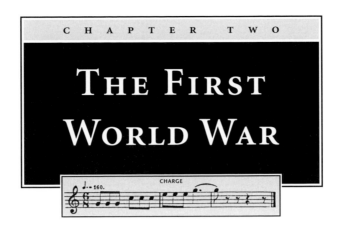

CHAPTER TWO

THE FIRST WORLD WAR

In Southern Ontario the early summer of 1914 was one of those memorable periods marked by a long period of hot, cloudless days without too much of the oppressing humidity that sometimes spoiled the enjoyment of that short season. Not many paid a great deal of attention to reports of the growing crisis in Europe. The old continent, after all, was a long way away, and there always were crises in strange places like the Balkans.

But the assassination of the Austrian Archduke Franz Ferdinand on 28 June 1914 in Sarajevo, the capital of the Austro-Hungarian province of Bosnia, set in motion a seemingly uncontrollable drive toward war between the two alliances that had grown up in the early years of the century. One after another, the major nations on the continent began to mobilize their massive armies, mainly to ensure that they would not be beaten to the draw and thus risk defeat by a country that reacted more quickly. First Austria mobilized against Serbia on 24 July, then Russia mobilized in support of their Serb allies, and then Germany mobilized out of concern at Russia's actions, and France mobilized because of the German threat. The sad thing was that mobilization set in train the implementation of national war plans, and, once begun there seemed to be no way this could be halted or delayed.

Germany's war plans were based on the need to avoid having to fight simultaneously against both the Russians and the French. Their first move would be a pre-emptive strike against France by means of a broad sweep through Belgium so as to knock France out of the war quickly before turning eastward to deal with the Russians. Thus on the early morning of 4 August 1914 four German armies with nearly a million men invaded Belgium en route to Northern France. The British, who years earlier had guaranteed Belgium's neutrality, issued an ultimatum to Germany: withdraw from Belgian soil by midnight or Britain would be at war. There was no reply.

Patriotic poster: Canada Putting on Arms and Armour.

Britain thus found herself involved in a war that would go down in history as one of the most terrible conflicts of all time. And, being part of the British Empire, Canada also was at war with Germany. There was no choice in the matter, even though the Canadian government did have the authority to

Nearly 400 men were recruited by the Governor General's Body Guard during the second week of August 1914. The photo above shows a group of young recruits, who have just been issued rifles, uniforms and basic kit. Note that while most of these young men are wearing the Body Guard's blue tunic, others toward the rear are wearing khaki uniforms. (City of Toronto Archives SC244-813)

(Left) Mississauga Horse recruits in scarlet tunics mustering outside the University Avenue Armouries, August 1914. (City of Toronto Archives SC637-1)

decide what sort of contribution the country would make to the war effort. In fact there had been extensive consultations with Britain over the looming crisis since 29 July, and on 1 August Prime Minister Robert Borden offered a Canadian contingent of 25,000 men. On 6 August the British government cabled its acceptance of this offer, but stipulated that infantry was what they wanted.

While there was a detailed plan already in the files in Ottawa for the mobilization of an overseas force of an infantry division and a cavalry brigade, the overbearing Minister of Militia, Sam Hughes, deliberately chose to ignore it, and instead decided to improvise. Rather than using the normal chain of command, Hughes sent telegrams directly to each of the 226 unit commanding officers with vague orders for them to begin the process of recruiting volunteers for the Canadian Expeditionary Force. The Minister, for reasons that have never been adequately explained, had decided not to mobilize any of the existing Militia units, but rather to raise a force of numbered battalions which had no connection to anything. The next weeks were a time of utter chaos, with orders and counter-orders flowing from Ottawa. It was especially confusing to

the cavalry units such as the Body Guard, who for several weeks were not certain whether cavalrymen were wanted or not.

The declaration of war was greeted with enormous popular enthusiasm over much of the country. In Toronto and in most other major centres there were huge patriotic rallies, and men flocked to the recruiting centres hastily established by the Militia units. There was a widespread belief that the war would be over by Christmas, and many didn't want to miss the opportunity to serve.

The Governor General's Body Guard rapidly enrolled nearly 400 men, all of whom fully expected that the Body Guard would form part of the cavalry brigade called for in the mobilization plan. It was not long, however, until Ottawa confirmed that the Canadian Expeditionary Force would not contain any cavalry: those who wanted to serve would have to do so as infantry.

It was a hard decision for loyal members of the Body Guard, Canada's foremost cavalry regiment. In the end, however, rather than forfeit the opportunity to serve overseas, 162 officers and men, including Major J.E.L. Streight, opted to join the 3rd (Toronto) Battalion, which was raised mainly from

among the Queen's Own Rifles. This Body Guard 'company' moved by train in late August to the new camp that had just been set up at Valcartier, Québec, to join the 3rd Battalion as it was being formed. After a month of rudimentary training in shooting and hardening up in many long hours of route marches, Major Streight's company sailed for England with the rest of the First Contingent on 3 October. (The wartime service of this company in the 3rd Battalion is not perpetuated by the Horse Guards, but by the Queen's Own Rifles.)

The newly minted 3rd (Toronto) Battalion paraded at the University Avenue Armouries on 22 August 1914 prior to boarding a train for Camp Valcartier, near Québec City, where the Canadian Expeditionary Force contingent was to assemble and train. Among the original members of this new battalion were 162 officers and men of the Body Guard. (City of Toronto Archives SC244-766B)

(Below) Horses donated to the Body Guard and the Mississauga Horse by the City of Toronto and the Mississauga's Honorary Colonel enabled both units to mount and train a full cavalry squadron while waiting for mobilization orders. (City of Toronto Archives SC244-822)

Rumours nonetheless persisted that cavalry would after all be needed, fuelled by an intimation from the Governor General himself that Egypt would be their likely destination. With this sort of unofficial encouragement, the commanding officers of both the Governor General's Body Guard and the Mississauga Horse established

their own voluntary training camps in late September. The Body Guard camp was set up at Aurora, while the Mississauga Horse located theirs near Long Branch where the unit had often trained in the summer. While the regiments conducted their training quite separately, both benefited from the generosity of the City of Toronto and the Honorary Colonel of the Mississauga Horse, Colonel H.C. Cox, who purchased 200 horses for use by the two units, enabling each to mount and train a full squadron.

The Toronto cavalry regiments didn't have long to wait. On 5 November 1914 Ottawa authorized the formation of six regiments of Mounted Rifles. The 4th Canadian Mounted Rifles, briefly called the Ontario Mounted Rifles, was to be raised in Military District No. 2, with an establishment of 28 officers and 577 NCOs and men. Command was given to Lieutenant-Colonel Vaux Chadwick, a former commanding officer of the Mississauga Horse, and one squadron was to be provided by each of the Governor General's Body Guard, the Mississauga Horse, the 2nd Dragoons and the 25th Brant Dragoons.

The Body Guard and the Mississauga Horse squadrons

Body Guard recruits moving into bell tents prior to beginning their training. (City of Toronto Archives SC244-751L)

81

were available immediately because of the astute action taken by Colonels Sanford Smith and Lockhart Gordon to organize unofficial training camps, and they were moved into quarters at the Canadian National Exhibition grounds on 16 November. Lieutenant Colonel Sanford Smith, CO of the Body Guard, was appointed second-in-command of the new regiment with the rank of major, and Lieutenant Colonel Lockhart Gordon, commanding officer of the Mississaugas, reverted to the rank of major to command a squadron. Major W.W. Denison of the Body Guard joined the 4th CMR as a squadron commander, as did Major J.F.H. Ussher of the Mississaugas. The Brant Dragoons joined the regiment in Toronto on 21 November, followed two days later by the troops from the 2nd Dragoons. Colonel Chadwick, knowing that he had to weld a unified regiment out of men from four different proud units, promptly put a troop from the parent regiments into each of his four squadrons.

Lieutenant Colonel Vaux Chadwick, a former CO of the Mississauga Horse, was selected to be the first commanding officer of the 4th Canadian Mounted Rifles on its formation in Toronto in November 1914. (GGHG Archives)

The 4th CMR did not have an easy winter in Toronto. The government had decided that the new units for the Overseas Force would not be sent to Valcartier but would train in their own garrison towns until they were sent to England. The Regiment was well supplied with horses: they inherited the 200 bought for the Body Guard and the Mississauga Horse, and another 500 were soon purchased by remount officers. But there were no saddles or bridles, and there was also a shortage of virtually every kind of equipment, including winter uniforms for the men. However, the unit's lack of winter clothing soon became known, and the people of Toronto came to the rescue, donating felt boots and sweaters, so the Regiment was able to continue training even in the harshest of weather.

The lack of saddlery could not be solved, however, even by borrowing some from the Mississauga Horse. The men thus had to be taught to ride bareback for the first three months, but the immediate result was that they became far better horsemen than if

Original badge of the 4th Canadian Mounted Rifles (left) and a variant. (GGHG Archives)

they had had proper equipment. Indeed, the Regiment's first review by the Minister of Militia, the notorious Sam Hughes, took place in December before any equipment arrived, but with the men in long cavalry greatcoats and with their excellent handling of the horses the deficiency wasn't even noticed.

While the 4th CMR went about its training for war, both the Body Guard and the Mississauga Horse did their best to carry on, but their main function over the next year was as a base for recruiting volunteers for other CEF units. For example, a large number of officers and men who had not been able to join 4th CMR were sent to the 7th Canadian Mounted Rifles. While this regiment was broken up in 1915 to provide reinforcements to the Canadian Mounted Rifles battalions, after the war the Horse Guards were granted the perpetuation of this unit. Among the junior officers of the Mississauga Horse who joined 7th CMR was Lieutenant William Avery Bishop, who later transferred to the Royal Flying Corps and won great distinction, including the Victoria Cross, as one of Canada's greatest aviation aces of the war.

The 4th CMR trained at a hectic pace during the winter of 1914-15, and every member became highly proficient in mounted rifle tactics and every aspect of horsemanship. The Regiment had become a thoroughly competent field unit. In the early spring of 1915 the Regiment was inspected by Governor General HRH the Duke of Connaught, and when he commented in glowing terms about the splendid appearance of the unit, many thought that this was a signal that the unit was about to be sent overseas – probably to guard the Suez Canal in Egypt was the barrack-room story. But this praise was followed by a series of great disappointments. First, in April the Regiment was ordered to supply their best horses as chargers for the officers of 2nd Canadian Division, which was about to depart for France. And then, in May, the Regiment was asked to volunteer for overseas service as a dismounted unit.

Morale sagged seriously for a short time, but the whole regiment soon accepted the inevita-

A 4th Canadian Mounted Rifles parade along University Avenue in Toronto in December 1914. At this time the unit was still desperately short of saddlery, and a close examination of the photo reveals that most of the men have no stirrups and thus are riding bareback. (City of Toronto Archives SC244-720C)

ble; everyone wanted to get into the field of action, even if it had to be as infantry. In June 1915 the Regiment was ordered to move to Valcartier, with only enough horses to bring the establishment to that of an infantry battalion. It was a sad parting when the unit said farewell to the remaining horses.

In Valcartier the Regiment joined 5th and 6th CMR to form the 2nd Canadian Mounted Rifles Brigade. But the unit also lost its leader. Lieutenant Colonel Vaux Chadwick had never become reconciled to the 4th CMR being a dismounted unit, and he was relieved. Lieutenant Colonel Sanford Smith, from the Body Guard, was appointed commanding officer, and Lieutenant Colonel Lockhart Gordon from the Mississaugas took over as second-in-command. The Regiment did its best to keep up its cavalry heritage: it still did foot drill in cavalry style, and the history of the 4th CMR recalls one of the efforts made to keep up the cavalry spirit while in Valcartier:

The famous drag hunts of the Canadian Mounted Rifles … would start with an innocent canter which would develop into a mad gallop through a wood followed by wonderful "fencing" on the flat. Then Lieut. D. MacKay would invariably challenge an unsuspecting officer to join in a race to

the finish. By the time they were going too hard to pull up they would come suddenly to a creek too wide to jump that ran into the Valcartier River. The first plunge would land the horses up to their chests; the next moment they had to swim and when attempting to climb up the opposite bank

Badge and collar badge of the 7th Canadian Mounted Rifles, formed in March 1915. Both the Body Guard and the Mississauga Horse contributed large numbers of officers and men to this unit, and it is officially perpetuated by the Governor General's Horse Guards. Originally, members of the 7th CMR wore the Army's standard General List badge. The regimental badge shown here appears to have been produced in very limited numbers just prior to the unit being broken up in England, and is very rare.

the majority of the riders would lose their seats and roll backwards into the water.

In early July the 4th CMR was inspected for the last time by the Governor General, and the regiment's horses were shipped to England along with the 2nd CMR on 9 July. Just over a week later the 4th and 5th CMR boarded the SS *Hesperian* in Québec harbour to begin their journey into battle.

In the meantime, back in Toronto, the Mississauga Horse and the Body Guard were busy recruiting jointly for the 75th Battalion, which was being raised by Lieutenant Colonel S.G. Beckett of the Mississauga Horse.

Lieutenant Colonel Sanford Smith, former CO of the Governor General's Body Guard, succeeded to command of the 4th Canadian Mounted Rifles in June 1915. (GGHG Archives)

ENGLAND

After a relatively calm nine-day crossing of the North Atlantic the *Hesperian* sailed into Plymouth harbour. 4th CMR disembarked early on the morning of 29 July, and was then moved by train to the Canadian camp at Shorncliffe, which overlooked the English Channel between Folkestone and Dover. Here they marched to a tented camp at Dibgate Hill, which was to be the Regiment's home for the next two months. Within days of arriving in England training took on a new intensity, for everyone expected they would soon be sent into action in France. The long route marches along the roads of Kent, which soon brought every man to peak physical condition, were most vividly remembered because they were so disliked. And there was field training of all sorts – fieldcraft, digging trenches, infantry platoon and company tactical exercises, and map reading schemes – on the picturesque rolling downs surrounding the camp. About once a week there was rifle and machine-gun firing on the nearby range at Hythe, and the Regiment was proud that they scored the highest average of all Canadian units that had shot there. At the end of the training day the men played baseball and soccer, and many made good use of the regimental canteen or the wonderful English pubs in the nearby villages. For most members the highlight of the brief stay in England was getting a two or three-day leave pass to go up to London.

On 23 September 1915 the Regiment abandoned the tented camp and was moved into an old British Army barracks called Caesar's Camp, where final preparations were made for the move to France.

Probably nothing was so significant in all these young soldiers' preparation as receiving their identification discs. Not even the field dressing or the rifle and its bayonet had the same sobering effect or was so indicative of the seriousness of the conflict in which they were about to participate as the reception of these little metal discs.

Training in infantry platoon tactics, Shorncliffe, England. (NAC PA004773)

This rather blurred photo shows the primitive conditions in the Canadian trenches in December 1915. (NAC PA5723)

The Regiment marched out of camp in full battle order on the evening of 24 October 1915 to board a packet boat in Folkestone harbour. A band led them down to the quay, and the local people shouted encouragement and farewells as they had done on so many occasions in the past year. After the men crowded on board, the ship slipped away from the jetty in the waning light of day. The 4th CMR was going to war.

THE YPRES SALIENT

The Regiment docked in the French port of Boulogne just two hours after leaving England and marched through the town to the large British base camp that now occupied the hills overlooking the port. Two days later a train was available to move the unit in behind the 1st Canadian Division, then occupying a section of the front south of Messines in Belgium. It was a long, circuitous journey for the men, crowded into the very basic French railway wagons marked "hommes 40, chevaux 8", and at every one of the many stops the troops would get out to stretch cramped legs or brew tea. Many hours later the train reached its destination at Bailleul, about 10 kilometres behind the front.

On 2 November the 2nd Mounted Rifles Brigade was moved forward for a week of indoctrination in trench warfare by the now highly experienced units of the 1st Division. Each squadron spent 48 hours in the front line, and for most it was an unpleasant and uncomfortable period, even though that section of the front was relatively quiet. The main enemy at the time, it seemed, was the weather: torrential rains had begun a week earlier, and temperatures hovered just above freezing. The trenches flooded, there was slimy mud everywhere, and with only one uniform the men were always wet and cold.

But they learned the essential harsh lessons about the deadly routine of war in the trenches.

Both the 1st and 2nd CMR Brigades were at this time grouped with the Canadian Cavalry Brigade, which had been serving as infantry with 1st Division since May 1915. Seely's Detachment was the official name of this ad hoc dismounted cavalry force, and on 23 November it was ordered to relieve the 2nd Brigade in a section of the front near Hill 63, on the north side of Ploegsteert Wood. The Canadian Mounted Rifles regiments thus had their baptism of fire, and each in turn held a section of the front line for four days and then served the next four days in reserve. The 4th CMR suffered their first casualties on 1 December, when Private Fulford and Lance Corporal Hodge were killed by a German shell and four others were wounded. Private Craig was killed the next day by a German grenade while on duty in a listening post in No Man's Land.

The Regiment's first real contact with the enemy came on 3 December, in the form of a raid on a German strong point

Cartoon depicting the abysmal conditions in the trenches in the late winter months of 1916.

being developed in No Man's Land. Some days before, artillery fire had felled a large tree across the Messines-Armentières road, about 120 metres in front of the Canadian line. The Germans had been seen working on this position, and General Seely asked for volunteers for a raiding party to get additional information. Lieutenant Rutter and twelve NCOs and men from 'C' Squadron were selected, supported by another group well forward of the trench and another in the line itself. The artillery bombardment meant to serve as a screen for the raid simply alerted the Germans, who brought down a hefty counter-bombardment

The 1914-15 Star, awarded to all Canadian troops that served in France and Flanders prior to the end of 1915.

that caused a number of casualties. The 'C' Squadron raiding group, despite being exposed by Verey flares and being under continuous fire from the German position, did manage to get across the cratered mud of No Man's Land and bring back a detailed report of what the enemy had done. The 2nd CMR, the Strathconas and finally the 5th Battalion all used this information to mount a series of raids during the next two weeks, but it was mid-month before the strong point was finally taken and demolished.

The regiments of Seely's Detachment were pulled back into the rear area on 9 December, bringing to a close 4th CMR's first experience of real operations. After the privations of the front the men enjoyed the relative comfort of their rude billets – at least they had showers and were able to keep dry. But at this very time decisions about the Regiment's future were being taken at the newly formed Canadian Corps headquarters.

3rd Canadian Division was officially formed on Christmas Day 1915, composed of the 7th, 8th and later the 9th Brigades. The 8th Brigade, commanded by Brigadier General V.A.S. Williams, a highly experienced RCD officer, was created by combining the 1st and 2nd CMR Brigades. But instead of the existing six mounted rifle regiments that had continued to operate on cavalry establishments, the 8th Brigade was to have four battalions, the 1st, 2nd, 4th and 5th, which meant disbanding the 3rd and 6th Regiments and bringing the new battalions up to the

normal infantry battalion strength of about 950 men. 'B' Squadron of 6th CMR officially became part of 4th CMR Battalion on 2 January 1916, and later that month the Battalion had a large infusion of men from the 8th CMR which had been disbanded in England.

Lieutenant Colonel Sanford Smith continued in command of the 4th CMR Battalion until early February, when he was relieved by Lieutenant Colonel J.F.H. Ussher, originally from the Mississauga Horse. Smith went to 3rd Canadian Division to take command of the division's mounted troops.

The 8th Brigade took over a section of the front south west of Messines on 1 February. While there wasn't a great deal of fighting, it was three weeks of demoralization. The rain that had begun at the end of October had never stopped.

There was no escape from it. The trenches … simply dissolved. The earth within the sandbags liquefied and oozed out. Everything collapsed. Every indentation in the ground filled with water, and to make things worse, the enemy, being on higher ground, delighted in draining his trenches across No Man's Land into those occupied by the Canadians.

Many spent days thigh-deep in stinking, muddy water because there were not enough high rubber waders to go around. The only small pleasure was the tightly controlled daily issue of $1^1/_4$ ounces (3 cl) of rum, and that did not compensate much for soaked uniforms and not having anywhere dry to sleep.

Following three weeks of drying out behind the lines, 8th Brigade was moved north to take over a section of the front on the eastern face of the notorious Ypres salient. The 4th CMR took over trenches in Sanctuary Wood on the night of 20 March. It was cold and raw, and, as everywhere in Flanders, the trenches were waterlogged. Because many vicious battles had been fought in this sector for over a year, the stench of half-buried decaying bodies permeated everything, and bloated rats were everywhere. Nothing could be done during daylight, as German machine guns could rake any above-ground activity from the flanks of the salient. Shelling was an ever-present danger, and the cause of most of the unit's casualties. 4th CMR

Badge of the 4th Canadian Mounted Rifles Battalion. In January 1916, the six regiments of the Canadian Mounted Rifles brigades were officially converted to infantry, becoming four battalions of the 8th Infantry Brigade. In 4th CMR, the new badge simply added an additional 'R' (for 'Regiment') in the title on the ribbon. (GGHG Archives)

rotated in and out of this sector until mid-May 1916, the standard routine being about a week in the front trench, a week in the second (support) line and a week in brigade reserve, followed by a week of rest and recreation in the rear area. On 16 May the Battalion finished another tour and headed for the division's rear. The leaves were by then sprouting on the trees in Sanctuary Wood, and the men sweltered in the hot sun as they marched through the ruined town of Ypres.

MOUNT SORREL

The whole of the Ypres salient had been fairly quiet since the fighting at St. Eloi in early April. For some time, however, the Germans had been preparing to attack into the sector held by 3rd Canadian Division, aiming to seize the high ground between the features known as Mount Sorrel and Hill 61, the only heights in the whole of the salient still in Allied hands. The Germans had effectively concealed most of their preparations for the attack, so no unusual precautions were taken on the Canadian side.

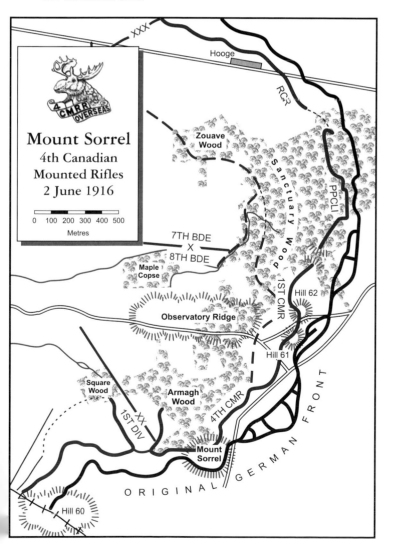

Lieutenant Colonel J.F.H. Ussher, commanding officer of 4th CMR February to June 1916.

The 4th CMR paraded in full marching order after supper on 31 May for yet another tour of duty at the front. This time they were to be on the 3rd Division's right flank, taking over a 1000-metre section of the front line forward of Armagh Wood, between Mount Sorrel and Hill 61. The 1st CMR was on their left, straddling a feature known as Observatory Ridge, and 5th CMR was some 600 metres in the rear in the support line centred in Maple Copse.

The trenches that 4th CMR took over that night from the 52nd Battalion were in the best condition of any that the unit had thus far occupied – there were good fire bays and clean shelters, and there was a deep tunnel on the reverse slope of Mount Sorrel that offered protection against shelling. The weather continued bright, clear and warm, and other than the appearance of several captive observation balloons there was no indication of any unusual behaviour by the Germans. Word was passed down that the Division Commander, Major General Mercer, would inspect the battalion area on the morning of 2 June, so an extra effort was made to tidy things up.

On 2 June the Battalion stood-to as usual at first light. At 0600 hours Colonel Ussher made a tour of the front trenches, and then went back along the communications trench to Battalion headquarters to meet Major General Mercer and Brigadier General Williams. The generals and their aides arrived promptly at 0800 hours. After giving a short briefing about the battalion, Colonel Ussher led the division and brigade commanders toward the front. Just before they reached the front trench, however, a violent artillery bombardment came down. The official history records:

For four hours a veritable tornado of fire ravaged the Canadian positions from half a mile west of Mount Sorrel to the northern edge of Sanctuary Wood. The full fury fell upon the 8th Brigade and the right of the 7th Brigade. Hardest hit was … the 4th Canadian Mounted Rifles, in front of Armagh Wood. Their trenches vanished, and the garrisons in them were annihilated.

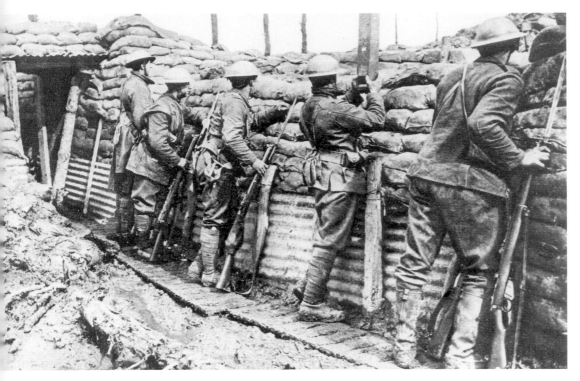

This photo of Canadian troops in the late spring of 1916 shows a well-constructed trench typical of those occupied by 4th CMR between Mount Sorrel and Hill 61 on the eastern side of the Ypres salient in late May 1916. Note the newly issued steel helmets. (NAC C6984)

During this terrifying rain of shellfire there were a great many acts of enormous bravery, most of them never officially recognized since decorations were not given posthumously. Three men did receive the Distinguished Conduct Medal. Lance Corporal E.C. Woodroof was cited for conspicuous bravery, having volunteered on two occasions during the bombardment to go forward into No Man's Land to get information on enemy activity. Private C.K. Hoag showed great courage on numerous occasions during the shelling by repeatedly exposing himself to go to the aid of wounded comrades. And conspicuous gallantry was demonstrated by Private C. Routledge during the German attack: "he rescued a Lewis gun, which he brought across the open, under heavy fire, firing at enemy bombers from shell holes. He also carried in many wounded men."

General Mercer was killed almost instantly by a shrapnel burst, and General Williams was badly wounded. Colonel Ussher managed to get General Williams to the entrance of the tunnel in Mount Sorrel, and they and a few men took refuge there from the devastating pounding of the intense enemy gunfire.

At 1300 hours the bombardment abruptly ceased, and at that instant four large mines under the 4th CMR trenches were exploded:

Private John Evans was with the Battalion machine gun platoon that morning. Some years later his story was published in *Maclean's* Magazine:

The morning of June 2 dawned clear and beautiful after a night of anxiety and alarms; and about 5:30 I turned in for a little sleep.... I had just nicely fallen off to sleep when it seemed as though the whole crust of the earth was torn asunder. I wakened to find myself buried under loose earth and sandbags. By a miracle I was not hurt and I finally managed to burrow out. A shell, I found, had blown up our dugout. Two of the crew were killed, but the fourth man had shared my luck.... Then the bombardment started in earnest. Shells rained on us like hailstones. The German artillery started a barrage behind us that looked like a wall of flame; so we knew that there was no hope whatever of help reaching us.

Our men dropped off one by one. The walls of our trench were battered to greasy sand heaps. The dead lay everywhere. Pretty soon only Wedgewood and myself were left.... As far as we could see along the line there was nothing left, not even trenches – just churned up earth and mutilated bodies.

[The explosion of the mines] hurled into the air a large part of the front line and its defenders. Sandbags, wire, machine guns, bits of corrugated iron and bits of men were slung skyward. After this final eruption all was quiet, even our own guns.

German infantry came forward at once, but since there were few members of 4th CMR left to offer any resistance the enemy were soon in possession of Mount Sorrel and Hill 61. Lance Corporal Wedgewood and Private John Evans were

This photo, taken about a month after the Battle of Mount Sorrel, shows clearly how the Canadian trenches in the area had been nearly obliterated by the German shelling on 2 June. (NAC PA811)

among those few who tried to do their duty. They manned their machine gun when the German assault came in, but they had only 300 rounds of ammunition, and that was quickly expended. Both wounded, they tried to get to the rear, but they were soon surrounded by German soldiers. Like so many other wounded survivors of the Battalion, they spent the next three years in German prisoner-of-war camps.

The 4th CMR had been annihilated. Of the 22 officers and 680 men who had gone into the trenches two days earlier, only three officers and 73 men got back. Of this small number, it is notable that a significant proportion were later decorated for bravery: Major Denison was awarded the Distinguished Service Order; Captains Coleman and Lee got the Military Cross; there were three DCMs and fourteen Military Medals. Eleven officers and 110 NCOs and men were taken prisoner, including Lieutenant Colonel Ussher, the command-

Lieutenant Colonel Lockhart Gordon, a pre-war member of the Mississauga Horse, was brought in to command 4th CMR after Lieutenant Colonel Ussher was taken prisoner. (GGHG Archives)

ing officer. And of those who died on 2 June, more than 50 are listed as 'missing presumed dead' as no trace of them was ever found. It was a dreadful toll.

1st CMR on the left suffered nearly as heavily as 4th CMR, and it was only because of the stiff resistance put up by the Princess Patricia's Canadian Light Infantry in Sanctuary Wood and 5th CMR in Maple Copse that the German attack was halted.

The remnants of the Battalion were kept at the front the next day to act as guides and carrying parties for the 1st Division units that had been rushed forward to re-establish the defence, and then on 4 June they were taken to billets in the village of Steenvoorde, where over the next month the Battalion was re-built. Lieutenant Colonel Lockhart Gordon, who had joined from the Mississauga Horse when 4th CMR was first formed, was brought from 3rd Division headquarters to take over as commanding officer. And Captain W.R.

The Defence of Sanctuary Wood. **This painting by K.K. Forbes depicts the battle in the PPCLI sector on 2 June 1916, about a thousand metres north of 4th CMR's location. It provides some insight into the fighting that took place on the 4th CMR front that fateful day. (Canadian War Museum 8157)**

Patterson, also one of the original members from the Body Guard, was brought from 8th Brigade headquarters as second-in-command. By 9 July some 563 reinforcements had arrived, and over the next week smaller drafts brought the unit up to its authorized strength. But a great deal of work remained to weld the new members into a fighting battalion.

As 4th CMR was beginning to re-form, 1st Division mounted a deliberate counter-attack in the early hours of 13 June, and in the space of little over an hour regained almost all of the ground lost on 2 June.

Colonel Gordon and his new company commanders set an ambitious programme to bring the unit to an acceptable level of operational competence over the next three weeks. The Battalion was inspected by the Army commander, the Corps commander, the new Division commander, and by Brigadier General Elmsley, the new commander of 8th Brigade, who had begun his military career years before with the Body Guard in Toronto. Companies went into the trenches for familiarization, platoons provided working parties at the front, and by mid-July the battalion was judged to be ready for operational

duty once again. The 'new' 4th CMR then took over a sector of the old front in Sanctuary Wood on 23 July. The author Rudyard Kipling described that very section of trenches in a history of the Irish Guards, who had occupied this trench in late June:

… for nearly half a mile [the line] was absolutely unrecognizable save in a few isolated spots. The shredded ground was full of buried iron and timber which made digging difficult, and, in spite of a lot of cleaning up by predecessors, dead Canadians lay in every corner. It ran through what had been a wood and was now a dreary collection of charred and splintered stakes, to the top of which, blown there by shells, hung tatters of khaki uniform and equipment.

Enemy shelling and sniper fire took an almost daily toll before the Battalion was relieved a week later, but warm summer weather helped to keep spirits up. Another brief period in rest billets far to the rear allowed the men to wash their clothes and at least briefly get rid of the lice that by now were an ever-present problem.

In mid-August it was time for yet another rotation to the front, this time into the southern-most section of the Ypres Salient. Despite the daily shelling, this tour in the forward line proved to be more challenging, in part because the trench line ran along the lip of a massive crater, and there was some scope for initiative in constructing wire obstacles to prevent enemy activity in No Man's Land. It soon became apparent the Germans were digging a tunnel for yet another mine: at quiet moments the sound of underground scraping and tapping could be clearly heard. There was some concern that the unit could be blown sky high at any moment, but then one day a large area caved in behind the front line, revealing the location of the tunnel and bringing the enemy's digging to an end. 4th CMR was relieved on the night of 22 August, and the Germans lobbed in a few shells as a parting gesture. It was not then known, of course, but this was to be the Battalion's last duty in the Ypres sector for more than a year.

A reserve trench in the Ypres salient in the summer of 1916. (NAC PA165)

Back in Canada, the Body Guard and the Mississauga Horse were again busy assisting in the raising of yet another battalion for overseas service, the 216th Battalion, known as the 'Toronto Bantams'. Lieutenant Colonel F.L. Burton of the Mississauga Horse was commanding officer of this unit.

THE SOMME

A major Allied offensive for 1916 had been in the making since December 1915. Despite the repeated failure of every offensive in 1915, the high command was still confident that a massive attack on a broad front could break through the German defences and maybe even bring the war to an end. The location of the 'Big Push' was to be the Somme valley, along the boundary between the French and British armies. But the ground selected was far from ideal: the Germans had held the high ground there for over 18 months, and they had constructed a series of interconnected trench lines, bunkers and concrete strong points in enormous depth, all protected by belts of thick wire entanglements.

The Somme offensive began on 1 July 1916, when eleven British and six French divisions attacked after seven days of the heaviest artillery bombardment yet seen during the war. But wave after wave of Allied troops were simply cut down in a rain of shrapnel and machine-gun fire. The first day's fighting cost the British over 57,000 casualties, and almost no ground was gained.

Throughout July and August the Allies repeatedly launched one attack after another, but there was never anything even close to a breakthrough. In two months of very hard fighting the Allied line had been pushed forward by at most 6,000 metres, but at the enormous cost of 200,000 British and 70,000 French soldiers. Attrition now governed the whole war effort, and fresh troops had to be brought in if the Somme offensive was to continue. The Canadian Corps was to provide some of them.

Beginning in mid-August the Canadian divisions were progressively pulled out of the Ypres Salient, and each in turn had a brief period of intensive training in offensive tactics. When 4th CMR was moved to Steenvoorde in the rear area on 22 August the Battalion immediately began its preparations for the Somme. Much of the training involved practice in a new form of offensive tactics – attack in successive waves behind a creeping artillery barrage. Dummy enemy trenches were marked out on the ground with white mine tape, and time after time the companies would rehearse the drills of attacking

Badge of the 216th Battalion, the Toronto Bantams, raised by the Mississauga Horse and the Body Guard in 1916. All its members were below the usual minimum height, many only 5 feet tall.

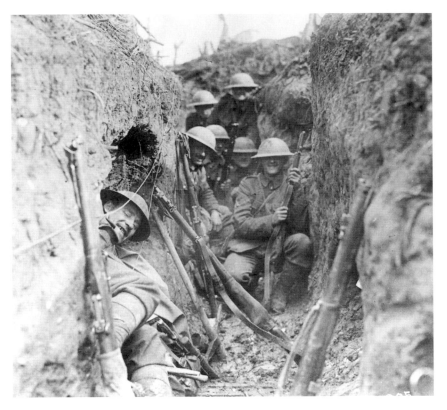

Troops in a communications trench near Courcelette, September 1916. Note the 'funk hole' carved out of the side of the trench as a shelter for sleeping. (NAC PA723)

Shrapnel bursting over a reserve trench in the Canadian lines, September 1916. (NAC PA733)

these positions while following closely behind a simulated creeping barrage of thunderflashes. Then too, there was a lot of emphasis on rifle practice and bayonet drill with the newly issued Lee Enfield rifles.

Along with the other units of 8th Brigade, the 4th CMR was moved southward by troop train into Picardy on 7 September, eventually reaching the rubbled town of Albert at midday on the 11th. As the unit neared the front the men came to understand the vastness of the operation they were about to enter: just about every piece of ground for many kilometres back was occupied by horse lines, ammunition and supply dumps, tented camps or row after row of guns of every size, and endless traffic moved in both directions along every road and track.

There was to be no time for gentle familiarization with the new area. That same night 2nd and 3rd Divisions were to relieve 1st Division, which had been at the front since 3 September. By 1830 hours 4th CMR was on the move, and the men soon saw first-hand the devastation of the Somme battlefields.

Not a tree was standing, [the village of] la Boiselle was a heap of rubble and the remains of its buildings had been used to fill the shell holes in the road. Shell cases were strewn along the roadside.... Tangled wire and mutilated trenches covered the barren waste as far as one could see.

It was pitch black by the time 4th CMR reached the 5th Battalion's support line, and this first tour at the Somme began badly as guides got lost in the pock-marked maze of cratered ground and old trenches as they led the companies toward the front trench. And to make matters worse the Germans bombarded the front with gas shells just as the Battalion got into position, causing a number of serious casualties.

The Canadians' first major assault was scheduled for dawn on 15 September. 4th CMR was to be in reserve during this opera-

Fixing bayonets prior to an attack into No Man's Land. (NAC PA683)

tion and had been relieved at the front the previous night. It was in this attack that tanks were to be used for the first time, and during the night some members of the Battalion saw a few of them from their rear positions as the tanks noisily crawled forward to their start line. The 8th Brigade attack, on the left flank of the Canadian Corps sector, went especially well, as did the operation in the 2nd Division sector, and all objectives were taken by 0700 hours, much earlier than anticipated. Deciding to push home his advantage, the Corps Commander decided to launch a second attack at 1700 hours, and the 8th Brigade commander, General Elmsley, ordered up 4th CMR and the 7th Brigade.

The Battalion was several kilometres behind the front when the warning order was received later that morning. Having

just come out of the line, Colonel Gordon knew it would take about four hours to move forward along the narrow and shell-scarred communications trenches so as to be in position to attack at Zero Hour, so he gave instructions to his second-in-command, Major Patterson, to begin immediately to march

Grisly scene on the Somme battlefield. (NAC PA639)

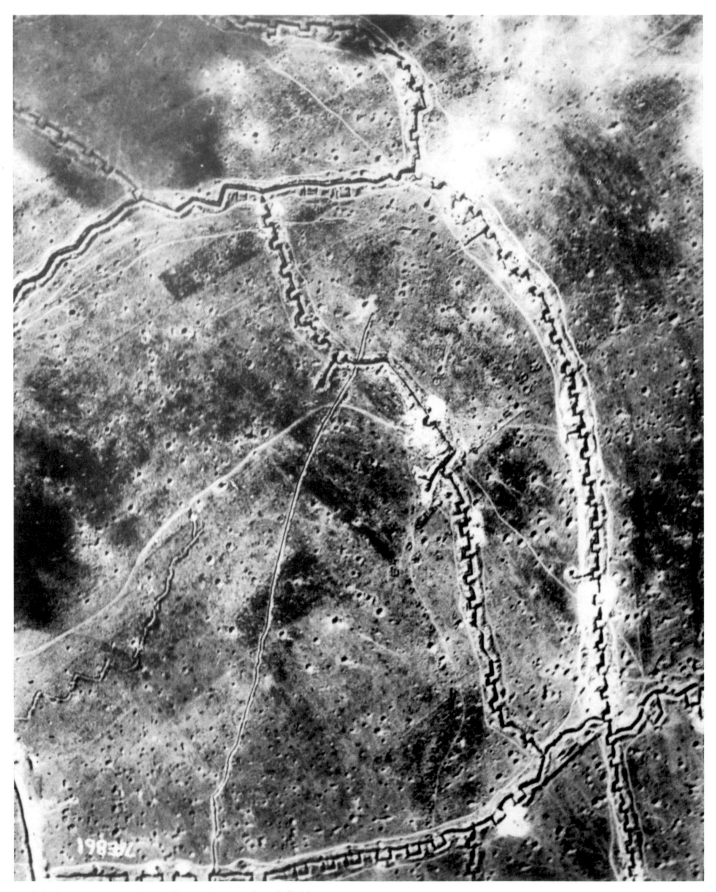

Aerial view of part of the shell-torn Somme battlefield.

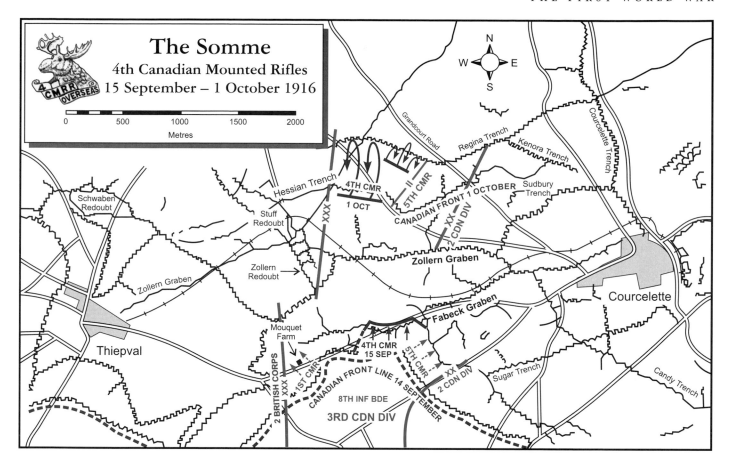

the battalion up to the 5th CMR position at the front and await orders there. Gordon then galloped to brigade headquarters where he learned the details of the plan. 4th CMR was ordered to attack on a 300-metre frontage from a jumping-off point 200 metres forward of 5th CMR. (The concept of having a secure start line was simply not understood in 1916.) The first wave was to capture a section of the German trench nearly 300 metres further on. The second wave was to occupy a portion of the Fabeck Graben trench about a hundred metres beyond the first objective, and establish contact with the 42nd Battalion advancing on the right. Zero Hour was set for 1730 hours.

Written orders were sent up to Major Patterson, who was to control the operation from a forward headquarters. 'B' Company (Major Coleman) was to attack on the left, and 'C' Company (Captain Hamilton) was to advance on the right.

'B' Company got into its jumping off point in front of 5th CMR in good time. 'C' Company, however, ran into serious difficulty before getting to the start line: the communications trench along which they were to move to the front had been blown in, and when Captain Hamilton tried to move his men cross country in the open they came under intense machine-gun fire which wiped out most of two platoons.

When 'C' Company failed to show up at the start line, 'B' Company was ordered to attack alone. At Zero Hour Major Coleman led his men forward, tucked in close to the creeping barrage, and as it lifted the leading platoons charged the German trench. The first objective was taken in minutes despite heavy enfilade fire from enemy positions on the left. The second wave of two platoons then pushed on to the second objective, Fabeck Graben trench. The Germans there put up a stubborn resistance, but this was soon overcome in large part because of the courageous leadership shown by Sergeant R.L. Layton. 'Bombers' (men armed with early hand grenades) under Lieutenant H.E. Moore then worked their way along the trench in both directions, clearing out or capturing the enemy who remained. Before dark, despite being under constant machine gun and mortar fire, 'B' Company had consolidated its hold on nearly 500 metres of the Fabeck Graben trench line, and had captured 50 Germans and two machine guns. It was indeed a truly heroic effort by every man in the company and an important part of the successes of the Canadian Corps in its first major offensive on the Somme. The gains on this one day had been greater than in any other single operation since the beginning of the Somme battle.

The severity of the fighting in this brief period is evident from the Battalion's casualties: two officers and 32 men killed and four officers and 52 men wounded. And once again a few members of the Battalion were rewarded for the great courage that had been demonstrated by the unit. Major Patterson got a well-deserved DSO; Captains Blake and Hepburn were both awarded the Military Cross; Sergeant Layton received the Distinguished Conduct Medal; Corporal Ingleby got a bar to his Military Medal, and five other men were awarded MMs.

Following further attacks by 7th and 9th Brigades, both of which failed, 4th CMR was relieved on the evening of 16 September and marched into rest billets some 15 kilometres to the rear. During the ten days that 4th CMR was out of the line, the battle for Thiepval Ridge continued to be fought by 1st and 2nd Divisions. Metre by metre gains were won against stiff enemy resistance, but the casualty list grew longer each day.

On 27 September 3rd Division was hurriedly brought back into the line to relieve 2nd Division. In 8th Brigade, 1st and 2nd CMR were tasked to man the front, while 4th CMR, all the while working under heavy enemy shelling, carried up supplies, ammunition and water and helped to clear the dead from the battlefield. Three days later 4th CMR relieved 2nd CMR at the front trench.

A fresh offensive had been planned for 1 October, with the objective of capturing the last of the main German lines, Regina Trench. Everyone knew that this would be especially difficult. The Germans had already shown they were determined to hold this pivotal ground, since losing it would mean having to pull back off Thiepval Ridge. To buttress the position they had strung several belts of concertina and barbed wire, each nearly 10 metres deep, and all were covered by machine-gun emplacements and planned artillery targets. To complicate matters, Regina Trench was going to be hard to get at: it was located on the steep reverse slope of the ridge, which made observed, and thus accurate, artillery fire virtually impossible. And accurate shelling was precisely what was needed to cut gaps in the wire entanglements and to keep the Germans' heads down during the assault.

The 8th Brigade was again to be the left pivot for the Canadian Corps, and 4th CMR was on the left of the brigade. The Battalion was ordered to attack from Hessian Trench at 1515 hours on a 600-metre frontage, in two waves. 'A' Com-

pany (Captain Gale) was to be on the left, 'D' Company (Captain Bishop) on the right, with one platoon of 'C' Company detailed to advance on the battalion's left flank to form a defensive block in Regina Trench as soon as it was taken. The remainder of 'C' Company was to form a defensive flank in Hessian Trench. During the morning before the attack, scouts had reported that the German wire had not been cut by the artillery barrage as had been planned. A further barrage was laid on, but it too failed to cut the essential gaps in the wire. 'A' Company was then ordered to crawl forward and get beyond the enemy's first belt of entanglements before Zero Hour, which they were able to do without being detected.

Two minutes before Zero Hour an exceptionally heavy barrage struck the area of Regina Trench. As it ended, both 'A' and 'D' Companies got up to move forward. In front of 'A' Company the barrage had, however, completely missed the enemy line, and the men advanced into a hail of machine-gun fire that stopped them as they began to move. Nearly the whole company was wiped out, with only a few survivors taking refuge in shell holes. 'D' Company had somewhat more success. While one of its first-wave platoons died almost to a man when it was hung up on uncut wire, the remainder of the company did find a gap and were able to fight their way into Regina Trench. Here they briefly held a short section, but only until the last man was killed.

For a time the survivors of 'A' and 'C' Companies made repeated attempts to fight along a communications trench leading into Regina Trench, but eventually their ranks were so depleted that they had to pull back and establish a defensive

Bodies of German soldiers after a Canadian attack, October 1916. Official photographers had instructions not to take pictures of Canadian dead. (NAC PA868)

Trench scene in the Vimy Ridge sector, December 1916.

block. The Germans mounted a counter-attack at 1630 hours, but Captain A.A. MacKenzie and his few remaining men, still in shell craters just short of the German trench, inflicted huge casualties and broke up the German attack.

5th CMR, who attacked on the right of the Battalion, did manage to get one company into Regina Trench, but they too were driven out the next morning. Their other attacking company was wiped out. Much the same thing happened on the 2nd Division front.

This first attempt to take Regina Trench had ended in a very costly failure. The failure was, however, not caused by any lack of determination or effort by the men who carried out the attack. The heavily wired and thoroughly prepared German position simply was too strong to be taken on by men opposed by numerous machine guns, however brave and skilled they might be. Six men from 'A' and 'C' Companies received the Military Medal, and Captain MacKenzie was awarded the Military Cross.

Another attack put in a week later by 1st and 3rd Divisions met with much the same results, and for the same reasons. There was clearly a pressing need for improved equipment that could cope effectively with the machine guns and barbed wire which had come to dominate the battlefield, such as the tanks that unfortunately had shown too many limitations a month earlier. There was also a need for better use of firepower to overcome battlefield obstacles. Fortunately, both were to come over the next year.

Before the Canadian Corps ceased operations on the Somme, the 4th CMR did another two tours in the trenches, including supporting the 4th Division during their introduction to the Somme battlefield. This fresh division made three attempts to take Regina Trench before finally succeeding in overcoming the German defenders on 11 November. In the meantime the remainder of the Canadian Corps began on 14 October to move northward to take responsibility for a sector of the front facing Vimy Ridge, where some months later the Corps was to have its greatest victory of the war.

The two and a half months of fighting at the Somme would forever leave its mark on the 4th Canadian Mounted Rifles. The Battalion had arrived overstrength, with nearly 1,200 men, and while there received over 200 reinforcements. The unit's casualties on this barren and scarred battlefield numbered over 1,000 magnificent men – killed, missing or wounded, and their sacrifice would never be forgotten.

VIMY RIDGE

As the deadly but inconclusive attrition battles on the Somme were petering out because of both sides' exhaustion, the Canadian Corps was moved north and assigned responsibility for a 6,500-metre section of the front that faced a feature known as Vimy Ridge, between the cities of Lens and Arras.

From the Canadian side, Vimy Ridge did not appear to be especially imposing, except in the northernmost third of the sector where the Canadian line was in a shallow valley. Elsewhere the ground rose very gradually, and in the south it was nearly flat. It was from the back – the German side – that the strategic importance of the ridge was apparent. The reverse slope was a steep, heavily wooded incline that quickly fell nearly 50 metres, and from the crest of the ridge the flat Douai plain below was open to observation to the east for many kilometres.

The Germans had held the heights of the ridge since early

1915, and in the intervening year and a half had constructed three, and in the south, four formidable defensive lines. The first of these positions overlooked and dominated the open forward slope of the ridge in the northern half of the sector. The front line in much of the new Canadian sector was sited within a hundred or so metres of the Germans' forward trench. In most circumstances this would have been a highly undesirable situation, but the underlying soft chalk was already a maze of natural caverns and tunnels dug in the Middle Ages, and it lent itself to the digging of underground bunkers and communications tunnels that reached many kilometres to the rear. The sector had seen little action since the French had lost nearly 130,000 men in a failed attempt to take the ridge early in 1915. This pattern of relative inactivity continued for several months after the Canadian Corps moved in.

8th Brigade initially took over the southernmost sector of the Vimy front on the night of 24 October, and 4th CMR did its first tour in the forward trench near Ecurie at the end of the month. For the next several months the Battalion followed the standard routine of four days at the front, four days in rest billets in the rear. When compared to the recent harsh experience at the Somme, life in the

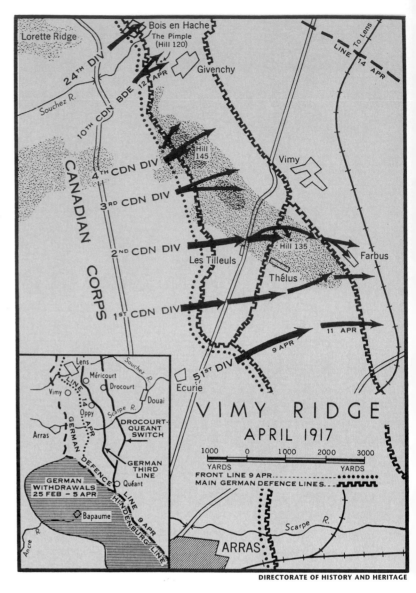

(Below) A detailed mock-up of the German defences on Vimy Ridge was put together behind the lines. Every unit went through intensive training in their part of the offensive, including walk-though demonstrations on models such as this. (NAC PA3666)

rear in these months was like being at a holiday camp. The Battalion had the use of a large shed where the men could sleep in warm, dry beds, and there were regular showers and issues of clean clothing. Heavy rain began in early December, and the 4th CMR spent a lot of their time repairing communications trenches that began to disintegrate because of the weather. Late that month the Battalion was ordered to mount a diversionary attack to cover a raid by 1st CMR. Unfortunately the ruse worked so well that it brought down an intense retaliatory bombardment which caused a large number of casualties, but it did enable the sister unit to do its job without a single man being hurt.

4th CMR's second Christmas in France was spent in the rear area, but only a few of the men who had been with the unit a year before were left to celebrate. The highlight of the holiday was a superb Christmas dinner, made possible because of money sent to the commanding officer by the Honorary Colonel of the Mississauga Horse, Colonel H.C. Cox, which paid for extra rations for the meal itself, as well as for special treats that the men at the front never saw – chocolate, oranges and a tot of whisky for every man.

The Battalion was back in the trenches for New Year's, but preparation for another major push began soon after they were relieved. Planning for an even broader grand offensive had been launched by the Allied high command even as the Somme battles were coming to an end. This time the French were to make the main effort, but it was up to the British to draw off the bulk of the German reserves before the French Army started out. The Canadian Corps was to have the task of anchoring the north flank of the British attack that would begin in April: they were to capture the formidable German positions on Vimy Ridge.

The Corps Commander was Lieutenant General Julian Byng, who after the war would become Governor General and Honorary Colonel of the Governor General's Body Guard. He knew that thorough planning and preparation would be the key to success, and a great deal of precise intelligence gathering was undertaken, much of which came from the Royal Flying Corps. Every piece of ground, every enemy position was examined in painstaking detail to determine what was needed to overcome the defenders. Then precise operational plans were made, and intensive training of every unit was begun, focused on their specific tasks. And the bitter lessons learned at the Somme began to have practical application: the tactical principle of fire and movement was rediscovered.

The great tactical change brought about by General [Arthur] Currie [then commanding 1st Division] was the emphasis on manoeuvre by platoons and sections: they were to use their own firepower to manoeuvre around enemy strong points. Platoons were taught that German defenders were to be pinned down by section Lewis light

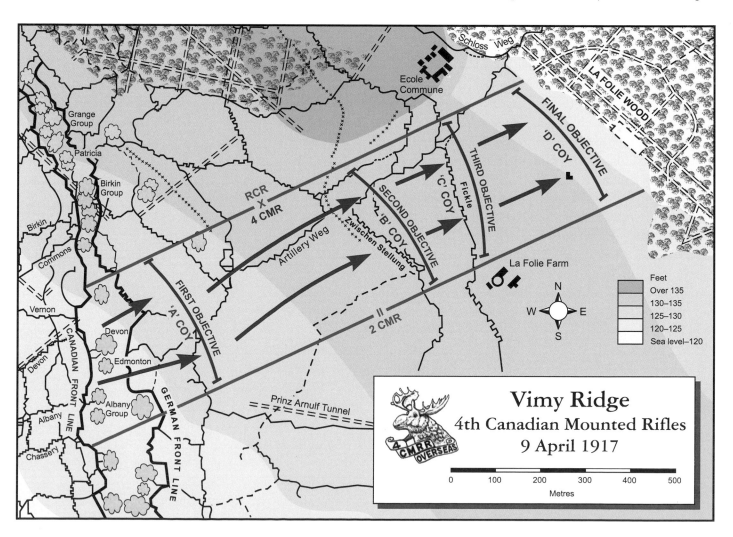

Vimy Ridge
4th Canadian Mounted Rifles
9 April 1917

machine guns, then outflanked by riflemen and 'bombers' throwing grenades.

Well behind the line a full-scale mock-up of the German defences was reproduced in great detail. Tapes showed the location of trenches, and flags indicated strong points. On 13 February 4th CMR began a five-week training session for their part in this great battle. Time and again the Battalion rehearsed their assault on taped trenches, and later all the 8th Brigade did the same thing together. In addition, there was a scaled-down model of the entire German trench system where demonstrations could show how all aspects of the plan were brought together.

Nothing was left undone which had any bearing on the preparations for an unimpeded assault. At the end of this time, every man knew exactly what he was to do, what his platoon had to do, what his company was expected to accomplish and what support would be available. This was probably the first time during this long, dreadful war that enough confidence had been placed in the innate initiative and common sense of the Canadian soldier to prepare him thoroughly for what had to be done, and the men's morale soared because they knew that every effort was being made to reduce the risk to them in the attack. General Byng himself injected great enthusiasm into these training sessions, "patiently accompanying battalions 'over the tapes' and explaining details to all and sundry". And to help the soldiers understand their own role and how it all fit together, over 40,000 maps of the terrain were distributed within the Corps, nearly one for every man in the assaulting battalions.

Even as this intense training took place, equally intense administrative preparations were being set in place. In most of the brigade areas tunnels were dug (or in some cases old tunnels were simply extended) from the front trench to points well behind the line so that troops could be brought up for the attack completely under cover. Most of these tunnels also incorporated large chambers to house battalion and brigade headquarters, ammunition stores, communications centres and dressing stations, all equipped with electricity and water, and several had narrow rail lines for the movement of stores and equipment. Enormous quantities of artillery ammunition was stockpiled for the crushing bombardment that was to precede the attack. And tunnels were also dug under the enemy's front line to place large 'mines' to be exploded at Zero Hour.

The usual defensive routine, of course, had to be kept up throughout this period, in part to ensure that the Germans did not notice anything unusual. And indeed part of the preliminary training was to familiarize battalions with the trench lines from which they would begin their attacks. Two companies of 4th CMR moved into the front trench on 18 March, and five days later the other two companies relieved them for a similar period.

A key aspect of the 4th CMR section of the front was that No Man's Land here consisted of a series of eleven deep craters clustered in three groups named Devon, Albany and Vernon. Most of these craters were about 100 metres in diameter, but two were nearly 200 metres wide. Part of the game played with the Germans at this time was over who could dominate No Man's Land during the hours of darkness, usually by deploying standing ambush parties in the craters and by periodic forays of small fighting patrols. One such patrol was sent out on the night of 30/31 March under Lieutenant Richards, with two three-man groups led by Corporals Martin and Dawson, and supported by others in Vernon and Devon craters. The raiding parties silently cut a small gap in the German wire and crawled up to the parapet and into the enemy trench without being detected. After moving a short distance along the trench they came across five German sentries and attacked with grenades. This, as expected, brought an immediate response: flares lit up the area, the Germans rushed reinforcements to the front, and a small but intense local battle raged while the raiders withdrew. Unfortunately, Lieutenant Richards was badly wounded by a stick bomb and died the next morning.

After this tour at the front, another brief respite in the rest area was devoted to final preparations for the offensive: one last rehearsal over dummy positions, and a thorough inspection of kit and equipment. Every man was issued with two days' "iron rations" (tinned corned beef and hardtack biscuits), five sand bags, two flares, four bombs and signalling flags. While the unit was in the rear the preparatory bombardment of the German lines was brought to a peak. "Shells poured over the heads of the Canadians onto enemy positions 'like water from a hose'", says one account. The enemy trenches were shattered, and their wire entanglements shredded over the period of a week.

The Battalion moved to the front through the Goodman tunnel on the night of 5/6 April. Two companies took up positions in the forward trench, while the other two – the lead-off companies – remained under cover in dugouts and tunnels. On the night of 6/7 April two parties were sent out to cut clearings through the Canadians' own wire entanglements, and on the following night parties from 'A' Company cut lanes

Troops advancing during the attack on Vimy Ridge, 9 April 1917. (NAC PA1020)

that they themselves would use through the German wire between the Devon, Albany and Vernon craters.

The Corps' plan for the operation called for a simultaneous assault by all four divisions abreast beginning before first light on the morning of 9 April, with the objective of capturing the heights of the ridge and the three German strong points at Farbus Wood, Thélus and La Folie Farm. Because of the layout of the German trench system, the attack was to have four phases. At each phase line fresh troops would take over the lead.

In the sector assigned to 3rd Division, 8th Brigade was in the centre, and 4th CMR was on the left of the brigade. Each battalion was to advance in four waves on a 350-metre front, one company up, with another company leapfrogging to take the lead at each phase line. Colonel Gordon issued his orders on the evening of 7 April. In 4th CMR, 'A' Company (Major Gale), with two platoons forward, was to capture the German front trench, mop it up, and then move several hundred metres beyond to consolidate. 'B' Company (Captain Hart) was then to pass through 'A' Company, first to capture a communications trench named Artillery Weg on the battalion's north flank, and then to take their main objective, Zwischen Trench, which was the Germans' second defence line. 'C' Company

(Major Menzies) was then to move through to take Fickle Trench, the German third line, which was about 1000 metres from the original Canadian front line. And finally, 'D' Company (Major MacKenzie) had orders to take the crest of the ridge between the Ecole Commune and the La Folie Farm strong point, and if need be assist the RCR on the left or 2nd CMR on the right. Zero Hour was to be 0530 hours.

While 'D' Company manned the forward trench, 'A', 'B' and 'C' Companies spent the early part of the night of 8 April in deep caverns and dugouts strategically sited just behind the front.

These concentration points were necessarily crowded. Companies were squeezed into the ordinary accommodation of a platoon. The men could not lie down with comfort, so they sat around the light of a candle and dozed or played poker for unusual stakes, collecting paper credits which were given freely by the pessimistic members who sat in the game.

Shortly after 0300 hours 'A' Company, who were to lead in the first phase, began to move out to occupy their jumping off points in No Man's Land.

Capture of a German Trench at Vimy. **W.B. Wollen's painting captures the vitally important moment in the battle for Vimy Ridge – the storming of the enemy's main defensive position. (Royal Canadian Military Institute)**

The bombardment had ceased. There was a deathlike silence. An occasional shell would scream across the sky and accentuate the stillness. The rattle of equipment, the muffled curses of the sergeants calling for less noise, added to the weird tension. All were hoping their movements would not be detected. Finally, the order to fix bayonets was given and a ripple of clicks passed along the line and died with the last obstinate rifle.

By 0400 everyone was in position, waiting for the appointed time. It was a far from comfortable wait, however. The temperature dropped sharply about a half hour before Zero Hour,

a strong westerly wind came up, and a blinding storm of snow and sleet swept the countryside.

At precisely 0530 hours the Canadian barrage opened, and seconds later a mine under the German line was exploded. As was happening all along the Canadian front, the men of 'A' Company rushed forward in heavy sleet, through gaps in the barbed wire between the craters. Even though it was still dark the company quickly crossed the hundred metres of No Man's Land separating them from the enemy's first trench, and five minutes later it was in firm possession of the German front line. Only minutes afterward troops were entering the Germans' immediate support trench.

Private Jack Harris of 'A' Company recorded his experience in his pocket diary:

> Left tunnel [at] 3:30 a.m. for jumping off trench. Mud to my knees as usual. At [5:30] a.m. came the order to go over. At the same time [a] terrible barrage from our artillery opened up. Terrific – no other word describes it. Walked over top (too overloaded to run). Lost track of rest of section. Very little return fire from Fritz.

Lieutenant T.W.E. Dixon was observing 'A' Company's progress from the lip of Edmonton crater, reporting by telephone line to Battalion headquarters. As soon as 'A' Company had consolidated on the 'Black Line', the first phase line, 'B' Company, which had been following just in rear, moved on close behind the rolling barrage. 'B' Company had to cover nearly 1,000 metres of badly torn up muddy ground before reaching its objective at Zwischen Trench, the second phase line, but very little opposition was encountered. By about 0615 the company was digging in just beyond the badly battered remnants of the German trench.

'C' Company then took over the lead to their objective, Fickle Trench, which was about 300 metres farther on. Again, they found only light opposition, and Fickle Trench was in their hands by about 0630 hours. La Folie Farm, just beyond the Battalion's right boundary – which had been reported to be an enemy strong point – was taken at about the same time by 2nd CMR. The farm was then simply a heap of rubble.

'D' Company carried on toward the crest of the ridge, under the command of Lieutenant Butson, who had taken over when Major Mackenzie had been wounded just after Zero Hour. The company soon ran into difficulties: German machine gunners and snipers had emerged from just beyond the crest of the ridge, and their fire cut a swath through part of the company. Lieutenant Butson was mortally wounded, but Lieutenant Gregory Clark, one of the platoon commanders, took charge and led the remainder of the company onto its objective at around 0730 hours. Clark had his platoons dig in just short of the crest of the ridge to defend against a counter-attack. Sergeant R. Mc-Quarrie was cited for his conspicuous gallantry in coordinating the re-organization of the company at this critical time, moving from one section position to another, all the while under heavy fire, until he was wounded. The company remained

4th CMR troops consolidating on Vimy Ridge after capturing their objective on the heights. (GGHG Archives)

under intense machine-gun fire throughout the whole of the day.

In the final stages of the assault a potentially serious gap had developed on 'D' Company's left flank when the RCR had veered slightly off to the north. Lieutenant B.C. Pierce, who at that stage was following behind 'D' Company with a platoon from 'A' Company, saw that this was happening and promptly took his men into the area. They arrived just in time to help the RCR beat off a counter-attack, but enemy pressure continued for some time, and 80 men from 'C' Company were brought forward by Major Menzies to reinforce the defence.

While many of the Germans who had manned the Vimy defences could be seen withdrawing to a rear line well out on the Douai Plain, the enemy for some time remained firmly in control of the wooded area on the steep reverse slope beyond the crest of the ridge, and they continued to harass the forward troops during the consolidation on the top of the feature. Most of the Battalion's casualties were in fact incurred in these latter stages of the battle.

Despite the fact that Hill 145, the highest ground on Vimy Ridge, still held out in the 4th Division sector, the Battle of Vimy Ridge had been an overwhelming success. All the training, and all the innovative tactical methods aimed at limiting the risk for the soldiers had paid off. Hundreds of prisoners were taken by the Battalion, along with seven machine guns, several trench mortars and a host of other trophies of war. In 4th CMR there were practically no casualties in assaulting the

first three objectives. But still, two officers and forty-three men were killed, and five officers and 131 men were wounded.

As in every earlier action, great bravery was shown by many members of the Battalion. Major Menzies, Captain Hart and Lieutenant Clark were awarded the Military Cross for their work that day. Sergeant (later Company Sergeant Major) McQuarrie was awarded the Distinguished Conduct Medal, and Sergeants Clark, Dougherty, Eade, Izzard, Miller, Pettie and Windsor and three junior NCOs received the Military Medal.

The Germans continued to shell the crest of Vimy Ridge throughout the day while the Battalion consolidated its gains. And as darkness finally fell on this momentous day, one of the sights remembered by the men of 4th CMR was of their padre, Captain W.H. Davis, steel helmet hung over his arm and oblivious to the shells dropping around him, prayer book in hand, burying the Battalion's dead.

On the following day, while the 4th Division attack on the fortified German positions still holding out on Hill 145 was renewed, a patrol led by Lieutenant T.W.E. Dixon was sent towards the village of Petit Vimy, on the eastern base of the ridge, to determine the locations and strengths of the enemy remaining in the wood on the reverse slope. Halfway down they were fired upon from a German trench supported by a machine-gun emplacement. The position was clearly too strongly held for the patrol to take out by itself, so Dixon and his men withdrew back to the Battalion's trench at the crest of the ridge. By the time Dixon reported to Colonel Gordon the whole of Hill 145 had finally been captured by 4th Division, leaving only the northernmost part of the Canadian sector, a low feature known as 'The Pimple', remaining in German hands.

The next task was to clear the Germans out of La Folie Wood, where several strongly held positions remained, including the one found by Lieutenant Dixon. 4th CMR was instructed to take out that trench on the morning of 11 April, but there was a problem: the artillery had only a very limited number of howitzer shells left and had no forward observer to direct the fire. Colonel Gordon decided that he himself would do that job, so he went with Lieutenant Dixon's troops and directed the supporting fire so essential to a successful attack. The bombardment controlled by the colonel was totally successful, even though he was nearly blown out of his observation post in the process because it was so close to the German strong point. Dixon was able to lead his men through the German position without a single casualty, and he was awarded the Military Cross for his gallant leadership.

The 4th CMR was relieved during a severe snowstorm on the night of 11 April, and an exhausted Battalion trudged back through the deep mud on the western slope of Vimy Ridge to a makeshift tented camp that had been set up near Neuville St. Vaast. The men had been in action for almost 63 hours in dreadful weather, and none had blankets or greatcoats with them. If they looked forward to some comfort behind the lines they were badly disappointed: the 'rest' camp was pitched in a field of mud, and the Battalion history records, "outside of the trenches it was the worst place the Battalion had experienced since arriving in France." While there, the Division commander, Major General Louis Lipsett, came to speak to the unit, congratulating the men on how superbly they had carried out their part of the operation.

Over the course of the next week the Germans were progressively pushed back from Vimy Ridge to a line on the Douai Plain running through the towns of Avion, Méricourt and Acheville, about three kilometres from the ridge. 4th CMR went into this line on the left boundary of the Canadian sector on 21 April, with orders to cooperate in an attack on Avion by the 5th (British) Division on the morning of 23 April. The Battalion's task was to protect the right flank of the British attack by carrying out a company-level raid on the German trench at the inter-di-

Lieutenant Colonel W.R. Patterson, commanding officer of 4th CMR May 1917 to demobilization in 1919. (GGHG Archives)

vision boundary. Two platoons of 'A' Company were to participate, Lieutenant M.W. MacDowell's platoon going forward on two separate axes to conduct the trench raid, with Lieutenant Fleek's platoon providing a firm base for the raiders out in No Man's Land.

At 0445 hours, only a half hour before dawn, the artillery opened up, and the raiding platoon rushed forward. The barrage, unfortunately, hadn't been heavy enough to destroy the Germans' machine-gun emplacements, and by the time both groups of MacDowell's men had got to within 50 metres of the enemy trench they were met by a withering rain of rifle and machine-gun fire. In but a few moments the 4th CMR casualties were so severe that the remaining men were ordered to take what cover they could in shell craters or folds in the ground. Lieutenant MacDowell, Sergeant Griffin and Sergeant Duncan all tried on several occasions to take out German machine-gun nests, but all day long their men were kept under fire. At dusk the Germans counterattacked with over 150 men, forcing the platoon to pull back. But they fought hard in the process, and with grenades and Lewis guns they practically wiped out the German company by the time they got back to Lieutenant Fleek's forward rifle pits.

Out on the Battalion's left the British division had been no more successful, and they too withdrew. This small action was, however, a costly one for 4th CMR: four men were killed, eight men were missing and two officers and thirty-four men had been wounded. Lieutenant MacDowell's heroic attempts to carry out his mission was rewarded with a Military Cross, and the equally gallant leadership by Sergeants Duncan and Griffin was recognized by the award of the Military Medal.

The next several months were relatively quiet as the unit took its turn manning sections of the front trench or providing the inevitable working parties to carry supplies to the front or to maintain the elaborate system of communications trenches that were again needed out on the Douai Plain. On 16 May there was a change of command: Lieutenant Colonel H.D.L. Gordon, who had reorganized the Battalion after the battle at Sanctuary Wood a year earlier, turned over command to Lieutenant Colonel W.R. Patterson, who by then was one of the few remaining officers who had joined the unit in Toronto in the autumn of 1914. Colonel Gordon was posted to take command of the 8th Reserve Battalion in England.

In June the Canadian Corps got a new commander, and this time he was to be a Canadian. When Sir Julian Byng was promoted to take command of the British Third Army, Major General Arthur Currie, who had commanded the 1st Division since after the Ypres battles in 1915, was knighted and promoted lieutenant general. Currie, a pre-war militiaman from British Columbia, was to prove that he was among the finest commanders on the Allied side during this entire war, and he was to lead the Canadians to ever greater distinction in the battles that followed.

By this time, conscription had become a very serious issue in Canada: after the large number of casualties taken at the Somme battles, the number of volunteers coming forward had dwindled greatly, and there was serious concern that the Canadian Corps could not be kept up to strength. Prime Minister Sir Robert Borden visited the Corps in May, and returned to Canada convinced that he had no choice but to introduce selective conscription. A Military Service Act was introduced in Parliament on 11 June, to become law on 29 August. In the meantime, however, there were enough troops training in England to keep units up to strength for several months.

On 1 July 1917, the 50th anniversary of Confederation, 4th CMR began a somewhat different task: to build an observation platform on Hill 145, the highest point on Vimy Ridge, for His Majesty King George V, who was coming to see his Canadians in action on 9 July. The Battalion was also to have provided a platoon from each company to line the road as His Majesty arrived at Vimy Ridge, but the King's visit was postponed by two days, and in the meantime 4th CMR was again sent into the front trenches on the western outskirts of Avion.

In mid-July the whole of the 8th Brigade was withdrawn into the rear area to train for an attack on the Méricourt-Achville line. The next month was a very busy time while the unit perfected the new infantry tactics that had been adopted just before the Vimy offensive, but the planned attack at Méricourt was called off in part because of the difficulties experienced by 1st and 2nd Divisions in their offensive on Hill 70, just north of Lens. Instead, 4th CMR spent another period of time rotating in and out of the forward defences.

The weather began to deteriorate badly by the middle of August: it rained incessantly, and daily temperatures were well below normal. The men talked of this time as being the most uncomfortable since the blizzards of early April. On the evening of 4 September the unit took over a sector of the front opposite Méricourt. It was a night the Battalion would not soon forget. Precisely at midnight the Germans laid down a heavy bombardment that lasted the better part of an hour and

The life of a soldier at the front during the First World War was one of constant discomfort. His clothing was filthy, often caked with dirt, and he was lucky if he had one extra pair of socks, his body was dirty almost all the time and most had a bumper crop of lice. He lived in the open when in the trench lines, so much of the time he was cold, and often he was wet. His food was spartan, all too often nearly inedible hard-tack biscuits and tins of corned beef. Here a soldier is shown trying for that little bit of luxury – a pair of dry socks. (NAC PA1571)

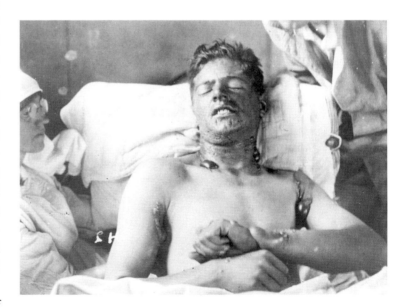

In the later years of the war, both sides often mixed gas shells with high explosive rounds during a bombardment. Mustard gas was more persistent than chlorine or phosgene, and it clung to the ground in craters and low spots in the ground. It rarely killed, but it caused crippling burns and blisters. (NAC C80027)

a half. But in with the high explosive rounds was a generous helping of gas shells. It was the first trial of mustard gas against the Canadian Corps, and the men were not aware of it because the gas shells simply sounded like duds among the rain of shrapnel.

The brunt of the shelling fell on 'C' Company occupying the brick fields, but they did not realize their danger until the morning when the sun rose and began to vaporize the gas which had lain dormant in the shell holes and on the cold damp bricks. The men going about without their helmets were suddenly stricken and collapsed in scores. Ten were killed and over one hundred seriously gassed. All the officers had to be evacuated because they remained all day looking after their men. While none of them died from the effects, only one returned to France.

The gas left a distinct odour of mustard in the air, it contaminated the ground and even penetrated their clothing; the men were not immunized merely by wearing their gas helmets. It made them vomit and remove their masks. Swellings, blisters and blindness resulted.

The Battalion spent another several tours in the trenches before being relieved again to prepare for an attack on Méricourt, which was again abandoned because the attention of the British high command was now very much focused on a disastrous offensive that had begun in the Ypres Salient in late July.

PASSCHENDAELE

The British offensive in the Ypres Salient, known officially as the Third Battle of Ypres, had been going badly ever since it had been begun on 31 July. Within four days the initial attack had ground to a standstill in the glutinous, deep mud that became synonymous with the name Passchendaele. A second major attack in mid-August was even less successful, and in those first weeks the British Army lost over 68,000 men for a gain of little over 4,000 metres. All thought of a major breakthrough had by then been abandoned, but the obstinate commander-in-chief, Field Marshal Haig, insisted on pressing on despite the enormous number of casualties. A third push was made in late September by Australian and British divisions, and in slightly dryer weather they managed to gain another

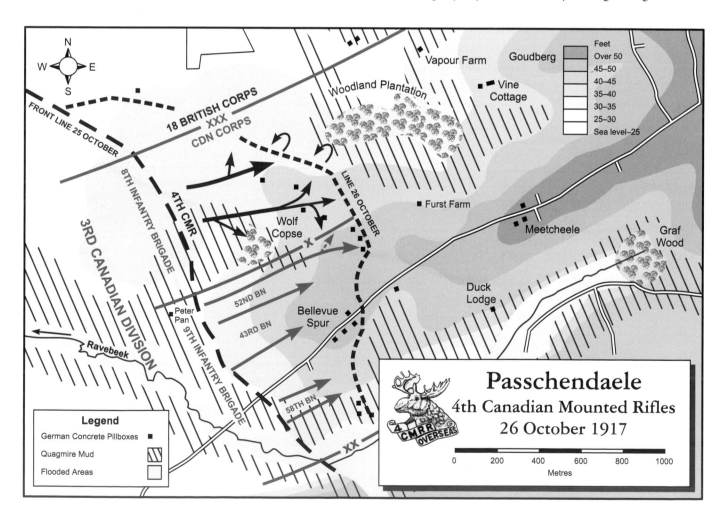

Passchendaele
4th Canadian Mounted Rifles
26 October 1917

(Above) When the Canadian Corps arrived in the Ypres salient in the third week of October 1917, much of the ground over which they were to attack was a quagmire of deep glutinous mud, pockmarked by shell craters filled with stagnant water. (NAC PA2195)

(Below) A contemporary aerial photo of the Passchendaele battlefield – looking to the north east – taken before the Canadian advance. The 4th CMR attacks on 26 October 1917 took place to the left of Wolf Copse, shown on the photo, and were held up at the southern edge of Woodland Plantation. The German blockhouse rushed by Private Tommy Holmes is in the area under the word 'Copse' in the photo. (GGHG Archives)

Thigh-deep mud so hindered the movement of men and supplies that wooden duckboards had to be laid over the mud to form pathways to the front line. In the foreground of this photo is one of the blockhouses or pillboxes used by the Germans as the hard core of their defences in this muddy sector where trenches could not be dug. (NAC PA2084)

few thousand metres before being halted by swamp and mud along the swollen Ravebeek Creek, still 2,500 metres short of Passchendaele. By this stage the British Army was stalled and on the verge of mutiny, and the commander-in-chief decided to bring in the Canadians, who from Vimy had earned the reputation of never failing.

In mid-October the whole of the Canadian Corps was moved northward into the Ypres Salient. 4th CMR began its journey aboard a troop train with the remainder of 8th Brigade on 15 October. After several brief pauses along the way they finally arrived in the heart of the ruined town of Ypres on the 21st, then marched three kilometres north east along a road congested with all manner of vehicles, pack animals and men to a bivouac where the village of Wieltje had once stood. The next day 4th CMR moved into the reserve trench line, where they relieved the New Zealanders.

General Currie, reluctant though he was to commit Canadian troops to this battle, had decided to attack in three separate phases, mainly because of the dreadful condition of the ground. The first assault was to be carried out by 3rd and 4th Divisions on the morning of 26 October; the second was to begin on 31 October; and the final phase was to be launched on 6 November by 1st and 2nd Divisions. In the 3rd Division sector, 8th Brigade was on the far left of the Canadian area,

and 4th CMR was detailed as 8th Brigade's lead battalion in the first attack on 26 October.

On the evening of 24 October the Battalion was deployed into the front line. Simply getting forward from the support to the forward 'trench' was a feat in itself. Three years of intensive shelling had reduced the terrain to a desolate wilderness of scummy, water-filled craters, ragged tree stumps and deep mud with the consistency of glue. The mud in places was thigh deep, and the only way to get forward was by duck-board pathways laid between the shell craters. It was pitch dark as the men trudged to the front, and it was difficult to keep to the duck-boards. The Regimental history recalls:

This was one of the worst reliefs the Battalion had ever experienced. Carried out at night in a heavy rain, it was almost impossible to make any headway through the sticky mud; the guides lost their way in the trackless swamp and it was 5:00 a.m. before the relief was completed. Rations arrived in their mysterious way but the water carriers had not navigated this endless sea [of mud].

The drizzle had stopped and it was sunny when dawn broke on the morning of 25 October, and the men had their first opportunity to see the ground over which they were to attack the next morning. The front trench was little more than a series of partially connected, slimy shell holes, but it was far worse just beyond: the Battalion was going to have to attack across a bog!

After seeing the ground, Colonel Patterson issued his orders. The Battalion would attack with 'C' and 'D' Companies forward, and with 'B' and 'A' Companies in depth and prepared to support the leading troops. 1st CMR would be immediately behind to reinforce the 4th CMR assault if necessary. The two forward companies would each have a section of two Vickers machine guns from the 9th Machine Gun Company. The Battalion's intermediate objective – called the Dotted Red Line – was the south-eastern end of a wood called Woodland Plantation, but the trees had long since disappeared and it was in reality simply a line on the map roughly 600 metres forward. The final objective – the Red Line – was a further 500 metres beyond.

The German defences opposite 4th CMR, and indeed over much of the Passchendaele battlefield, consisted mainly of individual strong points sited in depth, rather than a series of connected trench lines. Many of these strong points were centred on large, thick-walled concrete, above-ground pillboxes used as shelter during bombardments. The enemy soldiers were trained to come out of the pillboxes to man concrete machine-gun emplacements and field defences on both sides of the emplacement once a barrage had passed on. The pillboxes did not have forward-facing firing ports – they were too thick – and there was only a single door in the rear leading into a trench. So despite their formidable appearance they left their occupants blind while inside, and obstructed fields of fire to some extent when their twenty or so occupants manned the defensive positions on the sides.

As at Vimy, every effort was being made to ease the burden of the infantry. So as to wear down the enemy and mislead him as to the time of the attack, the gunners laid down intense bombardments each morning and afternoon for the four days preceding the attack. And because the mud would clearly slow any movement, the creeping barrage was timed to move only about a hundred metres in eight minutes, half the normal speed of advance.

It began to rain again during the early hours of the morning as the final preparations for the attack were being completed, and in the darkness of the pre-dawn of 26 October the leading companies moved into their jump-off points forward of the front line. The barrage began promptly at 0540 hours, and eight minutes later the first wave of 4th CMR started forward. Colonel Patterson was concerned that the barrage was "erratic and not uniform."

Shelled by their own guns, raked by German machine-gun fire, the Canadians found themselves struggling through what one 4th CMR man called 'porridge, a ghastly, dreadful porridge, thigh-deep, in which if you got it on the shoulder blade with a bullet that merely knocked you unconscious for two minutes you drowned'. We lost lots of men who simply drowned because they were knocked over or stunned and couldn't get recovered before they sunk in the mud.

In both the left and right hand companies the men moved slowly forward through the mire, dodging around shell craters brim full of water, and through what remained of the enemy's wire entanglements. All the while they were hampered by enemy machine-gun fire and heavy shelling, and casualties mounted every minute. During the first two hours neither company progressed more than 500 metres, and the rolling

A photo of Wolf Copse taken after the battle. (NAC PA 40139)

barrage, which had got too far ahead of the troops, had long since ceased to provide any protection.

On the left, 'C' Company (Lieutenant Nesbitt) struggled forward heroically, step by step, against stern opposition until eventually all its officers and many of its senior NCOs had been killed or wounded. Company Sergeant Major R.H. Sanders took over command, and continued doggedly to press forward until the company was so severely reduced by casualties that it was no longer an effective force. Sanders' DCM citation noted in part, "His example of courage and resource was solely responsible for holding the company together under the most difficult conditions". At this point 'B' Company (Major Hart) took over the lead, gathering in the remnants of 'C' Company as they passed through.

'B' Company continued to advance slowly on the Battalion's left, and there were many instances of extraordinary courage and inspiring leadership. When the company was held up by machine-gun fire from a pillbox, Corporal J.A. Post and Private D. Huyck worked their way forward "under a shower of enemy hand grenades". Huyck climbed onto the top of the structure with Corporal Post's help, and put it out of action by throwing a bomb through an opening in the roof. Both Post and Huyck were rewarded with the Distinguished Conduct Medal. Much of the company eventually reached the intermediate objective – the Dotted Red Line – but on gaining that position Major Hart realized that his left flank was completely exposed. The British battalion there had failed to keep pace, so he sent a message to the commanding officer asking for reinforcements to shore up that sector. Eventually platoons from 1st CMR came forward, and by mid-morning Major Hart had pulled his lead troops back by about 300 metres and established a firm defensive line to protect the vulnerable left flank.

On the Battalion's right, 'D' Company suffered much the same fate as 'C' Company on the left. They had a particularly difficult and costly battle in taking Wolf Copse, and when all other officers were killed or wounded, Lieutenant T.J. Rutherford (who would command Canada's armoured training groups in England during the Second World War) took command of a seriously depleted body of men. Sergeant N.

Private T.W. Holmes, VC (NAC PA2352)

Nicholas "set a magnificent example of courage and initiative" that morning when, from among the few remaining men, he collected a group and led them in a successful attack on a pill box that had caused many casualties in the company.

'A' Company (Major Scott) had overtaken what was left of 'D' Company by early morning, and both companies intermingled and advanced together. At about 0800 hours the advance on this flank was brought to a dead stop by a pill box manned by two machine-gun crews and a platoon. This position was also bringing fire to bear across the boundary into the 9th Brigade on the right and was holding up the advance of the 43rd Battalion. At this very time one of 4th CMR's most outstanding incidents of valour was enacted by a young man who only days before had joined the Battalion as a reinforcement. An article from the 20 February 1918 edition of the Toronto *Globe* told the story of the bravery of Private Tommy Holmes:

Ploughing through the mud and water, plugging from shell-hole to shell-hole, advancing over ground swept by relentless fire from Hun rifle and machine-gun they went forward but that death-dealing hail of bullets was taking an awful toll. Finally, in order to save themselves from what seemingly was going to be a complete annihilation, they were forced to take cover in convenient shell-holes. Unceasingly, the enemy fire raked the ground where they were, and over which they had to pass in order to reach the position that had been assigned to them to take.

It was during this halt that Holmes noticed that the fire which was holding up the company came from a concrete pillbox fort in their right flank.... Just beside the fort, two machine-gun crews had taken up a position, and it was quite apparent that it was the fire from these guns that had temporarily checked his company's advance.

Armed only with a Mills bomb, and without waiting for an order from anyone, his comrades crouching in shell-holes saw Holmes rush forward through the hail of bullets and spring into a shell-hole some yards ahead of the company. A moment later, he appeared, and on he rushed again, and again he disappeared. He did this several times, each spurt bringing him closer to the Hun machine-guns.

As Holmes got nearer to the guns, he noticed that occasionally there was a lull of a few seconds in the firing of one or the other of the guns, each pause indicating that the crews were changing the belts. Then suddenly there came a moment when both guns ceased firing simultaneously. Holmes knew that the crews of both guns were reloading at the same instant.

It was his opportunity, and, quick as a flash, before the machine-gunners could get their guns working, he rushed forward within fifteen yards of them, just in time to take cover in a shell-hole before the hail of bullets from both guns opened on him again. But he was within bombing distance now, and pulling the pin of the grenade he was carrying, he hurled it with unerring accuracy into the midst of the machine-gunners, then crouched and waited. He had not long to wait. 'Ping' sang out the bomb. At that same instant the firing from both guns ceased....

But there was still work to be done, for the pillbox remained full of enemy riflemen. Without hesitating a moment, and again risking his life, Holmes went toward his company, some of whom were beginning to advance again. From the foremost of his comrades he secured another bomb, then turned around and ran straight for the pillbox. Through the entrance at the rear, he threw the bomb. There was another explosion, and those of the Hun garrison that survived, nineteen in number, came out with their hands up, terrified, shouting 'Mercy, Kamerad', and surrendered to their youthful captor, who was standing outside the pillbox alone.

Major Scott watched in awe as Holmes carried out his brave deed but didn't know who he was, so he sent a runner to get his name so he could recommend him for his bravery. But before the runner returned Major Scott had been killed. Fortunately there were others who saw Tommy Holmes take on the pillbox all by himself and wanted to have his courage recognized. Private Thomas W. Holmes, a modest young man with a contagious smile, was eventually awarded the Victoria Cross, the Empire's highest decoration, for his valiant act.

Because of Private Holmes' initiative in clearing the blockhouse, 'A' and 'C' Companies were able to continue their advance, and despite taking casualties all along the way, they captured the intermediate objective, the Dotted Red Line, by about 0830 hours and continued beyond. One platoon fought through the Germans' Flanders I Line as far as the final objective at Woodland Plantation. At this point the combined 'A' and 'C' Company found themselves well forward of the 9th Brigade units on their right, and thus with a dangerously open flank.

In the 9th Brigade area, the 43rd Battalion had struggled forward as far as the Dotted Red Line after clearing a number of pillboxes on Bellevue Spur, but beginning at about 0900 hours the Germans rained a devastating bombardment on that battalion, and, with the exception of a small group that managed to hold out, the 43rd was forced to retreat. By 1030 hours the situation was critical in the 9th Brigade, and 4th CMR's right flank was in serious danger. 'A' Company of the 52nd Battalion, commanded by Captain C.P. O'Kelly, no doubt saved the day. Shortly after noon O'Kelly's company, which had worked its way forward, crater to crater, along the 4th CMR boundary, attacked the Germans between 4th CMR and the remnants of the 43rd Battalion. Then, reinforced by their 'B' Company, the 52nd then successfully moved against six German strong points from the rear. O'Kelly, who was awarded the VC for his gallant leadership, was thus instrumental in removing the flank threat to 4th CMR as well as restoring the Canadian hold on the vital Bellevue Spur. After the battle had ended, General Lipsett, commander of 3rd Division, gave credit to the men of 4th CMR for making the attack of 52nd Battalion possible by holding out and providing a secure base in their tenuous, isolated position.

Drawing of the remarkable ad hoc cease-fire and casualty exchange that took place because Padre W.H. Davis, at great personal risk, went into No Man's Land to mark the location of dead and wounded Canadians and Germans. (GGHG Archives)

The 4th CMR companies stubbornly held the ground they had taken in the face of heavy shelling and constant small arms fire until in the early afternoon when 'A' Company withdrew slightly to link up with the line established by the 52nd Battalion in the 9th Brigade area. The position was consolidated, and the forward locations were signalled to contact aircraft by waving helmets, as it proved to be impossible to light the water-soaked signal flares. The Germans kept up spasmodic shelling for the rest of the day, but the battle was over.

At about 1500 hours the Battalion was witness to a truly remarkable incident. The Battalion chaplain, Padre William H. Davis, who already was well known for his disregard for personal danger, went forward of the 4th CMR position to search for wounded men. Major Gregory Clark, who after the war became a noted journalist, wrote an account of this remarkable action in 1937 in *Legionary Magazine*:

He had a handkerchief tied to his walking stick. Padres are not allowed to bear arms, by international law. Holding his stick up and waving it every time a blast of fire came near him, he went plunging about, bending and straightening, and stabbing rifles into the mud. If it was a German wounded, he hung a German helmet on the gun butt. If a Canadian, a Canadian helmet.

Serenely, the Padre continued to quarter the dreadful ground this way, that way, while the crumps hurled in and the machine-guns stuttered and filled the air with their stomach-turning zipp and whisper.

Small parties of his own men tried to reach him or to carry in one of the wounded he marked. But they were flattened with enemy machine-gun fire. The Padre beckoned nobody. He called no man, Canadian or German, though he passed close to both. He simply stuck up the rifles, hung the helmets, and left them mutely there.

Then the heavens opened. But with silence. Shellfire ceased. Machine-guns died, all across that narrow C.M.R. belt. To north, to south, the fury raged. But out from this solitary figure, resolutely plowing his zig-zag course in horror, there radiated a queer paralysis.

In a matter of minutes, silence grew. It was as if the sun stood still. And there, all alone, in the middle of the silence walked the solitary figure, bending, rising and stabbing rifles into the earth.

From the Canadian side figures crouched up, ventured forward. From the German side men rose.... They ran to their own markers, the helmets, German or Canadian. Some of the wounded Canucks were far over amidst the Germans. Some of the wounded Germans lay back of the Canadian outposts. Canadians began to carry the Germans forward.

Padre Davis went and stood on the ruined remnants of a pillbox, a few vast hunks of concrete. Aloft, he stood and beckoned the parties to him. He had established a clearing house. They traded wounded. Cigarettes were offered.

This unofficial armistice lasted for nearly thirty minutes before some Canadian gunner called for fire on the German troops in the open, and everyone scurried for their holes. It was, however, one of those fleeting moments in this appalling war when compassion and the lack of animosity between the soldiers of both sides had an opportunity to be shown. Padre Davis received a Military Cross for his work that day.

In anticipation of a counter-attack, after dusk outposts were set out 50 metres forward of the line that had been established. And, as expected, the Germans did mount an attack on 'B' Company, on the Battalion's left front, shortly after 2200 hours. But the Germans had been spotted as they were assembling, and Major Hart's men were well prepared. Sergeant L. Harding, who had taken over his platoon earlier in the day when his platoon commander was killed and "set a splendid example of courage and devotion to duty" throughout the day, was instrumental in breaking up the German assault. Lewis guns were trained on the approaching enemy, and fire was opened when they were only a hundred metres away. The Germans quickly pulled back, leaving a few dead. Sergeant Harding immediately took a small patrol to pursue the enemy in No Man's Land, and returned with two prisoners. Harding was later awarded the DCM for his bravery and superlative leadership.

4th CMR remained at the front throughout the 27th, all the time under considerable shelling, but the enemy made no attempt to counterattack. Stretcher parties worked all day carrying wounded men to the rear, often going forward into No Man's Land to recover casualties. Two of the Battalion

Captain the Reverend W.H. Davis, MC, Chaplain of the 4th Canadian Mounted Rifles. (Canadian Army Photograph O2424, GGHG Archives)

Stretcher bearers bringing a wounded man to medical care in the rear. This man was lucky. It sometimes took six or eight men to carry a stretcher through the mud. Many of the wounded were never found. (NAC PA2140)

stretcher bearers were cited for exceptional bravery – Lance Corporal R.J. Clarke and Private H.E. Heggart, who already wore the Military Medal and bar – and were awarded the DCM. At 2100 hours the Battalion was relieved by 2nd CMR. In spite of the severe losses suffered the previous day, 4th CMR handed over a strong and well-constructed position.

There is no doubt that the 4th CMR paid heavily for its part in the capture of Passchendaele and the small amount of ground that was gained. Three hundred and twenty one officers and men had been killed, wounded or missing. The few hours of fighting had cost half of the officers and a third of the men.

Great bravery and devotion to duty were a constant element in the bitter fighting that took place on 26 October, perhaps even more than in the Battalion's other major actions. Private Thomas Holmes' Victoria Cross will serve as a perpetual honour to every member of the unit. Military Crosses were awarded to Captain W.H. Davis, the Padre, Captain H.C. Davis, the Medical Officer, Lieutenants A.W. Deacon and R.H. Warne of 'A' Company, and Lieutenant B.D. Poyser of 'B' Company. Major M.M. Hart, commanding 'B' Company, was recommended for a DSO but instead was awarded a bar to his MC. Ten men were awarded the Distinguished Conduct Medal, and another six received the Military Medal. And, as always there were many more who deserved recognition, but whose actions went unreported and unrewarded.

4th CMR played no active part in the subsequent attack by 3rd Division on 30 October, but did provide working parties to carry casualties from the forward area to the 9th Field Ambulance and to carry munitions and supplies to units at the front. This second phase of the Canadian Corps offensive proved to be as hard-fought as the first, but the 3rd and 4th Divisions managed to take the height of ground leading to Passchendaele, providing a truly firm footing for the final attacks by 1st and 2nd Divisions on 6 November.

On 31 October the 4th CMR was moved into a camp near Poperinghe on the Belgian border, where they had trained for the Somme offensive a year earlier. Here they encountered a new threat: enemy bomber aircraft that specialized in attacking Allied camps at night. To avoid these attacks, no lights were permitted after dark, so the men reported that their stay was dreary and uninteresting. Reinforcements were brought in to replace the casualties, and to prepare for winter the unit was issued with ill-fitting goatskin jerkins that were described as being "warm but not smart".

The Battalion was back in the forward area a week later, when the 1st and 2nd Divisions were making the final push on Passchendaele. This time, however, the men were there as labourers, helping to build a road through the putrid mud for the movement of supplies to the units at the front. Most of these five days the men were under shellfire, and they were always soaking wet and covered with mud. When the 4th CMR was pulled out on 13 November it was the last time they were to see the Ypres Salient. They left without regret, but they also left forever a battalion's strength of men in the soil of Belgium.

In mid-November the Battalion was moved well into the rear area for a month of training and refitting. It was a welcome change. The village of Enquin-les-Mines was out of the congested area, few troops had been billeted there before so the inhabitants were friendly and hospitable, and the local estaminet (pub) provided a congenial place to eat and drink. The highlight of this period was that leave was granted to the officers and men for the first time in nearly a year, and most

Digging new reserve trenches after the opening of the German spring offensive in 1918. (NAC PA 3802)

took the opportunity to spend some time in the luxury of Paris.

While the Battalion was enjoying this brief respite behind the lines, the final British offensive of the year took place at Cambrai on 20 November. This brief battle was notable because it signalled a conceptual victory over the battlefield stalemate created by machine guns and barbed wire, and marked the beginning of genuinely mechanized warfare. Cambrai was the first test of the use of tanks on a large scale: 474 of them were used to break through the formidable defences of the Germans' Hindenburg Line on a front of less than 10 kilometres. And the tanks succeeded magnificently, finally proving their worth after having failed in much smaller numbers (and over impossible ground) at the Somme and at Passchendaele. That this offensive was not decisive was because there were no reserves to exploit what the tanks had accomplished.

THE GERMAN 1918 OFFENSIVE

Just as the 4th CMR was preparing to move forward to take over a section of the line forward of Lens, just to the north of Vimy, the character of the war took an ominous turn for the Allies. In October 1917, the Bolsheviks (Reds) had gained the upper hand in the final stage of the revolution in Russia that had overthrown the Czarist government, and on 15 December Lenin signed an armistice with Germany. The Russian collapse meant that the 44 German divisions on the Eastern Front could now be transferred to the Western Front, giving the Germans a significant, if perhaps temporary, advantage over the Allies in manpower. The United States had declared war on Germany in April 1917, and once the great strength of the U.S. Army arrived in France the balance would tip in the Allies favour. The build-up of the American forces in France was, however, a very slow process, and it was not expected that they would be ready to take to the field until late spring in 1918. A major German offensive was thus expected as soon as they were able to move their vast army out of Russia, a last-ditch effort to win the war before the Americans could intervene. After Cambrai, the Allies settled down for the winter to prepare the defences against the anticipated German attacks.

For some time it was believed that the Lens-Vimy sector would be the prime target for the German offensive as it was thought that the Germans would want to take the important coal mines and communications centres close behind. The Canadian Corps, now undisputably the elite 'storm troops' of the British Army, was deployed to take over the area they had left in September 1917. The Corps was to spend the next seven months there.

On 21 December 1917 the 4th CMR moved into the trenches in front of Loos, just to the north of Lens, where they spent the next month in and out of the line. The traditional Christmas dinner was delayed until the Battalion was sent into reserve on 9 January 1918, and the War Dairy records that the Quartermaster did a sterling job of producing a sumptuous feast with generous quantities of rum punch. There was little enemy activity during the period, but there was always a great deal of work to be done to keep the trenches from deteriorating in the winter rain. And, because the high command was concerned about maintaining 'the offensive spirit', all units, including 4th CMR, were required to send fighting patrols into No Man's Land most nights, and to mount periodic trench raids.

Following three weeks of rest and rehabilitation in the rear, the Battalion was again moved to the front, this time to the Méricourt sector they had occupied after Vimy. For the next two months the now usual routine was followed: raids and patrolling when in the line, working parties to repair trenches and communications when in support. The patrols into No Man's Land, here a 600-metre-wide area of long grass and weeds, came to be very competitive events with the German unit on the far side, with carefully planned ambushes and other cat-and-mouse activities played out in the dark. Several of the subalterns, including Lieutenants A.J. Clarke, T.J. Rutherford and J.M. Dobie, along with a number of sergeants, became especially proficient in organizing and leading these ambush patrols. Following one of the numerous raids, Sergeant G.F. Price was cited for conspicuous gallantry and devotion to duty and awarded the Distinguished Conduct Medal:

During a raid on the enemy trenches he led a section of the raiding party … where he successfully rushed a machine-gun post, killing two of the garrison and scattering the remainder. Although severely wounded, he directed the retirement of his party with much skill, and himself carried a badly wounded comrade back to our lines. His courage and resource were responsible for the success of his portion of the enterprise.

The Germans finally launched their expected big offensive at dawn on 21 March 1918, but the centre of the thrust was about 60 kilometres south of the Ca-

nadian Corps' positions, and with the exception of a strong raid at Hill 70, the Canadians were unaffected. 4th CMR on that day happened to be well behind the front, with the men relishing the luxury of the first baths they had had in 32 days. But even at that great distance they did hear the continuous rumble of the massive German bombardment, and everyone knew that it was the German attack going in.

The forward defences in much of the British Third and Fifth Army areas were devastated by the German artillery, and there was little resistance when 80 German infantry divisions, using new 'infiltration' tactics, poured forward. By the end of the day, the Germans had penetrated to a depth of nearly five kilometres. And over the next three days, opposed only by confused and disoriented British troops, the Germans made rapid gains. There was a great risk that the enemy drive toward Amiens, thrusting along the boundary between the British and French forces,would penetrate between the two armies, and both the British and French rushed reinforcements into the area to stop the German onslaught. The only Canadians involved in this critical defence were the Canadian Cavalry Brigade and the 1st Canadian Motor Machine Gun Brigade, both of which made valuable contributions because of their mobility.

The immediate effect on the Canadian Corps was that it had to extend the length of the line it was holding to free up British units to be rushed southward. On 22 March, 4th CMR

Officers of the 4th Canadian Mounted Rifles, photo taken in the spring of 1918. (Canadian Army Photo 02473, GGHG Archives)

was hurriedly sent to man a front-line trench near Arleux, but they were moved back to the Lens-Vimy front six days later. By 31 March the German offensive in the south had been contained. Some have credited the Canadian Cavalry Brigade with halting the enemy advance with its stalwart actions at Moreuil Wood, but the Germans had also outrun their supply lines.

There was a great flurry of activity in the Canadian sector during the first week of April, when German shelling increased notably and it seemed that an attack was imminent. All units in reserve were employed on the construction of a new line of support trenches in the rear, in case the front line was overrun. But the next German thrust began on 9 April between Armentières and the La Basée Canal, just 10 kilometres north. Again the Germans rapidly overcame the British defences and penetrated to a depth of six kilometres. Armentières and Messines both fell the next day. By the 12th the enemy had again been halted, but not before Passchendaele had been given up.

4th CMR was ordered to take over a part of the front line at Hill 70 on 17 April. All 3rd Division units in the line were directed to conduct large-scale raids on the German line on 22 April to get confirmed identification of the enemy units. Captain Leslie Bumstead, commanding 'C' Company, volunteered to lead the Battalion's raid, along with Lieutenant Geoffrey Heightington, and they selected 60 of their most experienced men to take part.

At 1:30 a.m. on the 22nd, the barrage opened and as there were other raids in progress it made an imposing "shoot". Three minutes later the raiding party, which was divided, went forward. Both sections encountered wire and it took nearly fifteen minutes to cut gaps and get through. The left party under Captain Bumstead was at once faced by a machine-gun which was encircled, the crew of four killed and the gun captured. This party established "blocks" and proceeded to mop up the trenches. The enemy had fled down his communication trenches and only two wounded prisoners were found. The right party under Lieutenant Heightington proceeded to the corner of a wood where they found a vacated bombing post. A little further there was a machine-gun mounted at the entrance to a dugout. Half the crew fled over-land, the remainder taking shelter in the dugout. The party flung stick-bombs down the entrance wounding one German who gave himself up. The rest would not come out … so Lieutenant Heightington flung in enough Mills bombs to destroy the dugout.

When they had been out about an hour, the raiding party saw the green-red-green flare signal to withdraw. It was all a great success. Unfortunately Sergeant Boyce died of wounds, and four other men were wounded. Captain Bumstead and Lieutenant Heightington were both awarded the Military Cross.

On 29 April 3rd and 4th Divisions were moved into the rear to form a part of First Army's general reserve in case of further attacks against the British front. This time

Men of the 4th CMR in 'billets' somewhere behind the lines in the spring of 1918. Accommodation was scarce for units taken out of the line for a period of rest and rehabilitation, so improvised shelters such as this three-tiered arrangement had to suffice. The soldiers would have agreed that this was infinitely better than life in the trenches. (Canadian Army Photo O2076, GGHG Archives)

in reserve stretched to nearly two months of intensive training for 'open warfare' as the Canadian Corps prepared itself for the Allied offensives that everyone hoped might finally bring the war to and end. 4th CMR spent much of this period in its favourite billets in Enquin-les-Mines. On most days there was a 50-kilometre route march for physical conditioning, and a lot of emphasis on shooting, but the main focus was on tactical training at platoon level, such as movement under covering fire … bold patrolling and reconnaissance … rapid deployment and closing … infiltration … cooperation with tanks … use of smoke. But there was still time for recreation. The Battalion revived its baseball teams, and there were brigade and divisional sports meets. The most serious enemy confronted by the unit was an epidemic of influenza that had spread throughout the armies on both sides. In 4th CMR 70 men were affected, and all training and sports had to be cancelled until it was over.

3rd Division's interlude in the rear came to an end on 25 June, when it was ordered to relieve 2nd Division in the line at Neuville Vitasse, south of Arras. 4th CMR spent the first three weeks of July here. The front was quiet, the weather clear and hot, and there was plenty of material lying about to improve the 'bivvies' and 'funk-holes'. With the renewal of the daily rum ration this tour proved to be relatively enjoyable. The only notable action was a seventy-man trench raid on 13 July, led by Major W.V. Sifton, which ended somewhat noisily when the Germans counter-attacked the raiding party under cover of heavy machine-gun fire.

At this very time highly secret operational and administrative preparations were reaching their climax for a major British offensive east of Amiens which was to be spearheaded by the Canadians and Australians. Secrecy was deemed to be of paramount importance for the success of the offensive, and 4th CMR was to play a most interesting role in the plan to deceive the Germans.

The first information the Battalion got about this strange role came in a cryptic message from 8th Brigade headquarters on 29 July: 4th CMR was ordered to move almost at once to entrain in late afternoon "for a destination not yet notified". It was only once the train was under way that Colonel Patterson was given his mission: 4th CMR, along with the 27th Battalion, signals units and two casualty clearing stations, were to be deployed into the southern base of the Ypres Salient to induce the Germans into believing that the Canadian Corps was being moved northward, and that this was where the Allies would attack.

On 31 July this body of Canadians came under the control of the 41st British Division, and the next day were deployed into the front line opposite Mount Kemmel, which the Germans had taken in their offensive in early April. 4th CMR and the 27th Battalion spent only three days in the sector, but each night carried out raids on the German line, being careful to 'lose' bits of distinctively Canadian equipment and unit badges it was hoped the Germans would find. At the same time the Canadian signals detachments began transmitting dummy messages to indicate that headquarters of Canadian formations had been established behind the line. This foray at strategic deception unfortunately had a cost: Captain Thomas Dixon, MC, MM, the commander of 'B' Company, was killed by a German shell on the morning of 3 August, and Captain Beecher Poyser, MC, the second-in-command, was wounded. The loss of Captain Dixon, who had risen through the ranks and was one of the most respected officers in the Battalion, was sorely felt.

Early on the morning of 4 August 4th CMR was relieved, and after burying Captain Dixon in the cemetery at Wippenhoek the unit began its move southward toward Amiens, where they would join the rest of the Canadian Corps for the big offensive set for 8 August. After a lengthy journey by truck, train and on foot the Battalion arrived in its assigned billets in Boves, 12 kilometres south-east of Amiens, at about 0500 hours on 7 August. That night 4th CMR moved from Boves to an assembly area to be ready for the attack that would begin at sunrise the next morning.

THE BATTLE OF AMIENS

The plan for the Amiens offensive was very simple. There would be no preliminary bombardment, except in front of the French on the right. A rolling barrage would begin at Zero Hour, and tanks would lead the infantry through the enemy's forward defences, as at Cambrai. The main effort would be made in the centre by the four Canadian divisions and five Australian divisions, against three objective lines – the forward German defences, the reserve localities and gun lines, and then a final line well into the enemy's rear.

In the Canadian Corps sector, the initial break in would be made by 2nd Division on the left next to the Australians, 1st Division in the centre, and 3rd Division on the right next to the 31st French Corps. Each division was to have one brigade up. A second brigade would come into line as the frontage widened, the third brigade in each division remaining in reserve. 4th Division formed the Corps reserve, to take the lead when the 1st and 3rd Divisions reached the intermediate objective line.

In 3rd Division, the 9th Brigade was to lead the attack, followed by the 7th and 8th Brigades, one leap-frogging through the other. 4th CMR was not engaged in the fighting on the first

Infantrymen dig in on their objective as a Whippet tank moves through to continue the advance, 8 August 1918. (NAC PA2926)

mist that limited visibility to just a few metres. At 0620 hours 4th CMR started its move forward from an assembly area near Gentelles, moving in single file to a second assembly position near the village of Hangard. The Battalion was to follow behind 1st CMR, which was on the 3rd Division's left flank. By 0900 hours a message was received from brigade that all objectives had been taken, and that 2nd CMR had moved through 1st CMR and was beyond the village of Demuin, heading for Courselles. In mid-afternoon 4th CMR moved to a brigade rendezvous near Demuin, while the advance was being continued by 4th Division and the Canadian Cavalry Brigade, which was supported by a battalion of Whippet tanks.

day, but followed behind the advance until the second day, when 8th Brigade was to take the lead.

At 0420 hours on 8 August the artillery began a "hurricane" bombardment followed by a rolling barrage, and the tanks and infantry of the leading brigades went 'over the top'. There was little opposition as the attackers swarmed into a heavy

All day long the swift success of the morning was contin-

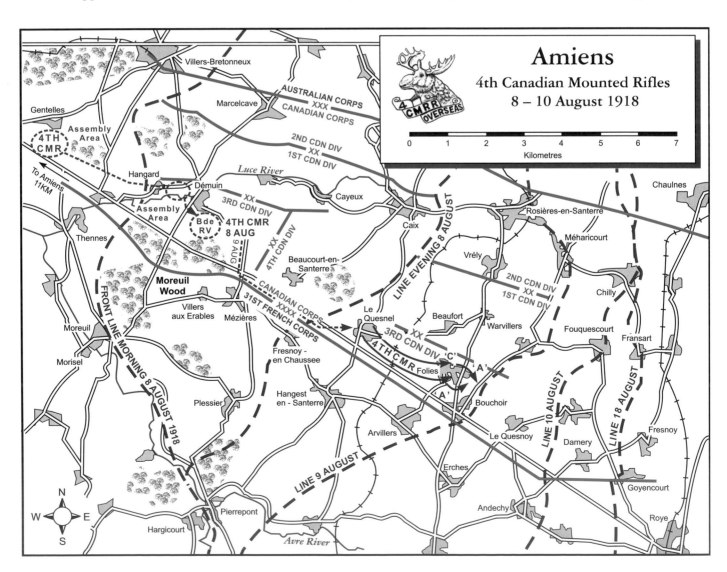

Canadian infantry (probably members of 4th CMR) advance along the Amiens-Roye road on 9 August 1918. The road was the boundary between the British and French armies; the soldiers in the right foreground are French troops. (NAC PA2925)

ued, even though German resistance was beginning to stiffen considerably as the final objective, a line of old British trenches from the Somme battle, was approached. The Canadian cavalry that had passed through earlier in the afternoon suffered heavily as enemy machine guns killed hundreds of their horses: they had no doubt been committed too early, before a real gap in the enemy defences had been torn open. But by 1800 hours the whole of the Canadian Corps had thrust forward by nearly twelve kilometres. By standards of this war it was already a magnificent tactical victory!

General Erich Ludendorff, the de-facto commander of the German forces, later called this "the black day of the German Army in the history of this war". And while the Germans were still far from being defeated in the field, the German high command was now convinced that they would lose the war!

Even as the Germans rushed up reinforcements, General Currie convinced the Army commander to carry on with the attack the next day.

8th Brigade did not receive its orders for the attack on 9 August until 0200 hours that same morning, but because of delays in the 4th Division's capture of its objective – the old British Somme-era trench line – new orders were issued at around mid-morning. Once the 4th Division's 75th Battalion had captured the village of Le Quesnel, 4th CMR would pass through to take the village of Folies, while 5th CMR, on the right, was to capture Bouchoir. Colonel Patterson gave orders that 'A' Company (Major Sifton) and 'C' Company (Captain Bumstead) would lead off, with 'B' Company (Lieutenant McDonald) in close support, and 'D' Company (Major Steer) in reserve. The Battalion moved off at mid-morning along the main Amiens-Roye road. Just short of Le Quesnel the water carts and ammunition mules were left under the Regimental Sergeant Major, and the companies turned onto a side road leading into Le

Quesnel. There they found that the 75th Battalion had not completely cleared the Germans from the area, so before beginning on their own task they had to help secure their own start line. Le Quesnel was then under heavy enemy shelling, and the Battalion suffered a number of casualties, including Lieutenant Warnica, who had taken over as acting commander of 'B' Company when Lieutenant McDonald was killed by shellfire.

At 1350 hours 'A' and 'C' Companies began their advance toward Folies, meeting heavy machine-gun fire and severe shelling as they started out. The Battalion had three Mark V tanks in support, but one was hit by an anti-tank gun and set on fire just as it began to move. Private W. Todd, a stretcher bearer, ran forward and at great personal risk rescued the wounded members of the tank crew from the burning hulk, dressed their wounds, and had them carried to the rear. Todd then rejoined his platoon for the remainder of the action. He was later awarded the DCM.

It was difficult ground that the Battalion had to cover to reach Folie: flat and open, but pock-marked with the remains of old trenches and rusted barbed wire, and with a railway embankment about half-way along the 3,500-metre approach to Folie. By 1430 hours, 'C' Company, advancing in a series of section-by-section rushes, had reached the railway line and were pursuing an enemy who seemed determined to fight every step of the way. As in every previous battle there were many acts of noteworthy bravery. Lance Corporal C.R. Salsbury was commanding the leading section when it came under intense machine-gun fire. Along with his platoon commander, who was immediately mortally wounded, "he rushed the enemy post, seizing their machine-gun and turning it on the fleeing enemy, after which he brought his wounded officer back under heavy fire". For this act of heroism, Salsbury was awarded the Distinguished Conduct Medal.

'A' Company, on the right, had a similarly difficult advance, at one point being stopped by a very determined enemy machine gun that eventually was destroyed by one of the accompanying tanks. As they neared Folies, 'A' Company was temporarily checked by an anti-tank gun firing almost at point-blank range, but the gun was forced to flee by the fire of two Lewis guns. By about 1620 hours 'A' Company was positioned on the south of the village, and 'C' Company had worked its way onto the north side. At this point 'B' Company closed in for the final assault into the village. Small groups of Germans continued to offer resistance, but they were finally beaten back and withdrew from the built-up area. Major Victor Sifton sent Lieutenant F.W. Rous' platoon to the east of the village to cut off the enemy's line of retreat. Rous was shot through the lung while leading his men, but he remained with them and organized the consolidation of the position. His gallant action this day won him the Military Cross. By 1700 hours 4th CMR was consolidating its hold on the village of Folie, and linking up with 5th CMR on the right and 1st Division on the left.

If there was one officer who deserves special mention during this action, it is Major Sifton. He was the senior officer with the fighting troops, and he commanded not only his own company, but also others who had lost their leaders. For his superb leadership he was awarded the Distinguished Service Order. His citation reads, in part:

> During the advance of about [four kilometres] under heavy machine-gun fire he directed the attack of his company and when two company commanders became casualties he assumed command of the attacking companies and directed the organization of the Battalion outpost line. His absolute disregard for his personal safety and his skill and initiative were a splendid example to all ranks and contributed largely to the success of the attack.

But there was also great sadness in the Battalion. Among those who were killed in the advance was Captain William Davis, the Battalion chaplain, who had been awarded an MC for his bravery at Passchendaele.

> If he knew what fear was he never showed it. His remarkable disregard for danger while carrying out what he considered his duty, became a regimental tradition. In the daily life of the Battalion, in billets or in trenches, he was always thinking of the men's welfare. On this day as on former occasions he was preparing to carry out his practical mission of mercy and was gathering around him his little band of stretcher bearers when he and one of his men were hit by a shell. No officer was more loved for his character or more admired for his bravery than Padre Davis.

Thirteen other officers and men were killed and a further 65 wounded, but 4th CMR contributed its part in extending the Canadian gains by another 5,000 metres, thus increasing the magnitude of the victory.

The offensive continued at a somewhat slower pace over the next three days before it was brought to an end. By then the Germans has been thrust back to extensive 1916-vintage trench lines, and they had been substantially reinforced. Any further attacks would have been far more costly than General Currie was prepared to accept. There would be another day, better prepared. The final victory in the war was now in sight.

The Battle of Amiens, another of the great laurels in the crown of the Canadian Corps, indeed marked the beginning of the end. It was the start of what came to be known as The Hundred Days.

THE HUNDRED DAYS

After the success at Amiens the Allied high command determined to press the Germans relentlessly in a series of successive attacks along different points of the front. For much of the next three months, the Canadian Corps would play a vital role in this plan, and it was almost continually in action until the enemy was defeated. The first task given the Canadians in this grand scheme was to break through the German defensive lines astride the Arras-Cambrai road, from positions the Corps had held just prior to the battle of Amiens. It was a daunting assignment, for the enemy defences in this area were among the strongest on the Western Front. There were five highly developed trench lines to overcome, and the ground favoured the Germans.

The 2nd and 3rd Divisions were moved from Amiens on 20 August to take over a section of the front forward of Arras on the night of 23/24 August, in preparation for an attack on the 26th. 4th CMR relieved a British battalion in trenches about 5 kilometres east of Arras, and had barely settled in when the Germans shelled the left-hand part of the Battalion with a mix of high explosive and mustard gas. The casualty toll was very high, especially in 'D' Company: five officers and 116 men were severely affected by mustard gas and had to be evacuated.

In what came to be known as the Battle of the Scarpe, 3rd Division was assigned to the Corps left, between the Scarpe River and the Arras-Cambrai road. Its task for the attack on 26

August was to break through the first German defence line, secure a north-south line just west of the town of Monchy-le-Preux, which stood on a hill north of the Cambrai road, and then to exploit as far east as possible. 8th Brigade was to lead, and 4th CMR was placed on the Brigade's left, just to the south of the Scarpe River. Here a long feature known as Orange Hill dominated the approaches, standing 20 metres above the surrounding countryside.

The attack went in at 0300 hours on 26 August. 4th CMR led off through low ground along the river, to the north of Orange Hill, while 2nd CMR followed in behind with the task of taking the hill from the north flank.

The barrage was strong and accurate and gave heart to the men as they went "over the top" at zero hour, the flashes from the guns, the blinding brightness of the flares, and the sudden lightning-cracks from the high-explosives increased the bewilderment of the darkness. The impedimentia of wire and old trenches which sprang into view with each artificial glare added to the difficulties in keeping up with the creeping barrage.

For the first 400 metres there was little opposition, then heavy machine-gun fire erupted from the enemy trench and from a railway line on the far side of the river. Captain Rounds, commanding 'A' Company, was killed, and the companies were forced to slow up and reorganize. Private J.W. Stewart, acting on his own, "crept round the flank and, single-handed assaulted the [enemy machine-gun nest], killing three of the team with his revolver and rendering two guns

useless. He saved the situation at a critical moment", and won for himself a DCM. A fresh assault was put in, and yet another DCM was won by Private G.A. Bell, who with two other men attacked a nest of four machine guns that had brought the 4th CMR advance to a halt. By 0535 hours the enemy trenches on the Battalion's right had been captured, and within a half hour 'D' Company had secured the Battalion's left.

2nd CMR then turned south to attack Orange Hill from the flank, and 1st CMR passed through the Battalion to mount an attack on the village of Monchy from the north flank. At the same time 5th CMR began a frontal attack on Monchy, which was in their hands by 0740 hours. 1st CMR was having difficulties in front of the Battalion's location, so 'D' Company was sent forward to assist in taking out enemy machine-gun positions near the river. 7th Brigade moved through the 8th Brigade units at 0930 hours, but advanced only about 2,000 metres before being stopped at the second German trench line.

4th CMR remained in the positions it had gained until the night of the 27th, when the Battalion was warned to be prepared for a further advance on the 28th, under command of 9th Brigade. In the meantime, 7th and 9th Brigades had, in most areas, penetrated through the Germans' second defensive line.

In the attack with 9th Brigade on 28 August, the mission was to break through the Germans' third defensive line,

This photo shows very clearly the type of defensive barbed wire barriers that by early 1918 existed in front of the German trench systems in France. Barriers such as this were almost always covered by fire from dug-in machine gun posts, and it is interesting to note that many decorations for bravery in the last year of the war were awarded for personal valour in knocking out machine gun emplacements. (NAC PA30372)

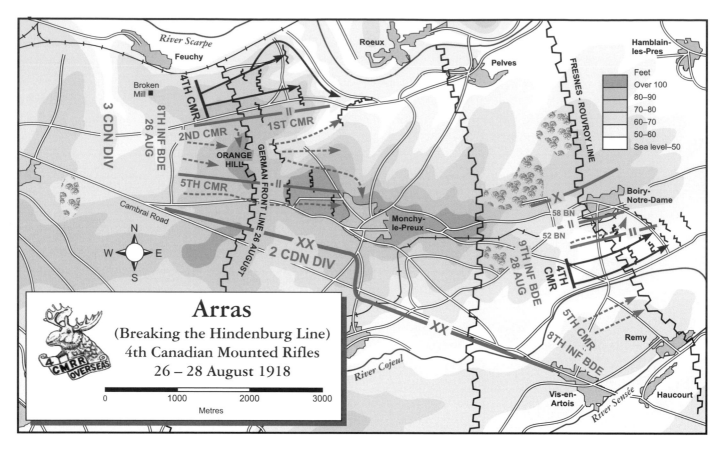

known as the Fresnes-Rouvroy Line, penetrating a distance of 2,000 metres. 4th CMR was assigned to the 9th Brigade's right, with a 1,200-metre front on the north bank of the Cojeul River. Zero Hour was set for 1100 hours, and the Battalion set out shortly after 0700 to move forward to its assembly area, which was about 6,000 metres distant. The march to the front proved to be extremely difficult; the ground was badly torn up, and the Battalion was shelled continuously. Only 'C' and 'D' Companies had managed to reach the assembly areas before the rolling barrage began at Zero Hour, but they advanced without waiting for the remainder of the Battalion. One of the innovations in this attack was that artillery forward observers moved with the companies, and they were able to provide valuable fire support throughout the advance by trailing out thousands of metres of telephone cable to communicate with their guns. The fire support they provided was especially helpful in dealing with enemy machine-gun posts that otherwise would have delayed the advance.

Both attacking companies successfully fought their way forward, although taking heavy casualties in the process, mainly from artillery. Six members of the Battalion were awarded the Distinguished Conduct Medal for their bravery, leadership and initiative in this action. Five of them – Company Sergeant Major W.R. Goodchild, Sergeant G. Carr, Ser-

geant L.O. Rule, Sergeant E. Skellern and Sergeant P. Turner – took over command of their respective companies when every one of their officers had become casualties, and each was credited with successfully leading their companies to the final objective. Private R.W. Wilson was cited for repeated acts of great bravery. With no concern for his own safety, he spent much of the day dodging machine-gun fire to rescue wounded men who were lying in the open, until finally he himself was seriously wounded.

By 1230 hours 4th CMR had broken through the Fresnes-Rouvroy defences, and by late afternoon all companies were consolidating on the final objective. "One more nick had been made in the German line…."

The 4th CMR was relieved during the night by a British battalion, and on 31 August the Battalion was sent into Army reserve in the rear area. The battle continued for another week. The vaunted Drocourt-Quéant Line was broken on 2 September, and by the 4th the Canadian Corps had reached the still uncompleted Canal du Nord. Once again 4th CMR had played an important role in a major Canadian victory. The stage was now set for an advance on Cambrai. But again the Battalion had paid a high price: on 26 August it lost 11 killed and 74 wounded; on 28 August a further 14 were killed and 152 were wounded.

The Canadian Corps had a lull in its offensive for nearly three weeks while the British and French to the south caught up with the Canadian advance. But this period of inactivity was used to good effect to make detailed plans for the next stage, the battles for the Canal du Nord defence line and for the city of Cambrai. The Canal du Nord was taken in heavy fighting on 27 September by 1st and 4th Divisions, and 3rd Division was brought forward to make the assault on the Marcoing Line on 28 September. This attack was made by the 7th and 9th Brigades, and 4th CMR, along with the other units of 8th Brigade, was in reserve and played no part. The Germans had brought in thousands of reinforcements in an attempt to hold the Marcoing Line, since it was the last of their prepared defensive lines, but the Canadians once more were victorious, albeit suffering huge numbers of casualties. General Currie again called a pause in operations to allow the Corps to recuperate.

Even though the Canadian Corps offensive had been halted temporarily, German artillery continued to bombard the lines, and the Battalion could never forget that it was in the forward zone. During this pause, yet another laurel was added to the already substantial list of 4th CMR honours. Lance Corporal W.C. Mitchell, the NCO in charge of signalling, was awarded a DCM for repeated acts of bravery in repairing telephone cables that were constantly being cut by enemy shelling.

On 9 October the attack on Cambrai was renewed, this time by 2nd Division supported by the 8th Brigade. 8th Brigade was given the task of advancing from the outskirts of the city and securing a crossing over the Canal de l'Escaut, which ran through the north-western part of Cambrai. If the attack was successful, the remainder of 3rd Division would come forward to secure the city.

The attack by 4th and 5th CMR went in at 0130 hours, on a clear, cool autumn night. In 4th CMR's sector, 'C' Company, in the lead, reached its objectives within an hour, thus gained the distinction of being the first Canadians to enter Cambrai. At daybreak the Battalion crossed the canal, passed through a badly damaged and nearly deserted city and by 0800 had reached the eastern edge of the built-up area. There was not a single casualty. With the capture of Cambrai the entire German front was on the verge of collapse, and it marked the beginning of a large-scale retirement across the whole front.

On 10 October the Battalion was relieved by a British battalion and went into billets in the old trench line west of the

4th CMR soldier taking cover behind a tree during the last stages of the advance into the city of Cambrai, 9 October 1918. (NAC PA3266)

city. The unit's War Diary for 10 October gives a somewhat sardonic view of this "relief":

> Well, we had no business to take Cambrai. Someone else, presumably the 3rd Army, wanted the city – volunteered to take it – and were very peeved that the Canucks were occupying and defending the place. We are ordered to clear out, which we do, and are all clear of the place by 13.30 and on our way to rest billets. Miles of wire, thousands of shell holes and dozens of ruined villages, without a single sign of civilization or civilians – but we shake down....

While continuing to fight occasional rearguard actions, after 17 October the Germans were pursued as they withdrew toward the Belgian border, initially by 1st and 4th Divisions. 3rd Division was brought forward on 21 October to take over from 1st Division, just as German resistance in the area of Valenciennes was stiffening. On 23 October 7th and 9th Brigades cleared the Forest of Raismes, and the division reached the west bank of the Canal de l'Escaut. Here the division halted to wait until a 4th Division attack on the city of Valenciennes on 1 November overcame the strong German garrison there.

For the units of 8th Brigade the immediate problem was how to attack across the wide Canal de l'Escaut just to the

4th CMR troops occupy the empty streets of the city of Cambrai which they have just liberated, 9 October 1918. (GGHG Archives)

north of Valenciennes. The Germans had destroyed all the bridges, and they had well-placed machine-gun nests on the east bank. On the evening of 1 November patrols were sent out to find suitable crossing locations and to determine how best to deal with the enemy machine guns. Major Charles McLean and a runner got across the canal on an improvised raft, but as soon as they touched the opposite bank they came under fire from a nearby machine gun. Major McLean killed one of the gunners with his pistol, and sent his runner back across the canal to get assistance. Company Sergeant Major W.R. Good-

A patrol entering Valenciennes, near the Franco-Belgian border, 2 November 1918. (GGHG Archives)

child quickly gathered a group of 15 men, crossing to help Major McLean under cover of a barrage of rifle grenades. With McLean, this group rushed the enemy and captured the gun and its ten-man crew. At the same time, Lieutenant Nodwell swam the canal and established a small bridgehead that enabled a makeshift bridge to be thrown across. These small garrisons on the far bank gave the Battalion a 600-metre toe-hold on the enemy-held side of the canal and greatly facilitated the crossing operations for the Battalion after dark.

For his initiative and bravery, Major McLean was awarded the Distinguished Service Order on the personal recommendation of the brigade commander, Brigadier-General Draper; Company Sergeant Major Goodchild was given a well-deserved bar to the Distinguished Conduct Medal he had earned two months earlier in the attack on the Fresnes-Rouvroy Line. Sergeant Major Goodchild was the only member of the Battalion to be awarded two DCMs.

On the morning of 3 November the Battalion attacked in conjunction with 5th CMR, but 'D' Company, on the right, came under withering machine-gun fire from a slag heap and made little progress. During the night the slag pile was bombarded and the enemy was driven out, but the Germans retaliated with high explosive and gas shells, killing three men and wounding fifteen. That day the Battalion advanced another four kilometres in a driving rain.

4th CMR's last battle of the war took place on 7 November, an attack with 2nd CMR on a strong German position in the village of Thulin. Despite the best efforts, this attack did not succeed. The Germans had well-positioned machine guns inside the stone houses of the village, and there was no artillery within range to assist in taking them out. Everyone knew that the war was in its very final stages, and there was great reluctance to accept unnecessary casualties. In the evening the Battalion was relieved by the Patricias, and marched to billets near the village of Quievrechain.

The Battalion was on the move again on 10 November, but spent much of the day helping to repair damage the Germans had done to the main Valenciennes-Mons highway. That night, as the unit moved into billets in St. Ghislain, about eight kilometres west of Mons, the enemy dropped in a few shells. Three men were wounded, the last casualties of the war.

On 11 November a despatch rider arrived at the Battalion to inform the CO that the Germans had agreed to terms of surrender, and that all hostilities would cease at 1100 hours. The war was finally over! As the word was spread throughout the Battalion, the reaction of the officers and men was strangely muted, "disappointing even to themselves", records the Battalion history. "To them it meant so much that nothing could express their feeling at the first announcement of the Armistice."

ARMISTICE TO DEMOBILIZATION

4th CMR marched into Mons on 12 November to join the remainder of 3rd Division, and it was then that the celebrations began in earnest. The streets were filled with throngs of exuberant citizens wanting to thank their liberators, the cafés and estaminets swarmed with soldiers and civilians, and this gaiety continued for most of the four weeks the Battalion stayed in Mons. The unit provided representative contingents to a number of enormous victory parades – for the commander of the First Army, for King Albert of Belgium and for His Majesty King George V.

While it was initially intended that the whole of the Canadian Corps would form a part of the Army of Occupation in the Rhineland, it was soon discovered that transportation resources simply could not support all four divisions in Germany, so 3rd and 4th Divisions were left in Belgium. On 11

December 4th CMR, along with other units of 8th Brigade were moved nearer to Brussels, and the Battalion was billeted in villages surrounding the historic Waterloo battlefield. By now, getting home was uppermost on everyone's mind. An early repatriation plan had called for a 'first in, first out' policy, but administrative reality simply ruled that out: 1st and 2nd Divisions were in the Rhineland, and as 3rd Division was nearest to the coast it was decided that its units would be the first to be sent back to Canada. Colonel Patterson made the happy announcement to the Battalion at the unit's Christmas dinner.

On New Year's Day 1919, 4th CMR began its journey toward the coast, arriving on 4 January in the small town of Dottignies, on the Belgian border eight kilometres east of Tourcoing. The Battalion spent a month here getting ready for the last voyage. Nominal rolls were prepared, medical boards and kit inspections were held, and spare time was filled with sports and vocational training to help prepare the men for their return to civilian life. On 11 February a remarkably slow train carrying the unit arrived in the port of Le Havre, and the Battalion crossed to England on the 14th.

The three weeks spent waiting for their ship in a repatriation camp at Bramshott seemed intolerably long, but one important ceremonial event was vividly remembered by all. On the afternoon of 7 March, despite a ferocious downpour, Colours were presented to 4th Canadian Mounted Rifles by Brigadier General D.L. Draper, commander of 8th Brigade. The King's Colour was received by Lieutenant W.A. MacLachlan, and the Regimental Colour by Lieutenant A.E. Dyke. They were proud, formal reminders of the enormous valour and the great sacrifices made by members of 4th CMR in the five years since the unit had been formed, and they were also a symbol of the bonds of comradeship that had grown in all who had served. These Colours were later deposited in St. James Cathedral in Toronto. On that occasion, only 36 of the original members remained who had joined the Regiment in Toronto on 16 November 1914. Of the 4,693 officers and men who had worn the Regimental badge, 839 would remain forever in the soil of France and Flanders, and 1,540 had been wounded during the years of war.

On the morning of 9 March 1919 the Battalion entrained for Liverpool, and later in the day, together with other 3rd Division units, boarded the SS *Carmania* for the voyage home. Eight days later the men crowded the decks as the Canadian coast came into view at dawn on 17 March. 4th CMR disembarked in late morning, and by mid-afternoon was en route to Toronto on two trains. The unit came home to Toronto in mid-evening on 20 March 1919.

Thousands of relatives crowded the station, throngs lined the streets and swelled the Armouries, making one of the greatest ovations which the city ever witnessed. The Battalion with difficulty formed up on Yonge Street, wearing their steel helmets and war regalia and marched in column-of-route to Bloor Street, through Queen's Park to the Armouries.... At the Armouries families and friends swarmed in, surrounded the Battalion and captured it with a last outburst of welcome. Lieut.-Colonel W.R. Patterson ... addressed the Battalion, every man of which he knew by name.... Finally, the Battalion, after four and a half years of honourable service to King and Country, was given its last command – "4th C.M.R. Dismiss".

POSTSCRIPT

The 4th Canadian Mounted Rifles was disbanded on arrival in Canada, along with all units of the Canadian Expeditionary Force. The valiant service of the Regiment throughout the years of the First World War was not, however, forgotten. On its reorganization in 1921, the Mississauga Horse was designated to perpetuate 4th CMR, and became entitled to emblazon the 4th CMR's battle honours on their guidon. Later, in 1935, the perpetuation of 4th CMR was also granted to the Governor General's Body Guard. The 4th Canadian Mounted Rifles is now perpetuated by the Governor General's Horse Guards, and the First World War battle honours of 4th CMR are proudly borne on the Regimental Standard.

The Governor General's Horse Guards also perpetuates the 216th Battalion, CEF, and the 7th Canadian Mounted Rifles. These units were in large part recruited by the Governor General's Body Guard and the Mississauga Horse, but both were broken up in England to provide reinforcements to other units at the front, and neither saw active service in the war.

The British War Medal, awarded to all men who served in the military forces of Britain or Commonwealth nations during the First World War.

The British Victory Medal, awarded to all who served during the First World War. All Allied nations issued a medal with a similar design and ribbon.

Presentation of the Battalion Colours to 4th Canadian Mounted Rifles took place in a parade in Bramshott, England on 7 March 1919. These colours were eventually deposited in St. James' Cathedral in Toronto, but by 2002 almost nothing remained of them (inset). (GGHG Archives)

CHAPTER THREE

THE INTERWAR YEARS

STAND TO YOUR HORSES

By the end of what was termed the 'Great War for Civilization' the Canadian Army had proven itself without equal among the Allied forces in operational competence and capability. Perhaps more important for the country, the valiant feats of the Canadian Corps on the battlefields of France and Flanders had contributed to a sense of nationhood unknown prior to the war. Thus when the many thousands of Canadian Expeditionary Force veterans arrived back in Canada in the spring and early summer of 1919 they were welcomed as national heroes. This was certainly true for the former members of the Governor General's Body Guard and the Mississauga Horse who had served with such distinction in many overseas units, including the 4th Canadian Mounted Rifles. Once at home, demobilization of returned units was accomplished quickly, often in less than a day, largely because much of the bureaucratic processing and paper work had been taken care of before leaving England. By mid-year the grand army that had been built at such high cost in blood and treasure had been dispersed. The country's defences once again rested in the hands of the Militia and the small Permanent Force.

RE-BUILDING THE REGIMENTS

Both Toronto cavalry regiments had continued to exist during the war years, but only in skeleton form. They had served mainly as bases for recruiting and training of reinforcements for the overseas battalions, and by mid-1919 both the Body Guard and the Mississauga Horse were in what might generously be called 'poor condition'. Strengths were low and members generally over-age or otherwise 'unfit for overseas service'. And as it had been impossible to carry out cavalry training during the war, the capability of the regiments was very low. It was not long, however, before a number of pre-war officers returned to their old units anxious to restore them. In the Body Guard, Lieutenant Colonel Sanford Smith resumed his pre-war position as commanding officer, as did Lieutenant Colonel H.D.L. Gordon in the Mississauga Horse.

Canadians had, however, grown extremely weary of war and things military, in part because there were so few who had been spared the sorrow of having some member of their immediate family killed or maimed during the conflict. Though there may have been enormous pride in the valour and the accomplishments of the veterans, that did not translate into public or political support for keeping a large and well-trained Army at home in peacetime. Even the returning veterans for the most part just wanted to get on with re-building their civilian lives. While a number of officers believed that they had a continuing obligation to serve in defence of their country, few of the battle-hardened NCOs or soldiers showed any interest in peacetime soldiering, at least initially, and the reconstruction of the old regiments was not an easy task.

The Department of Militia and Defence was very much aware of the problems that had to be overcome in making the transition to a peacetime military structure, and early in 1919 General Sir William Otter was appointed to head a committee to consider the reorganization of the Militia in Canada. There were several contending ideas. Many veterans wanted the

1908-pattern trooper's sword of the type issued to the Regiment after the First World War (GGHG Archives)

The University Avenue Armouries, Toronto, home to the Governor General's Body Guard from 1902 and the Mississauga Horse from 1905. (City of Toronto Archives, Fonds 1244, Item 1001)

numbered CEF battalions and regiments to replace the pre-war Militia structure; others wanted simply to reinvigorate the 'historic', pre-war named units; still others preferred some amalgamation of the two ideas. This last concept won the day: the Otter committee recommended that the new Militia should be composed of the old named units, but they would also perpetuate designated CEF battalions where there was a link through wartime recruiting or territorial association. Militia units that had not been mobilized because of Sam Hughes' unconventional notions in 1914 would thus become entitled to the battle honours that would be awarded to the now disbanded CEF units.

The Otter Committee, as much for reasons of internal Army politics as support of the strategic rationale, or any government direction on the matter, recommended a post-war Militia of eleven infantry and four cavalry divisions, with the whole range of supporting arms and services. This very large structural framework was accepted by the Department, and, while it was never formally approved by the government, it formed the basis for the organization of the Militia until the 1930s. For the Canadian Cavalry Corps, 33 regiments were authorized. Because the British had agreed to return to Canada most of the equipment of the four CEF divisions, less the mechanical transport, along with the weapons and the saddlery of the Canadian Cavalry Brigade, there was at least some reasonably useful kit for the many infantry and artillery units. But, with only the basic equipment of the three-regiment cavalry brigade, there was really not much in the stores for the cavalry. However, the major flaw in the plan was that there was absolutely no government commitment to provide enough money to man or to train a Militia of this size.

While the formal reorganization of the Militia was not officially authorized until May 1920, efforts to re-build both the Body Guard and the Mississauga Horse began well before that.

The Body Guard was first off the mark in the autumn of 1919, and Colonel Smith was given the princely sum of $300 as a grant to cover essential expenses incurred in reconstituting the Regiment. The initial task was to establish a slate of experienced officers and senior NCOs, and then focus on recruiting a cadre of men. By the time HRH The Prince of Wales made a visit to Toronto in late fall, the Regiment was able to provide a full mounted escort to the Royal party, but no training was attempted until 1920.

The Governor General's Body Guard was one of the early beneficiaries of the newly formed Battle Honours Committee, and the Regiment's first battle honour – **North West Canada 1885** – was awarded on 2 September 1919 by General Order 69/ 1919.

The Mississauga Horse was formally reorganized on 1 March 1920. The Regiment was designated to perpetuate the 4th Canadian Mounted Rifles, with entitlement to the Battalion's battle honours, and the unit at that time adopted the name The Ontario Mounted Rifles. Two reserve regiments were also created at this same time to perpetuate the 170th Battalion and the 216th Battalion.

Since defence was given a very low priority by every government in this era, the interwar period was to be a very difficult time for all Militia regiments, and this was certainly the experience of both the Governor General's Body Guard and the Mississauga Horse. Both regiments were, however, fortunate to be blessed with strong leadership throughout these years, along with a large group of dedicated and loyal NCOs and men willing to endure the harsh consequences of official neglect and still persevere in learning the art and science of soldiering. They were true patriots all, following in the footsteps of George Taylor Denison and an earlier generation of citizen soldiers who served their country and their Regiment without any thought of personal gain.

The Body Guard resumed its pre-war routine of holding evening training parades in January 1920 as regimental strength was gradually built up. It was allocated $2,300

Lieutenant Colonel Walter W. Denison, DSO, Commanding Officer of The Governor General's Body Guard 1921 to 1924. (GGHG Archives)

Warrant Officer Class I Harry W. Clarke, Regimental Sergeant Major of the Governor General's Body Guard 1923 to 1935. (GGHG Archives)

for pay for the entire year, but by common consent this whole sum was put into squadron and regimental funds. The financial strictures imposed by the government made peacetime soldiering very frustrating. The commanding officer later complained at the first post-war meeting of the Cavalry Association that the Regiment had no funding to pay a caretaker for the armoury, instructors, bands, or even for postage, and that much of the cost of maintaining the unit was coming out of the pockets of the officers!

There was not much improvement in the situation in 1921. The Body Guard, which had grown to 22 officers and 276 other ranks, was restricted to nine days of local training at the University Avenue Armouries, but the Ontario Mounted Rifles, with a strength of 171, was permitted to conduct its annual June training camp at Niagara. Command of both regiments changed this year. In January 1921 Lieutenant Colonel Walter W. Denison, DSO, took over from Colonel Sanford Smith, and in April Lieutenant Colonel J.F.H. Ussher, who had briefly been commanding officer of the 4th CMR until taken prisoner at Sanctuary Wood in June 1916, assumed the duties as commanding officer of the Ontario Mounted Rifles.

Financial difficulties continued to plague the units. In 1921 the Body Guard paid out over $300 to carry on schools of instruction, but Colonel Denison noted at the Canadian Cavalry Association: "from now on we cannot do it." A number of organizational issues were sorted out by the Militia Department during the year that affected both the Body Guard and the Mississauga Horse. The establishment strength of cavalry units was set at 346 all ranks, but in most years units were limited to a training strength of 200.

The cavalry versus mounted rifle training question was a hotly debated issue among senior officers of the Cavalry Corps at this time. Brigadier General Paterson, former commander of the Cavalry Brigade in France, argued that it was better to train units as traditional cavalry than as mounted rifles because cavalry knowledge allowed for all operational emergencies, while the other did not. The Cavalry Association agreed,

Badge of the Ontario Mounted Rifles, the name adopted by the Mississauga Horse on reorganization in 1920. The badge was patterned after that of the 4th Canadian Mounted Rifles, which the unit was designated to perpetuate. (Courtesy Major Louis Grimshaw)

ignoring the operational experience gained in South Africa and in France, and ignoring all of the arguments made so well by Colonel George Taylor Denison as early as the 1870s. Later in the year the Militia Department decided, mainly because of a shortage of equipment, that only four Militia regiments, the Body Guard, the Princess Louise Dragoon Guards, the Fort Garry Horse and the 19th Dragoons, along with the two Permanent Force units, would be equipped as "steel armed cavalry", that is, with swords. The rationale was that these units were all located in capital cities, so mounted escorts were part of their regular duties. All other regiments would continue to be equipped as mounted rifles. At the same time it was decided to man and equip a Hotchkiss machine-gun troop in the Body Guard, the PLDG and the Fort Garrys.

By 1922, one evening of voluntary training for ten weeks in the spring and ten weeks in the autumn were part of a well-established routine in both the Mississauga Horse and the Body Guard. The Body Guard paraded on Friday evenings, the Mississauga Horse on Mondays. The parade nights in both units followed much the same pattern: the whole regiment would form up for inspection at 1900 hours under the regimental sergeant major, the officers would fall-in, the commanding officer would inspect, there would be a march past, and then the troops would be dismissed to go to their training. Dismounted cavalry-style drill got a great deal of emphasis, since smart drill was still considered the hallmark of a good unit, but a variety of other subjects were also taught during these parades – military law, map reading, and signalling, for example, sword drill in the Body Guard, and there was machine-gun training for the Body Guard's Hotchkiss troop. Both regi-

ments also gave as much emphasis to equitation training as possible. Usually about 20 horses were hired each week – much of the pay donated to the Regimental fund was used for this purpose – and the troops took their turn in basic riding instruction. The whole regiment would be back on the armoury floor for a formal dismissal parade at 2200 hours.

The regiments were by now also playing a part in their members' social life. Each had its own Sergeants' Mess, and the units shared a recreation room for the men in the University Avenue Armouries. The Mississauga Horse in addition organized an annual gymkhana in the spring, as well as smokers and regimental rifle matches. And both regiments had baseball, hockey and boxing teams that competed in garrison leagues.

In both 1922 and 1923 a nine-day training camp was held in June at Niagara-on-the-Lake for the units of the 1st Mounted Brigade (the Body Guard, the Mississauga Horse and the 2nd Dragoons), but in both years the regiments were limited to taking only 40 percent of their strength. This was very frustrating for commanding officers, who were expected to recruit up to their authorized training strength, and equally so for the men left behind because they missed out on the excitement of the mounted work, which was what most had joined to do. Unfortunately, in June 1922 there was severe rain for the first several days, making the open horse lines too muddy for use, and the long grass on the common made dismounted training almost impossible, especially in the morning when there was heavy dew. Nonetheless, all units were happy to be able to return to some semblance of normality in mounted training, and the presence of RCD officer and NCO instructors ensured good quality training. The units were inspected by Major General Panet, the district officer commanding, and his report cited the Body Guard as a "well or-

Mississauga Horse tented camp and horse lines during a weekend scheme, ca. 1923. (GGHG Archives)

ganized unit", "efficiency of well above average". When a copy of the inspection report was forwarded to the Regiment some months later, it contained the following comment: "This excellent report has been noted by the Honourable the Minister and members of the Militia Council with much satisfaction. They desire to congratulate all ranks on maintaining a standard of efficiency worthy of the senior cavalry regiment in the Canadian Militia". The return to pre-war standards had taken only three years.

While training aspects were thus improving, the Body Guard still had to contend with frustrating administrative difficulties caused by a lack of funding from Ottawa. Colonel Denison commented: "We have had no grants, no paid adjutants, nor paid clerical assistance of any kind ... it is getting almost hopeless." "You cannot ask the young officers to put up more money, so it all comes out of the pockets of the COs."

In 1923 the training at Niagara was judged to be of a very good standard, especially because of the extra effort made by the RCD in providing not only the usual officer and NCO instructors, but also additional men in each squadron. That year improvement in the facilities for the cavalry at Niagara Camp had begun with the erection of permanent horse lines, and there was a plan to install drainage tiles under the horse lines before the next summer. One matter of serious concern to both regiments was that the official rate of pay for horses was reduced from $2 to $1.50 per day, raising doubt about the quality of horses that the regiments could hire.

New commanding officers were appointed in both Toronto cavalry regiments in February 1924. In the Body Guard, Lieutenant Colonel Thomas L. Kennedy took over from Colonel Walter Denison, who had been promoted and appointed commander of 1st Mounted Brigade. In the Mississauga Horse, Lieutenant Colonel

Lieutenant Colonel W.T. Brown, VD, Commanding Officer of the Mississauga Horse 1924 to 1927. (GGHG Archives)

Lieutenant Colonel T.L. Kennedy, VD, Commanding Officer of The Governor General's Body Guard 1924 to 1927. (GGHG Archives)

Badge of the Mississauga Horse, taken into wear in 1924 when the Regiment's original name was restored. (GGHG Archives)

W.T. Brown assumed command from Lieutenant Colonel Ussher. At that same time, the Regiment's name was restored when the seldom-used official title The Ontario Mounted Rifles was dropped.

Training in 1924 was adversely affected by a shortage of funding, and the Toronto regiments were allowed only to train at the armouries, but both organized regular shoots on the rifle range at Long Branch. The two regiments held a joint military gymkhana at the Eglinton Hunt Club in May 1924, which included jumping competitions as well as mounted pillow fights, bareback wrestling, tent-pegging with lances and a tug-of-war. Training was again at reduced levels in 1925, but both regiments were allowed to take 70 all ranks and 56 horses to camp at Niagara in June. Many of the NCOs and men thus had to be left behind in Toronto, and there was concern that they would lose interest and leave the Militia. The commanding officers of both units made it plain to District headquarters that they would not go to camp again under those circumstances.

Difficult times continued through 1926. That year the Body Guard and Mississauga Horse were again confined to training at the armouries, having only been allotted enough money to take 50 all ranks to camp, which the commanding officers chose not to do. The Body Guard trained 200 men in spring and fall parades, focussing on equitation in the spring. The Mississauga Horse trained 30 officers and 170 men, and they did equitation training in the autumn. The social highlight of the year was a Toronto Garrison Military Tournament in May. The Mississaugas held a regimental picnic and sports day in June, and spent a day on the rifle ranges at Long Branch in early October. Both units sent their full quota of officers and men to qualification courses.

The year 1927 began with a change of command in both Toronto regiments.

Mounted escort to the Governor General, Lord Willingdon, 1927. (GGHG Archives)

Lieutenant Colonel John Streight, MC, VD took command of the Body Guard from Colonel Kennedy, who like his predecessors went on to command 1st Mounted Brigade; he subsequently became Premier of Ontario. And in the Mississauga Horse, Lieutenant Colonel W.A. Moore replaced Lieutenant Colonel Brown. The 1st Mounted Brigade trained at Niagara Camp in June 1927 for the first time in several years, but each regiment was allowed only 100 all ranks and 75 horses. The Toronto units were again most unhappy to have to leave over half of their men at home, but commanding officers considered that good training for some was better than inadequate training for all. The camp followed the usual pattern: a day to march-in, a day of musketry training, a sports day, a day of rest on Sunday, four days of mounted drill and training, and a march-out day.

The Brigade camp at Niagara in June 1928 was twelve days instead of the usual nine, as had been requested for many years. Unfortunately the regiments were again allowed only 100 men and 75 horses. The additional three training days made an enormous difference in the overall quality of instruction, but the limited numbers that could go to camp made it necessary to give preference to new recruits. The training was hampered to some degree by many days of wet weather, and the horse lines became very muddy. Again, very long grass made dismounted training difficult. The Body

Guard this year had a strength of 304 all ranks, and the band, with 47 musicians, was noted to be "flourishing, but expensive to maintain".

General Order No. 6/1928 awarded five First World War battle honours to the Body Guard: **Mount Sorrel, Somme 1916,** Arras 1917, Hill 70, and Ypres 1917, the two shown in bold letters having been selected to appear on the Regimental Standard. These battle honours were awarded in respect of the overseas service of the officers and men who had been provided by the Body Guard for the 3rd Battalion, the 58th Battalion, the 75th Battalion, and the 124th Pioneer Battalion. There was, however, widespread dissatisfaction amongst veterans with the award of so few battle honours considering the large numbers of men the Regiment had recruited during the war. To many of them, it seemed that the important part that Body Guard men had played in the 4th CMR had simply been ignored, and a series of letters of protest to the Battle Honours Committee was begun.

Having noted the strength and effectiveness of the 4th CMR Association in the years since the end of the war, many former members of the Body Guard decided that it was time to give the regimental family a more formal structure. The result was the formation

Full dress uniform of the Governor General's Body Guard as worn in 1927. (GGHG Archives)

132

of the Governor General's Body Guard Association, which had its first meeting on 9 April 1929 at the Palais Royale. Lieutenant Colonel A.E.S. Thompson, for many years the Regimental quartermaster, was installed as president. Over 300 members of the Regiment attended this gathering of the clan, including two veterans of the 1866 Fenian Raid, twelve who had served in the 1885 North West Canada campaign and two Boer War veterans.

Lieutenant Colonel J.E.L. Streight, MC, VD, Commanding Officer of the Body Guard 1927 to 1931. (GGHG Archives)

Lieutenant Colonel W.A. Moore, VD, Commanding Officer of the Mississauga Horse 1927 to 1931. (GGHG Archives)

Warrant Officer Class I Fred Dewhurst, Regimental Sergeant Major of the Mississauga Horse 1929 to 1935. (GGHG Archives)

The addition of a machine-gun troop in the Body Guard in 1929 provided a fresh focus for the Regiment that year. 1st Mounted Brigade again held a twelve-day camp at Niagara in late June, and while the regiments were still limited to 100 men and 75 horses, both in fact took about 25 extra men for so-called 'duties'. This year all the horses were rented from a local Indian band, and it was commented that they were the best the units had ever had. It was also noted that the band could, if necessary, provide good horses for a wartime-strength brigade. A considerable amount of time was spent on musketry, including training on the Lewis and Vickers machine guns, and on judging distance. This was the first occasion that the Body Guard took their own trucks to camp.

The official perpetuation of the 4th Battalion, Canadian Mounted Rifles by the Mississauga Horse was recognized in 1929 by the award to the Regiment of the 4th CMR battle honours: **Mount Sorrel, Somme 1916,** Flers-Courcelette, Ancre Heights, Arras 1917, '18, **Vimy 1917,** Hill 70, **Ypres 1917, Passchendaele, Amiens,** Scarpe 1918, Hindenburg Line, Canal du Nord, **Cambrai 1918,** Valenciennes, Sambre, and France and Flanders 1915-18. Those in bold type were authorized to be emblazoned on the Regimental Guidon. The granting of these First World War battle honours prompted interest in acquiring a guidon for the Mississauga Horse, and a design was locally produced at about this time. There was, however, no attempt to gain official approval, and the guidon was never made.

Warrant Officers and Sergeants of the Governor General's Body Guard, 1930. (GGHG Archives)

Design of a guidon for the Mississauga Horse, produced locally in 1929. The dire financial straits of the Regiment caused by the onset of the Depression halted all work on the project, and the guidon was never made. (GGHG Archives)

DEPRESSION YEARS

If tight funding had caused serious problems for the Body Guard and the Mississauga Horse in the 1920s, the situation for both units grew immeasurably worse in the 1930s. The collapse of the stock markets in 1929 was now being felt around the world, and by 1930 Canada was caught firmly in the grip of the Great Depression. Among the measures taken by the government to reduce spending was a 78 percent cut in the defence budget, a proportion of which inevitably came from money allocated to Militia training. All units of the 1st Mounted Brigade elected to conduct spring and fall training in the armouries in 1930 and 1931 instead of going to a brigade camp. There was heavy attendance at all training parades in these years, even though members of the regiments were asked to donate their pay to the regimental funds.

Perhaps it was because of the financial hardships suffered by much of the population during the Depression years that both the Body Guard and the Mississauga Horse came to be the central focus in the lives of many of their members in this period. Both were usually well over their authorized training strength, and as there were long waiting lists of potential recruits, the units had the ability to accept only the very best sort of young men. Many junior officers were graduates of Royal Military College, and those that were not generally came from the private high schools such as Upper Canada College, Trinity College School, Ridley College or the University of Toronto Schools.

In 1929 Lieutenant Colonel R.Y. Eaton, Chairman of the Board of the T. Eaton Company, was appointed the Body Guard's Honorary Lieutenant Colonel, and until his retirement in 1954 he was a stalwart supporter of every aspect of the life of the Regiment. Twice each year, after the garrison church parade in May and the regimental church parade in the autumn, he would entertain the officers and their ladies at his home, and he was present at every important regimental function over the years.

In the early 1930s many of the men belonging to the units were out of work, and the regiments went to great lengths to take care of their members. While there was no pay, men were given streetcar tickets on parade nights, and afterwards provided with sandwiches and coffee. The messes and canteens in fact became centres for the social life of their regimental families. In addition to the formal training parades, men came to the armouries for smokers and other social gatherings, they played baseball and hockey, and there were dances and picnics and dinners. And for those over 21, the messes were popular for another reason: as Prohibition was still in effect, they were the only places in Toronto where it was legal to buy alcoholic beverages. In the Body Guard, a regimental dance was given each year at the Columbus Hall for the NCOs and men.

Lieutenant Colonel John Webb Graham, who joined the Body Guard as a second lieutenant in October 1930, recalled:

For the unmarried officers, the Regiment was our avocation and our recreation. This was where our friends were. For us, the main social activity of the week was the Officers' Indoor Baseball League. All of the infantry regiments in the garrison had a team in the league, but because the cavalry regiments were much smaller, the Body Guard and the Mississauga Horse combined to form a "Cavalry" team. A dou-

Badges of the Allied Regiments of the British Army, The Queen's Bays (2nd Dragoon Guards), allied with the Governor General's Body Guard in 1930, and of The 1st, The King's Dragoon Guards, allied with the Mississauga Horse. (GGHG Archives)

Colonel R.Y. Eaton, president of the T. Eaton Company, Honorary Lieutenant Colonel of the Governor General's Body Guard 1929 to amalgamation in 1936, and of The Governor General's Horse Guards until 1954. (GGHG Archives)

Bands were also an important part of regimental life, contributing greatly to ceremonial occasions and to social events. The Body Guard band had a strength of 48 in 1930, and it was always kept busy with engagements to play at parades, concerts and dances. The Mississauga Horse brass band had a strength of 40 at this time, and in 1930 the bandsmen were outfitted with scarlet tunics of pre-war pattern.

February 1931 marked the change of command in both regiments. Lieutenant Colonel Walter Rawlinson, MC, VD took over from Colonel Streight in the Body Guard, and Lieutenant Colonel N. King Wilson, VD assumed command in the Mississauga Horse from Lieutenant Colonel Moore.

The inability to take the regiments to camp in 1931 led to a great deal of emphasis on making garrison training interesting for the troops. In the Body Guard, special attention was given to the Hotchkiss gun detachments. One Vickers machine gun was issued, and men were recruited and trained to man it. Competition shoots for prizes were held weekly on the short range in the armouries and occasionally on the range at Long Branch, and several officers qualified at the Small Arms School. One major training innovation was that arrangements were made with the Eglinton Hunt Club to carry out equitation training in their indoor ring on two evenings each week, using 20 of their horses. In the Mississauga Horse, the formation of a second Vickers machine-gun troop spurred interest, and they too conducted equitation training in the evenings both at the armouries and at the Eglinton Hunt Club. This year an officers' mess was opened at the University Avenue Armouries.

Mississauga Horse full dress uniform, ca. 1930. The collar and cuffs were in myrtle green, the Regiment's facing colour, as was the pugaree on the cork helmet. (GGHG Archives)

ble-header game was played every Saturday evening on the floor of the University Avenue Armouries, although a few years later some of the games were played at Fort York. This was where you took your best girl for an evening out. Usually we would start out with something to eat in the Queen's Own or 48th Highlanders officers mess, both of which were on the main floor of the armouries. Our mess would be open after the game if the Cavalry team was playing. Everyone turned out to support the team. It was always a lot of fun, and equally important at this time when nobody had much money, it was cheap entertainment.

Alliances with British regiments were formed by both the Body Guard and the Mississauga Horse in 1930. The Body Guard was formally affiliated with The Queen's Bays (2nd Dragoon Guards), and the Mississauga Horse entered an alliance with The 1st, The King's Dragoon Guards.

Mounted sports were an integral part of regimental life in the Body Guard in 1931. NCOs and men won events at the Acton Fair, and a complete troop in full dress was paraded at the Open Air Horse Show, and eight ribbons were won. The riding highlight of the year was, however, produced by a group of youthful officers. A team made up of Lieutenant Donald Hunter, Second Lieutenant Marshall Cleland, and two of the Honorary Lieutenant Colonel's sons, Second Lieutenant Erskine Eaton and Second Lieutenant John Eaton, competed at their own expense at the Olympia tournament in London and at the Dublin Horse Show in Ireland, the first time in 22 years that a Canadian military team had entered competitions in Britain. At Olympia the Body Guard team won nine ribbons and the trophy for the team with the best average of points. In Dublin, riding against the very best riders the European armies could produce, they won four ribbons, and the Individual Grand Challenge Cup was won by Lieutenant Cleland for the only perfect performance of the competition. The whole of the Regiment was extremely proud of these fine young horsemen. Shortly after their return from Britain, Lieutenants Hunter and Cleland went to riding competitions in Boston and New York as part of the Canadian Army team. Both claimed second prize ribbons in events in Boston, and in New York the team won five ribbons, with Lieutenant Hunter taking first place in the bareback jumping event with what was described by the *New York Herald Tribune* as "a game exhibition of dazzling riding".

Lieutenant Colonel W.L. Rawlinson, MC, VD, Commanding Officer of the Body Guard 1931 to 1934. (GGHG Archives)

Lieutenant Colonel N. King Wilson, VD, Commanding Officer of the Mississauga Horse 1931 to 1935. (GGHG Archives)

The Governor General and Honorary Colonel of the Governor General's Body Guard, The Earl of Bessborough, inspecting a guard of honour, 1931. (GGHG Archives)

On 22 November 1931 the Regiment provided a guard of honour for the Governor General, the Earl of Bessborough, during His Excellency's first official visit to Toronto. On that occasion Sergeant Major John Finnamore was congratulated by Lord Bessborough on the superb appearance of the men.

The Minister of National Defence gave internal departmental approval to Defence Scheme No. 3 in late January 1932, an outline plan for the mobilization of an expeditionary force for overseas service, consisting of two infantry divisions, one cavalry division, and the usual support troops. This plan was never given formal government blessing, but it came to be used as the rationale for the future, much reduced structure of the Militia, and planning for a major reorganization of the Army was begun in secret at this time.

In 1932, the Body Guard carried on with the practice of ten spring and ten fall parades, and it held its own camp at Niagara for seven days in July, when 130 all ranks and 45 horses trained. In addition to the usual mounted and dismounted drill, two days were devoted to a field exercise that demanded initiative on the part of even the troopers. The end of training was marked by a gala garden party given by the Regimental officers, attended by hundreds of guests who came by steamer from Toronto.

Both the Signals and Machine Gun troops paraded twice a week all year, and the very popular equitation training at the Eglinton Hunt Club was continued. A number of the men attended courses of one sort or another at Royal Schools, but there always seemed to be more eligible men than available vacancies, and these courses were very desirable 'perks' in part because there was real pay involved that did not have to be turned over to the regimental fund. Musketry practice on weekends continued to be well attended, and the Band, 36 strong, turned out regularly with the Regiment and had many civilian engagements.

On 7 June 1932 the design of a Regimental Standard for the Governor General's Body Guard was approved by His Majesty King George V on the recommendation of the College of Heralds in London, according to records in the Directorate of History and Heritage in Ottawa.. This Standard, which was to bear the battle honours 'North West Canada 1885', 'Mount Sorrel' and 'Somme 1916', was, however, never made because the Regiment could not afford the cost during the depth of the Depression.

The Body Guard was extremely well represented in riding competitions in 1932. Five officers and eight NCOs from the Body Guard took part in the Open Air Horse Show on 1 July, and won the first prize in every event entered. The officers' jumping team entered shows at Boston, New York and Toronto and won many ribbons. A Body Guard team of Lieutenant Colonel Rawlinson, Lieutenant Marshall Cleland and Lieutenant D.F. Hunter won the Merritt Challenge Cup for 1932. This was the first time that the Regiment had won this competition since 1913, and it was notable that Colonel Rawlinson had been a member of the winning team nineteen years earlier.

In addition to the usual evening parades in spring and fall, the Mississauga Horse conducted three overnight camps, and four weekend recce exercises by mounted troops in 1932. This year, in an effort to maintain the interest of the longer-serving men, the Regiment divided the standard training syllabus into progressively advanced blocks so as to avoid repetition of rudimentary training for the more experienced soldiers. As a further effort to keep interest at a high level, 200 swords were bought from Ordnance in England at the Regiment's own expense, since as a mounted rifles unit they were not entitled to an issue of swords.

The Mississauga Horse experienced a windfall in the spring of 1932 when 20 excellent riding horses were donated to the Regiment on condition that the officers arrange for their upkeep. Through the generosity of the mayor and city council of Toronto, the unit was granted the use of a superb stable at Sunnybrook Farm, along with the exclusive use of a 3½ acre field for outdoor training. In addition, the chief of police granted the unit part-time use of the police covered riding school at Sunnybrook. The stable was in full operation by the beginning of April, and from that time the horses came to be

The stables at Sunnybrook Farm, used by the Mississauga Horse for equitation training from 1932. (GGHG Archives)

the focal point of activity in the Regiment. Equitation training for the men was carried out five evenings a week, with an average of 125 men riding each week, while the officers rode on Saturdays and Sundays. This training had immediate results: at the Open Air Horse Show in July, Mississauga Horse riders took 16 of the 20 prizes.

"AT NO COST TO THE PUBLIC"

Militia appropriations were again cut in 1933, this time to the lowest point in the century, and Militia units across the country had great difficulty just continuing to exist. Regimental funds, where there were any, had to be used to pay for a whole range of things no longer supplied by the Department of National Defence. "At no cost to the public" thus became the unofficial motto for the Canadian Militia, because it applied to almost every activity in which the units were involved.

The Body Guard continued to train at the armoury in the spring and fall of 1933, with a strength of just over 300. The Regiment was honoured to have the Governor General, Lord Bessborough, visit the unit on the final parade night of the spring training in May. His Excellency presented long service medals to Regimental Sergeant Major Clarke, Squadron Quartermaster Sergeant Large, Regimental Farrier Sergeant Major Wilson, Squadron Quartermaster Sergeant Harbour and Farrier Quartermaster Sergeant Surtees.

The highlight of that summer's training was a two-day tactical exercise conducted near Woodbridge, which involved a 'mechanized' attack on the town of Bolton by a force of some 20 automobiles. The second day of the scheme focused on troop tactics for the junior officers and NCOs. The exercise attracted a lot of attention in the local area: officers and NCOs were billeted in homes, and the officers held a mess dinner in

(Left) A variant of the Body Guard cap badge with an oval-shaped garter, was taken into wear in 1933. A new collar badge (right above), with the top of the maple leaf squared off to make the badge less fragile, was also brought into use at this time. A new officers' collar badge – a miniature of the cap badge – was adopted in 1935 (lower right) but was not commonly worn. (GGHG Archives)

the home of the reeve, Major Lex MacKenzie, a former officer of the Regiment who had served with great distinction in 4th CMR and who later was a member of the Provincial Parliament. (Major MacKenzie Drive is named after him.) The Regimental band added greatly to the festive atmosphere, and among their performances they entertained the town at a presentation of trophies to the local cadet corps.

Equitation training continued as in the previous years at the Eglinton Hunt Club on Monday evenings, with 25 horses, while the Regiment continued to parade most Tuesday and Friday evenings. Musketry continued to receive particular attention, and every Saturday 20 to 50 men fired on the ranges at Long Branch. The unit's machine gunners became especially proficient.

In March 1933 the Body Guard officers celebrated the 111th anniversary of the formation of Denison's Troop with a dinner at the Royal Canadian Military Institute. The guest of honour on this occasion was Lord Wakefield of Hythe, who made a presentation to the Regiment of a mahogany and sil-

ver mess case to be used as a trophy for annual competition by squadrons.

By 1933 the correspondence with the Battle Honours Committee begun some years earlier was beginning to show results, for, by General Order 60/1933 the Governor General's Body Guard was awarded the battle honour **South Africa 1900** in belated recognition of the contribution made by the Regiment to the Royal Canadian Dragoons in Canada's Second Contingent in the Boer War. No explanation was given, however, for not recognizing the even larger group of men from the Body Guard that had served with the 2nd Canadian Mounted Rifles in South Africa in 1901.

The superb quality of the Regiment's horsemanship was again demonstrated when the Body Guard team – Major F.H. Wilkes, Second Lieutenant Erskine Eaton and Second Lieutenant Allan Burton – won the Merritt Challenge Cup in 1933, the second year in a row that the unit took top place, and the Regiment's second team tied for second place in the Cavalry Association's rigorous annual competition.

The new regimental stable continued as the focal point of the Mississauga Horse in 1933, and over 4,000 riding hours were logged by members of the Regiment during the year. A new Vickers Machine Gun Troop was recruited from amongst former high-school cadets, and both brass and trumpet bands maintained full schedules. Three squadron camps and three troop rides were carried out in spring and early summer, with about 200 men participating, and a regimental field day was held in November.

The reorganization of the Militia, and especially the cavalry, was *the* topic of the year in 1934. A conference had been held in Ottawa in the autumn of 1933, where the plan concocted by National Defence Headquarters was presented to representatives of the military associations, and then in 1934 district commanders and unit commanding officers were brought into the consultation process. The essence of the plan was that in the event of a major overseas war Canada would be asked to contribute a Corps of six infantry divisions and one cavalry division, a significant change in numbers from Defence Scheme No. 3. The cavalry element of this force would be two brigades (six regiments) and five infantry division cavalry regiments, for a total of eleven regiments, plus two ar-

The trophy box presented by Lord Wakefield in 1933 to mark the 111th anniversary of the founding of the Body Guard. (GGHG Archives)

The Body Guard team – Major Wilkes, Second Lieutenant Eaton and Second Lieutenant Burton – that won the prestigious Merritt Challenge Cup in 1933. (Courtesy Lieutenant Colonel Allan Burton)

Lieutenant Colonel A.J. Everett, MC, VD, Commanding Officer of the Governor General's Body Guard 1934 to 1936, and of the Governor General's Horse Guards 1936 to 1937. (GGHG Archives)

moured car regiments. Some additional cavalry regiments were to be allowed for reinforcement generation, thus bringing the total number of allowable cavalry units to about 15. Also included in the plan was a proposal to create six tank regiments. The reorganization plan was discussed in detail at the October 1934 meeting of the Canadian Cavalry Association, and while there was obvious reluctance to see fine old regiments disappear, general approval was given, with the hope that consultation would continue as the plan was refined.

In January 1934 Lieutenant Colonel Arthur Everett, MC, VD took over command of the Body Guard from Lieutenant Colonel Rawlinson. A new Cavalry Wing had been added to the University Avenue Armouries, a Depression-era public works project, and beginning in the spring of 1934, equitation training was carried out there, with each member getting three hours of instruction, and senior NCOs special training in jumping. In addition to its usual evening parades, the Body Guard organized a 10-day camp at Niagara in June 1934, attended by 125 men and 53 horses, "at no cost to the public". Much of the time in camp was devoted to tactical training, and as a grand finale a garden party was held for over 300 guests who came to Niagara by boat for the day. Lieutenant Colonel Allan Burton, who had joined the Regiment in January 1933 as an eighteen-year-old second lieutenant, remembered this summer training:

Jack Eaton and I and our sergeants were chosen as the rough-riding detail to go to Niagara-on-the-Lake in the advance party to accept the horses which came from the Indians on the Caledonia Reserve after careful examination by veterinarians. Our task was to saddle and ride each horse, or attempt to ride it, to get it ready to issue to the incoming troopers….

It is not hard to imagine the dust, confusion, hullabaloo, and pandemonium that existed the first day of mounted drill, trying to get unbroken horses saddled, bridled, and ridden by city boys, some of whom had never been on horses before. An apparently impossible task, yet a miracle was in the making. In under a week Regimental Drill was performed mounted on the new horses, complete with sabres and lances, as if we had been doing it for months….

One officer, Alec Roberts, was over six feet tall and over 250 pounds … and finding him a suitable horse was a serious problem. Jack and I found a huge black mare, so strong she could have carried a knight in full armour…. Her nickname was Stagnant Stella. She had two speeds, slow and stop, and once stopped she was not easily coerced into shuffling forward again in her parody of a trot… At the end of each parade the colonel would call "Officers!". Each one of us would surround him smartly in a semi-circle, salute, and wait to be dismissed. Poor Alec would still be kicking, beating, pleading, and trying to convince Stagnant Stella to join the other officers' smarter chargers, when we would be off parade and in the Mess tent. One day the sergeant behind Alec's mare, thinking to help him respond to the call for Officers, jabbed the mare under the tail. Stagnant Stella screeched and sprang forward one leap, much to Alec's surprise. Unseated, Alec fell off one side with his foot still caught in the stirrup, hanging upside down in front of the whole regiment, while Stagnant Stella breached herself and cascaded a torrent of urine on the parched ground near his head. It would have been a dangerous situation with any other horse, but once Stella relieved herself, she sighed and looked around in calm contentment at her rider's unusual antics.

As a contribution to the city of Toronto's centennial celebrations in 1934, the Regimental band was mounted for the first time. The horses for the band, all greys, were Eaton's store delivery horses, and the bandsmen received their riding training under the supervision of some of the Regiment's very talented riders. This was a major undertaking, and not without its humorous incidents, for not many of the bandsmen were comfortable in the saddle, and some of the horses didn't espe-

cially like drums beating or trumpets blaring in their ears, and let it be known. The band paraded with the Regiment and appeared at many events that were part of the city's centennial celebrations.

Mounted sports continued to be a popular activity, with unit officers and NCOs winning prizes in competitions at the 1934 Royal Winter Fair and the Toronto Horse Show. The Toronto Garrison Military Tournament, held on 23 and 24 May 1934 to bring Militia activities to the public's attention, was an enormous success. The Governor General and Lieutenant Governor were in attendance to watch the performances of the unit bands, the RCD musical ride, displays of arms drill and gymnastics and jumping competitions. The Body Guard's mounted band proved one of the highlights of the programme, and many of the Body Guard officers and NCOs won prizes. When the Canadian Corps held its 20th anniversary reunion in Toronto, Senior NCOs of the Regiment put on an

The Mounted Band of the Governor General's Body Guard (below) and on parade for the centennial of the City of Toronto, 1934 (right). (GGHG Archives)

Pay parade for Mississauga Horse troopers, ca. 1934. (GGHG Archives)

Body Guard troop moving off on a weekend patrol, ca. 1934. (GGHG Archives)

conducted weekend recce exercises in the countryside north of Toronto. In addition, sand-table exercises were used regularly to teach tactical deployment to officers and senior NCOs. An annual sports day was held in the spring, and unit teams continued to enter competitions in local tournaments and horse shows.

The restructuring of the cavalry units in central Ontario was an issue that was uppermost in the minds of the senior officers throughout 1935, as district headquarters was required to provide its plan to National Defence Headquarters by the autumn of the year. Among the decisions made was that the two Toronto regiments, the Governor General's Body Guard and the Mississauga Horse, were to be amalgamated. While this came as no surprise, a great deal of planning had to be done by the senior officers of both regiments to determine how this would be accomplished with the least harm.

1935 was a busy year for the Body Guard, despite the continuing financial straits. The Regiment conducted dismounted parades and equitation training during the fall, NCO classes, weapons and signals training and recreation during the winter, and dismounted training and equitation in the spring. Regimental activities at the University Avenue Armouries were made easier this year when the Toronto Scottish Regiment was moved to the new Fort York Armouries and more space became available for offices and training rooms. In late April the Regiment conducted a mounted exercise near Markham to train officers and NCOs in cavalry tactics, and the unit held a nine-day camp at Niagara in June with one troop from each squadron, "at no cost to the public", where the focus was on mounted tactical training. Regimental strength fell off a bit, but the enthusiasm of members of the Regiment was kept high, despite receiving no financial remuneration for their efforts. The regimental grant for the year was $3287.55.

The Body Guard's continuing prowess in horsemanship was once again demonstrated when the Regimental team, consisting of the commanding officer, Lieutenant Colonel Everett,

impressive display of tent-pegging for the thousands of veterans who attended.

Throughout 1934 the Mississauga Horse maintained a strength of some 215 all ranks. Weekly parades were held on Monday evenings, and in line with a new training syllabus issued by District headquarters, considerable emphasis was placed on shooting and other operational skills. The regimental stable at Sunnybrook was in full use four nights a week except in the heat of summer, each squadron using the facilities one night a week. Many of the young troopers took full advantage of the fact that the Regiment's horses were available to members at no cost for riding on weekends. Each squadron conducted two weekend tactical exercises, and three troops

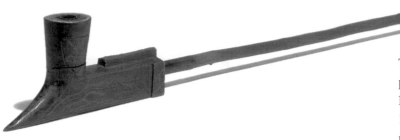

Chief White Cap's peace pipe, given in 1885 to Lieutenant William Hamilton Merritt, was presented to the Body Guard by Colonel Merritt's sister in 1935. The pipe apparently originated in what is now the south-western United States; the tradition was that the pipe would be passed to whatever new tribe with whom peace had been concluded. (GGHG Archives)

Lieutenant Hunter and Lieutenant Cleland, won the Merritt Challenge Cup in the 1935 competition. The Regiment's social life was also very full. The Sergeant's Mess held its annual dinner in February, and in November there was a special ceremony at which the peace pipe given to Lieutenant Colonel Merritt by Chief White Cap in 1885 was presented to the Officers' Mess by Merritt's sister. The Governor General, Lord Tweedsmuir, joined the regimental officers for lunch at the Military Institute in early November, and the annual regimental dance was held on 15 November.

There was great satisfaction in the ranks of serving and former members of the Body Guard when on 15 October 1935 the Regiment was granted joint perpetuation of the 4th Canadian Mounted Rifles with the Mississauga Horse. The Battle Honours Committee in Ottawa had finally recognized that the Body Guard had contributed more men to 4th CMR in 1914 than any other unit, and the Mississauga Horse, which already perpetuated the Battalion, was most gracious in agreeing to the joint perpetuation. This decision brought with it the award to the Body Guard of 4th CMR's seventeen First World War battle honours.

In February 1935 Lieutenant Colonel Albert E. Nash, MC, VD succeeded Lieutenant Colonel Wilson as commanding officer of the Mississauga Horse. Training in the Mississauga Horse in 1935 followed the pattern of previous years: weekly parade nights in spring and fall and equitation throughout the year at the Sunnybrook stable. This year somewhat more attention was given to musketry, and there were regimental and squadron shoots, with prizes for the best shots. A four-day regimental camp was

held at Long Branch during the summer for 150 men, "at no cost to the public", and three troops did a weekend recce scheme. The annual sports day was well attended, and unit teams competed in the Royal Winter Fair and the Toronto Open Air Horse Show. The Regiment's brass band was disbanded in 1935, mainly because of the expenses involved, but the trumpet band was maintained. The training grant for the year was $2958.70.

Both regiments participated in a Toronto garrison parade held on 5 May 1935 to mark the Silver Jubilee of His Majesty King George V. Five members of each of the regiments were awarded the King's Silver Jubilee Medal, including the commanding officers and regimental sergeant majors.

Early in 1936 a joint committee of the commanding officers and seconds-in-command of the Body Guard and the Mississauga Horse was established to make detailed plans for the amalgamation of the regiments that was to take place later in the year. Many things had to be agreed on beforehand, and Captain (later Lieutenant Colonel) John Graham, then the adjutant of the Body Guard, recalled that all preparations proceeded in the most amicable manner because everyone understood that amalgamation was inevitable and that it had to work. Early on it was decided that the new regiment's name should be The Governor General's Horse Guards, thus maintaining the Guards status and precedence of the Body Guard, but also incorporating the 'Horse' part of the Mississaugas' title. As 'Horse Guards', the new regiment would retain the blue full-dress uniform of the Body Guard, but with a broad red guards stripe on the overalls instead of the double white stripe.

The new regimental badge would keep the form of the Body Guard badge, with the Mississauga Horse's unicorn replacing the maple leaf as the central device within a garter bearing the Royal motto. The collar badges would be the Mississauga Horse badge with the motto changed to read *Nulli Secundus*. Captain Allan Burton,

Lieutenant Colonel A.E. Nash, MC, VD, Commanding Officer of the Mississauga Horse 1935-1936, and of The Governor General's Horse Guards 1937 to 1939. During the early part of the Second World War he served at Army Headquarters in Ottawa as Inspector General for Central Canada in the rank of Major General, the highest rank attained by any member of the Horse Guards. (GGHG Archives)

who had trained as an architect, was given the task of producing the drawing of the new badge for submission to the College of Heralds.

Combining the slate of officers was somewhat more difficult, as both regiments already had full officer establishments, and eventually nearly half would have to be let go. The commanding officers decided they would alternate in the position, Colonel Everett taking the first six months and Colonel Nash the next eighteen.

Training in the Body Guard continued in 1936 much along the same lines as in previous years, with equitation training being carried out in the Cavalry Wing of the Armouries, although the Eglinton Hunt Club continued to be used for preparations for special events Trumpet Major Al Banner, who had joined as a trumpeter in 1936, recalled being sent to pick up horses for a parade:

One Thursday Sergeant Frank Farris came to me and said that there was a ride going on at the Eglinton, and could I ride some horses down from a stable up at Hoggs Hollow. So another fellow and I went. The deal was to ride one and lead four – three on the off side, one on the near side. As we came down Avenue Road there were cars behind and the silly buggers would blow their horns. There was one horse who didn't like what was going on and wanted to go sideways, so my arm was stuck way out. I guess he didn't like my arm out there either, so he got in close and bit me. There I was, flailing away with my spurs trying to get him to stop, and he pulled off and took a chunk right out of my tunic…. I didn't know that leading horses could be so hazardous, so I said to Farris, 'You'll have to get somebody else to take the horses back; they tore me to pieces'.

The usual training camp was held at Niagara-on-the-Lake for nine days in June, with 151 all ranks and 86 horses. Two interesting training innovations were introduced during the camp. A trial was conducted of cavalry working with an aircraft manned by two regimental officers, Major A.G. Cameron and Lieutenant Cleland, and the Signal Troop ex-

Warrant Officer Class I John W. Finnimore, Regimental Sergeant Major of the Governor General's Body Guard 1935-36, and first RSM of the Governor General's Horse Guards 1936 to 1940. (GGHG Archives)

perimented with the use of radios in passing information between motor cars on the move. The Regiment was very proud when the Regimental Machine Gun Troop won the Stockwell Challenge Cup in the Dominion of Canada Rifle Association's Vickers machine-gun competition. Lieutenant Cleland again brought honours to the unit when he won the International Jumping Championship at the Montreal Horse Show.

In the Mississauga Horse, unit strength was kept up during the year, and the quality of recruits continued to be high. Training was carried out as in past years, emphasis being given to rifle and machine gun shooting. Equitation training continued on four nights a week at Sunnybrook Farm. Tactics training was done on a sand table during winter months, and brief weekend recce exercises were conducted in spring and fall, and four squadron camps of three-days length were held in the summer. This year a Scout Troop of 20 men was formed. The regimental trumpet band grew in proficiency, and added greatly to the pomp and ceremony of unit activities. The Regiment held a sports day in the spring with the usual dismounted and mounted competitions, and unit teams entered mounted competitions in Toronto and at Chicago. A regimental team of a corporal and three troopers won the Leonard Challenge Trophy for horsemanship, and an officers' team took second place in the Merritt Cup competition.

The magnificent Canadian War Memorial on the heights of Vimy Ridge was formally unveiled on 26 July 1936 by His Majesty King Edward VIII, in the presence of a large group of Canadian and French dignitaries. The Royal Canadian Legion had made special arrangements for thousands of First World War veterans to be present, and among this contingent was a large group of 4th CMR veterans, who returned to honour the 839 of their comrades who had fallen during the war.

Warrant Officer Class I John Burry, MSM, Regimental Sergeant Major of the Mississauga Horse 1935 to 1936. (GGHG Archives)

Practising cavalry troop formations: the Body Guard at Niagara Camp in the summer of 1936. (GGHG Archives)

Mississauga Horse tent lines at Niagara-on-the-Lake, summer 1936. The cavalry was showing signs of significant change. Note the automobile in the background; several were used in cooperation with aircraft on elementary reconnaissance schemes, and the Vickers machine guns herald a change toward greater firepower. (GGHG Archives)

THE GOVERNOR GENERAL'S HORSE GUARDS

The most momentous event of the year for the Regiment was, of course, the formal creation of the Governor General's Horse Guards on 15 December 1936 by the amalgamation of the Governor General's Body Guard and the Mississauga Horse. The Horse Guards was placed first in the order of precedence of Militia cavalry units, and it was designated as part of 1st Cavalry Brigade, which had its headquarters in Toronto, and was thus a component of the planned cavalry division.

The formal restructuring of the Militia was made on the same date. In this process, the Cavalry Corps retained 20 regiments in all, 16 horsed regiments and four armoured car units. At the same time, giving at least half-hearted recognition to the great change in military technology that was underway, six tank regiments were created, but they were not part of the Cavalry Corps, and it would be several years before any of them would have any form of armoured fighting vehicles.

The place of cavalry in a modern army was highly controversial at this time. The extent of the mechanization of the German Army was widely known, as were their experiments with armoured units in the civil war in Spain. Britain had been slow to adapt, but even there the cavalry had already been transformed into mechanized units, and the Royal Tank Regiment had several units equipped with tanks, albeit light and not very reliable. A Canadian Tank School had been formed in London, Ontario the same year, but it too would not have any tanks for several years to come.

At the 1937 meeting of the Canadian Cavalry Association, the Minister of National Defence referred to "the passing mania for mechanization". General Ashton, the Chief of the General Staff, at the same meeting talked about the tendency toward mechanization in all modern armies, but cautioned that mechanization was extremely expensive and that no final decisions had yet been made about how far it would proceed in Canada. In the meanwhile he advised the Association to go on with cavalry training, teaching the principles of reconnaissance and attack by a mounted unit, but he also noted that it was advisable to interest the men in mechanical training "so that in the event of change they may be ready to take over their new type of mounts." There was no doubt that the more forward-thinking cavalry officers in Canada saw that the days of horsed cavalry were numbered, and their main concern was that Ottawa recognize that the cavalry should continue to be the mobile arm on the battlefield regardless of the form of mobility.

The Horse Guards effectively blended the training pattern of the two parent regiments, parading on Tuesday evenings in spring and fall, and continuing equitation training four nights a week at Sunnybrook Farm. Shooting was given much emphasis, especially by the Vickers and Lewis gun troops, and map reading, distance estimation, gas training, tactics and

Officers of the Governor General's Horse Guards meet at the home of the Honorary Lieutenant Colonel, Colonel R.Y. Eaton, only weeks after the formal creation of the new amalgamated Regiment. (Courtesy Major Eric Taylor)

Segment of a panoramic photo that showed all members of the Horse Guards at camp in Niagara, summer 1937. The new Horse Guards badge was not yet available, so members continued to wear Body Guard or Mississauga Horse insignia. (GGHG Archives)

care of horses were among the subjects covered. The Scout Troop, formed the previous year in the Mississauga Horse, trained twice a month, and both the brass and trumpet band were maintained. The Regiment took 220 all ranks and 155 horses to the brigade camp at Niagara in June.

The Regiment took first prize in the competition for the Leonard Challenge Trophy in 1937, and second place in the Merritt Cup competition. The Horse Guards were well represented in the Canadian Contingent sent to the Coronation of His Majesty King George VI in London on 12 May 1937. Colonel J.E.L. Streight, then commander of 1st Cavalry Brigade, was named as the contingent commandant, and Major F.H. Wilkes was the adjutant. A garrison parade to mark the Coronation was held at Queen's Park on 12 May, and Coronation Medals were awarded to five members of the unit. As had been agreed prior to the amalgamation, Lieutenant Colonel Everett handed over command of the Horse Guards to Lieutenant Colonel A.E. Nash, MC, VD in September. Lieutenant Marshall Cleland was given a signal honour on 10 December 1937, when he was named as the most outstanding Canadian sportsman of 1937, and awarded the Lou Marsh Memorial Trophy for his exceptional record of victories in equestrian events during the year.

Badge of The Governor General's Horse Guards, designed in 1936 and brought into wear in 1938. (GGHG Archives)

The Horse Guards continued to prosper in 1938 under Colonel Nash's leadership, with an average regimental strength of over 300, 40 new recruits having been taken in during the spring. Equitation training at the regimental stable at Sunnybrook Farm continued to be a focal point in the unit's training, and it was rewarded when the Regiment won both the Merritt Cup and the Leonard Trophy that year. Regimental teams also performed well in competitions at the CNE Horse Show, the Lake Forest Horse Show in Chicago, and the Toronto Winter Fair. Nine days were spent at camp at Niagara in June, with 30 officers, 206 other ranks and 162 horses. Here cooperation of the signals motorcyclists and a newly formed Light Car Troop demonstrated how cavalry operations could be speeded up and made more effective by the use of motor vehicles. Once again there was a demonstration of cooperation with aircraft. The Regiment hosted the Governor General, Lord Tweedsmuir, to lunch on 16 March, and in May provided an escort to His Excellency when he attended the running of the King's Plate at Woodbine Race Track. Two church parades were held, and a special parade was held for presentation of regimental awards. A dance was held for all ranks, and smokers and social evenings helped maintain regimental morale.

(Left) Consecration of the Standard of The Governor General's Horse Guards on the floor of University Avenue Armouries, 23 November 1938, by the Archbishop of Toronto. After the Governor General and Honorary Colonel, Lord Tweedsmuir, presented the Standard to the Commanding Officer, Lieutenant Colonel Nash, it was handed over (right) to the custody of Squadron Sergeant Major George Craven. (GGHG Archives)

The highlight of the year occurred on the evening of 23 November 1938 when the Governor General, Lord Tweedsmuir, Honorary Colonel of the Horse Guards, presented the Regiment's first Standard in a dismounted parade in the University Avenue Armouries. The *Toronto Telegram* reported that "thousands thronged the galleries" for the grand ceremony. After His Excellency was received with the customary Royal Salute, the Standard was consecrated by the Archbishop of Toronto, assisted by the Regimental chaplain, Major N. Clarke Wallace. While a fanfare of trumpets was sounded, the Governor General then presented the Standard in the King's name to the commanding officer. Colonel Nash in turn passed the Standard to the senior sergeant major, Sergeant Major George Craven, who had the honour of being the Standard Bearer. So that every member would get a good look at this sacred Regimental symbol, the Standard was then trooped through the ranks of the Regiment, escorted by Squadron Quartermaster Sergeant William Harbour and Sergeant James Keir, as is cavalry tradition. When the ceremony had ended, His Excellency took the salute as the whole unit marched past to the Regimental march "Men of Harlech". This gala event was concluded with a reception in the officers' mess and an all-ranks dance on the floor of the armouries.

The Standard presented to the Regiment in 1938 was perhaps somewhat unusual. The regimental badge of the Horse Guards was not used as the central device, as is customary on regimental colours, but instead the basic design of the Standard that had been approved for the Body Guard in 1932 was followed, with the maple leaf instead of the unicorn being used in the centre of a surcingle bearing the new regimental name. The abbreviated unit title GGHG, in the upper left and lower right corners, was embroidered on a white background – the facing colour of the Body Guard – instead of being on the Horse Guards' red facing colour. The reason for these variations can no doubt be traced to the fact that the initial application for the Standard was made by the commanding officer of the Mississauga Horse on 11 December 1936, before the amalgamation took place and before the design of the Horse Guards badge and the new facing colour had been approved. In this application for the Standard, the authorities were asked to "hasten the decision and preparation of the Standard", so as "to promote unity and harmony in the newly organized regiment". For 29 years this first Standard was carried by the Regiment with great pride, and it was not until 1967 that these anomalies were corrected with the presentation of the second Standard.

The beginning of 1939 was marked in the Horse Guards by a change of command. Lieutenant Colonel Russell P. Locke,

The first Standard of the Governor General's Horse Guards. (GGHG Archives)

VD, who at one time had been expected to take command of the Body Guard in 1937, reached the pinnacle of regimental soldiering, command of his Regiment, succeeding Lieutenant Colonel Nash in January. His was not to be a normal peacetime tenure.

Training in the Horse Guards followed the now standard pattern in the spring of 1939: Tuesday night parades at the University Avenue Armouries, and riding lessons at Sunnybrook Farm four nights a week. The Regiment, with a strength of 435 and a huge surplus of excellent officers, had in many respects never been in better form.

The Royal Visit of the King and Queen to Toronto on 22 May 1939 was a day of great pomp and pageantry, to which the Regiment was honoured to contribute. A mounted Sovereign's Escort was provided by the RCD and the Horse Guards, and they accompanied the Royal couple's limousine through the crowd-thronged streets of the city wherever Their Majesties were taken. The escort had in fact practised for months beforehand, and the horsemanship was superb.

Money for training in 1939 was more plentiful than for many years, and the Regiment spent twelve days in camp at Niagara in late June with over 400 men and 140 horses. The report on the Regiment's final inspection prior to the war was,

The Regimental band, May 1939. (GGHG Archives)

however, not entirely complimentary. While the unit was described as "very smart and well-turned out", the report went on to state that the Regiment "was very disappointing in camp. Too high a percentage of the other ranks had only a very elementary knowledge of riding which curtailed the tactical training. It would appear that the unit concentrates too much on ceremonial at the expense of other training".

Despite the comments by the inspector, this summer camp was a magnificent experience for members of the Regiment, for besides being good training in practical cavalry work, it had been great fun for everyone. When the Regiment returned to Toronto at the end of the month, little did members of the Horse Guards know that they had seen the end of an era, the end of horsed cavalry in Canada. Nor could they know that less than two months later the country would be at war and that they would be flocking back to the Regiment as it mobilized for battle.

Their Majesties King George VI and Queen Elizabeth pass in front of the Horse Guards' Royal Escort during the Royal Visit to Toronto, 23 May 1939. This was the first occasion when the Regiment provided an escort to the reigning sovereign. (GGHG Archives)

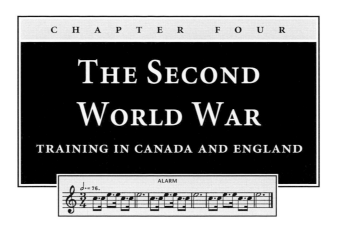

CHAPTER FOUR

THE SECOND WORLD WAR

TRAINING IN CANADA AND ENGLAND

Then outbreak of the Second World War came as no great surprise to anyone who had been following world events. War clouds had been building over Europe since Adolf Hitler and his National Socialist (Nazi) party came to power in Germany in 1933. The Nazis quickly consolidated their dictatorial grip on the country, and their aim of dominating the whole of Europe became apparent within just a few years. In 1935 Germany began a massive rearmament programme which included the creation of mechanized and tank formations. In 1936 the Rhineland, demilitarized by the Treaty of Versailles in 1919, was re-occupied by the German Army. That year Germany and Italy created a Fascist alliance known as the Rome-Berlin Axis, and Hitler intervened on the side of Franco's Fascists in the Spanish Civil War, where the *Wehrmacht* was able to test its new aerial and mechanized weapons and tactics. In 1938 German troops marched into and annexed neighbouring Austria. That same year Hitler browbeat the British and French into accepting German annexation of the Czech Sudetenland, and only months later, in March 1939, Germany seized most of the rest of Czechoslovakia. Hitler's attentions then focused on Poland. Britain and France, by that time appreciating his intentions, promised support to Poland in the event of aggression.

The German-Polish situation deteriorated steadily over the spring and summer of 1939, and it was considered but a matter of time before Germany took action. A non-aggression pact on 21 August between Russia and Germany opened the way for Hitler's troops, and on 1 September, supported by a massive fleet of fighter-bombers, German mechanized divisions raced across the Polish frontier. Few images capture the essence of this *blitzkrieg* campaign better than the gallant but futile charges made by Polish cavalrymen, armed only with lances, against advancing German tanks. Acting on their commitments made to the Poles, Britain and France declared war on Germany on 3 September.

The Canadian government followed these developments very closely. While Prime Minister Mackenzie King had a personal preference for neutrality, he understood clearly that Canada could not stand aside if Britain were involved in a major war. On 25 August precautionary measures were taken, in accordance with the Militia Act, to call out units that had been detailed in district plans for the guarding of vulnerable points. On 1 September orders were telegraphed to district headquarters across the country to place "on active service" all the units designated in Defence Scheme No. 3 as part of 1st and 2nd Divisions. The Governor General's Horse Guards was not among the units thus mobilized.

Captain (later Lieutenant Colonel) John Graham, then the adjutant, recalled the Regiment's first, if futile, efforts to prepare the unit for mobilization. Early on the morning of Saturday, 27 August, while at the family cottage in Muskoka, he got a call from the district duty officer and was told to report immediately.

I called Ian Cumberland, whose family had a cottage just down the lake, and we quickly drove to Toronto and put on our uniforms. I recalled that it was Warrior's Day at the [Canadian National] Exhibition, and we knew that the men would be wearing their uniforms to get into the grounds for nothing. So we went to the midway at the Ex and collared every Horse Guard we came across, loaded them into a truck and took them down to the University Avenue Armouries. But, of course, despite the excitement it all came to nothing: there were no orders for the Regiment, and everyone was sent home.

The Horse Guards were not alone in being left off the list of units to be mobilized for the Canadian Army Active Service Force. A revision of Defence Scheme No. 3 in February 1939

LICK THEM *over there!* **COME ON CANADA !**

sooner or later the Horse Guards would be needed. A few chose not to wait. Among the members of the Regiment who joined units that were already mobilized was Captain John Graham, who went to the First Hussars.

Canada declared war on Germany on 10 September. Over the next weeks recruiting for the units of 1st and 2nd Divisions proceeded at a hectic pace. The government decided on 19 September that the 1st Division would be sent to England as soon as possible, but by then many of the real, practical difficulties of raising a field army were becoming apparent. The main problem was a nearly complete lack of essential equipment, the result of grossly inadequate defence budgets over the previous two decades. Other than a quantity of First World War rifles, there were practically no war stocks of anything that was needed, and the shortages included such basic items as uniforms, boots, beds and blankets. With almost nothing to issue to the newly enlisted men, general recruiting was stopped on 24 September. The men of 1st Division would go overseas in early December 1939 with only their uniform and a rifle, counting on the British to supply everything else.

GUARDING THE WELLAND CANAL

Within the Regiment, there was a great flurry of activity on 25 September 1939. The Horse Guards received orders to mobilize a complete horsed squadron to guard the Welland Canal, and a smaller dismounted squadron to protect vital points in Toronto, including the University Avenue Armouries. Then-Lieutenant Allan Burton later wrote:

> The "call up" was high-school drama at its worst. Suddenly we were all ordered to report to the armouries under orders of silence. ... We fully expected to be able to phone home

had eliminated all cavalry units from the mobilization plan, with the exception of the First Hussars from London and the Fort Garry Horse from Winnipeg. The plan was, of course, classified secret, so few cavalrymen knew that nearly all their arm had been excluded from the call up, and that certainly applied to members of the Horse Guards.

In the days that followed Britain's declaration of war a host of members of the Regiment flocked to the University Avenue Armouries, fully expecting that their services would be needed immediately, just like their infantry comrades. But the most that Colonel Russell Locke could do was to tell them to stand by, that

The first wartime duty: a Horse Guards cavalry section patrols along the banks of the Welland Canal, October 1939. The Horse Guards squadron was the only Canadian horsed cavalry mobilized during the Second World War. (NAC PA 5127)

150

from the armouries, once we knew our destiny. But we were incarcerated, held incommunicado, for the next forty-eight hours, while our wives and families feared the worst. Meanwhile, we were passing pseudo-medicals, while the quartermasters issued uniforms reeking of mothballs, stiff and itchy with the warmth and feel of steel wool, boots in two sizes too large or too small, Lee-Enfield rifles from World War I plastered with grease, mess kits, blankets, and so on, to a long line of bewildered and excited troopers.

The Welland Canal squadron, commanded by Major Ian Cumberland – the only horsed cavalry to see service in the Canadian Army during this war – was quickly deployed to the armoury in St. Catharines, which was to be the squadron's base camp. Horses proved invaluable during the month the Regiment performed this duty, for many parts of the canal embankments were inaccessible by any other means. While this was not quite the war service that had been expected, the duty was taken very seriously. The Welland Canal was unquestionably a vital part of Canada's transportation system, and sabotage of the locks and bridges seemed at that time a most logical action to be taken by enemy fifth columnists who were presumed to be lurking behind every bush. The introduction to the history of the Regiment in the Second World War recalls:

In due course all is well and we are scattered out along the Canal, patrolling night and day with horses and cars. ... We have more patrols, more sleepless nights and many more scares. Bingos are invented. There are surprise night surveys of the entire canal zone. Then we have an accident, much to our sorrow, with a horse on the Railway Bridge, and the animal has to be destroyed. ... One of the highlights is the adoption of a bear as our Mascot. Much to the amusement of everyone he can consume quantities of soft drinks from the bottles and toss the "empties" quickly to one side when they are of no further use to him.

On 3 November the squadron was relieved by the RCMP and moved back to Toronto, where security guards were needed at the airports.

While patrolling as security guards may not have been quite what members of the Regiment had expected in time of war, the Horse Guards were employed as usefully as most other Canadian soldiers during the autumn and winter of 1939-1940. Even in Europe nothing was happening, and this time came to be known cynically as the Phony War.

The Horse Guards received a new task in November 1939, the provision of a dismounted squadron for security guard duty at the RCAF station at Camp Borden. In late November the squadron relieved the Toronto Irish Regiment and began the job of guarding the fighters and medium bombers that were being used in flying training. Lieutenant Allan Burton recalled:

We took our job of protecting the air station much more seriously than the Irish, and it became much more dangerous for the pilots! At night, when ordered to halt and be recognized, the pilots used to ignore the order. But when the Horse Guards took over, ignoring an order to halt

(Below left) While on patrol duty on the Welland Canal, the troops adopted a young bear named Judith as a mascot. There is no word about her fate once the squadron was relieved. (Below right) The return to Toronto of the Welland Canal cavalry squadron on 3 November 1939, Major Ian Cumberland leading. (GGHG Archives)

meant a rifle round fired into the trunk of the departing officer's car. Most of our troopers at the time were almost untrained and certainly not good shots, but fortunately during this episode there were no casualties.

For a few months in early 1940 the Regiment was led to believe that it might be mobilized as the divisional mechanized cavalry unit for the 3rd Canadian Division, and training was adjusted to reflect the anticipated role. The Regiment continued to parade on Tuesday and Friday evenings during the late winter and spring of 1940, and planned for the usual two-week camp at Niagara in June.

Lieutenant Colonel Russell P. Locke, ED, Commanding Officer of the Governor General's Horse Guards 1939 to 1941. (GGHG Archives)

The so-called Phony War came to an abrupt end in April 1940 when the Germans attacked Denmark and Norway and quickly overran the defences of these countries, including a small British force at Narvik in north Norway. A month later Belgium, the Netherlands and France were invaded. The *blitzkrieg* offensive swept around the French Maginot Line and pushed rapidly toward the Channel coast, separating the French army from the British Expeditionary Force. On 27 May the British began a hasty evacuation of their army from Dunkirk, but they had to leave behind almost all of the guns and heavy equipment they owned.

MOBILIZATION AS 2nd CANADIAN MOTORCYCLE REGIMENT

The Canadian government's reaction to the military disaster in Europe was to ship to Britain the 2nd Division, only recently recruited to full strength, and to order the raising of the 3rd and 4th Divisions. One of the consequences of the mobilization of the 3rd Division was a decision taken in early July to authorize the formation of five motorcycle regiments as light reconnaissance units, three with the brigades of 3rd Division, one for the Niagara District, and one for the West Coast. Motorcycles were chosen essentially because they were a cheap alternative to armoured cars, which the Canadian Army in 1940 did not have and could not get quickly. If the government learned one lesson from the swift

WO I George Craven, Regimental Sergeant Major 1940 to 1941. (GGHG Archives)

German conquest of France, it was that the coming war was going to require mechanized forces. The motorcycle regiments were all to come from the cavalry. The 1st was a composite unit formed from the RCD and the Strathconas, the 2nd was raised from the Horse Guards, the 3rd was from the 17th Hussars in Montreal, the 4th was formed by the 8th New Brunswick Hussars in Sussex and the 5th was raised by the British Columbia Dragoons in Kelowna.

On 14 July 1940 orders were received late in the morning from Military District No. 2 that the Horse Guards were to mobilize as the 2nd Canadian Motorcycle Regiment (Governor General's Horse Guards), with their base in Camp Borden once recruited to strength. Before noon, the adjutant, Captain 'Swatty' Wotherspoon, had reported to the district headquarters for further details, and he then informed the commanding officer. All officers were briefed at a meeting that same evening. The new regiment was to have a strength of just over 400 all ranks, in three squadrons, although the actual establishment was still somewhat vague. The Militia regiment was to continue to exist as the Reserve or 2nd Regiment.

The next day was spent in completing the formal organization procedures. Officers were 'boarded', and the following slate was submitted to the district officer commanding: Lieutenant Colonel R.P. Locke was to be commanding officer, second-in-command – Major G.D. Thomas, adjutant – Captain G.D. Wotherspoon, quartermaster – Captain K.V. Stratton, paymaster – Lieutenant J.H. Kent, medical officer – Captain J. Magnus Spence. The squadron commanders nominated: 1st Squadron – Major H.M. Sharp, 2nd Squadron – Major I.H. Cumberland, 3rd Squadron – Captain W.A. Boothe. Other officers selected were Captain A.K. Jordan, Captain J.M.R. Berwick, Captain R.E.H. Ogilvie, Lieutenants Donald Hunter, Marshall Cleland, Dennis Fitzgerald, Alan Burton, Mark Auden, Harry Appleton, Joseph Cornish, Fred Struthers, and Second Lieutenant Michael Rawlinson. The regimental sergeant major was Warrant Officer Class I G. Craven.

A group of Regimental sergeants and warrant officers, 1940. Back row: Sgt H. Craven, WOII W.E. Surtees, WOII W. Hardy, Sgt L.S. Payne, SQMS W. Harbour. Front row: WOII R.L. Wedge, RSM George Craven, WOII J. Anderson, Sgt W.G. Murray.

The enlistment of other ranks was begun on 16 July, and the first man attested was Trooper R.J. Greer. Documentation and attestation of the recruits continued until 23 July. There was an abundance of volunteers, but preference was given to men who already knew how to ride motorcycles, and about a hundred expert motorcycle drivers and mechanics who were members of local motorcycle clubs were quickly enlisted. In many cases these men brought their own motorcycles. When recruiting was over it was clear that the Regiment had secured a "splendid body of men". "Their only fault it would seem was the visible over-eagerness at first. Many of them fondly imagined that all they had to do was get sworn in, get uniform and equipment (rifle), get on their machines and away to war. Tally ho! And all that, but after the first disappointment was over, all settled down to the serious business of training". These experienced cyclists were soon to prove invaluable as instructors, since training on the motorcycles had to be conducted in groups of three or four men.

When a tentative War Establishment was received a week later it caused more confusion than clarification of the Regiment's new organization and role, for it was simply a 1931 organization table of an infantry motorcycle battalion with one troop cut from each squadron. The War Diary complained that "No consideration can have been given to new developments in [mechanized] attack." Meanwhile, as the Army had finally started to cope with supplying necessities to the thousands of men brought into the ranks, new uniforms made of heavy khaki denim were issued to everyone, but they proved a great disappointment. "They were the same as … battle dress,

in two pieces, very sloppy looking in that the fit was simply atrocious. The Horse Guards, long noted for their smartness, looked very strange."

At the end of July the Veterans Guard relieved Regimental guards at Malton airport, the University Avenue Armouries and the Ordnance Depot on Spadina Avenue. By this time the strength was up to 23 officers and 353 men.

On 6 August 1940, the Active Service Force Regiment paraded at the University Avenue Armouries with the Militia Regiment for one last time before taking up its new station at Camp Borden. After the formal parade, 32 men mounted on privately owned motorcycles led the two regiments on a march around downtown Toronto. Sea Biscuit, the regimental mascot – a pony of 13 hands that had been presented by the Master of the Eglinton Hunt Club to remind the Regiment of its origins – was also on parade for the first time.

The Horse Guards departed for Camp Borden on 14 August, 42 men on their own motorcycles, some in private cars and the remainder by special train. The Regiment detrained at Borden shortly after noon, and then went into temporary quarters in the infantry lines since permanent quarters in the cavalry section were not yet available. A composite squadron, led by Major Cumberland, that had been guarding the Air Force training camp was relieved and joined the remainder of the Regiment.

Sea Biscuit, a pony presented as a mascot by the Eglinton Hunt Club, paraded for the first time on 6 August 1940, just as the Regiment began its move to Camp Borden. Trooper Avery Sharpe, holding the pony, is dressed in khaki denim battledress, one of the most un-soldier-like uniforms the Horse Guards were ever required to wear. (GGHG Archives)

The Minister of National Defence for Air, The Hon. Charles Power, inspecting the airfield guard provided by the Horse Guards at Camp Borden, July 1940. (GGHG Archives)

For the next two months the Regiment concentrated its efforts on learning to use their new mounts. The riders recruited from motorcycle clubs were given a quick course in techniques of instruction by Major Thomas, and they taught the rest of the Regiment the fundamentals of how to ride the bikes. Initially privately owned motorcycles were used, but in early September the unit was issued with 66 military combination motorcycles – powerful cycles with sidecars – along with a variety of trucks for the echelon. The training first focused on basic handling of the machines on the roads in the camp, but it soon progressed to cross-country driving in the sand of the training area, crossing water and mud obstacles, climbing steep embankments, driving through woods, emergency stops by sliding the machine on its side and other hair-raising manoeuvres. Most thought the driving was enormous fun, but some of the officers and NCOs whose job it was to ride in the sidecar admitted to long periods of white knuckles.

By the time the Regiment reached Camp Borden they found that they were no longer in the cavalry. The Canadian Armoured Corps had been founded on 13 August, and the motorcycle regiments were a component of the new Corps. While the Horse Guards were still formally a unit of Military District No. 2, in Borden they came under Colonel F.F. Worthington, the commandant of the Canadian Armoured Fighting Vehicles Training Centre, who for some years had been the driving force behind the creation of a mechanized arm in the Canadian Army. Colonel Worthington was of great assistance in sorting out the peculiarities of the unit's war establishment with authorities in Ottawa.

By the end of September, all of the hard training on the motorcycles in the Camp Borden training area was showing good results. The Regiment entered a team of Second Lieutenant W. Shenstone and Troopers Harry Van Shalk and S. Willis in the British Empire Motorcycle Club's annual 65-kilometre trial at Woodbridge, and they took top honours for the Horse Guards.

In the meanwhile, the senior officers had been grappling with questions about how to use the cycles tactically. Motorcycles were not armoured cars, even though they were intended as an expedient and inexpensive substitute for them, but it was after all mechanized operations for which the unit was to prepare. On the other hand, cavalry reconnaissance operations were not new to the Regiment, but adapting cavalry concepts to the much faster motorcycles was still a challenge, especially since there were no radios for command and control and passing information.

The Horse Guards team – Trooper S. Willis, 2Lt W. Shenstone and Trooper Harry Van Shalk – which took first place in the British Empire Motorcycle Club's competition in September 1940. (GGHG Archives)

The Horse Guards leading the division-size column from Camp Borden, 'showing the flag' in Hamilton at the end of the first large-scale wartime exercise in Canada, October 1940. (GGHG Archives)

During the first three days of October the Regiment had a magnificent opportunity to practice some of its newly devised operational concepts when it was detailed to provide a motorcycle squadron as the advance guard of a 5,000-man motorized column from the division based in Camp Borden during a three-day exercise. The exercise, the largest conducted in Canada for many years, was designed to practice the division in advancing to repulse an enemy landing on the shore of Lake Ontario. During the advance to the lakeshore the squadron had a reconnaissance troop in the lead and others delivering messages to units up and down the 500-vehicle column, acting as traffic control at junctions, and generally keeping the column moving smoothly. At the conclusion of the tactical scheme, the column was routed through Hamilton and Toronto to show the flag, and the streets of both cities were lined with people who waved and cheered the troops. By later standards the tactics were no doubt very primitive, but the exercise was useful in employing an entire squadron of cycles on a variety of tasks.

Soon after the end of this exercise the Horse Guards moved back to Toronto, where the Regiment was quartered in the Government Building at the Dufferin Street entrance to the Exhibition Grounds. The band of the Militia Regiment, mounted on a truck, met the unit convoy at St. Clair and Dufferin Streets, and led the convoy through the centre of Toronto to its new home.

The Horse Guards were destined to remain in Toronto for the next five months. While many of the men were happy to be home and close to their families, this period is not remembered as one of the highlights of the Regiment's war service. The quarters assigned were very crowded, and it took well over a month and a bout of spinal meningitis among the soldiers to persuade the district headquarters staff to allocate additional space. Equipment was still in very short supply and training facilities were decidedly limited, especially for the slightly more advanced tactical work that the Regiment was ready to undertake.

A great deal of effort was devoted to make training both useful and interesting for the men, but in truth much of what was done over the fall and winter months was designed as much to keep the troops busy and out of trouble as it was to prepare the Regiment to go to war. The Regiment routinely went shooting

Horse Guards motorcycles parade in front of the Princes' Gates shortly after taking up quarters at the Exhibition Grounds in Toronto, October 1940. (GGHG Archives)

at the Long Branch ranges or at the miniature range in Fort York Armouries. High Park was often used for fieldcraft training, there were many map-reading exercises, and there were long route marches to keep the men physically fit. And, because it was difficult in a city environment to maintain a high level of skill in driving the motorcycles, squadrons routinely took their men outside the city on tactical schemes. The exercises at this time were kept at a fairly basic level to give troop and section leaders practice in deciding on how best to provide mutual fire support while advancing by tactical bounds.

In early November the Regiment received 31 solo Indian 1200 cc motorcycles, which added to the 66 combination bikes certainly aided in keeping up the men's interest. At this same time, to show the troops there really was a war on, identity discs were issued, along with coloured field service caps which may have had the opposite effect.

WO I William Huggett, Regimental Sergeant Major of the Reserve Regiment 1940 to 1942. (GGHG Archives)

But Regimental tradition was not ignored. For the annual Remembrance Day parade on 10 November, the Reserve contingent fell in behind the 1st Regiment to march to the Timothy Eaton Memorial Church, and, continuing his long-established practice, after the parade the Honorary Lieutenant Colonel, Colonel R.Y. Eaton, entertained the officers and their ladies at his home in Rosedale.

Winter arrived with a vengeance on 27 November. That day the Regiment was to be reviewed by Major General T.V. Anderson, the inspector general. It proved to be a difficult day, as over 12 centimetres of snow fell, and the march past was "a bit of a shambles" because of the deep snow on the parade square. 'C' Squadron conducted an exercise in the afternoon in driving on snow-covered roads, and practised pushing motorcycles through snow banks.

The unusually harsh weather made outdoor training somewhat of a challenge. One squadron experienced great difficulty with their Ross rifles at the Long Branch ranges, as sub-zero temperature congealed the oil on the bolts, and only about 30 percent of the rifles could be fired. Some might have recalled stories of the problems that troops in the trenches at Ypres had with these very rifles during the First World War! Despite the weather, however, all squadrons continued with field exercises to practice fire and movement and defensive drills. As a break from the bone-chilling outdoor routine, one day the medical officer gave a very graphic lecture on the consequences of venereal disease. Another day a captured German propaganda film depicting the rapid advance of the *Wehrmacht* through Belgium, Holland and France was shown to all ranks. And perhaps as much for the troops' amusement as anything, the officers were required to begin their work day with thirty minutes of physical training.

The approach of the Christmas season brought a lightening of the workload, and every effort was made to make it a jolly

Training to drive motorcycles in the snow was one of the big challenges for the Regiment in the bitterly cold winter of 1940-1941. (GGHG Archives)

time for everyone. On 20 December a Christmas party for children of the married men was held at Fort York Armouries, and on Christmas Day a traditional dinner was given for the men at noon at the Gerrard Hotel. A few days later the officers gave a lunch at the Military Institute to mark a visit by Major General A.E. Nash, a former commanding officer.

While part of the Regiment was allowed 14 days' leave in early January 1941, the remainder continued the usual syllabus of training, and in mid-month several day-long tactical exercises were held west of Toronto. Recreation was not forgotten in the bitterly cold winter: a skating rink was built, with lighting so that it could be used at night. The Regimental hockey team was active, and each squadron also had its own team, but there was, unfortunately, always a shortage of equipment.

Governor General The Earl of Athlone, the Honorary Colonel, paid a visit to Toronto on 20 January 1941, and in traditional fashion the Regiment provided a mounted escort to His Excellency. This time, however, the mounts were motorcycles. Lieutenant Marshall Cleland and 20 men, in 11 combination motorcycles, escorted the Governor General from Union Station to the Royal Canadian Military Institute, where he was to address the Canadian Club. During the dinner His Excellency mentioned to Colonel Locke that he thought that the oldest regiment in the Canadian Army ought to be allied with his own regiment, the Royal Horse Guards, the senior regiment in the British Army. When Colonel Locke politely indicated that this would be most appropriate, the Governor General said that he would do something about it. Unbeknownst to the Regiment, he did just that: he wrote to his old friend Field Marshal Lord Birdwood of Anzac, Colonel of the Regiment of the Royal Horse Guards, to propose the alliance. This somewhat unorthodox method of creating a regimental alliance apparently caused considerable consternation among the

authorities in Army Headquarters, but Colonel Locke was able to maintain that the whole matter was Lord Athlone's personal initiative and he knew nothing about it.

3rd ARMOURED REGIMENT

It was a momentous day for the Regiment when on 21 February 1941 the commanding officer announced that effective the next day the Horse Guards were to become the 3rd Armoured Regiment (Governor General's Horse Guards). The War Diary entry for 23 February noted: "This gives us the action we crave and a chance to achieve distinction in this Modern Arm of the Service. A very important and sweeping change from M/C to TANKS." For the moment, however, the conversion took place in name only, and for the next two months the Regiment continued to train with its motorcycles, although with a noticeable lack of enthusiasm.

The Regiment's distinguished past was remembered on 4 March at the funeral of Sir Frederick Banting, one of the discoverers of insulin, who had been the unit medical officer in the early 1920s. Major Boothe commanded a detachment representing the Regiment, and the Last Post was played by the trumpeters under Trumpet Major Grealis.

The conversion from motorcycles to armour brought a significant increase in the authorized strength of the Horse Guards, so a concerted recruiting drive was begun in late March to fill the many vacancies. But because the Regiment was not, however, overwhelmed with eager applicants, more aggressive methods of attracting recruits were adopted. Beginning in early April, rallies were held at a number of locations throughout the city. The band was used to draw crowds, and the commanding officer would then deliver a heart-wrenching patriotic speech which concluded with an invitation to fit young men to join with the Horse Guards in defeating the

The Regimental guard for the funeral of Captain Sir Frederick Banting, MC, former medical officer of the Body Guard, who was renowned as the discoverer of insulin, 4 March 1941. (GGHG Archives)

2nd Armoured Brigade. This brigade was made up of cavalry regiments which had been mobilized as motorcycle units – the Horse Guards, the 8th New Brunswick Hussars and the British Columbia Dragoons, with the brigade Headquarters Squadron coming from the 7th/11th Hussars.

The Horse Guards travelled to Camp Borden in convoy on 7 May and were quickly reacquainted with its peculiarities: "Sand blowing in great clouds and very annoying…. Sun, sand and wind – what a combination…. It is sand in one's eyes, ears, mouth, food, bed, clothing and then more sand." The next day was, according to the War Diary, "the real beginning of an epoch in the old regiment": the unit received its first tanks – two 1918-vintage Renault light tanks – part of the batch that Colonel Worthington had bought from the Americans as scrap iron. Over the next few weeks the tank strength grew to 14 of the old Renaults. The War Diary commented: "Apart from some of them seeming to be as temperamental as women, the men are enjoying the running of them, albeit they are very, very dirty indeed and awfully cramped inside. It is common for them to 'conk' out and stop, with the result that towing is the order of the day. However, they are better than none at all…." The Renaults also provoked a few pranks, as Lieutenant Allan Burton recalled:

When the Regiment received some extra Renault tanks, our fitters cannibalized several machines to create one 'hot rod'. The fitters' 'secret' run happened one day when I was Orderly Officer. The race track, the road past the Brigadier's headquarters, was vacant at noon until a hopped-up version of a Renault stormed past at 20 mph with steam hissing from every part. The idea was to hide the tank in the

Hun. By mid-April the recruiting drive had achieved good results, and the Regiment was close to full strength.

Major General E.W. Sansom, the commander of 1st Canadian Armoured Division, inspected the Regiment at Exhibition Camp on 25 April, and only days later orders arrived to move to Camp Borden to become part of the newly formed

A typical view of wartime H-Hut barracks in Camp Borden, home to the Regiment from May to early October 1941. (RCAC(A) Archives)

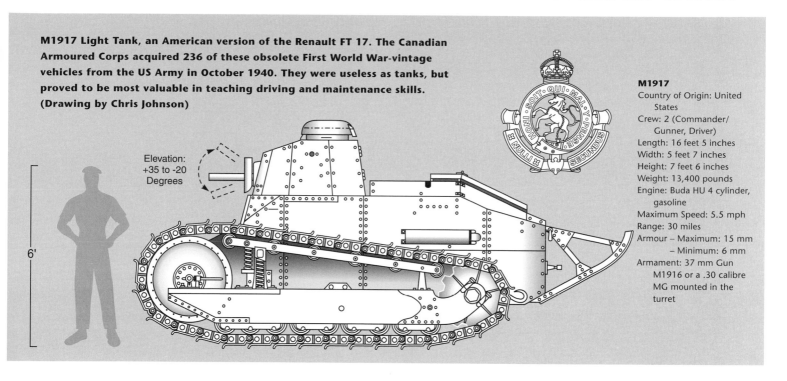

M1917 Light Tank, an American version of the Renault FT 17. The Canadian Armoured Corps acquired 236 of these obsolete First World War-vintage vehicles from the US Army in October 1940. They were useless as tanks, but proved to be most valuable in teaching driving and maintenance skills. (Drawing by Chris Johnson)

Elevation: +35 to -20 Degrees

6'

M1917
Country of Origin: United States
Crew: 2 (Commander/ Gunner, Driver)
Length: 16 feet 5 inches
Width: 5 feet 7 inches
Height: 7 feet 6 inches
Weight: 13,400 pounds
Engine: Buda HU 4 cylinder, gasoline
Maximum Speed: 5.5 mph
Range: 30 miles
Armour – Maximum: 15 mm
        – Minimum: 6 mm
Armament: 37 mm Gun M1916 or a .30 calibre MG mounted in the turret

woods at the end of the road – and the crew to depart – but they hadn't counted on the geyser of steam betraying them. The Brigadier was furious, but fortunately decided the best thing to do was pretend it never happened.

In the six months since the Regiment had last been in Borden, the camp had become a very different place. It was now home to all of the regiments of 1st Canadian Army Tank Brigade and the two armoured brigades of 1st Armoured Division. While H-huts seemed to be going up everywhere on the sand dunes of Camp Borden, there simply weren't enough of then to house all of the units. The Horse Guards were thus extremely cramped in the few buildings assigned, and there were many complaints that the unit lines were too far away from the training facilities. One squadron – the 'duty' squadron – was housed in bell tents for a week at a time to enable two of the huts to be used for lecture rooms, an armourers' shop and storage. The men in fact found that they far preferred the tents to the H-huts, which tended to be stuffy. The major source of grouching at this time, and a problem that was never fixed, was a totally inadequate supply of hot water. For men whose work covered them every day in dust, grease and grime, this was a serious issue.

Training was the sole focus of the Regiment

Badge of the Royal Horse Guards, with whom the Governor General's Horse Guards was allied in 1941.

throughout the late spring and summer of 1941, even though a severe shortage of equipment limited what could be accomplished. Every day began at 0605 hours with 15 minutes of physical training. The Regiment conducted continuous courses in Driving and Maintenance, Signals, and Gunnery, as well as courses for 'Drivers Wheeled' on unit trucks. Additionally, there was usually a basic training course in process to train a continuous influx of new recruits. Many of the NCOs were attached to A8 Canadian Armoured Corps Training Centre for instructors courses, and large numbers of men were sent off to places like the Tracked Driving and Maintenance School at Woodstock, the Canadian Army Trade School in Hamilton, which conducted a course for vehicle mechanics, the Central Technical School in Toronto, which had a course for driver-operators, or the International Harvester Company in Hamilton, which ran an automotive course.

Even with a considerable number of their men away at any time on formal courses, the squadrons did their best to carry on with their own schedule of advanced practical training, getting out in the field as much as was possible. Very little tactical training was attempted, however, as the few Renault tanks that could be made to run were usually used for advanced driver training. Occasionally, however, troop leaders were able to practise troop formations and elementary tactical drills in the sand on Camp Borden's Salisbury Plain.

As mentioned, the Camp Borden sand was all-pervasive and could not be escaped. On windy days it filled the air and found its way into everything, and on more than one occasion there were sandstorms that reduced visibility to just a few metres. In an almost futile effort to tame the effects of the sand, all units were instructed to lay sod around the buildings in their unit lines, which kept the duty squadron busy for many weeks.

Throughout the war years the Women's Auxiliary of the Horse Guards proved to be a pillar of strength for everyone in the Regiment. This fine institution took on the job of providing comforts from home for all members of the unit, as well as taking care of each other, especially the wives and families of the junior men who occasionally needed some form of assistance or support while the men were far away from home. Their members were tireless in organizing fund-raising teas and bazaars so that they could do the many things that were needed. One of the first of their big events was a bazaar and "frolic" at Casa Loma on 16 May 1941, and many men from Borden were given a short leave to attend. The Regimental Band provided the music, and many prominent Torontonians attended. The WA made a tidy profit of over $2,000, quite a sum

at that time, which was used later in the year to provide a Christmas package for each of the men. The War Diary noted on this occasion: "It is such things as this that make one proud to belong to a first class unit with such hearty support behind it and sets all ranks on their mettle not to let down their friends."

Little by little the Regiment received bits of equipment that made training more realistic and much more interesting. At the end of May two 37mm tank guns were delivered , and in mid-June the unit received a RYPA. "This is a very ingenious machine which is built to train personnel in firing from a constantly moving platform and one which moves in an extremely eccentric manner. The name is made up from the initials of Rolling, Yawing, Pitching and Alteration of Course, and these words aptly describe the contrivance."

By early June the extremely hot and humid weather for which Camp Borden is well known had arrived in full force, and there is no doubt that the discomfort had its effect on the men's span of attention on the subjects that were being taught in the D & M, Gunnery and Wireless Schools. In these circumstances, the commanding officer wisely decreed that the Regiment was in need of convoy training, the route for which just happened to include Wasaga Beach. There were many of these convoy exercises during the course of the summer, and, of

Officers of the Governor General's Horse Guards, Camp Borden, summer 1941. (GGHG Archives)

Renault tanks, probably broken down, in the Camp Borden training area in the summer of 1941. (GGHG Archives)

course, the men were permitted to swim for an hour or so during the mid-point break at the beach.

In late June 1941, 'A' and 'C' Squadrons participated in a major exercise with an ad hoc Camp Borden force of some 12,000 men. The objective of the exercise was to take control of all vulnerable points within the city of Toronto, simulating a Quisling-like coup. The Horse Guards squadrons, mounted in trucks, acted as the advance guard for the force, leaving Borden well before dawn and arriving at University Avenue Armouries at 0730. By noon the city was firmly 'held' – with all public buildings, newspapers, radio stations, telephone exchanges and many offices 'taken over'. Everyone entering or leaving the buildings was required to produce identification, which created a lot of public resentment on a day that was extremely hot and humid even by Toronto standards. When the exercise was ended in late afternoon, the Horse Guards bivouacked on the grounds of Osgoode Hall, many of the men spending the evening visiting with families. The exercise force left Toronto the next morning, moving back to Camp Borden in a long show-the-flag convoy via Hamilton, Brantford, Paris, Guelph and Orangeville. Whether or not the exercise had any real training value, it was generally great fun.

Elements of the Regiment took part in yet another exercise on 30 June in a violent sandstorm that limited visibility to about 20 metres. This time the emphasis was on harbouring. The scenario painted the picture that the enemy had landed a tank and an infan-

WO I Arthur J. Finn, Regimental Sergeant Major 1941 to 1942. (GGHG Archives)

try division on the shore of Lake Ontario. 1st Armoured Division was given the task of intercepting the enemy along the Alliston-Cookstown road, and the armoured regiments were required to harbour for the afternoon to replenish and rest, thus avoiding aerial observation. It proved to be a good day, a useful introduction to the camouflage and concealment of large vehicles.

At this time the government was making many crucial decisions about the size and composition of the field army that it was prepared to commit to the war, and among them was that divisions were to be numbered sequentially, whether they were infantry or armour. Thus on 10 July 1941 the name of 1st Armoured Division was formally changed to 5th Canadian (Armoured) Division, although for the remainder of the war it was known simply as 5th Canadian Armoured Division.

Formal inspections by one's formation commanders are one of the unpleasant realities of military life, but unit pride always demands they be taken seriously and the best effort put forth. Brigadier A.C. Spencer, the commander of 2nd Armoured Brigade, and his full entourage came to inspect the Regiment on 22 July. This event was recorded in the War Diary:

All ranks paraded in full web with respirator, steel helmet, etc. The band played very well indeed and all in all we made a smart turn out. However, the day was awfully hot with a fierce sun and NO wind and, as is usual on occasions such as these, the men were kept standing so very long, that many began to fidget and generally displayed distinct unsteadiness, which finally resulted in the collapse of some 6 or 8 troopers. What a thing to happen on a Brigade Inspection! Eventually we marched past Brigadier Spencer, who took the salute, but prior to this the regiment had been minutely inspected, the Brigadier and his staff missing nothing. Then followed the real ordeal of the day, the Brigade officers making what proved to be the most searching inspection of our lines that we have so far had to undergo. Nothing passed unnoticed. No corner was too small. The lines hummed like a beehive all through the long day.... We are showing ourselves just what we are, namely, a hardworking unit with no window dressing or 'spit and polish'.

The Regimental Band, September 1941. (GGHG Archives)

Just over a week later the report from Brigade Headquarters was received: the Regiment was rated as 'poor'. "All in all, the report was disappointing, very much so, and we expect a thorough 'house cleaning' so to speak, with somewhat stricter discipline." The whole process was repeated on 7 August when the Chief of the General Staff, Major General Crerar, along with the Division commander, Major General Sansom, did the honours. "The inspection was extremely thorough and before the day was over every nook and corner, every detail of administration, every vehicle, etc. was under close scrutiny, and we came through with flying colours!"

The well-established training routine continued throughout August and early September, despite the fact that so many unit officers were away on courses that the unit had "barely enough to carry on the general duties." Sports occupied much of the men's free time, and the Regiment proved to have many good athletes. The Horse Guards team won the Camp Borden and the Toronto garrison softball championships, and members of the Regiment took top honours in five out of seven events in the camp boxing tournament.

By early September 1941 rumours were rampant of an impending move of 5th Armoured Division to England. Training continued, but War Diary entries noted a high level of boredom with the routine. The rumours, of course, turned out to be true, and on 18 September notice of general embarkation leave was received. This generated great excitement and a lot of activity getting equipment cleaned and checked in preparation for turning it in to Ordnance stores. The next week was a flurry of kit inspections for the half of the men who had not been sent on their seven-day leave.

The formal notification that the Horse Guards were to go overseas brought the need for an important ceremonial event. By military custom, units going off to war are obliged to deposit their colours in a church for safekeeping until their return. In keeping with this tradition, the Regimental Standard was deposited in Timothy Eaton Memorial Church on 28 September. It was a large and impressive occasion. Both the Active Service and the Reserve Regiments were on parade, nearly 1,000 officers and men in all, the 1st in khaki with black berets, the 2nd in full dress uniform. All three unit bands played appropriate marches and martial airs as they led the long column of Horse Guards along St. Clair Avenue. The Standard was carried by Squadron Sergeant Major Len Binns, who was flanked by Regimental Sergeant Major Arthur Finn of the 1st Regiment and Regimental Sergeant Major William Huggett of the 2nd Regiment. After a very moving ceremony in the church, both units marched past a saluting base set up in front of the Granite Club, where Major General Sansom took the salute in company with the Honorary Lieutenant Colonel, Colonel R.Y. Eaton. This was the last occasion when both Active Service and Reserve components of the Horse Guards paraded together. The men from Borden were then dismissed to allow them to visit their families. Later that night it was a long, chilly ride to Borden in the backs of unit trucks.

The following day was also significant in the history of the Regiment. In a moving parade at Camp Borden, Lieutenant Colonel Russell Locke relinquished command of the 1st Regiment to Lieutenant Colonel H.M. 'Buff' Sharp. The War Diary noted that just as the commanding officer and second-in-command had passed the saluting base, Colonel Locke turned to Colonel Sharp with the words, "It's all yours now, Buff". Major Ian Cumberland became second-in-command, and Captain R.E.H. Ogilvie took over command of 'C' Squadron.

During this frenzy of activity a letter was received from Lord Birdwood of Anzac, Colonel of the Regiment of the Royal Horse Guards, giving formal announcement of the alliance of the Governor General's Horse Guards with 'The Blues'. Other than the Governor General, the Earl of Athlone, who had made the arrangements with quiet dignity, no one knew anything about this, but it was welcome news. As the Regiment was about to move to England, it was hoped that there would be many occasions for close contact with the new Allied Regiment.

By the beginning of October nearly all of the equipment destined to accompany the unit to England had been packed, and fatigue parties were busy loading freight cars. The War Diary, however, noted cynically on 2 October: "With nearly all packing completed, Ordnance must now begin to send us stores indented for in the misty past, most of which must then be returned as we cannot take them with us. This is usual Ordnance procedure." A great deal of effort was made by the Regimental Sergeant Major and the NCOs to ensure that the area of the camp occupied by the Regiment would be left in spotless condition, no doubt to the immense consternation of the troops. With the imminent departure from Canada, one more of the links to the cavalry past came to an end. By divisional decree, all former cavalry units were required to adopt infantry foot drill.

The Horse Guards left Camp Borden on 4 October 1941 on the first leg of the journey to England. The Regiment paraded in Borden for the last time at 1930 hours, and in pouring rain the men were detailed to railway coaches. The train arrived in North Toronto station just before midnight to find hundreds of people there to say farewell. As the wartime movement of troops was supposed to be a matter of the greatest secrecy, there were more than a few comments about breaches of security. The train pulled out a half hour later, and the officers spent the next several hours counting and re-counting the men to be sure that everyone was present that should be, and that no one else had slipped aboard. "All this counting nearly drove all ranks crazy."

The train reached Truro, Nova Scotia, in the early afternoon of 6 October, where there was a grand welcome by the women of the town who gave out coffee,

cigarettes, apples and cookies – something these stalwart women did every time a troop train passed through, and the Horse Guards were genuinely touched by this generosity. Halifax was reached in late afternoon, and soon the Regiment was comfortably aboard the RMMV *Capetown Castle*, a luxury liner that still retained all of her best qualities since this was her first voyage as a troop ship.

The ship remained in Halifax harbour for the next two days while baggage and stores were loaded. Finally, on 9 October the *Capetown Castle* formed up in Bedford Basin with the other five troop carriers in the convoy, along with a Royal Navy supply ship and six destroyers which were serving as the escort. Soon afterward the convoy got under way. The crossing of the North Atlantic was without problems, although in the cold, high winds the ship rolled and pitched fairly violently throughout most of the voyage, and many were seasick. Late in the afternoon of 16 October land was sighted, presumably a hill in Northern Ireland. By the next morning the ship was off

Lieutenant Colonel H.M. Sharp, Commanding Officer of the Governor General's Horse Guards in Canada and England 1941-1942. (GGHG Archives)

(Below) Laying up the Standard in Timothy Eaton Memorial Church on 28 September 1941, as is required of units going off to war. (GGHG Archives)

the Welsh coast. A pilot came aboard, and the ship docked in Liverpool harbour shortly after noon.

"On the way into the Mersey many interesting sights were to be seen – sunken ships, with parts showing above the water, coastal barbed wire entanglements and so forth, but probably the most interesting thing seen was the balloon barrage. There were literally scores of these enormous balloons and a formidable defence they must make, particularly at night." The Regiment had entered the war zone. It was pouring rain, and a strong, cold wind was blowing; an appropriate introduction to England.

TRAINING IN ENGLAND

After an early morning disembarkation on 18 October 1941, the Regiment boarded trains that would carry them on a circuitous route through the Midlands to their first home in Eng-

land, Ogbourne St. George, some 20 kilometres north of Salisbury Plain. The squadrons detrained at the village station after dark, and after marching to the camp site, everyone made haste to bed down. The men awoke the next morning to find themselves in an altogether unwelcoming environment.

It was not the England they had been told about. Ogbourne St. George Camp appeared to be in the middle of nowhere on the bleak, windswept Marlborough Downs, a location described in the War Diary as "an English version of Podunck Corners". The barracks, of relatively new wartime construction, were long, single-storey brick buildings, heated (if one can use the term) by "puny little stoves [which] made no impression on the damp chill in which so many centuries of Englishmen have thrived with stubborn perversity". The tiny hamlet was three kilometres away, but it offered no pub, no diversions and no amenities. The weather was cold and unbelievably wet for much of the Regiment's stay in Ogbourne, and few veterans

The RMMV *Capetown Castle* (left) carried the Regiment from Canada to England 9 to 17 October 1941. (Below) The Regiment assembled on the deck on docking at Liverpool. (GGHG Archives)

have anything good to say about this interlude. The relative discomfort of the troops was not helped at all by an initial period of incredibly bad food. The Regimental cooks had enormous difficulty in adjusting to a very changed scale of rations, greatly reduced quantities and things that were never on any list of Canadian favourites – tinned bully beef, mutton, Lord Woolton sausage (which everyone swore contained sawdust), powdered eggs, brussels sprouts and a very artificial-tasting margarine. On top of that, the cooks initially couldn't cope with the British Army 'cookers', which burned poor-quality coal. Half-cooked meals were a prime source of discontent.

Perhaps even worse for troops who believed they were coming to England to help win the war, there was no equipment. The tanks that 5th Armoured Division had expected to be waiting were not yet available, and there were not even any trucks. On instructions from brigade headquarters, the Regimental hierarchy quickly set about organizing a re-hash of a basic training programme that was designed more to keep people busy and tired than anything else: parade square drill, map-reading exercises, lectures on small arms, and lots of 'hardening' training that usually took the form of route marches over the hills and valleys.

The process of adjustment to life in wartime rural England soon had the men in better spirits. The Navy, Army and Air Force Institute (NAAFI) canteen provided a snack bar and social amenities and, as important as anything to soldiers, it sold beer. The NAAFI, staffed by English girls renowned for their cheeky good humour, came to be the centre of social life for the Regiment in Ogbourne St. George, and indeed in every camp the Horse Guards were to occupy over the next two years. And when the men did venture into the town of Marlborough, eight kilometres to the south, they found the local people friendly and most hospitable, often inviting these strangers from Canada into their modest homes for meals or a drink. A 'landing' leave of seven days, which was granted to everyone in early November, greatly assisted in giving all members a measure of familiarity with British customs and ways.

On arrival at Ogbourne the Regiment was assigned a young Roman Catholic padre, Father Percy Johnston, even though only about two percent of the unit were Catholics. The new padre immediately set out to meet the troops, introducing himself, saying, "My name is Percy, what is yours", and he quickly became known as 'Percy Purple Pips' because of the colour of the Chaplain Corps rank insignia. Padre Johnston did a great deal for regimental morale, organizing sports and entertainment. He also converted some Protestants to pseudo-

Unpacking equipment, Ogbourne St. George camp, November 1941 (NAC PA142611)

Catholics because if a man attended his early Sunday-morning Mass he got the rest of the day off.

Within a month of arrival the general perspective had changed very significantly. Nearly half of the men were sent to advanced courses at Royal Armoured Corps training regiments, and a large number of officers and senior NCOs attended instructors courses at the Royal Armoured Corps School at Bovington. The Regimental complement of wheeled vehicles – 15 cwt (¾ ton) and 30 cwt (1½ ton) trucks – began to be delivered in early November, allowing much needed wheeled-vehicle driver training to proceed. Because these trucks were configured for right-hand drive, drivers needed considerable practice in driving on the left side of the road, as well as in negotiating the very narrow, winding country lanes of England.

The real highlight of this period, however, was undoubtedly the delivery of the Regiment's first tanks on 25 November 1941. A throng of men gathered to watch and admire as two unfamiliar tanks were unloaded from transporters. No one had seen either variety before, and there was a lot of chatter about what 'breed' they might be. The Regiment soon learned that one was a Stuart light tank and the other a Lee medium tank, part of a small batch on loan to the division from the British until Canadian-built Rams could be shipped to England. Over the next weeks three more Lees and one more Stuart were delivered, and with them came six Royal Armoured Corps instructors to teach the rudiments of D&M and gunnery. At this same time the Regiment's Light Aid

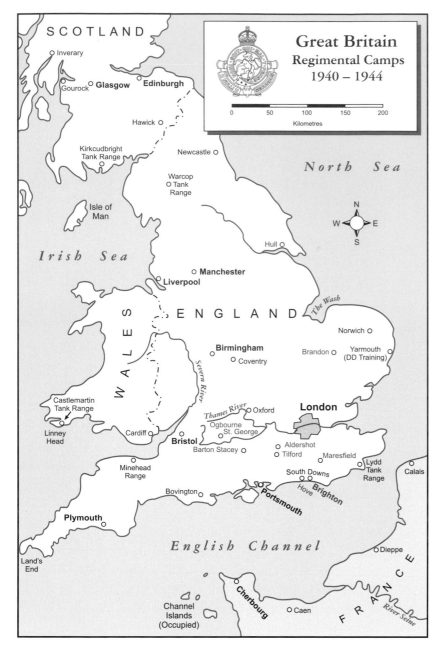

Detachment (LAD), mechanics and artificers then part of the Ordnance Corps, were posted to the unit. While the number of tanks was too small for anything but basic trades instruction, the men at least sensed that the Horse Guards really were, or at least were becoming a real armoured regiment.

The 27-ton Lee was a strange beast that gave every appearance of having been designed by the proverbial committee. It had a crew of six, and mounted a small turret with a 37mm gun and a machine gun on top of a large, rivetted hull. The main armament, a 75mm gun with limited traverse, was mounted in a sponson on the right front of the hull. There were more than a few comments about the strange location of the main gun, which would mean that the whole tank would be exposed when

firing at an enemy. The design of the fighting compartment also left a great deal to be desired. But perhaps the greatest inconvenience was that there was no workable intercom system, and so a variety of means – shoulder kicking and even reins attached to the driver – were used to overcome this handicap. The tank was, however, mechanically very sound, using the same basic lower hull and engine as the Canadian Ram, and it proved to be useful for early training.

The first Christmas in England was celebrated with as much merriment as could be mustered so far away from home, the festivities going a long way to relieving the monotony of the bleak surroundings. Squadron parties were held on Christmas Eve, and these continued with considerable zest and enthusiasm throughout Christmas Day. Every member received a parcel of greatly appreciated practical necessities from the Women's Auxiliary – wool socks, shaving cream, razor blades and other things hard to find in wartime England. And at noon the officers served the men their traditional Christmas dinner, turkey with all the trimmings, which the quartermaster staff had gone to great lengths to acquire, legitimately and otherwise.

The Regimental Band was a great morale booster in this period, giving concerts in camp and in the local villages, providing music at dances held in the NAAFI and playing for parades for the Regiment and other units. The band built an excellent reputation, and twice it was sent to London to broadcast over the BBC. Unfortunately, regimental bands were considered an anachronism in this age of mechanization, and in early April 1942 it was disbanded. Many of the bandsmen were, however, posted to the Canadian Armoured Corps Band formed at the 3rd Canadian Armoured Corps Reinforcement Unit, and they continued to serve the whole Corps until the end of the war.

In early January 1942 the Regiment's place as part of 5th Armoured Division was made more prominent when the first divisional patches were issued for wear on the arms of the uniform jackets. The original issue, which a Regimental sergeant had designed, had been a maroon rectangle bearing an embroidered maple leaf with a spur centred on the leaf. In that the embroidered rendering of the spur had some resemblance to male genitalia, the troops quickly gave the patch a rather rude description. This version of the division insignia was very soon taken down, as some expert on heraldry objected to the spur 'defacing' the national emblem. This patch was even-

The M3 Lee tank, a British variant of the American Grant tank, was provided to the Horse Guards in small numbers between November 1941 and July 1942. While mechanically sound, and thus a good driver training vehicle, the Lee was a strange and essentially unsound design as its main armament, a 75mm gun, was located in a sponson on the right hull and had limited traverse to the left. The secondary armament in the turret was a 37mm gun and a .30 calibre machine gun. It had no intercommunications system, so communications between the crew commander and the other crew members was difficult to say the least. (Drawing by Chris Johnson)

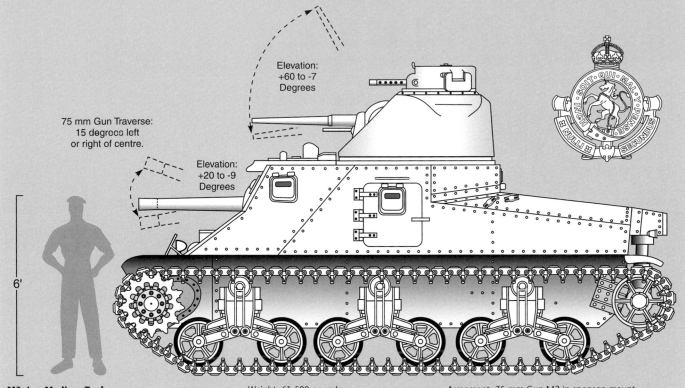

Elevation: +60 to -7 Degrees

75 mm Gun Traverse: 15 degrees left or right of centre.

Elevation: +20 to -9 Degrees

6'

M3, Lee Medium Tank
Country of Origin: United States
Crew: 6 (Commander, 2 x Gunners, Driver, 2 x Loaders)
Length: 18 feet 6 inches
Width: 8 feet 11 inches
Height: 10 feet 3 inches

Weight: 61,500 pounds
Engine: Continental 9-cylinder radial, gasoline
Maximum Speed: 24 mph
Range: 120 miles
Armour: Maximum: 37 mm
　　　　Minimum: 12 mm

Armament: 75 mm Gun M2 in sponson mount
　　37 mm Gun M6 in turret
　　.30 calibre MG M1919A4 in turret cupola
　　.30 calibre MG M1919A4 co-axial to 37 mm in turret

tually replaced by the maroon rectangle on which the abbreviation of each unit's name was embroidered, in green for 1st Armoured Brigade, in red for 2nd Armoured Brigade and in gold for divisional troops.

In an effort to concentrate the two armoured brigades of 5th Division, in late January 1942 the 2nd Armoured Brigade was moved from Ogbourne St. George and Marlborough into the area south of Aldershot, where 1st Armoured Brigade had been based since its arrival. The Horse Guards left Ogbourne in convoy early on the morning of 28 January. The War Diary noted:

Reveille at 0500 hrs, breakfast at 0600 hrs, then the hurry and bustle and scurrying around in pitch darkness. Road convoy got away early and, apart from very slippery roads, journey passed without any particular incident. Of course we pass lightly over the tank which skidded sideways down a long hill, presenting a formidable yet marvellous side-view to an upcoming and rather scared looking motorist, who hastily pulled over as far as he could…. Again we pass, also lightly, over the various DRs [despatch riders] who did parts of the trip skidding along the roads on their backsides….

5th Division patches, worn on the sleeve of uniform tunics. While the Horse Guards were part of 2nd Armoured Brigade the lettering on the patch was in red. Later, when the Regiment became the divisional reconnaissance regiment, the lettering on the patch was in gold.

The Regimental band leading a parade in England, probably early 1942. (GGHG Archives)

By evening, the Regiment had begun to settle in to its new quarters. Regimental Headquarters was in the village of Elstead. 'B' and 'C' Squadrons were three kilometres west in the village of Tilford, while 'A' Squadron was billeted in Milford, some three kilometres in the opposite direction. The squadrons came to enjoy their relative isolation, and the comfort of the requisitioned civilian accommodation, but splitting the Regiment between the three villages created many administrative difficulties; separate squadron kitchens had to be operated, and vehicles had to be used every day to transport the men whenever they needed to get to sick parade or to the clothing stores. However, the climate in the region south of London was considerably milder than on the windswept Marlborough Downs, and the men found plenty of off-duty distractions in the pleasant and friendly villages.

Since the shortage of tanks would not be remedied for many months, training followed much the same pattern as in Ogbourne. Driver training, map reading and elementary trades training were given emphasis in the syllabus laid down by the operations staff at Division headquarters. While no one was happy that training had to continue at such a basic level, equipment limitations did not permit more. Severe restrictions on the use of gasoline (or petrol, as the troops now called it) hindered the amount of tank or wheeled vehicle driver training that could be carried out, and 'vehicle days', when all transport was grounded unless specifically authorized by the commanding officer, were a weekly inconvenience. Fitness training continued to be stressed, and the compulsory Saturday five-kilometre run was as unpopular as ever, especially when augmented by having to wade through an ice-cold stream near the end.

Field Marshal Lord Birdwood of Anzac, Colonel-in-Chief of the Royal Horse Guards, came to visit the Regiment on 13 February, and the men put on a splendid showing on the parade and during the training demonstrations. Lord Birdwood, as mentioned, had been instrumental in approving the formal affiliation of the Regiment with the 'Blues'(The Royal Horse Guards), and he became a warm friend of the Regiment. To bring the unit more firmly into the family of the British Guards, he even suggested that the Regiment adopt the badges of rank worn by officers of the Brigade of Guards.

Major General Sansom, the commander of 5th Armoured Division, made a formal inspection of the Regiment on 9 March 1942. The day began with the usual ceremonial parade, and all ranks gave a very impressive display of smartness and bearing. Teams of men were then picked at random for a series of tests on basic skills, while the general and other members of his staff inspected the mens' quarters, the kitchens and the vehicle lines. To cap the day, a convoy of vehicles was sent out after dark on a night map-reading test. When the inspection was over, there was general satisfaction that the Regiment had done reasonably well. A few days later, however, the staff report on the inspection was received, and it revealed that General Sansom was not at all pleased with the standard of training he had observed. This was apparently also the case with the other regiments in 2nd Armoured Brigade, so it was decided that the Horse Guards, the 8th Hussars and the British Columbia Dragoons would trade places with the units of 1st Armoured Brigade (Strathconas, 1st Hussars and Fort Garry Horse) located in Aldershot garrison, where training facilities were significantly better.

The Horse Guards marched the twenty kilometres north to

Aldershot on the morning of 1 April. Willems Barracks, which was to be the Regiment's home for the next four months, was one of many similar complexes in Aldershot built in the heyday of the British Army in the 19th century. The grey stone buildings were "of plain and soldierly design, facing across their parade squares to the tree-lined streets of Aldershot. They [were] Spartan in the simplicity of their appointments, but nevertheless contain[ed] all the necessities of a soldier's life."

Training now took on a level of intensity which the Regiment had not thus far experienced, and a great deal was accomplished over a short period. Regimental schools in D&M, wireless and gunnery were set up under instructors who had attended advanced courses at British centres, and these courses operated for eighteen hours a day, in three shifts, over a period of six weeks. The RYPA miniature range enabled crew commanders and gunners to gain a thorough grounding in fire orders, and a small-arms range at nearby Caesar's Camp permitted regular firing of all the unit's weapons except the large-calibre tank guns. Sten guns, sometimes described as a bit of a plumber's nightmare, were issued to replace Tommy guns as individual crew weapons. The newly-acquired No. 19 Wireless Sets brought a significant change for the better in the training of the radio operators, for the tedious use of Morse code could be de-emphasized and more time spent on voice procedure and quick and accurate netting of the sets. By the end of May this hectic pace had given the Regiment a profusion of highly skilled tradesmen and an excellent grounding in all of the unit's operational equipment.

Still, it wasn't all work. The men had abundant opportunity to enjoy the facilities of the nearby pubs, with their barmaids and dartboards, and there were several cinemas within easy walking distance of the barracks. As important as anything, among the population of the town were many young ladies who never lacked for attention from the Horse Guards or members of other units, and dances in the NAAFI and in the messes became a feature of many weekends.

Regimental M3 Stuart Light Tanks training near Elstead, south of Aldershot, February 1942. (Canadian Army Photo 617-16)

(Below) A group of Lee tanks, the first issued to the Horse Guards in early 1942. (GGHG Archives)

Driver training in Lee tanks, March 1942. (NAC PA167118)

While the intensive training was taking place, the regiments of 5th Armoured Division on 24 April had the great honour of a visit by the King and Queen. Their Majesties spent nearly an hour with the Horse Guards, "inspecting the activities quite thoroughly, and stopping to speak to a number of NCOs and men. At the end of the visit, all ranks gave three very hearty cheers, waving their berets vigorously." The King and Queen stayed for lunch, "a simple meal by special request on the part of our rulers" prepared by Sergeant A.E. Tanner, chief cook in the Men's Mess.

A new phase of training was begun in early June, with the focus on troop drills and tactical movement. The intention was to move beyond individual skills and begin to weld the tank crews into efficient fighting teams within the troops. While each day began with a spit-and-polish inspection and a period of squadron drill, the majority of the day was under the control of the troop leaders. A cloth model room was provided for basic instruction in troop formations and drills, and a training area on nearby Ockley Common was used by squadrons in rotation for practical field training with the few tanks the Regiment owned. Officer training also took on the new thrust, with emphasis on Tactical Exercises Without Troops (TEWTs). During these exercises the officers would be taken to selected locations in the countryside, and at each site a theoretical tactical problem would be posed for that piece of ground. Each officer was then required to go through the standard military analytical process of "appreciating the situation". The steps in this process, which each officer learned by rote, were selection of the aim; examination of the factors which might affect achievement of the aim, such as 'enemy', 'ground', 'time and space', 'weather'; comparison of the advantages and disadvantages of courses open; and, finally, formulation of a tactical plan to deal with the problem at hand. One or more of the officers would be selected to present their solution, which would then be critiqued by the senior officers. These TEWTs were generally considered great fun, especially on a pleasant day, but on occasion some of the participants returned to camp with badly bruised egos if the colonel showed himself displeased with their tactical prowess.

In early June the Regiment participated in Exercise "Ram III", the first conducted by the division. It was designed primarily to work the brigade and divisional staffs, so units sent only a skeleton organization to function as 'lower control' stations on the wireless net. The Horse Guards contribution consisted of Regimental headquarters in four Lees, one tank from each squadron, and a representative group from 'A' and 'B' echelons. While there was no tactical realism, it was still a valuable experience for those who participated because they gained an insight into how brigade and division headquarters functioned in an operational scenario.

On 19 June 1942, Lieutenant Colonel Sharp passed command of the Regiment to Lieutenant Colonel Ian H.

Drawing of a No. 19 Wireless Set, the remarkable radio that enabled tanks and other vehicles to talk to each other on the battlefield, and which included an effective intercommunications system so that tank crew members could talk to each other. (Courtesy of Don Graves)

It wasn't all training, of course. Sports have always been an integral part of life in the Horse Guards, and the Regiment was fortunate to have a number of very talented athletes. On 11 July the entire Regiment attended the first 5th Division track and field meet in the Aldershot Stadium, in which winners of the brigade trials participated. The Horse Guards were represented by Lieutenants J.D. Crashley and J.B. Essery and Lance Corporal C.P. Burgess, together with the regimental tug-of-war squad. Lieutenant Crashley won three of the four jumping events, and came second in the fourth. Lance Corporal Burgess came third in the 220-yard dash.

On 12 July the Horse Guards moved by train to the Castle Martin tank gunnery range at Linney Head in south Wales for a fitting climax to this phase of intensive training – the first experience in firing the tank main armament. The week spent at Linney Head was described as "the most solid and realistic experience which the Regiment had ever encoun-

Cumberland, who had served continuously with the Horse Guards since joining as a subaltern fresh out of RMC in 1933. Colonel Sharp was posted to take command of the training wing at No. 3 Canadian Armoured Corps Reinforcement Unit. At this time Major Alec Boothe took over as second-in-command. Throughout his tenure of command, Colonel Cumberland set exceedingly high standards for the Regiment, both in training and in operations in Italy, and while he was considered somewhat hard, he was greatly respected by all ranks.

A period of intensive squadron-level field training was begun on 22 June. The Regimental tanks were pooled so that each squadron in turn could move into the training area for five full days of tactical manoeuvres during daylight hours. The squadron practised harbouring in the field at night, and the 'A' Echelon also got much-needed practical experience in bringing up supplies after dark. The level of training within 5th Division was at this time judged to have reached the stage where the division could undertake limited operational commitments if necessary and it was placed under command of First Canadian Army on 24 June.

(Right upper) His Majesty King George VI talking to the commanding officer, Lieutenant Colonel Sharp, as crewmen demonstrate changing an engine in a Lee tank, 24 April 1942. (NAC PA 168021)

(Right lower) Her Majesty Queen Elizabeth talks to a Horse Guards corporal during the Royal inspection. To the right is the brigade commander, Brigadier C.R.S. Stein. (NAC PA193937)

Truck drivers putting 'scrim' on camouflage nets, Willems Barracks in Aldershot camp, April 1942. (GGHG Archives)

Lee tanks practicing the 'charge': tactics training on a heath near Aldershot, April 1942 (GGHG Archives)

tered." The Regiment took over 28 Ram I tanks early on 14 July, and began firing familiarization practices with 2-pounder guns and Browning machine guns on three separate squadron ranges for the 260 men who were members of tank crews. Later in the day the gunners and driver operators fired additional practices, which were scored. The firing of elementary range practices continued over the next four days. Six crews were selected to fire the complete range practice with the 75mm guns on Lee tanks, using both armour-piercing and high explosive rounds. On subsequent days squadrons progressed to 'battle range practice', in which a troop of three tanks would advance over a five-kilometre battle run, engaging a series of moving targets or stationary pop-up targets that would appear briefly at different ranges. During the battle runs each tank fired 10 rounds of armour-piercing and 200 rounds of .30 calibre machine-gun ammunition, and emphasis was placed on fire control at both crew and troop levels. Those not involved in the battle runs had the opportunity to swim in the rather cool ocean and visit the magnificent castle at Pembroke.

When the Regiment arrived back at Aldershot there was good news: four brand-new Mark II Ram tanks had been delivered on 17 July, marking yet another stage in the evolution of the Horse Guards. Unfortunately, however, these Rams were missing their 6-pounder guns; the production of the guns had apparently fallen behind the assembly of the tanks. With only 23 tanks among the three squadrons at the end of July, the lack of tanks continued to hamper the Regiment's ability to train effectively for much of the remainder of the year. And since the same situation prevailed in all of the other regiments of the division, the Division commander extended the time allocated to troop- and squadron-level tactics training to the end of December.

One of the training innovations made by Colonel Cumberland was to make every Monday an officers training day, when the colonel himself could lead the officers in practical tactics training, sometimes mounted in tanks in the local training area and at other times in more thoughtful, theoretical discussion. In time this would pay enormous dividends in operations, as all officers developed a common understanding of how tactical principles should be applied in practice within the Regimental setting.

In yet another change of locations,

WO I George Bentley, Regimental Sergeant Major 1942 to 1946. (GGHG Archives)

Lieutenant Colonel Ian H. Cumberland, Commanding Officer of the Governor General's Horse Guards in England and Italy, June 1942 to June 1944. (GGHG Archives)

the Horse Guards, along with other units of the division, were moved in mid-August to a variety of camps in East Sussex, near the south coast of England. The Regimental home until mid-October was Maresfield Camp, a cluster of modern one-storey yellow brick buildings. Many remember Maresfield as the best camp in which the Regiment was ever quartered in its time in England.

The large training area allotted to the Regiment in Ashdown Forest enabled us to intensify greatly our policy of troop training. Although one squadron was required each week for duties and fatigues, the remainder moved out each day in their tanks and carried on their manoeuvres. During the week we dispensed with regimental parades, while the squadrons concentrated on training, one squadron remaining in the training area for four days of the week.

While the Horse Guards were busily occupied with their training in the summer of 1942, one of their sister regiments, the Calgary Regiment, prepared for the first experience of battle of any of the Canadian armoured regiments. The Calgarys, part of 1st Canadian Army Tank Brigade, supported units of the 2nd Canadian Division in a large-scale amphibious raid on the French port of Dieppe on 19 August. The Dieppe Raid, which had little real purpose other than to demonstrate to the Russians that the Allies were doing 'something' to hit at the Germans, was badly flawed from the moment of its inception, and it has gone down in Canadian military history as one of the worst disasters of the Second World War. Over 800 Canadian soldiers lost their lives that day, and nearly 2,000 more were taken prisoner. In the aftermath, only three members of the Calgary Regiment's tank crews got back to England, so there were no lessons for the Corps about how to conduct an amphibious landing.

Later that same month, the first units of 4th Armoured Division's two armoured brigades began to arrive in Britain, oc-

Major General Sansom (right), Commander of 5th Armoured Division 1941 to early 1943, with his aide-de-camp, Lieutenant Douglas Crashley. (Courtesy Lt Col Crashley)

cupying the camps near Aldershot recently vacated by 5th Armoured Division. There was little real effect on the Horse Guards or on other units of 5th Division, other than slowing the provision of the new Ram II tanks, which were still in short supply.

On 9 October 1942 the Regiment was inspected by the new brigade commander, Brigadier G.R. Bradbrooke, who had taken over from Brigadier Stein. Brigadier Bradbrooke, who had a magnificent sense of humour as well as great operational knowledge and a truly charismatic presence, was undoubtedly "the most popular and best loved brass hat under whom the regiment was ever privileged to serve".

One of the Regiment's officers, Lieutenant Lawren Harris, was at this time posted to Canadian Military Headquarters to serve as a war artist. Lawren Harris was in later years to become known as one of Canada's foremost painters, following in the steps of his father who was a member of the famed Group of

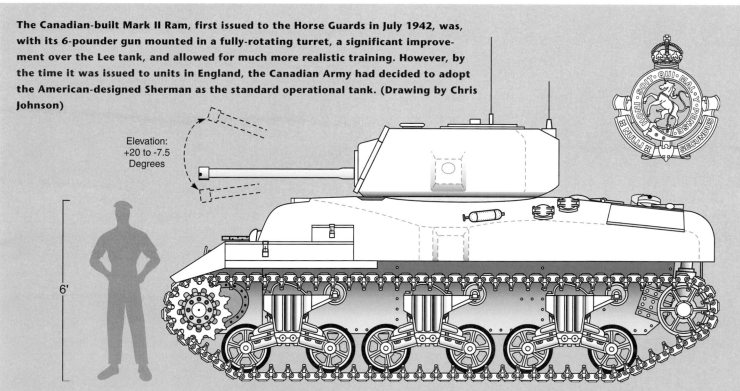

The Canadian-built Mark II Ram, first issued to the Horse Guards in July 1942, was, with its 6-pounder gun mounted in a fully-rotating turret, a significant improvement over the Lee tank, and allowed for much more realistic training. However, by the time it was issued to units in England, the Canadian Army had decided to adopt the American-designed Sherman as the standard operational tank. (Drawing by Chris Johnson)

Elevation: +20 to -7.5 Degrees

6'

Ram II Cruiser Tank
Country of Origin: Canada
Crew: 5 (Commander, Gunner, Driver, Assistant Driver, Loader)
Length: 19 feet
Width: 9 feet 1 inch
Height: 8 feet 9 inches
Weight: 65,000 pounds

Engine: Continental 9 cylinder radial, gasoline
Maximum Speed: 25 mph
Range: 144 miles
Armour: Maximum: 87 mm
Minimum: 25 mm
Armament: – 6 pdr Ordnance Quick Firing Mk 3 (Early) or Mk 5 (Late) in turret

.30 calibre MG M1919A4 co-axial to 6 pdr Gun
.30 calibre MG M1919A4 in hull auxiliary MG turret (Early)

NOTE: Late production versions visually distinguished from early production versions by the following:

– Side doors removed from the hull.
– Access plate on rear of turret eliminated.
– Auxiliary machine-gun turret removed from the hull.
– Improved 6 pdr main gun.
– Improved vertical volute suspension.

Seven. During the Italian campaign he was to paint one of the Canadian War Museum's best-known works, depicting a Regimental tank in the Liri Valley battle.

The Horse Guards made yet another move on 20 October, this time to Hove, a pleasant suburb of the seaside resort of Brighton. Here the Regiment was quartered in requisitioned houses near the waterfront. The only disadvantage of this location was that the unit's tanks and vehicles had to be kept in a park a considerable distance from the unit lines, and trucks therefore had to be used to transport the men back and forth. Being on the Channel coast, with enemy-held France only about 15 minutes flying time away, the Regiment was now very vulnerable to air attack, and the howl of air-raid sirens was an everyday occurrence.

Canadian Tanks Manoeuvring. **Painting by W.A. Ogilvie depicting Ram IIs on exercise in England. (Canadian War Museum 13268)**

The nearby rolling hills of the South Downs, just west of Brighton, provided a superb training area, with plenty of room for the tank squadrons to manoeuvre. For much of the two months spent in Hove, troop and squadron tactics were the predominant activity, each squadron taking its turn in the field with a full complement of tanks for four days and nights. By the end of November the tank troops had all achieved a sufficiently high standard to enable the focus of training to shift to squadron-level tactics. Even Regimental headquarters spent a four-day period in the field to establish procedures for operating the headquarters from tanks, and on several occasions the entire unit operated on a single radio frequency to practice the use of a regimental wireless net. Throughout December, night training was practised once a week to develop the skills needed to work efficiently during hours of darkness, despite Armoured Corps doctrine that insisted that tanks could not operate at night.

One of the Regiment's long-serving officers left the unit at this time. Major 'Swatty' Wotherspoon was promoted to the rank of lieutenant colonel and posted to the staff of the Senior Officers' School. Later he was to be appointed commanding officer of the South Alberta Regiment, with which he served with very great distinction for the remainder of the war.

New equipment continued to arrive throughout the autumn months. By the end of December, the Horse Guards were the proud possessors of 31 Ram I and Ram II tanks, seven Ford scout cars, two Daimler scout cars, three Universal Carriers and one jeep. The combination of more and better equipment, even though not yet complete, coupled with the high standard of trades training and the recent period of intensive tactical training, brought the Horse Guards to the stage where it was finally capable of operating in the field as a tank regiment, although admittedly it still required a great deal more practical experience as part of a larger formation.

If there was a single aspect of the Regiment's time in Hove that was not remembered with any joy, it was the divisional Assault School. This three-week course was intended to simulate battlefield conditions, accustom people to functioning under live fire, and generally provide 'hardening'. Clearly, it was a painful experience for those required to attend. The Regimental history notes:

No battle of this war was ever half as tough or gruelling as the battering experience of the 5 CAD Assault School. In order to prevent death, desertion and a revision of the reinforcement program, the school was finally abolished. No one wept.

Christmas 1942 in Hove was a very different affair from that of a year earlier in Ogbourne. The sergeants held a party for local children whose fathers were casualties of war, and on Christmas Day the officers served dinner to the men. The next day the Regiment moved back to Maresfield.

3rd ARMOURED RECONNAISSANCE REGIMENT

The Horse Guards had just settled back into the familiar surroundings of Maresfield Camp when it was announced early in the New Year that the unit was to have a new role, a new organization and a new official name. In the course of a major reorganization of 5th Armoured Division, the Regiment had been selected to be the divisional reconnaissance regiment as the 3rd Armoured Reconnaissance Regiment (Governor General's Horse Guards).

The structure and operational employment of the Canadian armoured divisions had been under intense scrutiny since the spring of 1942, when the British had decided to reorganize their own armoured divisions based on the lessons of the large tank battles in North Africa. The British had concluded that a division of two armoured brigades was both unwieldy and tactically unbalanced – too many tanks and too few infantry – and that far closer tank-infantry cooperation needed to be fostered. Their pared-down armoured divisions thus came to consist of one armoured brigade and an infantry brigade, and two regiments of artillery. After a great deal of consultation between London and Ottawa, the Canadians decided to conform to the new British war establishment for an armoured division, beginning on 1 January 1943. With two armoured brigades in England thus being surplus to requirements, there was a shake-up in the structure of the whole of the Canadian Armoured Corps in Britain, which included the disbandment of a number of fine regiments and a change in role and employment of a number of others.

When Colonel Cumberland briefed the officers on the important change in the Regiment's role, he stressed that this was a great honour, but that everyone would have to work very hard to develop the knowledge and skills needed in reconnaissance operations. As a recce unit, the Regiment was to have three fighting squadrons, each with three troops of three tanks and three troops of four Universal Carriers. The squadron headquarters would continue to have four tanks, and Regimental headquarters would get its own recce troop, consisting of twelve scout cars. While the new role was to provide 'close reconnaissance' for the division – officially defined as "reconnaissance carried out to obtain detailed information of the ground and of the enemy's strength and movements" – no one, not even the commanding officer, was quite sure what that might mean in terms of tactical employment of the new regimental structure. In the meantime, as this was worked out, squadrons were to continue with training that had been planned before the change of role.

Almost at once, however, the squadrons began to structure their troops based on the new organization, even though it was to be some time before the Universal Carriers would arrive to equip the carrier troops. And, anticipating that the Regiment's most probable tasks were likely to be those of an advance guard – finding and making contact with the enemy; determining his strength and dispositions; identifying weak points in his defences; eliminating the enemy position if possible, or, if unable to break through, pinning down the enemy for the armoured brigade; and, following-up a withdrawing enemy – the officers began to discuss the tactical drills that might best employ the new combination of tanks and carriers.

Another innovation during the period was the construction of a Lorried Command Vehicle, the LCV, mobile mad house or what you will. This was a three-ton lorry, converted into an office for Regimental Control, with a large map board running down its length and resting on a table. The operators cowered behind the map board, coping with two wireless sets on a rear and forward frequency and wishing they were anywhere but trapped in the LCV. On the

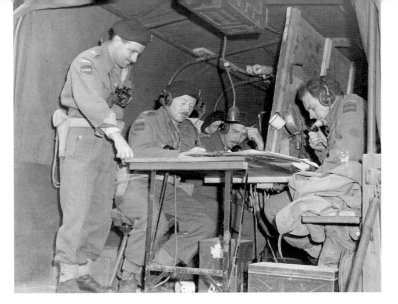

other side sat a clerk, the adjutant and the intelligence officer, keeping a log of the regimental net, marking the battle map and wishing they were someplace else too. The remaining space was occupied by the CO, who presided in the centre, while the 2 IC and the signals officer faced each other across the end of the table, logging the rear link to Division. All in all, it was quite a little vehicle.

It was at Maresfield that the Regiment suffered its first casualty of the war. One day, while the men were lined up outside the mess hall waiting for lunch, German Me109 and FW 190 fighters strafed the camp, wounding Trooper Stan Pilcher, the Regimental tailor.

EXERCISE SPARTAN

Military authorities had decided that the spring of 1943 would be an appropriate time to put Canadian formations in Britain to the test. Exercise "Spartan", the largest field exercise in which Canadian troops participated while in England, was thus planned for early March. It was to involve the headquarters of First Canadian Army and both I and II Canadian Corps, along with six divisions, three of them Canadian. The exercise scenario pictured the army breaking out of an established bridgehead on the continent, a role that was indeed intended for the Canadians in the eventual invasion of France.

For the exercise, 5th Armoured Division and the British Guards Armoured Division were placed under II Canadian Corps, which had only recently been formed. General Andrew McNaughton described "Spartan" as

designed as a strict test of the physical condition and endurance of the troops, their proficiency in movement and tactics and of the ability of commanders and staffs to administer, handle and fight their formations.

In reality, the exercise was intended mainly to test the competence of formation commanders and their staffs. The units involved were essentially just training aids, meant to provide verification of the effectiveness of command, control and planning procedures, although of course they were never told this. Even though there was a 'live' enemy of two British divisions, there was to be very little free play, for the operational situation was tightly controlled by a large force of umpires. Nonetheless the units did get worthwhile experience in living in the field under simulated battle conditions, with little sleep and irregular meals, as well as in the passage of orders and information.

With the recent reorganization of the division barely completed, and without having conducted a field exercise of its own at division level, 5th Armoured Division was in most respects ill-prepared for an intensive exercise of this scale. Certainly the Horse Guards were neither properly equipped nor adequately trained to serve as the divisional armoured reconnaissance unit. In fact, to bring the Regiment up to its establishment strength, 40 Universal Carriers and their drivers had to be brought in from the South Alberta Regiment, the armoured reconnaissance regiment of 4th Armoured Division.

On the afternoon of 25 February the Regiment, along with the other units of 5th Armoured Division, began its move to

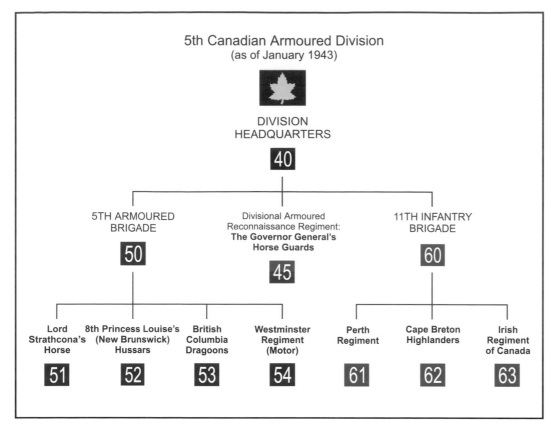

5th Canadian Armoured Division
(as of January 1943)

DIVISION HEADQUARTERS
`40`

5TH ARMOURED BRIGADE
`50`

Divisional Armoured Reconnaissance Regiment: The Governor General's Horse Guards
`45`

11TH INFANTRY BRIGADE
`60`

Lord Strathcona's Horse	8th Princess Louise's (New Brunswick) Hussars	British Columbia Dragoons	Westminster Regiment (Motor)	Perth Regiment	Cape Breton Highlanders	Irish Regiment of Canada
`51`	`52`	`53`	`54`	`61`	`62`	`63`

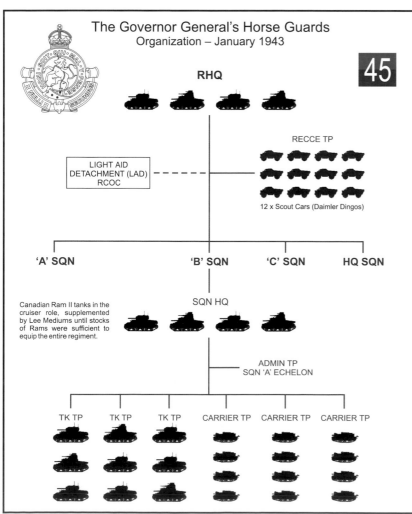

The Governor General's Horse Guards
Organization – January 1943

`45`

RHQ

RECCE TP

LIGHT AID DETACHMENT (LAD) RCOC

12 x Scout Cars (Daimler Dingos)

'A' SQN **'B' SQN** **'C' SQN** **HQ SQN**

Canadian Ram II tanks in the cruiser role, supplemented by Lee Mediums until stocks of Rams were sufficient to equip the entire regiment.

SQN HQ

ADMIN TP
SQN 'A' ECHELON

TK TP TK TP TK TP CARRIER TP CARRIER TP CARRIER TP

the divisional concentration area near Winchester, which was reached two days later. The unit remained in a comfortable harbour here until deployed into a forward assembly area near Andover on 2 March.

The exercise proper began as a conventional advance to contact in the early hours of 3 March, when the Horse Guards, under command of 11th Brigade, moved northward on three routes toward the River Kennet as part of the divisional advance guard. 'A' Squadron was the first to make contact with the 'enemy', and they were able to 'seize' a crossing of the river at Marlborough and take a few 'prisoners'. 'B' and 'C' Squadrons, however, had their first of many such encounters with umpires wearing white arm bands, who ruled, as they would on so many other occasions over the next days, that all bridges over the river had been 'blown'. This being duly reported to the Regiment, who in turn informed brigade headquarters, the squadrons were pulled back into harbours while the infantry went forward to take on the entrenched 'enemy' on the far bank, and engineers were brought up to 'build' bridges. The next day the Regiment reverted to divisional command, and once again pushed forward about 20 kilometres, only to be halted by strong enemy positions near Wantage. So, again into a laager to await the deployment of the infantry. Finding that the enemy had withdrawn during the night, the advance continued on the third day for a further 20 kilometres only to find that all bridges over the Thames River had also been 'blown'.

With its intended axis of advance thus blocked, 5th Division began a swing to the south-west on a wide, left-flanking manoeuvre to capture a crossing of the Thames in the vicinity of Swindon, 30 kilometres west. This move took all night, and no one got any sleep. Toward morning:

THE SECOND WORLD WAR: TRAINING IN CANADA AND ENGLAND

The enemy had reversed a sign post a few miles east of Swindon, so that 'B' Squadron, who were leading, took a wrong turn and the Division was led through the town by the embattled but slumbering LCV, while the figure of Major Jordan was seen leaping through the night, howling with fury at the malevolence of fate and attempting to turn 'B' Squadron around with his bare hands.

And so it went for the next six days, a seemingly endless succession of thrusts, moves and counter-moves blocked by 'blown' bridges or some other umpire artifice. Everyone became increasingly exhausted from continual activity and always too little sleep. Map reading errors became more common, 'cock-ups' became more frequent, senses of humour disappeared and tempers flared. The Regimental history noted: "In comparison with the easy operation of later manoeuvres, it was a scene of hectic disorder, frenzied, sleepless, and often misdirected effort."

As part of the battle-hardening experience of the exercise, an edict was issued that only the British 'compo ration' would be used:

We were forbidden to purchase any local food-stuffs, but the English farmers' addiction to bully [tinned corned beef] was soon discovered, and many an English egg was smuggled to a secluded petrol fire. In lieu of meals, which were frequently irregular, we munched away at hard tack and bully, hard tack and jam and just plain hard tack until our mouths ached and our jaws stiffened.

The ordeal came to an end on the morning of 12 March near the town of Huntington, just as the Regiment had been halted by yet another line of 'blown' bridges. The order "Spartan, Cease Fire, Spartan" came over the radio. "With the greatest of haste and no confusion, we dashed back to our harbour and

cooked hot breakfast." Two days later the Regiment, barely recovered from its near-exhaustion, set out on the journey back to Maresfield. As an indication of the level of effort, the unit's tanks had logged over 600 kilometres in less than two weeks.

In later years we were to pass through days of grim and punishing endurance, but Spartan was a combination which was never really equalled. It will remain in our memories forever, the battle to end all battles, the scheme to end all schemes.

DEVISING ARMOURED RECCE TACTICS

For the first weeks after returning to Maresfield, maintenance was the first priority, as most vehicles had been driven to their limits during Exercise "Spartan". Once the vehicles had been looked after, training in the new armoured reconnaissance role was soon in full swing. The most pressing issue clearly was how the carrier troops could best be employed in a mixed tank-carrier squadron. There was no established doctrine to use as a guide, and it became necessary to develop the tactics from scratch. In early April a senior officer came from Division headquarters to lecture on the role of the armoured recce

Universal Carrier. This versatile vehicle, often called a 'Bren Gun Carrier', was widely used during the war in motorized infantry battalions and some were employed in the infantry division recce regiments. It was not, however, a particularly good vehicle for the armoured divisions' heavy armoured recce units such as the Horse Guards because it was such a mismatch with tanks. It could not keep up with tanks moving cross country, and its lack of armour protection and open top made it especially vulnerable to enemy fire of all sorts. (Drawing by Chris Johnson)

Universal Carrier
Country of Origin: Great Britain
Crew: 2 (Commander, Driver)
Length: 12 feet
Width: 7 feet
Height: 5 feet 3 inches
Weight: 9,800 pounds

Engine: Ford 8-cylinder, gasoline
Maximum Speed: 33 mph
Range: 80 miles
Armour: Maximum: 10 mm
        Minimum: 7 mm
Armament: .303 inch Bren MG

6'

Mail from home, May 1943. (Directorate of History and Heritage)

regiment, which opened the way to discussion among the officers about the specific operational tasks of the carrier troops, and how drills could be developed to accomplish them. The procedures tentatively adopted based on these discussions were then tried out and refined in a series of exercises in the South Downs training area.

During this period the new War Establishment was received. At Regimental headquarters the Recce Troop was to have ten Lynx Scout Cars, while each of the three squadrons was to have three tank and three carrier troops. Carrier troops were each officially to have three Universal Carriers. The tank troops would now consist of two Rams as well as one close-support Sherman equipped with a 75mm gun, which was to be crewed by the troop leader. The great advantage of the Sherman was that its 75mm gun fired a very effective high-explosive shell, in addition to a much more deadly armour-piercing round than the Ram's 6-pounder. The first of the new Shermans arrived on 3 April. Ten days later the tank troops were deployed to the nearby tank ranges at Beachy Head and Lydd, on the coast west of Brighton, for five days of shooting. While there wasn't yet much ammunition for the Shermans, this proved to be a good introduction to their capabilities.

Much of May was devoted to short squadron schemes on the nearby South Downs to practice the drills that had been devised for the use of the mixed tank/carrier squadrons. In the first of these trial exercises, Colonel Cumberland found the work of the carrier troops to be most unsatisfactory, and a fresh set of officer discussions was initiated before yet another series of test manoeuvres was undertaken.

At the same time a great deal of effort was made to convert the mind-set of the troops in the operational squadrons from thinking in terms of fighting as 'pure armour' to the more inquisitive nature demanded of reconnaissance troops. There was a great deal to be learned about what sort of information was needed at higher headquarters that could be converted into intelligence. The troops needed to be taught about engineer recce and the type of information needed about bridges and fords, about conducting a road recce, about patrol reports, and especially about enemy vehicle recognition and enemy tactics.

Even under Ian Cumberland's rather stern regime, training was tempered with relaxation and entertainment, and as the weather got better squadron and regimental sports got increasing attention, baseball being very popular. In mid-June a divisional sports meet was held, which the Regiment won by a large margin, Lieutenant Doug Crashley again being the star. Later in the month the Regiment took second place at a Corps tabloid sports meet. At another 5th Division sports day on 30 June the Regiment won the Division Cup. It was quite a record.

Tank gunnery was the main focus of training during June 1943. All three squadrons spent three days in early June carrying out live firing with the main armament on the nearby ranges at Lydd on the Channel coast. Then, two weeks later the Regiment deployed to the much more sophisticated ranges at Linney Head in Wales, where the unit got eight full days of shooting. The allocation of ammunition was far from generous, but on the first day on the firing points all members of the tank troops were able to fire nine rounds from the 6-pounder gun and 120 rounds from the coaxial machine-gun. Over the next few days the gunners and radio operators fired additional practices from static fire positions and on troop battle runs. During the battle runs the carrier troops supported movement from bound to bound with their 2-inch mortars. The highlight of the period was, however, the introduction to the Sherman's 75mm gun. Major F.E. White of the Strathconas, fresh from exchange duties with the British in Tunisia, lectured on Sherman gunnery techniques, and in particular on the use of the Sherman's 75mm high-explosive round and the bracketing method of bringing fire onto a target.

While at Linney Head the Horse Guards suffered the first fatal casualty of the war. On 13 June 1943, Lieutenant Jack Coleman accepted a ride in a Coastal Command Sunderland aircraft from a nearby aerodrome. Unfortunately, the plane was shot down over the Channel, and no survivors were found.

On departing from Linney Head, the Regiment was once again shifted to another camp, West Tofts, near Brandon in Norfolk. A collection of cold and drafty Nissen huts, it was

Carrier crew during Exercise "Snaffle", 10 August 1943. (Directorate of History and Heritage)

one of many camps that had been hastily constructed on the periphery of a large area recently cleared of civilians to allow large-scale tactical manoeuvres. In fact, all of 5th Armoured Division was in similar camps nearby, and the division's most intensive period of field training was about to begin.

5th DIVISION COLLECTIVE TRAINING

For five weeks it was one exercise after another, each a little more demanding than the last, starting at troop and squadron level and progressing to full-scale divisional mock battles. The Norfolk countryside, a mix of rolling, open fields interspersed with woods, was somewhat like Canada, and it was close to being ideal tank training country. After a brief work-up at

troop level, squadrons carried out a series of one-day exercises, and then in mid-July each squadron got an opportunity to take part in a 5th Armoured Brigade scheme. For the last two weeks of the month, the exercises were at regimental level, focusing on one aspect or another of the divisional reconnaissance role: all three squadrons covering the withdrawal of the division while in contact with the enemy, squadrons advancing to contact, crossing obstacles, patrolling to find gaps in enemy defences, deep reconnaissance, harbouring and the like, all the while stressing accurate and complete passage of information. At the end of the month Regimental headquarters, along with the squadron headquarters in their tanks, each with their three carrier troops, took part in Exercise "Hardtack", the first divisional exercises designed to test the operational fitness of the two brigade headquarters and the units of the entire division.

The next of the major divisional exercises, Exercise "Grizzly", took place in early August. The scenario painted was somewhat akin to what was expected to happen during the long-awaited invasion of France: 5th Armoured Division was to break out of a bridgehead just established on a hostile coast, thrusting deep to keep the enemy off balance and prevent him from reorganizing his defences. And as the armoured recce regiment was to be well out in front of the rest of the division in this scenario, the Horse Guards played the main role. For three days there seemed to be a standard drill: every day the Regiment would push the enemy force, played by the 12th Manitoba Dragoons, back as far as the next river line, where umpires would rule that the bridges had been blown. Every day the Regiment went into harbour while engineers con-

An 'orders group' during a field exercise, May 1943. In the centre of the photo is one of the Regiment's new Sherman tanks; the tank on the right is a Ram II. (GGHG Archives)

Learning to use the Universal Carriers on the South Downs. (GGHG Archives)

Ram IIs in the field. (Canadian Forces Photo Unit)

structed bridges and the infantry seized a bridgehead on the far side. Then next morning, off again for the same drill.

The final three-day divisional exercise in Norfolk, called "Snaffle", pitted 5th Division against the Polish Armoured Division, and was to be the culmination of the division's preparation for operations. Again it was a classic advance to contact, but this time the opposing divisions were both ordered to advance as rapidly as possible to seize a notional 'vital chrome mine', located in the centre of an interposing neutral country, before the enemy could get it. Most participants remember this exercise as being a series of 'mad dashes', with little real opportunity to practice tactical manoeuvre. But, in an exercise of this magnitude, it really was not the recce or tank troops or infantry platoons which were being exercised: it was the commanders and staffs of the unit, brigade and division headquarters who were perfecting their ability to deploy and move ever larger bodies of troops and keep them supplied with food and fuel. In these circumstances some strange tactics were played out. The War Diary describes how on the last night the carrier troops were sent off on their own at 0200 hours, encountering minefields and enemy rearguard resistance, while the remainder of the Regiment remained in their harbours until first light, about two hours later.

By 12 August the Regiment was back in West Tofts Camp, maintaining the tanks and vehicles before returning to the south of England. At about 1545 hours there was an accidental explosion of a round in a fully loaded ammunition truck in the vehicle park, which set off a chain reaction as the rest of the ammunition started to explode. Everyone was ordered to take cover, but Trooper R.A. Johnson, realizing the truck was dangerously close to the ammunition hut, got into the cab and drove the lorry away even though ammunition was exploding all around him. Johnson's quick thinking and courageous behaviour was later recognized by the award of the British Empire Medal, the Regiment's first decoration of the war.

Instead of returning to

'B' Squadron tanks and carriers at the training camp at West Tofts, near Brandon in Norfolk, where the Regiment spent the summer months of 1943. (GGHG Archives)

their usual billets on the Channel coast at the end of the field training, the Regiment, with the rest of 5th Division, was sent to Barton Stacey, a large camp some 10 kilometres north of Winchester. No one thought this especially strange as moving from camp to camp without explanation was simply the way the Army seemed to work, and this was to be home until early October. During this time Colonel Cumberland placed a lot of emphasis on improving the tactics employed by the carrier troops, which had not worked at all well during the exercises in Norfolk.

The real reason for being sent to Barton Stacey was so the division could participate in Exercise "Harlequin", which began on 8 September. Harlequin was an enormous pre-invasion exercise intended to practice the intricacy of moving a large formation through a series of temporary holding areas and ultimately to a Channel port for embarkation. It was also very much part of a grand deception scheme designed to convince the Germans that the Allied invasion of France really would take place on the Pas de Calais coast, opposite Dover.

Once Harlequin was over, the unit resumed tactical training, and for two weeks the sole emphasis was on practising cooperation between carrier and tank troops. But in reality, the training was very much intended to try to work out satisfactory tank/carrier troop drills and standard procedures because no one seemed to be able to devise practical ideas about how the two were to work together on the battlefield. The differences between the vehicles in protection, mobility and firepower were just too great. The culmination of this period of tactical experimentation was a demonstration put on for the Division commander, Major-General Stein, on 1 October. Carrier troops were shown working across an open piece of ground, supported by tanks, and

The Defence Medal, awarded after the end of the war to all members with six months service in Great Britain.

since it had been carefully rehearsed it looked relatively effective.

More divisional-level field exercises followed in the first half of October 1943 and, as had become the rule, they focused exclusively on the offensive, with the Horse Guards in the role of advance guard. But the exercises were becoming increasingly sophisticated as the Regiment was made into an all-arms battle group, with two infantry companies, artillery observers and engineer recce detachments in support. The four-day Exercise "Ditto" was certainly more lively than most. While 'A' and 'B' Squadrons advanced on either side of the division centre line, 'C' Squadron did a right flanking of an enemy defensive position holding up the attack. When the inevitable river line was reached, the umpires actually allowed one squadron to cross to capture and hold a shallow bridgehead. On the final day the Regimental Recce Troop managed to get behind the enemy's main defensive line, and, by reporting detailed information on the locations and state of the enemy positions, tank troops also got behind the position and forced the enemy force to withdraw.

While it was not known at the time, this exercise marked the culmination of the Horse Guards' operational training.

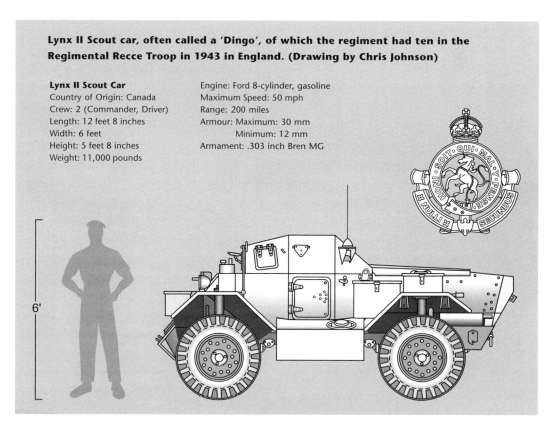

Lynx II Scout car, often called a 'Dingo', of which the regiment had ten in the Regimental Recce Troop in 1943 in England. (Drawing by Chris Johnson)

Lynx II Scout Car
Country of Origin: Canada
Crew: 2 (Commander, Driver)
Length: 12 feet 8 inches
Width: 6 feet
Height: 5 feet 8 inches
Weight: 11,000 pounds

Engine: Ford 8-cylinder, gasoline
Maximum Speed: 50 mph
Range: 200 miles
Armour: Maximum: 30 mm
Minimum: 12 mm
Armament: .303 inch Bren MG

6'

The Regimental 'B' Echelon, 1943. (GGHG Archives)

Never again would they take part in training at this level; the next time it would be for real. All the squadrons, and all their troops had mastered the essentials of armoured recce operations. The drivers, gunners, radio operators, mechanics, echelon truck drivers, cooks, clerks and other tradesmen all knew their jobs, and the Regimental family – for that was what it had become – knew and trusted each other and got along about as well as any family does.

OPERATION "TIMBERWOLF"

When 'Ditto' was over on 15 October 1943, the Regiment was again moved to the south coast, this time to Preston Park on the outskirts of Brighton. It proved to be a delightful location. The troops were comfortably billeted with families in the town, and the Regiment was assigned a former college building large enough to house all of the offices and orderly rooms and a sizeable vehicle park. But this was not to last.

Operation "Timberwolf", the plan to deploy a second division and a corps headquarters to Italy, had been in train since the summer of 1943, when the Prime Minister first raised the matter with Winston Churchill at the Quebec Conference. The problem, it seemed, was that Canadian politicians and some influential newspaper editors were questioning what the Canadian Army was doing sitting on its 'duff' after several years of training in England. Many senior military officers also thought that providing operational experience to another division would be beneficial to the overall standard of training for the invasion of North West Europe. The British initially were opposed, but eventually gave in to Canadian political pressure. There were conditions, however: it was to be strictly an exchange of personnel – the Canadian division would have to take over equipment left behind by British formations being returned to England. And, even though General Sir Harold Alexander, commander of the Eighth Army, insisted there was

no need for an additional armoured division in Italy, that was what the Canadians insisted on providing. The deployment was approved by the British and Canadian governments on 12 October 1943, and implementation began almost immediately under cover of a move of 5th Armoured Division to Ireland.

On the afternoon of the second day in Brighton, the colonel called the officers together to announce that the Regiment would very soon be moving to Northern Ireland, where a complete set of new American equipment would be drawn. The next day the men were briefed, but by then the news had already leaked out.

The next three weeks were filled with a frenzy of preparations. Sten guns were exchanged for Thompson sub-machine guns; everyone was jabbed several times to immunize against typhoid, smallpox and sundry other dreaded diseases; and there was one kit inspection after another. The issue of tropical uniforms and equipment on 22 October brought rife speculation about where the division really was being sent. If there was one thing everyone agreed on about the destination, it wasn't going to be Northern Ireland! As final sign, on 4 November the Regiment's complement of tanks and carriers were driven in convoy to be turned in at an Ordnance depot in Woking. Then on 12 November the main body moved by train to Bristol, and by 1900 hours everyone was safely aboard HMS *Scythia*. The Strathconas and the headquarters of 5th Armoured Brigade were also aboard, and with a human cargo of close to 1,700, the troop decks were very crowded.

After two days of strong winds and rough seas, reminiscent of the crossing of the Atlantic just over two years earlier, the ship dropped anchor off Gourock on the Clyde River on the morning of 15 November while a convoy was formed. Just after 2030 hours the ship got underway again. The Horse Guards unceremoniously said farewell to Great Britain.

CHAPTER FIVE

THE SECOND WORLD WAR

OPERATIONS IN ITALY AND HOLLAND

♩ = 108. PURSUE

The first part of the voyage to an as yet unknown clime was without incident, and the weather became progressively warmer and the sea increasingly calmer. The men had ample free time to wander on the open decks, watching seagulls or the other ships in the convoy, but the daily boat drill to see how quickly the troops could evacuate the troop decks was a constant reminder that German submarines might be lying in wait. On the fourth day, Brigadier Bradbrooke, the armoured brigade commander, spoke over the ship's public address system to tell the troops that 5th Armoured Division was now part of I Canadian Corps and that their destination was Italy.

The convoy passed through the Straits of Gibraltar just after dusk on 24 November 1943. In neutral Spain the coastal towns were brightly lit, a pleasant if unfamiliar sight after two years of blackout. Two days later the ship dropped anchor in Algiers harbour. It certainly looked like an exotic place, and the War Diary comments that watching the lethargic Arab dock hands provided considerable amusement. The Regiment offloaded from the *Scythia* in the early afternoon, then was split into two parties. Regimental headquarters and the Headquarters Squadron – which were to form the Regimental vanguard in Italy, along with a group of drivers and mechanics from 'A' Squadron – were immediately put aboard a smaller French ship, the *Ville d'Oran*. They were taken further along the Al-

gerian coast to the port of Phillippeville, where they boarded HMT *Cameronian* for the rest of the trip to Italy.

In the meantime, back in Algeria, the three fighting squadrons were moved by truck to a British staging camp sited under huge umbrella pines in the Forêt de Ferdinand, some 25 kilometres west of Algiers. Here, in the company of all of the other units of the division, they were to enjoy three weeks of relative indolence in the Mediterranean sun while waiting for ships to take them on to Italy. Major Allan Burton, in charge of the Canadian camp, recalled:

We were located next to a Ghurka battalion, the famed Nepalese soldiers. Their CO bet me that they could steal our flag one night, even if we ringed the flagpole with soldiers side by side. That night I put two rings of our men, almost interlocked, around the pole, but the Ghurkas, true to their promise, somehow got through and 'stole' the flag without raising any alarm or even being seen.

THE ITALIAN WINTER

As the *Cameronian* sailed into the Bay of Naples on the morning of 1 December 1943, the passengers had a magnificent view of the famed Isle of Capri, the lush coastline of the Sorrento peninsula and the historic volcano Mount Vesuvius. However, the picture changed markedly with the approach to the docks in Naples harbour. Here, the detritus of war – sunken ships with broken masts rising out of the water, rubbled buildings and

Idyll in the Forêt de Ferdinand in Algeria: Major Hugman, Lt. Brown, Lt. Essery, Lt. Jamieson, Lt. Hood, Capt. Baker, Lt. Dawson, Capt. Chant. (Courtesy LCol Baker)

bombed-out quays – reminded everyone this was a war zone.

It was late afternoon before the Regimental party disembarked. Major Alec Boothe and some of the advance party men were waiting on the docks to lead them through the narrow streets of old Naples to a group of beat-up trucks parked in a nearby square. After a 12-kilometre journey beyond the outskirts the trucks came to a halt and unloaded their human cargoes at the edge of a sodden potato field in the village of Afragola in which dozens of pup tents had been set up, home for the next five days.

Bright and early on the morning of 2 December the drivers, fitters and mechanics set to work. The advance party had already taken over trucks and scout cars from the 11th Hussars, an elite British cavalry regiment known as the 'Cherry Pickers', who had served through the bitter battles of the North African desert campaign as a recce regiment with 7th Armoured Division (The Desert Rats). In polite terms, the vehicles were somewhat the worse for wear, having crossed the Sahara from El Alamein to Tunisia under fire from the *Afrika Korps*. In less polite terms, the majority of the vehicles were absolute junk – the worn-out crocks left over from the war in Africa. Very few were even in running condition, and most needed an enormous amount of work just to get the engines going. The divisional War Diary quoted the British officer in charge of the vehicle handover as being "frank to admit that units of Eighth Army had picked over the equipment before any was delivered." There were, however, no options; the Canadian military authorities had agreed as a condition of getting 5th Armoured Division into action in Italy that they would take over the vehicles of British units being sent back to England. The new commander of 5th

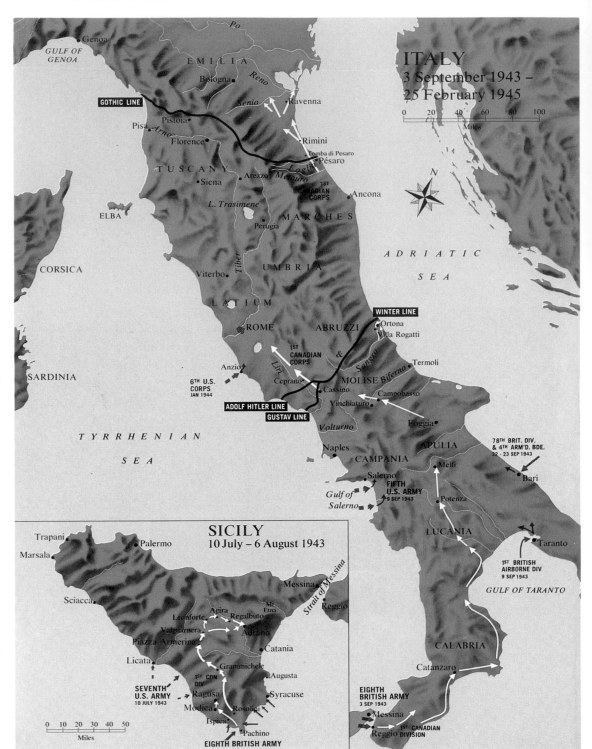

DEPARTMENT OF NATIONAL DEFENCE

Division, Major General Guy Simonds, had, however, made a very smart decision: the division was going to get brand new Shermans and Honeys rather than take over 7th Armoured Division's tanks. But they were going to have to wait for some weeks until the new tanks came.

General Simonds, who had taken over command of the division only on 1 November, had made arrangements for it to be concentrated for training and refitting in southern Italy, around the towns of Matera and Altamura. So while the mechanics did their best to get the unit's wheeled vehicles in running condition, Colonel Cumberland set out for Matera to get the lay of the land and plan for the Regiment's arrival. The convoy of Regimental vehicles started in convoy with other 5th Division units on the morning of 7 December. It took two full days to get to Matera, mainly on narrow, twisting, mountainous roads which severely tried the diminished capability of the trucks, jeeps and scout cars. It was a great testament to the skill and ingenuity of the Regimental fitters that not one vehicle broke down during this 260-kilometre move, quite in contrast to the performance of the other units of the division, which left vehicles strewn from one end of the route to the other.

Passing through innumerable villages and towns along the way, the drivers had a close view of the dismal living conditions in southern Italy – the desperate poverty, no doubt made worse by the war; the poorly clothed, dirty and nearly starved

Scene in Naples harbour about the time the Horse Guards advance party arrived. (GGHG Archives)

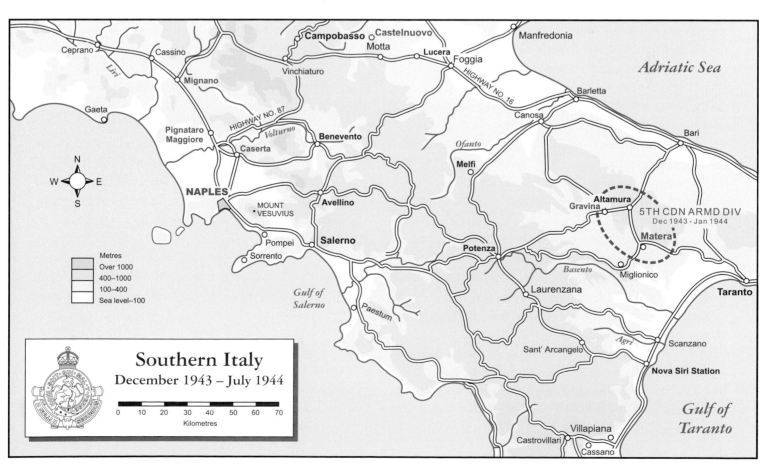

Southern Italy

December 1943 – July 1944

0 10 20 30 40 50 60 70
Kilometres

Contemporary postcard depicting the centre of Matera. The owner of the card has marked (X) where he spent Christmas 1943. (GGHG Archives)

children who crowded around in throngs to beg every time the vehicles halted; the obvious lack of basic sanitation and thus the vile smells that pervaded the atmosphere. It was not an inviting place.

Matera, an ancient centre of about 20,000 people, was like so many southern Italian towns perched on the crest of a hill. The principal buildings – an elaborate baroque ducal palace, a 13th-century cathedral and the town's administrative buildings – surrounded the main square or piazza. Narrow, winding streets led to the lower levels, with the hovels of the poorest, often still caves, at the lowest level. Somehow the Horse Guards managed to lay claim to the grandest buildings in the centre – the provincial government building for Regimental headquarters, the cathedral school for mens' quarters, the palace of the Duke of San Candida for the Officers' Mess and an adjoining mansion belonging to a Count Gattini for the Sergeants' Mess and quarters. There was considerable competition for the few buildings that could be used as accommodation, since both the Strathconas and the British Columbia Dragoons were also billeted in Matera. As a consequence, the three fighting squadrons were all placed in tented camps a considerable distance from town, although one squadron was always kept in Matera for guard and picquet duties.

Back in Algeria, the Regimental officers attended a mess dinner given in their honour by the officers of the Queen's Bays, one of the unit's allied regiments in the British Army, who were located nearby. This was the first occasion when the officers of the two regiments had met at a social occasion, and by all accounts liquid refreshments flowed freely and it was a

very memorable evening. The unit sergeants participated in a similar event a few days later. However, the troops found their brief holiday in the sun ended on 16 December, when the main body of 5th Division began its move to Italy. The Regiment embarked on the SS *Antenor* the next morning and on 19 December arrived in Naples with the other armoured units of the division. After a brief halt in the Naples holding camp, the fighting squadrons arrived in Matera on 23 December, just in time to settle in at tented camps near Gravina before celebrating Christmas.

Veterans of the Italian campaign were unanimous in the view that Christmas 1943 was the best in all the years overseas. Foraging parties had scoured the area for turkeys and other large fowl, so the traditional dinner could be served to everyone, even though a shortage of space meant that squadrons had to come in to the dinner over three successive days. Everyone got a bottle of Canadian beer, a great luxury, and a group of Headquarters Squadron sergeants put on a superb concert party. Technicolour movies of the Women's Auxiliary picnic were shown, giving the men the welcome opportunity of watching moving pictures of wives and children they had not seen in over two years. And, of course, there was far too much indulgence in Italian wine, with the inevitable consequences the next day. But it was a grand time while it lasted.

The Second World War history commented eloquently on living conditions in the squadron camps during the first winter in Italy:

Canteen tents were erected to provide a centre for the men; but the two-man one-room pup tent was the basic housing unit and no prefabricated palace was ever subjected to so many variations. Pup tents were built up and pup tents were dug down. Pup tents were fitted up with tin can stove pipes and tin can fires. Pup tents were flooded and pup tents were burned to the ground. In pup tents one lived and in pup tents one slept. In pup tents one fought lizards and the ravages of the weather. There was never anything quite like a pup tent.

The first major divisional activity organized in Italy was a senior officers' study conference, which took place in the first week in January 1944. Each of the arms and services units had to make a three-period presentation explaining their organization, roles and tactics, and preparing it kept the colonel, the second-in-command and the squadron commanders very busy for several days. This group drove to Division headquarters in Altamura on 27 December to rehearse the presentation for General Simonds. Colonel Cumberland made a brief introduction about the armoured recce regiment and its roles, after which Major Jordan briefed on the organization of the unit and how it should be used as the division advance guard. Then the other squadron commanders provided skits which brought out how the tank and carrier troops were employed, and how all-arms cooperation could be coordinated during an advance guard operation. At the end, General Simonds rather took the wind out of their sails by announcing that he was not at all satisfied with the Regiment's organization. He also made it plain that he thought tanks had a very limited role in the mountainous Italian terrain, and that the armoured regiments and infantry battalions of the division were probably quite capable of performing whatever reconnaissance was needed. This attack on just about everything the Regiment had been training to do for the past year was hardly what the colonel and squadron commanders expected to hear from Simonds, but, dutifully, the presentation was appropriately simplified and altered.

Perhaps the most useful thing to come out of this study period was far better comprehension by the officers of the nature of warfare in the Italian campaign. As the next few months passed and the Regimental officers came to understand the limitations imposed by the Italian terrain, they also came to recognize that Simonds' views were pretty much on the mark. There would be no bold and sweeping divisional offensives where the Horse Guards would dash forward as the advance guard to pinpoint the locations of a withdrawing enemy. Serving as a flank guard was a much more likely role,

One of the infamous pup tents in the area of Gravina, typical of the improvisation so common at this time. Note the 'foundation' of bricks to raise the roof, and even the brick 'patio'. (NAC PA204151)

and even then a lot of the work would probably have to be dismounted.

Despite Simonds' dim views about the need for armoured recce, the Regiment seemed to have a high priority within the division for being equipped with the new Shermans. In the first week of January 1944, thirty were delivered out of the Regimental entitlement of 43, and this before the tank regiments in 5th Brigade got their allotment. However, this apparent good fortune didn't last. On 9 January the Regiment was ordered to turn over all the Shermans to the Strathconas, who had suddenly been ordered to the Arielli front to gain battle experience.

Without tanks or carriers there was not much armoured recce training that could be done, so the unit spent most of January doing a variety of elementary training which while no doubt useful was more than anything intended to keep the men busy. It included a heavy dose of physical fitness training and basic infantry work such as obstacle courses, cliff climbing, bayonet practice and foot patrolling, along with firing small arms and the 2-inch mortar. Thrown in were some essential recce skills such as a map-reading refresher, judging

A group of Horse Guards in Matera, January 1944. (GGHG Archives)

distance and setting up observation posts, and the engineers gave interesting lectures on enemy mines and booby traps. The officers were briefed by the commander of the artillery regiment on directing artillery fire. In addition, perhaps inspired (or intimidated) by General Simonds' doubts about armoured recce, Colonel Cumberland decided to form a Regimental Assault Troop by taking the men from the Anti-Aircraft Troop, which was not needed in Italy because the Germans had such limited air capability.

Then, on 22 January 1944, the Regiment was informed that its War Establishment – the authorized organization and scale of equipment – had been significantly changed. Each of the fighting squadrons was authorized to have five instead of six troops, but instead of the separate tank and carrier troops of the recent past, the recce troops were now composite organizations of two Shermans and two Stuart light tanks. The Regiment would retain eight White wheeled scout cars for the RHQ Recce Troop, but it was going to have to give up the Daimler Dingo scout cars taken over from the British in Naples.

The new structure of the squadrons led to renewed discussions about tactics by the unit officers. The new recce troop organization was a true bastard structure – it could not conduct heavy recce as done by tank troops, nor light, 'sneak-and-peek' recce as could be performed by Universal Carrier troops. Faced with having to work out basic tactical movement, the officers decided that the two light tanks should generally move in front, with the two heavier Shermans giving fire support from the rear. It was also recommended that the troop leader be in one of the Shermans.

It was 30 January before tanks once again began to appear; that day 'C' Squadron got its first three Stuarts, and over the next two weeks all 30 of the unit's Stuarts were drawn from Ordnance. (These Stuarts still had turrets with 37mm guns; the turretless or cut-down Stuarts used in operations were not issued until late March.) Shermans started to arrive on 15 February and most had come by the end of the month.

Major General E.L.M. Burns, who took over as division commander in late January, continued the practice begun by General Simonds of ensuring that all units got a relatively gentle introduction to actual operations up at the Arielli front. Because vehicles simply could not move in the deep mud of the forward area, when it came to the Horse Guards' turn it

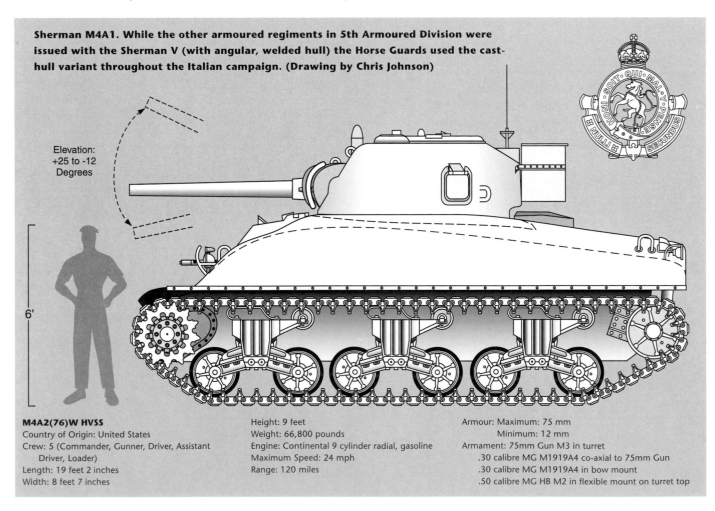

Sherman M4A1. While the other armoured regiments in 5th Armoured Division were issued with the Sherman V (with angular, welded hull) the Horse Guards used the cast-hull variant throughout the Italian campaign. (Drawing by Chris Johnson)

Elevation: +25 to -12 Degrees

6'

M4A2(76)W HVSS
Country of Origin: United States
Crew: 5 (Commander, Gunner, Driver, Assistant Driver, Loader)
Length: 19 feet 2 inches
Width: 8 feet 7 inches

Height: 9 feet
Weight: 66,800 pounds
Engine: Continental 9 cylinder radial, gasoline
Maximum Speed: 24 mph
Range: 120 miles

Armour: Maximum: 75 mm
Minimum: 12 mm
Armament: 75mm Gun M3 in turret
.30 calibre MG M1919A4 co-axial to 75mm Gun
.30 calibre MG M1919A4 in bow mount
.50 calibre MG HB M2 in flexible mount on turret top

was to be dismounted battlefield inoculation. Thus, on 2 February an ad hoc Assault Squadron, with Captain Classey in command, was created out of the fifth troop of each of the three recce squadrons and christened 'D' (known to all as 'Dog') Squadron. The Assault Squadron spent from 11 February to 1 March serving as infantry at the front, under the command of the Westminster Regiment. While conditions in the defensive positions were primitive and uncomfortable, the Regiment's assault troopers acquitted themselves well, participating in several independent patrols into No Man's Land, much like their Regimental forebears in 4th CMR during the First World War.

The rather dismal living conditions in the squadron camps took its toll. Major Allan Burton wrote:

My squadron is decimated with dysentery, and nowhere to send the sickest of the men. Some are too weak to walk, so slit trench latrines have been dug within crawling distance of the pup tents. And we have become infested with scabies. The treatment entailed stripping to the buff and having someone paint every square inch of you, including your privates, with a liquid poison. Eight hours later you had a shower and all the burrowing lice rose to the surface and were washed away.

Back in the area of Matera, an ad hoc tank gunnery range was set up by the division mid-way between Matera and Gravina. On 16 February, 'A' Squadron was on the range firing the 37mm guns of its Stuarts, and 'C' Squadron was firing with its Shermans. The gradual delivery of the rest of the Shermans allowed the squadrons to devote the better part of three weeks to training the Sherman and Stuart gunners, all of whom were new to these vehicles.

By this time, however, it was clear that the Allied offensive in the Adriatic sector had ground to a muddy halt, and that a major revamping of the strategy for the Italian campaign was now essential. And even though an Anglo-American landing at Anzio had been contained by the Germans and an Ameri-

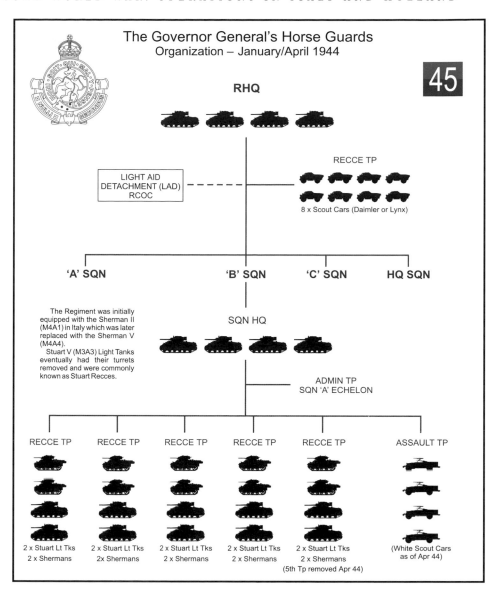

can attack stalled at Cassino, the Mediterranean side of the peninsula offered far better prospects than did the Adriatic. At the end of February, the high command decided to give overriding priority to the capture of Rome and concentrate the bulk of the Allied forces west of the Apennines for a major offensive intended to begin in May. The gradual redeployment of troops for this offensive began in early March. The Canadian Corps was relieved in the Ortona sector on 7 March 1944, and 5th Division moved into reserve in the area of Castelnuovo, in the Daunia Mountains west of Foggia, to train and prepare for the coming offensive.

Strategic decisions of this importance are, of course, not communicated down to regimental level. So the Horse Guards, tasked to provide two ad hoc dismounted squadrons to take over defensive positions held on the Arielli front by the Irish Regiment, sent the squadrons forward on 4 March. The

191

convoy was halted en route by Lieutenant Murdoch, then liaison officer at Division headquarters, and told that the tasking had been cancelled. The squadrons were directed to harbour temporarily near Santa Croce, some 25 kilometres south of Termoli, while the rest of the Regiment redeployed to the new camps immediately south of Castelnuovo over the course of the next ten days.

The division barely had time to get settled in the new area when, on 20 March 1944, Major General B.M. 'Bert' Hoffmeister took over command of 5th Armoured Division. General Burns had been promoted to take command of I Canadian Corps, so the division had its third commander in just over four months. Hoffmeister, who had commanded the Seaforth Highlanders and 2nd Infantry Brigade in quick succession, was to serve as division commander with great distinction for the remainder of the war. The Horse Guards were his personal eyes and ears over the course of many operations, and he developed very close ties to the Regiment.

The Regiment's first encounter with the new commander came on 25 March, when a demonstration was staged of tank and assault troops cooperating in an attack. The squadron assault troops at this time were completely unauthorized, and Colonel Cumberland hoped to convince the corps and division commanders to allow two assault troops in each squadron – one troop in White scout cars, the other in Daimler scout cars. While both commanders were impressed, the commanding officer was told that the unit War Establishment could not be changed, but that "for the interior economy of the regiment" he would be permitted to structure the unit pretty much as he saw fit. However, he could not have any Daimler cars; there were too few of them. The decision was thus made: the squadrons were to remain with four recce troops, with the fifth troop, equipped with four White scout cars, serving as an Assault Troop. In the Assault Troop, each of the scout cars had a crew of eight: a section leader, driver, Bren gunner, grenade thrower and four men armed with Tommy guns. The assault troops were to be able to function both as normal infantry and as pioneers capable of minor engineering tasks. And just in case there was a need to put them back into a recce role, the Shermans and Stuarts of this fifth troop were to be held in the Regiment as spares.

The relatively short stay in Castelnuovo was a period of intensive training for the upcoming offensive, often under General Hoffmeister's personal supervision. Squadrons spent a considerable amount of time firing the tank guns on a makeshift range located behind the RHQ harbour, and in the process all members of the crews honed their battlefield skills. The officers

were introduced to the use of air photos to supplement or replace the nearly unreadable and grossly inaccurate Italian survey maps that were available for issue to crew commanders, and they also attended several demonstrations of how tank-infantry cooperation was supposed to work in deliberate attacks.

Beginning at the end of March, the squadrons began to trade turreted Stuarts for the cut-down versions equipped with .50 calibre Browning machine guns. For the first time since leaving England a full-scale Regimental exercise was conducted, this time practising the protection of a divisional flank, for it was by now clear that there would be no grand advance to contact led by the Regiment during the campaign in Italy. The whole Regiment also deployed for the divisional scheme, Exercise "Thruster", which proved to be a bit of a disappointment as only 'A' Squadron was called on to play an active part before the ceasefire.

"Hang on to the cat. We'll test this one next."

'Herbie' cartoons, drawn by Sergeant Bing Coughlin of the Princess Louise Dragoon Guards and published weekly in the Army newspaper, *Maple Leaf*, tickled the fancy of most Canadian soldiers in Italy. Herbie was always getting into scrapes that the men identified with. Post war Horse Guards reunion booklets were never complete without a half dozen or more of these cartoons. (GGHG Archives)

Surprise orders – for the Regiment at least – were received on 10 April: the division was to move across Italy to the Mediterranean coast, with 'A' and 'B' Squadrons' Shermans leaving almost at once to be loaded on trains. The rest of the Regiment's tanks were loaded the next day, and the wheeled vehicles set out by road. By the morning of 12 April the Regiment had been concentrated near Caserta, on the Volturno River north of Naples. Later that day the squadrons turned in their multi-bank-engine Shermans to a British tank delivery regiment, and had them replaced with M4A1 Shermans with radial aircraft engines.

Scene in 'The Camouflage Camp', near Pignataro Maggiore, early May 1944. (GGHG Archives)

was regularly changed as the leaves dried out. All vehicle movement was severely restricted, and even the movement of large groups of men was discouraged. There was also an elaborate deception scheme involving placing Canadian unit signs in Salerno and fake radio traffic intended to convince the Germans that the Canadians were preparing for a landing on the coast north of Rome.

Finally, on 11 May, the suspense came to an end: the commanding officer and the officers were briefed on the outline of the Eighth Army plan of attack, and for the next week the Regiment made its preparations for battle. As the unit began its

There was not a great deal of opportunity for much tank training in the next several weeks as there simply were few places for it. Everyone, however, greatly enjoyed the arrival of warm, sunny weather and the opportunity for brief excursions to Naples and Pompei. One of the memorable events of this period occurred in mid-April: the first of the Regiment's own 'commissioned from the ranks' officers arrived back after completing their training. Lieutenant Roy 'Fuzz' Richards had left as a sergeant major, while Lieutenants Denny Gallagher, Gord Base and Allan Martin had been sergeants. Later in the month, Trooper Charles Lampman was unfortunately killed in an accident on a tank gunnery range.

While certain security precautions had been taken prior to the deployment of the division to Caserta, such as the removal of unit insignia and division patches, these measures were greatly tightened beginning on 26 April. The word was that "5th Division must vanish on its next move" forward to the zone of intended operations, so extra camouflage nets were issued and all daylight movement restricted. The anticipated move began on the night of 1 May, when 'C' Squadron's tanks were carried on tank transporters to a new harbour area near Pignataro Maggiore, nicknamed for obvious reasons the Camouflage Camp.

In this new camp, vehicles were as much as possible parked in the cover of olive groves and other trees, nets were stretched over every vehicle, and these were covered with foliage which

move forward, Lance Corporal George Bohas was killed in a motorcycle accident near Capua.

During the night of 18/19 May the division continued its progressive deployment toward the front. The Regiment completed its move into harbours in the area of the village of Mignano just after first light. The War Diary describes the reception received by one of the squadrons:

Shortly after our arrival, 'B' Sqn became involved in a pitched battle with a vast and extremely violent family of Italian peasants. Hostilities broke out when the troops began to cut the surrounding bush in order to camouflage their vehicles. As the bush alluded to included their orchard, there was probably a certain amount of justification for their wrath. In no time at all a complete chorus of Italian harpies was formed up in line abreast, screaming all the imprecations at their command in a wild, continuous howl that must have lasted for at least an hour…. The main body finally retired to the safety of a ruined house, occupied apparently by the entire local population, leaving one crippled old crone as a standing patrol. Armed with a face that would have stopped a battleship and brandishing a hatchet, she circled her domain and defied all comers. The affair ended with a remark from one of the troopers, "It's a bloody good thing Mussolini didn't put women in the army".

THE LIRI VALLEY OFFENSIVE

From its beginning south of Cassino, the Liri Valley runs northwest for 24 kilometres to Ceprano, where it joins the valley of the River Sacco that runs much of the way to Rome. The valley is six to ten kilometres wide throughout this length. The Liri River runs generally along the southwestern side of the valley, with a range of low mountains between it and the coastal plain. On the north side of the valley is Highway 6, the main road to Rome, and beyond it a rugged mountainous massif centred on the 1,700 metre-high Monte Cairo, which dominates the first sixteen kilometres of the valley. General Alexander proclaimed it to be the "gateway to Rome", but the Germans also knew this and had taken advantage of every natural barrier to ensure that the valley would not be the easy route to Rome the Allies hoped it might be.

At the entrance to the valley ran the Gari River, also known as the Rapido in the area of Cassino, and as the Gargliano south of its junction with the Liri. The Gari – 20 metres wide and with a swift current – was a tank obstacle throughout its length. Immediately beyond the Gari the ground rose to a series of hills that dominated the river line, and beyond these hills the ground, even though heavily cultivated with olive groves and vineyards, was rough country – small hills, mean-

The Canadian Voluntary Service Medal. Every volunteer member of the Canadian Army with 18 months service was eligible for this medal. The bar was issued to all those who served 'overseas'. Members of the Horse Guards became eligible for the medal in January 1944, and were required to wear the ribbon on their tunics. The actual medal was not awarded until after the war.

dering, steep-sided ravines, scattered woods, narrow sunken farm trails, innumerable small streams and isolated stone farm buildings. Nine kilometres beyond the Gari was a deep gully called the Forme d'Aquino, another tank obstacle over much of its length, and five kilometres further on came the River San Martino. Seven kilometres beyond that was the Melfa River.

The Germans had constructed two formidable defensive lines. The Gustav Line, anchored on Cassino, followed the line of the Gari. The second, the Adolf Hitler Line, its complex of

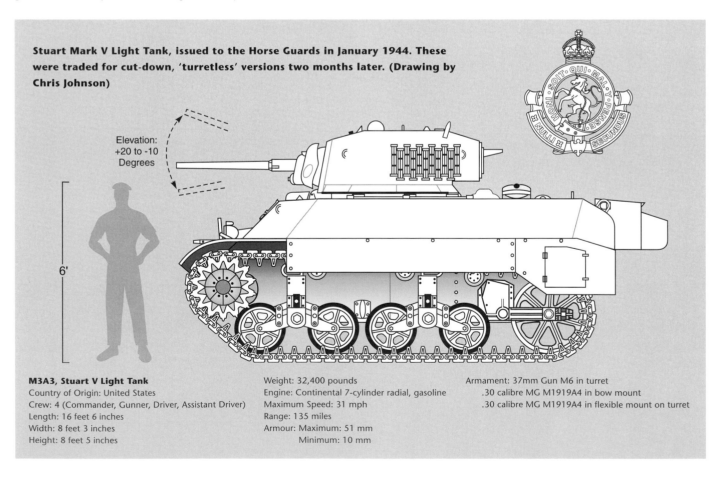

Stuart Mark V Light Tank, issued to the Horse Guards in January 1944. These were traded for cut-down, 'turretless' versions two months later. (Drawing by Chris Johnson)

Elevation: +20 to -10 Degrees

6'

M3A3, Stuart V Light Tank
Country of Origin: United States
Crew: 4 (Commander, Gunner, Driver, Assistant Driver)
Length: 16 feet 6 inches
Width: 8 feet 3 inches
Height: 8 feet 5 inches

Weight: 32,400 pounds
Engine: Continental 7-cylinder radial, gasoline
Maximum Speed: 31 mph
Range: 135 miles
Armour: Maximum: 51 mm
      Minimum: 10 mm

Armament: 37mm Gun M6 in turret
.30 calibre MG M1919A4 in bow mount
.30 calibre MG M1919A4 in flexible mount on turret

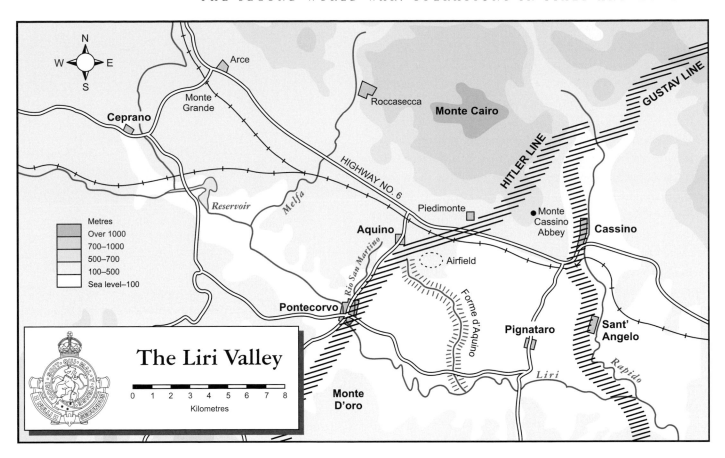

The Liri Valley

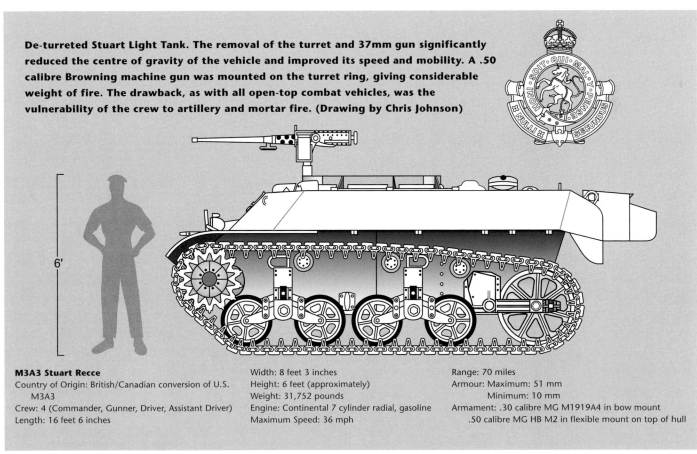

De-turreted Stuart Light Tank. The removal of the turret and 37mm gun significantly reduced the centre of gravity of the vehicle and improved its speed and mobility. A .50 calibre Browning machine gun was mounted on the turret ring, giving considerable weight of fire. The drawback, as with all open-top combat vehicles, was the vulnerability of the crew to artillery and mortar fire. (Drawing by Chris Johnson)

M3A3 Stuart Recce
Country of Origin: British/Canadian conversion of U.S. M3A3
Crew: 4 (Commander, Gunner, Driver, Assistant Driver)
Length: 16 feet 6 inches

Width: 8 feet 3 inches
Height: 6 feet (approximately)
Weight: 31,752 pounds
Engine: Continental 7 cylinder radial, gasoline
Maximum Speed: 36 mph

Range: 70 miles
Armour: Maximum: 51 mm
         Minimum: 10 mm
Armament: .30 calibre MG M1919A4 in bow mount
          .50 calibre MG HB M2 in flexible mount on top of hull

anti-tank gun positions and machine-gun posts never quite completed but still a major barrier, ran just in front of Aquino and Pontecorvo, 11 kilometres behind the Gustav Line. For the most part, the ground between the two lines was not good tank country, but in comparison with much of the Italian countryside, it was as good as it got.

The Liri offensive, code named Operation "Diadem", was to be carried out in three broad stages. First, XIII British Corps, with 1st Canadian Armoured Brigade under its command, would make an assault crossing of the River Gari just south of Cassino and break through the vaunted Gustav Line, while at the same time II Polish Corps was to capture the town of Cassino and the ruins of the abbey at the top of Monte Cassino. Then the Canadian Corps would be brought in to take over the southern half of the valley, below Highway 6. Units of 1st Canadian Division would carry the attack through the next set of heavily prepared positions, the Hitler Line. And finally, 5th Armoured Division would exploit through the gap in the Hitler Line to Ceprano, which would open the way to the beleaguered Anzio bridgehead and then to Rome.

Within 5th Armoured Division, General Hoffmeister broke his plan into two main phases. He assigned the task of pushing through whatever gap was created in the Hitler Line to 5th Armoured Brigade, but in an unusual tactical departure for this stage of the war he created two all-arms battle groups for this mission – Vokes Force, consisting of the British Columbia Dragoons supported by the Irish Regiment of Canada, and Griffin Force, the Lord Strathcona's Horse with 'A' Company of the Westminster Regiment. The mission of 5th Armoured Brigade was to seize a bridgehead over the Melfa River – 8 to 10 kilometres behind the Hitler Line. Because of the expected stiff German resistance, this thrust was to be made on a very narrow front. In the first stage, the BCD and the Irish were to advance to a line two kilometres short of the Melfa and create a firm base. Then the Strathconas would push through to take a bridgehead beyond the Melfa.

The narrow frontage of the attack, meant that a large part of the 5th Division sector would be left uncovered, and the Horse Guards were tasked to fill this void on both flanks of the 5th Armoured Brigade thrust.

The Regimental plan for the flank guard mission initially called for two squadrons forward – 'A' on the right, covering the area between 5th Armoured Brigade and the division boundary at Highway 6, and 'B' Squadron on the left, covering the area to the north bank of the Liri River. 'C' Squadron was to be in reserve. The plan was, however, to be very flexible, since it was not known where or when the first major gap

Major General Bert Hoffmeister, the Regiment's immediate 'boss' in Italy, giving a briefing on the tasks of 5th Armoured Division in the Liri Valley offensive, May 1944. (NAC PA189922)

would be forced through the Hitler Line defences by the 1st Division. An interesting sidelight to the development of the unit plan was the arrival back in the Regiment of Lieutenant Doug Crashley, who had served as aide-de-camp to General Burns both at 5th Division and I Corps. At Corps headquarters, Crashley had prepared all of the maps for the Liri Valley attack: "I obviously knew more about the plans than Colonel Cumberland, but I briefed him in as much detail as I could."

The 1st Division attack on the Hitler Line – two brigades up, each supported by a British armoured regiment – went in on 22 May on a 3,000 metre front south of the village of Aquino. For the most part the attack was an unmitigated disaster. The 2nd Brigade was stopped almost immediately, and the supporting tanks of the North Irish Horse lost 41 out of their 58 tanks to well-sited anti-tank guns and *panzerturm* – Panther tank turrets mounted on camouflaged concrete bases. Immediately to the south, in 3rd Brigade, the story was quite different. Despite a vicious fight, the Carleton and York Regiment broke through the German defences and reached their objective just behind the Hitler Line, astride the Pontecorvo-Aquino road. Even so, most of the supporting tanks of 21st Royal Tank Regiment were knocked out during this fight, leaving a battlefield of burning hulks. But this singularly important if still limited success prompted the division commander to commit his reserve, the Royal 22e Régiment and the West Nova Scotia Regiment, along with the tank squadrons of the Three Rivers Regiment.

The two infantry battalions, each supported by a Three Rivers squadron, moved through the gap held by the Carleton and Yorks late in the afternoon, and to everyone's surprise they met very little resistance. By early evening the infantry had advanced well over two kilometres, but the tanks initially had great difficulty getting across a very small and insignificant river, the San Martino, because of its steep banks and a very soft, muddy river bed. This barely passable crossing of the San Martino was to play an important part in the early stages of 5th Armoured Division's exploitation beyond the Hitler Line; it seems it was the only place where tanks could negotiate this supposedly minor river obstacle.

On learning of the successful breaching of the Hitler Line by 3rd Infantry Brigade, General Hoffmeister got permission from Corps headquarters to begin the 5th Division advance on the evening of 23 May. But the heavens opened just after 1800 hours, and the extremely heavy rain had its inevitable effect: by early evening all roads and tracks had become impassable for tanks, so the attack was delayed until the next morning. One part of the plan affecting the Horse Guards was changed at this time. General Hoffmeister was very concerned about protecting the armoured brigade thrust from interference by German troops still holding the entire northern section of the Hitler Line, and he therefore gave instructions to Colonel Cumberland to send in 'C' Squadron to carry out this task.

The British Columbia Dragoons moved up to the San Martino shortly after 0600 hours on 24 May 1944. It was a cold, misty morning, and visibility was very poor. The engineers were supposed to have constructed a Bailey bridge over the San Martino, but heavy shelling had prevented this. The BCD Recce Troop searched for an alternative crossing site, but the only place which looked at all suitable was the spot where the Three Rivers squadrons had crossed the day before, and it was even more of a quagmire than on the previous day. It was thus nearly 0800 hours when the BCD and the Irish were across and on their way. As soon as the crossing was clear, the Strathconas, who were some hours later to take over the lead from the BCD, moved up to begin their crossing.

The Horse Guards began to move toward the gap in the Hitler Line soon after 0830 hours, first 'B' Squadron, then 'C'. 'A' Squadron meanwhile remained in its forward assembly area west of Pontecorvo until early afternoon, (1400 hours) when it moved up with the second wave of 5th Armoured Brigade. The move to the Start Line, the crossing over the Rio San Martino, was, however, painfully slow because an enormous traffic jam backed up on the east side of the river. As the three squadrons operated quite independently during the next several days, their experiences are told separately.

'B' SQUADRON

'B' Squadron reached the San Martino crossing site at about 0930 hours and almost immediately came under heavy fire from German artillery and multi-barrelled rocket projectors called *Nebelwerfers* – known by Canadian troops as 'Moaning Minnies' because of the strange howling sound the projectile made as it descended. Major Tim Hugman was warned by his lead troop leader, Lieutenant Gibsone, that the crossing site had been very badly churned up by the tanks of the armoured brigade, so for fear of bogging his tanks, Hugman decided to try to find a more suitable crossing to the south. It was a time-consuming and as it proved fruitless search, and one that provoked considerable enemy anti-tank fire, which fortunately did no damage. Eventually word was passed on that the original crossing had been repaired by the engineers, so the squadron dutifully returned. It was 1115 hours before it was able to report all vehicles across the river.

'B' Squadron, responsible for guarding the left flank of the thrust to the Melfa, had a considerable piece of ground to cover, its sector being nearly 5 kilometres wide in places, and some 8 kilometres deep from the San Martino to the Melfa River. Major Hugman quite rightly appreciated that his squadron's mission was not literally to defend the 5th Armoured Brigade column or search every metre of his sector – he simply did not have the strength to do that. Rather, the squadron's role was to advance on a parallel axis at

Sherman and 'bivvy' belonging to Lieutenant Bob Murray's crew "just before the Gustav Line", May 1944. The note on the back reads: "Ready for a good night's sleep in the mud and rain." (Courtesy Captain Robert Murray)

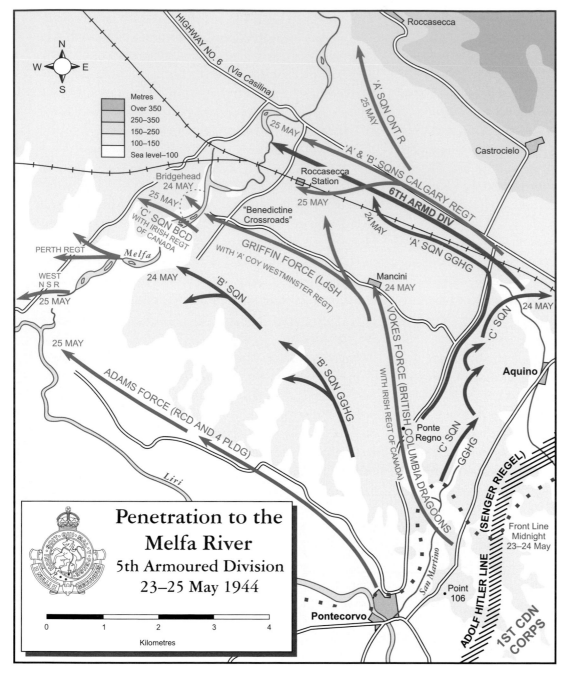

Penetration to the Melfa River
5th Armoured Division
23–25 May 1944

been registered as targets, and German observers high in the mountains to the north were able to see and thus track every move of every unit in the comparatively flat Liri Valley.

Movement was exceedingly slow in the early stages of the advance, in part because of the understandable caution being exercised by crew commanders in this their first experience of battle, but it was largely caused by the enormous difficulty in moving through the many olive groves and vineyards. The main problem was the guy wires supporting the grape vines; they were usually stretched tightly just at the height of the Sherman gun mantlet, so when a tank moved through a field of vines the wires would often slide over the front of the turret before breaking. Many an unwary crew commander was nearly decapitated! The vines themselves also seriously obstructed a Sherman commander's view, for most of the time he could see little or nothing underneath them at ground level. The Stuart

roughly the same pace as the lead tank unit in the armoured brigade so as to be able to detect any major concentration of enemy troops that could interfere with the main thrust. In the process, however, small enemy rearguard pockets would have to be taken out for the squadron's own security.

As soon as the vehicles were clear of the crossing, 'B' Squadron came under nearly continual shelling from enemy artillery and *Nebelwerfers*. The persistency and accuracy of enemy shelling and mortaring throughout this operation was noted by all units. It is clear that all important landmarks such as roads, road junctions, open fields and buildings had already

crew commanders, just that little bit lower, got the vines, and the wires, right in the face. Since crew commanders could rarely see each other because of the vines or olive trees, troop leaders, and indeed all crew commanders, had an almost insurmountable problem in coordinating the tactical movement of their vehicles. Then too, the maps issued were inaccurate and hard to read, and since terrain features could not be clearly identified few crew commanders ever knew exactly where they were. This certainly was the case with 'B' Squadron's Third Troop; the War Diary notes that "they were hopelessly lost for the greater part of the day."

Despite the range of difficulties, 'B' Squadron nonetheless leapfrogged forward by troops, covering the central part of their sector some 2,000 to 3,000 metres south of the 5th Armoured Brigade centre line. The first encounter with the enemy was about noon, some three kilometres from the start point at the San Martino, when a First Troop crew spotted German infantry beside a house. Coax machine-gun fire cleaned out the position, and several prisoners were taken. A short time later Second Troop attacked another enemy infantry position, killing a number of the German defenders and taking a further 25 prisoners. As the squadron had no means of looking after prisoners of war, they were marched to the rear under the watchful eye of a Stuart crew and handed over to the first Canadian infantry encountered, a company of the Irish Regiment. Lieutenant Doug Chant, the troop leader, also spotted a self-propelled 88mm anti-tank gun. Chant was awarded a Military Cross for his gallant leadership during this operation, and his citation for the award expands on this story:

> During the advance the troop was held up by an 88-mm anti-tank gun and, finding it impossible to bring his own fire to bear on the target, this officer directed the fire of one of our own 105-mm guns on it with the result that the enemy gun was destroyed shortly after. Lieutenant Chant then moved his tank over a crest where he spotted and destroyed an enemy machine gun post, killing six of the occupants and taking twelve others prisoner. At the same point he cleaned out a house of enemy who had been causing considerable trouble to our troops. ... Throughout this action, Lieutenant Chant showed outstanding powers of leadership. His dogged determination, initiative and unselfish devotion to duty were an inspiration to his men and were largely responsible for the continued advance of the infantry whose flank he was protecting.

The citation goes on to expound on the same sort of exceptional leadership he demonstrated the next day when supporting the Perth Regiment.

By late afternoon, elements of 'B' Squadron had advanced in almost continual contact with the enemy to positions overlooking the Melfa River. Having determined there was no major enemy threat on the division's left flank, the squadron moved back toward the main body of the armoured brigade. During this move the Regiment suffered its first fatal battle casualty. A Sherman commanded by Corporal Dave Bradshaw took a direct hit from an 88mm anti-tank gun and quickly brewed up. With Corporal Bradshaw's help, all of the crew got out except Trooper Howard Conn, the driver. Conn had been injured or knocked out by the force of the explosion, and despite desperate efforts by the others, the driver's hatch could not be opened from the outside before the tank was engulfed in flame. At last light the squadron harboured with an 8th Hussars squadron.

Night Attack before the Hitler Line. **Painting by the Regiment's own war artist, Lawren Harris, depicting the night move prior to the attack on the Hitler Line on 22 May 1944. (Canadian War Museum**

Back in Canada, the Reserve Regiment was busy training anti-tank gunners, shown here counting holes in a tank target on the range at Niagara-on-the-Lake. (GGHG Archives)

'C' SQUADRON

'C' Squadron crossed the San Martino at about 1130 hours, then proceeded northward from the crossing site in the direction of the town of Aquino. Readers may recall that 'C' Squadron had been intended to be in reserve for this operation. However, a change in plan directed personally by General Hoffmeister brought it into the action to cover the back side of the Hitler Line defences which had not yet been captured, especially in the area of Aquino and Highway 6. It was here that five days earlier the Ontario Regiment (in 1st Armoured Brigade) had lost 13 tanks in an unsuccessful attack on Aquino, and there had since been intelligence reports that large numbers of German tanks were still in the area.

This squadron of course confronted the same dismal conditions at the river crossing when they arrived. Major Allan Burton asked permission to divert to the right (the north), since to carry out his mission in rear of the Hitler Line defences at Aquino he did not have to cross the San Martino, but could advance between the river and the Pontecorvo-Aquino road. The squadron did not have a particularly auspicious beginning for this move, however, as it soon passed a troop of knocked

Lieutenant Colonel Alfred Bunting, Commanding Officer of the 3rd (Reserve) Armoured Regiment (Governor General's Horse Guards) in Toronto, 1944 to 1946. (GGHG Archives)

out Shermans and a still-smoking German Mark IV tank. Very soon the forward tanks were shelled and came under anti-tank fire, a vivid reminder that the section of the Hitler Line north of the crossing site had not yet been cleared of the enemy. Sergeant Sewell pinpointed the location of an 88mm self-propelled gun that was source of much of the squadron's difficulties. Lieutenant Pat Murphy went forward in his Sherman to engage it, but his tank got bogged almost immediately and had to be towed out while under fire. As soon as the tank had been recovered, Major Burton was told that the original crossing was now passable, so the squadron moved south and crossed immediately behind 'B' Squadron. The Assault Troop's White scout cars could not negotiate the deep mud at the exit from the crossing and had to be left behind, so two Honeys were left at the crossing as protection for them.

From the moment they started out in the direction of Aquino, 'C' Squadron encountered difficulty in moving cross-country through tangled vineyards or along sunken farmers' tracks that meandered aimlessly and were not on the map. And because they were advancing just in behind what until very recently had been a major German defensive line – and one where at least some of the German occupants were still in position, as they had discovered before crossing the San Martino – their movement was cautious and deliberate. It took the squadron the better part of two hours to cover about 2,000 metres, all the while being shelled by mortars and artillery. By the time it reached its initial objective southwest of Aquino in early afternoon, Major Burton noted that his troops "had settled down and recovered from their initial battle nervousness".

The first physical encounter with the enemy came as two troops swung left toward a farm complex called Massa di Falco, about 2,000 metres directly west of Aquino. Lieutenant Cy Gaskin, troop leader of Second Troop, reported sighting a 75mm anti-tank gun and crew located beside one of the buildings at Massa di Falco. Major Burton directed all the Shermans to fire high explosive at the target while several Stuarts cut in behind to get more information on the position. The War Diary reports, "Everyone was still tense and the firing was a bit erratic. At this point, the ripe, Irish brogue of Sergeant Bill Sewell [troop sergeant in

Fourth Troop] took charge of the air, as he bitterly complained, 'Yerr firrin' at me. Toimes is hard enough as it is'. The diversion broke the tension. Everyone had a good laugh and settled down." One of the Stuarts had, however, reported an 88mm self-propelled anti-tank gun (mistakenly referred to as a *Ferdinand*) hidden behind one of the buildings.

In the meanwhile Lieutenant Gaskin charged toward the farm buildings in his Sherman, machine guns blazing. On reaching the farm he put the 75mm gun out of action by running over it with the tank. He then dismounted and ran toward the entrance of the farm house, Tommy gun firing from the hip, and, kicking in the door, threw in a couple of grenades. He soon found himself with nearly 70 prisoners of war. Major Burton later wrote:

We also found the officer in charge of the Ferdinand shot through both legs and in great pain. The medical kit in his vehicle was full of pills of all descriptions, but no regular supplies, so we eased his pain with our morphine kit. We had the foresight to make a note of the frequencies on their radio equipment and found a code book which appeared to be current. The Germans were unaware of its capture for the next three weeks.

The code book quickly made its way to the intelligence staff at division headquarters, and there were later reports that the codes and radio frequencies enabled the locations of German anti-tank weapons and artillery to be tracked over the next several days of the battle.

What does an armoured unit do with a large number of prisoners? One cannot simply take a crewman out of one of the tanks to escort them to the rear, and the administrative echelon people, who might be able to cope, are well behind the fighting troops. Major Burton again:

We had no instructions except to send them back to our lines. We had no desire to have them attack our rear, but we could not spare any vehicles or men to escort them.

So I had them pile all their arms and helmets and remove their boots, and I ran the tanks over the pile, destroying them. Then, barefoot, they began the march back to our lines carrying their wounded.

Burton was never sure that these prisoners did get back safely. The previous day, one of the infantry units in behind had taken a large number of casualties when surrendering Germans opened fire, and there remains some suspicion that this batch of prisoners may have been 'done in'.

The "first bag" – a dug-in German Panther turret knocked out by 'B' Squadron on 24 May 1944. (GGHG Archives)

Knocked out German self-propelled 75mm Marder III gun near Aquino, 25 May 1944. (NAC PA167298)

Tank Advance, Italy. **Painting by Lawren Harris depicting Horse Guards tanks advancing behind the Hitler Line on 24 May 1944. Note the abbey on Monte Cassino in the background. The somewhat surrealistic treatment of the tank camouflage is, of course, exaggerated. (Canadian War Museum 12722)**

Having cleared the area to the immediate west of Aquino as well as possible, the squadron continued its methodical advance toward the railway line and Highway 6 north of the town to well-separated troop positions sited to cover likely German approaches. Along the way there were innumerable brief encounters with small German rearguard parties. One such instance is recorded in the War Diary:

One of Mr. [Pat] Murphy's tanks had been ditched and as he could not get it out without the aid of a recovery vehicle…. As Mr. Murphy was standing on the back of his tank, cheerfully reporting to the Sqn Comd that there were no enemy in sight, he was fired on by two very real and hostile machine guns. Mr. Murphy hastily went to ground and the

troop opened fire with their ground guns and the coax. The engagement lasted from 1630 hrs to 1745 hrs, and during its course Tpr Dickenson distinguished himself by dashing across the bullet swept ground to man a machine gun….

Trooper Thomas Edwin Dickenson was given an immediate award of the Military Medal for his brave conduct that evening. The citation for his decoration reads in part:

As darkness came on, the troop was engaged by a small but determined force of enemy paratroopers and were pinned, the majority being outside their tanks repairing a track. Trooper Dickenson left his cover and under the concentrated fire of the two MG 42's and rifles, dashed across the open and manned a Browning machine gun on a ground mount forcing the enemy to cease fire and allowing his troop to reorganise, man their guns and beat off the attack. Trooper Dickenson's prompt action undoubtedly saved the lives of many of his comrades, and averted what might quite easily have been the partial or even complete annihilation of his troop.

A short time after the enemy had been driven off, squadron headquarters got a report that enemy tanks were approaching from the north, so Murphy's troop, less the disabled tank, moved to new fire positions facing to the north of Aquino. A quarter of an hour later one of the crew noticed a puff of dark smoke by the ditched tank: the engine had just been started, and a small group of Germans were trying to move it. When the crew rushed back, covered by one of the Stuarts, the Germans hastily abandoned their immobile prize without doing any damage. But, indicative of the unstable situation still prevailing on the division's flanks, this tank remained under machine-gun fire until the squadron later withdrew into a night harbour.

Trooper Thomas Edwin Dickenson, MM. Dickenson was the first member of the Regiment decorated for bravery on the battlefield. (GGHG Archives)

At about 2000 hours squadron headquarters was firming-up the arrangements to move the entire squadron to a night harbour south of Mancini, beside the 8th Hussars harbours. Enemy mortars, which all afternoon had been firing on elements of 'C' Squadron from the high ground to the north, suddenly concentrated their fire on the headquarters position. One of the bombs scored a direct hit on the open-topped White scout car belonging to the troop leader of the Assault Troop. Four of the crew – Lieutenant Roy Richards, and Troopers Les Hawgood, Louie Axtell and Bill Forsythe – were wounded. When there was a pause in the mortaring, Sergeant Rex Rolfe and Trooper Jesse Smith carried the wounded men to a nearby road, where they were picked up by a Stuart and taken to a nearby medical aid station. Trooper Axtell later died of his wounds. He was the first battle casualty in 'C' Squadron.

The "large number of enemy tanks" that intelligence reports had warned of were in fact nowhere in the area, nor did any approach the 'C' Squadron sector. While the Germans did indeed continue to hold Aquino and parts of the Hitler Line to

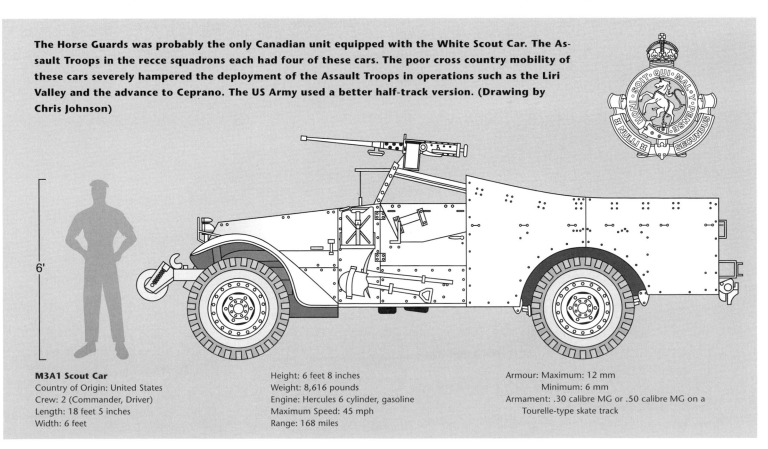

The Horse Guards was probably the only Canadian unit equipped with the White Scout Car. The Assault Troops in the recce squadrons each had four of these cars. The poor cross country mobility of these cars severely hampered the deployment of the Assault Troops in operations such as the Liri Valley and the advance to Ceprano. The US Army used a better half-track version. (Drawing by Chris Johnson)

6'

M3A1 Scout Car
Country of Origin: United States
Crew: 2 (Commander, Driver)
Length: 18 feet 5 inches
Width: 6 feet

Height: 6 feet 8 inches
Weight: 8,616 pounds
Engine: Hercules 6 cylinder, gasoline
Maximum Speed: 45 mph
Range: 168 miles

Armour: Maximum: 12 mm
      Minimum: 6 mm
Armament: .30 calibre MG or .50 calibre MG on a
    Tourelle-type skate track

the south throughout the day, it seems likely that the German tanks reported in and around Aquino had already pulled back to the Melfa, where late that afternoon the Strathconas became enmeshed in one of the most vicious tank-versus-tank battles of the Italian campaign. In the midst of this heavy fighting, the Strathcona Recce Troop, followed somewhat later by a Westminster company, did get across the

Major Allan Burton, DSO. (Courtesy Lieutenant Colonel Allan Burton)

Melfa, and this small body of men managed to hold this precarious toehold against repeated counter-attacks during the evening and night.

Both Colonel Cumberland and General Hoffmeister were greatly impressed with the performance of 'C' Squadron during this crucial baptism of fire for the division and for the Regiment, and they gave much of the credit to the superb leadership shown that day by Major Allan Burton. He was given an immediate award of the Distinguished Service Order, and his citation reads in part:

> Although his headquarters was under intense mortar fire throughout the day, this officer placed and controlled his troops with superb skill and coolheadedness, succeeding in locating them in every position ordered.
>
> The Squadron destroyed at least three 75mm guns and one 88mm self-propelled gun, capturing approximately 100 of the enemy as well as killing many others. This resulted in the right flank of the Division being kept entirely free from any interference by the Germans throughout the day in the Hitler Line in the Aquino area.... The bold, skilful way in which he handled his Squadron without thought of personal danger was of material assistance to the general advance of the Division and the success of subsequent actions.

'A' SQUADRON

By late in the day, the main German threat to the success of the division's thrust to the Melfa was to the front and to the forward part of the right flank. 'A' Squadron, which came into the forward area across the San Martino immediately behind the 8th Hussars at close to 1500 hours, followed a slow-moving column to the north along the main Pontecorvo-Castrociello road, now being used as the main 'up' route. About 2,000 metres beyond the river the column came under a massive and pin-point accurate enemy artillery bombardment, and for a considerable time the vehicles could not move off the road to comparative safety because a large number of infantrymen were sheltering in the ditches. The Assault Troop's open-topped White scout cars were especially at risk, and Lieutenant Joseph 'Mickey' McBride very courageously dismounted in the worst of the shelling to lead his men to safety and then returned with two drivers to move the vehicles through the infantry. McBride was wounded in this action and died of wounds the next day. Major Frank Classey soon tired of letting his squadron serve as a static target, so he led the tanks away from the stalled column. It was still slow going, however, in part because the Germans were jamming the squadron's radio frequency, and the shelling continued, knocking the track off one Sherman.

The headstone marking the grave of Lieutenant J.B. (Mickey) McBride, killed in action on 26 May 1944. The graves of all Regimental members killed overseas are exceptionally well tended in cemeteries maintained by the Commonwealth War Graves Commission. (GGHG Archives)

Eventually, 'A' Squadron reached its initial objective, a position near the Aquino railway station just short of Highway 6, and west of the area held by 'C' Squadron. The Germans obviously had the squadron under close observation from the nearby slopes of the mountain just beyond Highway 6, for soon an 88mm gun opened fire. The squadron quickly dispersed to a new position in the thick vineyards, but within minutes the Germans had targeted them again, forcing yet another hasty move before it at last found a position under cover.

In early evening Major Classey contacted the Strathconas, who had just suffered very heavy casualties in an especially heavy shelling of their harbour. The Strathconas were forming a defensive line along the near bank of the Melfa to support the still weakly held bridgehead, so 'A' Squadron moved forward to tie in with them and protect their right flank. By just short of midnight the troops were in position, some overlooking the Melfa in the area of Roccasecca Station, others across the railway line immediately north of Mancini. It was an extremely tense night, everyone at full alert, as the threat of an enemy counterattack was very real. The sounds of nearby enemy tanks and vehicles were heard all night, no doubt the vehicles that several times mounted counterattacks on the small bridgehead. Enemy patrols several times tried to infiltrate the squadron's position but withdrew as soon as they were fired on.

The Westminster company and Strathcona Recce Troop earned a lasting place in the annals of great Canadian military exploits by holding out in their shallow bridgehead on the far bank of the Melfa against extreme odds. The gallantry demonstrated by the two leaders, and indeed by many of their men, earned Major John Mahoney, the Westminster company commander, a Victoria Cross, and Lieutenant Ed Perkins of the Strathconas a Distinguished Service Order, a "subaltern's VC", as it was called.

In this first battle, the Horse Guards acquitted themselves with the professional aplomb of the highly trained and proficient soldiers they had become over the course of the past three years. Every squadron saw considerable action, even if most of it was against small parties of enemy soldiers. And all squadrons endured a day of nearly continuous mortaring and shelling. The Regiment had done a thoroughly creditable job of protecting the flanks of the divisional attack, and there was no enemy interference. During the action the squadrons accounted for at least 50 Germans killed and an equal number of prisoners. There was, of course, a cost; Lieutenant McBride and Troopers Conn and Axtell had been killed in action, and three men were wounded. If casualties were light in comparison to other units in the division, these Regimental comrades, the first to die in combat, were very sorely missed. But from this baptism of fire came an increase in confidence and determination so pervasive that it could be sensed everywhere in the unit.

With the arrival of first light on 25 May, the high state of alert was relaxed. 'A' Squadron held tight in their positions, but saw no further action during the day. 'C' Squadron, on the other hand, got an early start. Division headquarters was still getting reports of enemy tanks at Aquino and numerous small enemy rearguards that had been bypassed during the thrust to

---

LESSONS LEARNED: POINTS FROM 'A' SQUADRON O-GROUP

1. White scout cars are hopeless for following tanks.
2. Be recce conscious.
3. Don't become careless when in positions; e.g., personnel wandering about.
4. Get information from units you meet.
5. Do not rely on information sent to you.
6. Information must be sent back about leading troops.
7. Tracks shown on maps are inaccurate
8. Stay off tracks because of dust.
9. Stay away from places that might be registered as enemy targets.
10. Use air photos to confirm locations.
11. Never try new things in action.
12. Note targets for artillery.
13. Try to spot Jerry first.
14. Arrange meeting point or covered approach for the echelon going up to the front.
15. Be sure petrol tins are filled with petrol.
16. Always have your rear covered.
17. Use dismounted patrols for bad ground.
18. Always two men in the turret when in action.
19. Expect Jerry anti-tank guns in crazy positions.
20. Take the spring off hatches; no hatches to be locked.
21. Men on the ground must be covered by fire.
22. Send map references in clear when possible.

---

the Melfa, so "C" Squadron was ordered to conduct a sweep of the entire right-flank sector, from Aquino to the Melfa, in the area of Highway 6 and the railway line. As the squadron moved back toward Aquino from their harbour (midway between Pontecorvo and Mancini), several small groups of enemy soldiers were encountered and nine were taken prisoner. As the lead troop approached the town, a column of camouflaged vehicles was seen moving from the north side of Aquino, across the squadron's front. Warned that they might be friendly, Major Burton ordered First and Fourth Troops to keep them covered until they could be identified. The vehicles turned out to belong to the Derby Yeomanry, the XIII British Corps recce regiment, leading that Corps' advance to the Melfa. 'C' Squadron nonetheless carried on with its mission to sweep the ground on the south side of Highway 6. However, it wasn't long before the squadron was overtaken by the leading elements of 6th British Armoured Division who as it happens were advancing well inside the 5th Division's northern (right)

Melfa River Crossings. **Painting by Lawren Harris depicting his impression of the advance beyond the Melfa River, 26 May 1944. (Canadian War Museum 12705)**

boundary. With 'C' Squadron's task now overtaken by events, Major Burton obtained permission at about 1500 hours to withdraw to a harbour near Mancini.

By this time, 'B' Squadron, had orders to provide a flank guard for the second of two 11th Brigade attacks across the Melfa, this one slated for late in the afternoon. The intention of this attack was to further enlarge the bridgehead, already slightly expanded by a thrust earlier in the day by the Irish Regiment and the BCD. The first order of business for the squadron was to find a crossing over the Melfa well to the left of the main brigade crossing site, so two troops set out at about 1730 hours. In this sector the Melfa, at this time of year, was only a shallow stream barely two metres wide, but the river's flat bottom, from one steep bank to the other, was a hundred or more metres wide. This gravel-covered bottom land may have looked solid, but the heavy rain of two days earlier had made it a deep bed of sticky mud. The troop leader of First Troop, Lieutenant George Gibsone, made the first attempt to cross, but he quickly got his Sherman thoroughly bogged. When the other troop vehicles attempted to help, all became

totally immobilized in the mire. Lieutenant Doug Chant and his troop continued to search for a useable crossing further to the south, but when they had no success the troop was recalled to the brigade main crossing.

The Cape Breton Highlanders and the 8th Hussars went across at 1630 hours, and, following a ferocious hour-long battle in which the Hussars lost four Shermans, reached the objective, a thousand metres beyond a lateral road taken earlier. The Melfa bridgehead was now firmly consolidated.

It was 1930 hours when the Horse Guards half-squadron (Second and Third Troops), under Captain Bud Baker, drove across the Melfa and moved off along the far bank of the river to the left flank of the brigade. Not long afterward, Third Troop made contact with a company of the West Nova Scotia Regiment, the right-flank unit of the 1st Division brigade which had also crossed the Melfa closer to the junction with the Liri. The West Novas' attack had ground to a standstill because of a well-sited German machine gun and mortar roughly 1,500 metres from the line of the Melfa, so Third Troop advanced and, following a brief but stiff fight, took out the German weapons. This minor engagement was nonetheless important in the grand scheme, for the West Novas were able to take their objective without further casualties. After nightfall, the Regimental elements committed forward of the Melfa were withdrawn to prepare for the next day's attack.

MONTE GRANDE

The breakout from the Melfa bridgehead began on the morning of 26 May, with an 11th Brigade attack aimed in a northwesterly direction. The objective was to force a crossing of the Liri River at Ceprano, and then seize the line of a road just beyond, thus setting the stage for a subsequent phase. It was an ambitious plan for an inexperienced brigade, calling for an advance of nearly ten kilometres against an enemy who had already shown they were not beaten. Once again, the Horse Guards were placed on the division's flank, this time to secure the very vulnerable right flank. (The left flank was already being well guarded by elements of 1st Canadian Division, especially the 4th Princess Louise Dragoon Guards with elements of the RCD.)

Shortly after first light on 26 May, three 'B' Squadron troops crossed the Melfa and set out to guard the right flank of 11 Brigade's attack toward Ceprano. They initially intended to move in the general area between Highway 6 and the railway line roughly 1,000 metres to the south of the road. Then, once near the village of Coldragone, the squadron would swing to the west into the area of a hill named Colle Leone. Since the 11th Brigade units moved very slowly and cautiously, the 'B' Squadron troops were soon well out in front of the infantry, not a bad thing since 6th British Armoured Division was supposed to follow close behind along Highway 6.

Almost as soon as the lead troops were on their way, Major

Tim Hugman went back to Regimental Headquarters (still behind the Melfa), and Colonel Cumberland instructed him to drive immediately to the division's tactical headquarters to get personal orders from General Hoffmeister himself. The commander told Hugman he was particularly concerned about a strong German rearguard reported to be taking up positions on hills on the north side of the division's sector at Monte Grande and Monte Piccolo. Hoffmeister was concerned that the Germans could mount a counterattack against the right flank of 11th Brigade as they swung toward Ceprano. Before returning to the squadron, Major Hugman stopped in at 11th Brigade headquarters to tie in with Brigadier Snow, and he briefly joined the other squadron commanders at the Melfa crossing for a conference.

By late morning the recce troops had, with difficulty, worked their way into the area of Coldragone station. The 'going' was exceptionally bad: woods interspersed with heavy brush that concealed one ravine and ditch after another. Fields of view were very short, and it is no doubt fortunate that not a single enemy position was encountered during the course of the advance into the area south of Monte Grande, for small rearguards could have taken the tanks by surprise almost at any moment.

Shortly after noon the leading elements of the squadron arrived in positions in the lee of Colle Leone, about 2,000

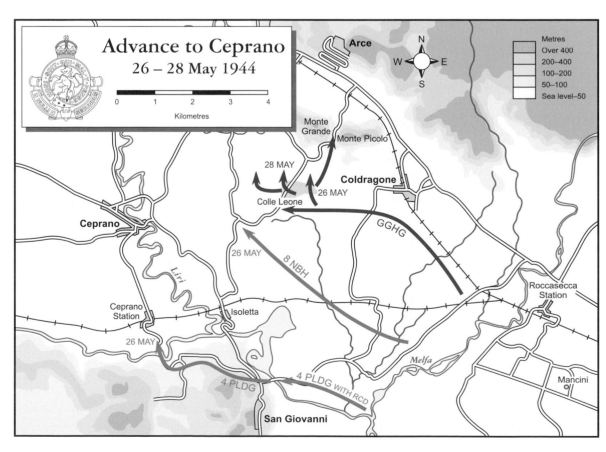

metres south of Monte Grande. From this area, enemy movement could be seen on the high ground to the north. Closer examination revealed several dug-in enemy positions, including a concrete gun emplacement at Point 358 (the summit of Monte Grande), and heavy vehicle movement – tanks or self-propelled guns – was noted at the base of the hill. While Fourth Troop continued to observe, First Troop's Stuarts winkled their way forward in folds in the ground to the very base of Monte Grande. They couldn't go any farther without exposing themselves, but before pulling back they were able to confirm that the area was strongly held by infantry, supported by self-propelled 88s. During this time one unfortunate piece of misinformation got passed to squadron headquarters, and subsequently to Regiment and division: someone erroneously reported having difficulty at a map reference that happened to be the top of Monte Grande, and for some time all the higher headquarters thought that the hill was in our hands, when of course that was far from the case. 'B' Squadron remained in position on Colle Leone throughout the day, keeping a close watch on the Germans on Monte Grande and Monte Piccolo, until about 1900 hours when, adhering strictly to the doctrine taught in England that armoured troops would withdraw from contact during hours of darkness even if no one replaced them, the squadron pulled back into a night harbour. German mortars on Monte Piccolo continued to shell sporadically, but fortunately there were no casualties.

'A' Squadron, tasked to move forward on the right flank and eventually relieve 'B' Squadron, got caught in dense traffic congestion at the Melfa crossing. As the 11th Brigade units were well on their way to Ceprano by the time the squadron was beyond the Melfa at about 1030 hours, Major Frank Classey decided to keep pace with 'B' Squadron by moving along the southern spur of the railway line, rather than keeping strictly to the right flank. The same exceptionally difficult ground that 'B' Squadron had encountered severely hampered the advance, and in fact the Assault Troop had to be left behind as the White scout cars could not cope with the rough terrain. The War Diary reports:

> The many streams and valleys, which lay at right angles across the line of our advance, made the going tortuous for our tks. Although we did not contact any enemy resistance, the bad going made our progress very slow and we were still near the RR [railway line] … at 1700 hrs.

At close to 1800 hours the colonel put pressure on the squadron to move more quickly. Two troops were to relieve 'B' Squadron on Colle Leone, but the remainder of the squadron was now to push further west to the bank of the Liri River north of Ceprano, where 11th Brigade intended to capture crossings. The distance to Colle Leone was only about 4,000 metres as the crow flies, but three and a half hours later the squadron was still short of this first objective, so the task of reaching the Liri was put off until morning. Eventually, First and Third Troops made contact with a troop from 'B' Squadron, but after being mortared they pulled back about 500 metres behind the observation posts.

The ground conditions that had been encountered during the move to the front made it far too risky to attempt to get the 'A' Echelon wheeled vehicles forward during the night, so Major Classey decided to carry on toward Ceprano in the morning without being resupplied with fuel and ammunition. As it happened, just before midnight the order to proceed to the Liri was cancelled. On reaching the bank of the river, the Perth Regiment – then in the lead in 11th Brigade – found that all bridges had been destroyed, and any attempt to cross in strength would have to wait until the engineers could build a bridge. 'A' Squadron was thus told to remain in position overlooking the Monte Grande-Piccolo area until further orders, so each troop went into its own separate harbour behind its assigned sector.

The strength of the German positions on Monte Grande and Piccolo became apparent on the morning of 27 May, when the Guards Armoured Brigade of 6th British Armoured Division – now advancing astride Highway 6 on the right of the Canadians – launched an attack on Monte Piccolo. The weight of an entire British brigade simply could not dislodge the German rearguard there!

Throughout the daylight hours of 27 May, two troops were kept in forward positions where they could keep a watchful eye on enemy activities. Lieutenant Harry Tye's Fourth Troop repeated the feat that a 'B' Squadron troop had managed the day before; moving cautiously and carefully along the bed of a narrow stream, the troop's vehicles patrolled forward to the base of Monte Grande and got to within 400 metres of their objective before being detected. Unfortunately, Sergeant Hank Starkey's Stuart threw a track just as the troop came under enemy small-arms fire from Monte Piccolo, and the Shermans had to be backed out until they could get into cover behind a small hill. Leaving the drivers with the tanks, the rest of the troop went forward on foot. Even though every move drew fire, the troop gathered several bits of important information. There was a dug-in 88mm emplacement on the very top of Monte Grande, a self-propelled 88 was positioned in the saddle between the two features, and another gun and a mortar position were pinpointed on Monte Piccolo. Working with Lieutenant J.W. Southwick, Tye repeatedly worked his way to and from his Sherman – often under small arms and mortar fire – to direct artillery fire onto the gun positions in the saddle and on eastern slope of Monte Grande. In this action Trooper Thomas Scollick was killed. When the lead troops were pulled back in mid-afternoon, Lieutenant Tye and Corporal Brown remained on the forward slope of Colle Leone to maintain observation, but being under constant mortar fire they too were withdrawn behind the crest.

By early afternoon many of the tanks were running short of fuel, the inevitable consequence of being unable get the 'A' Ech-

'B' Squadron Sherman setting out to protect the division's right flank in the sector Monte Grande-Monte Piccolo, 26 May 1944. (NAC PA168022)

elon up to resupply petrol and ammunition the night before. This might also have had an unfortunate operational effect, for shortly after 1300 hours the squadron was asked to move west to support the 11th Brigade crossing of the Liri at Ceprano, but a combination of lack of petrol and close engagement with the enemy made that impossible. Resupply became the top priority, so First and Third Troops were sent back after dark to meet Squadron Sergeant Major Larry Britten and lead the echelon vehicles forward to a central harbour. The ammunition and fuel trucks had an extraordinarily difficult time getting over the nearly impassable ground, in addition to being harassed by enemy snipers, but in true echelon tradition they made it to the squadron harbour and replenished the vehicles.

Meanwhile, during the evening of 27 May, 'C' Squadron moved forward to relieve their 'A' Squadron brothers. By this time there was a greatly heightened concern that the Germans in the area of Monte Grande would interfere with the crossing of the Liri River south of Ceprano by attacking the division's vulnerable right flank. The infantry battalions of 11th Brigade, crossing the river by boat, had taken a bridgehead on the far bank, but it was a tenuous one because they had no heavy weapons or equipment. A 40-metre Bailey bridge was to be built during the night of 27/28 May to get tanks and guns across, and so – to give some protection to this effort, or at least early warning – Major Burton was instructed to position two of his troops well west of Colle Leone to cover possible enemy approaches toward Ceprano. However, because of the near impossibility of moving over the rough ground in the

dark, the whole squadron harboured for the night south of Colle Leone after getting a hand over briefing from Major Classey and Lieutenant Tye.

At first light on 28 May, 'C' Squadron's troops deployed to their positions, Second and Third well off to the left to cover the roads leading from behind Monte Grande toward Ceprano, with First Troop facing Monte Grande and Fourth opposite Monte Piccolo. Almost immediately, Lieutenant Bud Wass' First Troop vehicles came under fire from the 88mm gun on Monte Grande. The wartime history recounts this story:

Regimental Sergeant Major J.H. Bentley (far right) passing out some liquid refreshment to the crew of an Assault Troop White Scout Car before they move to the front. (NAC PA 168025)

Lieut. Wass was instructed to get the exact location of the 88 and he attempted to spot it from his OP on the ground. As he could not get adequate observation, he moved forward to a house which he knew the enemy had registered and which he had been warned to avoid. Nevertheless, he proceeded to a second floor window; as soon as he raised his binoculars the 88 opened fire. Although the shots came very close he escaped without injuries and by 1030 hours had secured the exact location....

An artillery stonk was then requested to take out the gun, but it was refused as the British, on the right, had reported that the Grenadier Guards were on Monte Grande. Captain Doug Crashley recalled:

We knew the Grenadiers weren't there because a short time before they had retreated through our position. Major Burton tasked me to find the CO of the Grenadiers so they could withdraw the objection. He gave me a runner armed with a Tommy gun for protection, but I outdistanced him in the first hundred yards. I ran behind the Grenadiers' dug-in positions during a mortar barrage and finally, after about a mile, located their regimental headquarters. The British brigade commander and the CRA [Commander Royal Artillery] of 6th British Armoured Division happened to be visiting, and the objection was immediately withdrawn. Down came the 5th Division artillery. Later I got a radio message from the British brigadier: "Well done Canada".

For his bravery here and elsewhere in this battle, Lieutenant Bud Wass was awarded the Military Cross.

Meanwhile, elsewhere in the vicinity there were a number of significant developments in the operational situation. The Bailey bridge over the Liri just below Ceprano collapsed into the river just as it was being pushed into position, so the 5th Armoured Brigade units waiting to cross into the bridgehead were diverted on a long detour south of the Isoletta Reservoir to a 1st Division crossing over the Sacco River. This long diversion also included 'B' Squadron, which had been placed under 5th Brigade for their attack beyond Ceprano. Closer to home, Monte Piccolo was captured in mid-morning by the Grenadier Guards of 6th British Armoured Division, but an attack

on Monte Grande by the Coldstream Guards was repulsed with heavy casualties. It was clear that even at this stage the Germans had no intention of easily giving up their hold on the high ground north of the Liri.

At noon the two troops on the left were ordered to move forward to a low hill about 600 metres south of Highway 6, so that they could better observe to the north and west of Monte Grande. Before reaching there, however, Second Troop encountered a patrol of German paratroopers. Following a sharp if brief fight, two prisoners were taken and the remainder of the enemy scattered. Then, just as the troop arrived at the new position, enemy armoured vehicles were seen only a few hundred metres to the west. One of Third Troop's Shermans then broke a track, and almost at the same time the Germans opened fire with armour-piercing rounds. Hastily backing down into a fire position, Lieutenant Bruce Steele bogged his own Sherman. As the troop was now in no position to fight, Major Burton gave instructions to abandon the Shermans and get the crews away in the Stuarts while Second Troop tanks covered their withdrawal with fire. Lieutenant William 'Pat' Murphy's Fourth Troop, having been withdrawn from the Piccolo area, was also sent to bolster the west flank. Sporadic fighting continued over the next two hours. Shortly after 1500 hours Second and Third Troops came under heavy shellfire, and Lieutenant Steele and two of his crew, Corporal Frank Ryan and Trooper C.H. Wood, were wounded by shrapnel and had to be evacuated in one of the Stuarts. In one of the unfortunate if all too common accidents of war, this shelling was friendly fire, brought down in error by 6th British Division guns. 'C' Squadron's involvement in this phase of the battle came to an end at around 1700 hours, when a Derby Yeomanry squadron made contact and relieved its troops. Both 'A' and 'C' Squadrons then moved back to a Regimental harbour in the area of the Melfa crossing.

While 'C' Squadron was battling Germans on the slopes of Monte Grande, 'B' Squadron was placed under 5th Armoured Brigade to serve as a flank guard on the right of the brigade advance from Ceprano which was to be launched on the morning of 29 May. Accordingly, at mid-morning on the 28th, the squadron moved forward to join the 5th Brigade units in an assembly area on the near bank of the Liri, about 1,500 metres south of Ceprano. The squadron arrived to find a state

Thompson .45 calibre sub-machine gun, commonly known as a Tommy gun, used by crew members in Italy. Tank crews often removed the butt stock to make it easier to store and handle the weapon in the confined space inside the vehicle (GGHG Archives)

of utter confusion caused by the collapse of the Bailey bridge into the Liri.

While waiting for a decision about what was to happen, the squadron went into a harbour about two kilometres short of the bridge site. It wasn't long before the harbour came under heavy shelling. Lieutenant George Yavis, one of the most promising of the new subalterns, was hit by shell fragments and killed instantly. Lieutenant A.J. Dobie, the squadron liaison officer, was also hit and had to be evacuated. Late in the afternoon Captain Bud Baker, the second-in-command, was given instructions to move the squadron with the BCD on a 10-kilometre detour south of the Isoletta Reservoir and thence to a crossing over the River Sacco near Ceprano Station. This rather lengthy move would bring the BCD into their intended start point on the far bank of the Liri, south of Ceprano. It was well after dark when the squadron got into a harbour near Ceprano Station, and Major Hugman made contact with Colonel Vokes, commanding officer of the British Columbia Dragoons, to tie in plans for the next morning.

THE ADVANCE BEYOND CEPRANO

'B' Squadron set out at 0600 hours on 29 May. The squadron was to advance on the right of two BCD columns aimed west toward the village of Pofi, but first it had to move about two kilometres north toward Highway 6 to get into position. Just short of Ceprano the squadron encountered a minefield which the sappers were reported to have gapped. When no cleared lane could be identified, Major Hugman decided the squadron had to find its own way through, which it did, fortunately without hitting any mines. First and Second Troops, commanded by Lieutenants Gibsone and Chant, led off in a westerly direction along the south side of Highway 6. The road was already clogged with 6th British Armoured Division vehicles, but the British were completely uninterested in the Canadians on their left flank.

The advance progressed at a snail's pace because of exceedingly rough terrain. Much of the ground was covered in trees and thick scrub brush, with steep-sloped

hills and a succession of streams, ditches, sunken trails and impossibly thick hedges, all seeming to run at right angles to the line of advance. To make matters worse, every bit of low ground appeared to be boggy. Fortunately, no enemy were encountered until about 1300 hours, by which time the lead troops were about a thousand metres apart, on the general line of the Meringo River and a road running south from Highway 6 to Pofi. But once the Germans spotted them, they brought down a rain of shells which lasted for the whole of the afternoon.

While there had been no obvious enemy defensive position or line, the squadron had indeed penetrated into an area where many small groups of Germans were still holding out. About this time, squadron headquarters, about 3,000 metres to the southeast of the First Troop position, came under mortar and shellfire. As a result of a direct hit on the side of one of the tanks, Trooper John Getty was killed and Troopers John O'Halloran and H.C. McPhail were badly wounded. The second-in-command, Captain Baker, loaded the wounded men in a Stuart and took them back to medical assistance, but O'Halloran died soon afterwards. Baker had no sooner left than two of the three remaining headquarters tanks got thoroughly bogged. When every effort to get them out failed, Major Hugman, in the only headquarters vehicle that could move, headed for the rear to find the recovery vehicles. He was thus out of contact for the next several hours, and during this critical time the squadron was by default under command of

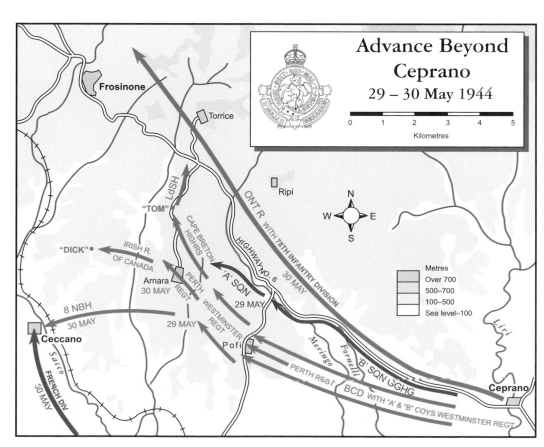

Lieutenant George Brown, the liaison officer, from one of the bogged tanks.

One of the truly unfortunate incidents of this battle took place at about 1400 hours. For nearly an hour a German sniper had been firing on Lieutenant George Gibsone's troop from a hill on the far side of Highway 6. Neither machine-gun fire nor high explosive rounds put the sniper out of action, so Gibsone decided to take out the sniper himself, and went off alone on foot. The War Diary reports: "As he passed over the crest of the hill, his troop heard a burst of M.G. and he failed to return". Some time later, Sergeant Bill Gardiner, the troop sergeant, went forward with Trooper S.A. Uppington to see what might have happened. But, coming under heavy small-arms fire as they approached the crest of the hill, they had to pull back, and it had to be assumed that Gibsone, a gifted leader who never showed fear, had been killed or captured. The padre, Major Bill Prior, found his grave the next day near an enemy machine-gun dugout, where his body had been buried by British troops.

The situation became progressively worse over the course of the afternoon. The First Troop tanks were targeted so accurately that about 1830 hours they had to be pulled back to safety. Shortly afterward 5th Armoured Brigade passed orders that the squadron was to take on a new task: providing protection to an artillery regiment moving their guns into a sector just south of Highway 6. The squadron was expected to establish a defensive perimeter along Highway 6 over a distance of nearly six kilometres. However, the immobile squadron headquarters tanks had by that time also come under fire from machine guns. When an 88mm gun opened fire on them from a hill on the far side of Highway 6, Lieutenant Brown ordered the crews to gather all codes and classified documents, change the frequencies on the radios and abandon the vehicles. At close to 2100 hours a German patrol closed in on the squadron headquarters position. Captain Baker had by then re-appeared, and under his guidance the forward elements of the squadron withdrew to a central harbour two kilometres to the southeast, leaving the bogged headquarters tanks to the mercy of the enemy.

Major Kitch Jordan, who was serving as Regimental liaison officer at 5th Brigade headquarters, sent word in unmistakably terse terms on the regimental net that it was imperative a protective screen be deployed immediately to guard the gun positions during the hours of darkness, as ordered several hours earlier. Following a discussion with the troop leaders who knew the area, it was decided that this could best be done on foot. Every last man in Second and Third Troops volunteered for the mission, and they soon deployed with every form of machine gun they could carry. Fortunately the night was without incident or contact with the enemy, and at first light the entire squadron pulled well back from the Meringo River.

During the morning of 30 May, 'A' Squadron moved forward into the positions on the Highway 6 to Pofi road covered the previous day by 'B' Squadron, but when it arrived the squadron found the situation very much changed: the Germans, it appeared, had begun a general withdrawal, so the squadron was ordered to move forward to the village of San Antonio, some five kilometres northwest of Pofi on Highway 6, where they were to establish a position to cover the divisional units operating in the rough ground south of the highway.

The ground, bad as it was to begin with, became progressively more difficult as it became more mountainous. 'A' Squadron never did reach its objective: it was brought to a complete halt by a deep, rocky gully about a thousand metres east of the village of Arnara. A few Stuarts got part way down the steep, boulder-strewn near slope, but were then stopped by huge rocks they could not get over or around. Nor could they get back up!

Fourth Troop, 'C' Squadron, Italy, summer 1944. (GGHG Archives)

It was obvious that none of the Shermans had any chance of crossing. Enemy patrols were still very active in this area, and they made a point of harassing the two Stuarts stuck in the gully. Trooper Cyril Fairhead, one of the Stuart crewmen, was unfortunately shot in the head and killed. The squadron spent much of the day searching for a place where the vehicles could get across the gully, but none was ever found, even though it was known that the Strathconas were engaging enemy tanks northwest of the position. That night the troops bivouacked with Westminster Regiment companies.

On 31 May, the Regiment withdrew completely: 5th Armoured Division was pulled out of the line and replaced by the 6th South African Division. For the next two weeks the 5th Armoured Division was held in temporary camps near Ceprano, where rest and maintenance were the order of the day. The advance on Rome was being intensified by both the Fifth US Army and the Eighth Army, and it was essential that Highway 6, the only main road in the Eighth Army sector, be kept free for supply convoys. Rome was liberated on 4 June: the Americans were given the 'honour' of being the first to enter. The War Diary entry for 6 June notes that the 'Second Front' had finally been opened with the successful Allied invasion of Normandy.

The most significant event of the brief period in the Sacco valley was a Regimental change of command. Lieutenant Colonel Ian Cumberland was promoted to Brigadier and appointed commander of 5th Armoured Brigade on 5 June. The new commanding officer was Lieutenant Colonel Kitch Jordan, who for some time had been second-in-command.

The Regiment received a notable pat on the back in a congratulatory letter written on 5 June by General Sir Oliver Leese, commander of the Eighth Army, to General Hoffmeister. It read in part:

> You then advanced with great dash to the Melfa Line, where brilliant actions were fought; in particular by The Governor General's Horse Guards, Strathcona's Horse, and the Westminster Regt…. I am very proud to have the 5th Canadian Armoured Division in the Eighth Army; and I have learned in this battle how greatly I can rely on you in the future….

Lieutenant Colonel A.K. Jordan, DSO, commanding officer of The Governor General's Horse Guards June 1944 to January 1946. (GGHG Archives)

Indeed, the Horse Guards had performed very well in its first week of operations. At least seven and probably as many as 10 enemy anti-tank guns were destroyed or put out of action, approximately 200 German soldiers were killed, and some 150 prisoners-of-war were captured. The cost to the Regiment was relatively light in comparison with other units in the division: nine members were killed and 25 were wounded. Only one tank was completely destroyed, while four others disabled by enemy action were recovered and repaired within 24 hours.

Not everyone, however, was happy with the way 5th Armoured Division had performed in this its introduction into battle. Many things had indeed gone wrong, and among the more serious problems was an obvious lack of understanding of all-arms cooperation on the battlefield. On General Hoffmeister's personal order, all units conducted a thorough, soul-searching examination of their performance during the course of the battle of the Liri. A written report on the Horse Guards' performance, submitted just before Colonel Cumberland departed, was somewhat self-congratulatory in comparison to those of other armoured units in the division. The main areas for improvement centred on improving the passage of information to the rear by the squadron headquarters and on the need for squadron commanders to remain at their headquarters:

> it is necessary to resist the temptation to go [forward] to look and see what is going on. This possibly applies to our Sqns more than any other unit as they are working on such a wide front, it is impossible for a Sqn Comd to see his tps while they are working and it has to be controlled from a map (like playing chess).

The authors of the wartime history of the Regiment were perhaps a bit more open:

> During the May offensive our role had always been subsidiary, and we were never flung head on into the teeth of the enemy defences. We had done our job well and efficiently, with many instances of courage and physical endurance, but we emerged with a rather distorted impression of what it was all about.

In mid-June the whole of 5th Armoured Division was moved south into generally the same area near the Volturno that had been occupied prior to the Liri Valley battles. The Horse Guards' tanks and wheeled vehicles drove to the new area along Highway 6 on 14 June. It was the first time that members of the Regiment had actually seen the ruins of Cassino, and among the sights everyone noted were the hundreds of 'brewed up' Shermans, "lined up in batches" along Highway 6.

The camp near Dragoni which the Regiment occupied for the next month and a half was in a grove of woods on the bank of the Volturno River. Many remember this interlude as one of the best times of the Italian campaign. Because of the extreme heat, the working day ended at 1100 hours, and if they felt inclined the men could swim in the river. Rest camps were set up on the Mediterranean coast, with squadrons in turn spending three or four days at the beach. And there were also organized visits to Rome, undamaged by the war because the German commander in Italy, Field Marshal Albert Kesselring, would not permit the wanton destruction of antiquities that were important to the whole of Western civilization and had declared Rome an open city. It was not until well into July that training once again became the prime focus of the Regiment.

One of the major changes that occurred within the division was the creation of 12th Infantry Brigade from troops that were already in Italy with I Canadian Corps. The battles in the Liri Valley had made it obvious that 5th Armoured Division – with one armoured and one infantry brigade – was operation-

ally unbalanced for the terrain likely to be encountered for the remainder of the war in Italy. The division needed an additional infantry brigade, but where to get it was the problem. A request to provide an additional brigade from England was rejected outright; all the troops there were needed for the more vital battles in

The 'hard life' in the camp near Dragoni on the Volturno River, late June 1944. (Courtesy Sgt Finbow)

North West Europe. The only solution was to find the troops from within existing units. 12th Infantry Brigade thus came to have as its battalions 4th Princess Louise Dragoon Guards, which had been the divisional recce regiment for 1st Division, the Westminster Regiment from 5th Armoured Brigade and an ad hoc battalion created out of anti-aircraft artillery units that was eventually named the Lanark and Renfrew Scottish. One of the effects of the creation of this new brigade was that increasingly the Horse Guards would be used as light armour rather than strictly as armoured reconnaissance.

Toward the end of July there was a flurry of activity surrounding an inspection of the division on 31 July by a British VIP named General Collingwood. Steel tracks were replaced by rubber-padded tracks, and the tanks were all repainted a

(Left) His Majesty King George VI inspecting the Governor General's Horse Guards, 31 July 1944. (NAC PA204158)

(Below) The King speaking to Lieutenant Colonel Jordan, 31 July 1944. (GGHG Archives)

darker green. Then, on 29 July, all fighting vehicles were moved into a field beside Highway
6, lined up sergeant-major fashion in long,
straight rows, scrubbed and dusted until they
were spotless, and then rubbed down with engine oil to make then glisten. Shortly before
noon on 31 July, His Majesty King George VI
arrived in a staff car in front of the Horse
Guards. Pressed for time because he had to inspect all of the division's units, the King spoke
briefly to Colonel Jordan, took him into the
staff car, and drove slowly along the front of the
Regiment's tanks. His Majesty complemented
the colonel on the fine appearance of the men
and their vehicles, and then was off to the next
unit. If the Royal inspection was brief, its effects
were lasting; there wasn't a soldier that day who
did not consider it an honour to have paraded
for his Sovereign. When it was over, Colonel
Jordan called the men together, passed on His
Majesty's compliments, and told them that the
holiday was over. The division was moving
north to return to battle.

THE GOTHIC LINE OPERATIONS

After the fall of Rome on 4 June, a battered and
much reduced German army was rapidly
pushed back from one improvised position to
another. The German high command finally
decided to make a firm stand on a new defensive line, known to the Allies as the Gothic Line,
which ran across the peninsula from the Apennine Mountains
north of Florence to Pesaro on the Adriatic coast. In late July,
just as the Allies were poised to enter Florence, a major change
was made in the strategic plan for the Italian campaign: the
main thrust to break through the Gothic Line would now be
made on the Adriatic front instead of north from Florence
through the mountains.

The Eighth Army plan was to thrust northward from a secure area on the Metauro River, along the coastal plain and
into the flat Po Valley, which was expected to force the Germans to withdraw to the Alps. The Canadian Corps was to
play a major role in the offensive, initially between II Polish
Corps and V British Corps. Everyone understood full well that
speed was of the essence: by early October the usual heavy autumn rain would turn the ground along the coast into a veritable sea of mud, limiting vehicle movement and thus making

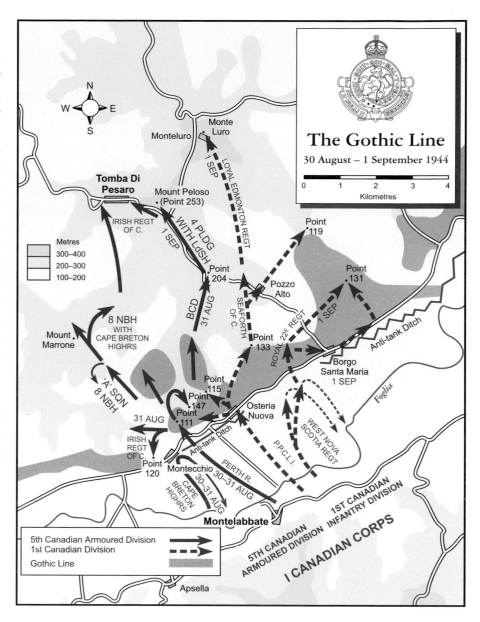

offensive operations virtually impossible. The redeployment
of the Canadian Corps began almost immediately, with 5th
Armoured Division beginning its move across the peninsula
to the Adriatic on 16 August.

In the previous two weeks, the Horse Guards had been al-
most continuously on the move – first to Cassino, then to
Rome and Lake Bolsena, then to Foligno in the very centre of
Italy, the wheeled vehicles preceding the tanks by several days.
On 20 August the Regiment concentrated just to the north-
west of the town of Jesi, 30 kilometres south of the Metauro
River, where the division was being assembled for the forth-
coming offensive.

A briefing on the Corps plan of attack was given by the
commanding officer on 24 August. Beginning on the night of
25/26 August, 1st Canadian Division was to lead off, attacking
from the line of the Metauro to the Foglia River, some 18

215

A group of Horse Guards, Italy, summer 1944 (GGHG Archives)

kilometres to the north. The partially prepared Gothic Line defences were located in a 3- to 4-kilometre-deep belt on the north bank of the Foglia. At this point 5th Armoured Division was to be brought in – for a deliberate attack on the Gothic Line if necessary, but to 'bounce' through if possible. Once the flat plain of the broad Po Valley was reached, Allied superiority in armour was expected to sweep away whatever enemy resistance remained. An equally vague and hopelessly optimistic distant objective was laid out: the Horse Guards were to lead the division in a pursuit to Ferrara, an ancient city on the bank of the Po River, 150 kilometres to the north.

The 1st Division started out as planned at midnight on 25/26 August, and four days later the Canadians were on the south bank of the Foglia. The infantry battalions of 11th Brigade moved up to take over the left-hand sector from 1st Division so that 5th Armoured could control its own front as it went into action. On the evening of 29 August, General Hoffmeister went forward with his reconnaissance group to a position overlooking the Foglia and the village of Montecchio on the far bank. Later he recalled:

> We could, by careful examination, pick out the odd concrete gun emplacement, and we could see the barbed wire, and we saw the minefield; but there was no life around the place at all. I did not expect German officers to be swanking up and down but the whole thing looked terribly quiet. There was not a shell coming our way, and the road that led out of the position we were occupying at the time, due north, … was still in operation and you could see it going up through the line itself, obviously still in use by the Germans.

In fact, the Germans had not yet fully occupied this part of the Gothic Line, but it is now known that a large number of enemy troops were on their way forward. Hoffmeister's sense that the German defences were nearly unmanned was, however, reinforced by a patrol from the Cape Breton Highlanders that went forward into Montecchio village and came back to report that the town and the high ground just beyond were unoccupied. Based on this information, on the morning of 30 August Hoffmeister decided not to wait to put in a time-consuming deliberate attack, but to press forward almost immediately – to 'bounce' the German defences. Orders were given to 11 Brigade to launch a 'hasty' attack at 1730 hours, on a two-battalion front. The Cape Breton Highlanders were to take the village of Montecchio and the neighbouring escarpment known as Point 120, while the Perths were to capture Point 111 a thousand metres to the right.

The mere possibility that the Germans were not going to defend the Gothic Line set in motion a whole range of contingency planning for exploitation. Accordingly, the Horse Guards were warned to get ready to lead the division on the planned mad charge to Ferrarra – the very role the Regiment had been trained to do in all the exercises in England. Colonel Jordan attended Hoffmeister's orders at 1600 hours on 30 August: placed under his command were an anti-tank battery of 4th Anti Tank Regiment and two carrier-borne platoons from 11th Brigade; in support was the whole of the 8th Field Regiment RCA. The War Diary notes that "there was a great flap and all the tracks moved forward post haste". Over the next hours the whole of the Regiment concentrated just northwest of the village of Sant' Angelo waiting for the order to go.

In the late evening hours of 30 August, during the tense period of waiting to see if a crack could be wedged open in the vaunted Gothic Line, there was an incident that might be classified as almost amusing if it did not have its serious side. An 8th Hussars squadron was moving up toward the Foglia to give fire support to the CBH attack on Montecchio when a very officious military policeman stopped the column of tanks. The Hussars were told very firmly that the Governor General's Horse Guards had priority on the road, and that they were immediately to get off to the side. Indeed, the division plan for exploitation did give the Regiment priority – but the brigade plan that had to be carried out first understandably had a different set of priorities. Then too, a lot of emphasis had been given to effective control of traffic since the Liri Valley battles almost choked on traffic jams. It was nearly half an hour before the Hussars squadron commander decided that his tanks could simply ignore the provost corporal's barrier and got on with his mission.

The order for the Horse Guards to "go" never did come. While the Perth Regiment and a squadron of the 8th Hussars managed to fight their way up onto Point 111, the Cape Breton Highlanders were thrown back, despite several attempts to capture Montecchio and Point 120. Shortly before 0100 hours on 31 August "the great pursuit was called off completely … as it looks like we will have to fight our way through after all." There was enormous disappointment; the Regiment had been on the verge of mounting an operation that might have gone down in history.

The 31st of August 1944 is one of the red-letter days in the history of the Canadian Army: the Gothic Line was decisively breached by units of 5th Armoured Division! It was, however, a near-run thing, with the proverbial fog of war affecting the outcome almost as much as good leadership and valiant soldiers.

At daybreak only the Perths and one squadron of the 8th Hussars had a tenuous toehold in the German defences, but enemy positions on Point 120 continued to dominate the flat, treeless Foglia valley. Then shortly after first light the Irish Regiment and Hussars captured Point 120 in a daring attack from the rear, and another Hussar squadron got part way to Monte Marrone before it was stopped by anti-tank guns. The decisive action was, however, carried out by the British Columbia Dragoons, when in a bold if almost foolhardy move their CO sent his regiment thrusting toward Point 204 – 5 kilometres into the German lines – without infantry or artillery support. The BCD got to their objective, but they lost all but 18 Shermans and had to be relieved at last light by the Strathconas. The Horse Guards, ordered to occupy positions on Monte Marrone to guard the Division's left flank as soon as it was taken by 11th Brigade, sat in harbour throughout the day waiting for instructions that never came.

The overall situation was still very unsettled at dawn on 1 September. During the night the Germans had mounted several strong counterattacks against the Strathcona/Perth Regiment position on Point 204, and there seemed to be pockets of Germans hidden at every turn in the barren brown hills. Nevertheless, there was a mood of great optimism, and

during the early afternoon the Regiment moved to a new harbour on the north bank of the Foglia to be in a better position to react quickly when the order came. In the meantime, the 4th Princess Louise Dragoon Guards, now dismounted as an infantry battalion, captured Point 253 (Monte Peloso), the highest hill in the 5th Division's sector, supported by the Strathconas. Soon afterward, in the 1st Division sector on the right, Monte Luro, the only other prominent height of ground, was taken. The Gothic Line defences had been broken! The German high command accepted the inevitable: German troops were ordered to withdraw north, leaving only rearguard elements to delay and harass.

Just after 1800 hours Colonel Jordan got the expected order: the Regiment was to move at once to relieve the 8th Hussars on Monte Marrone, and from there be prepared to advance on the division's left flank to the River Conca, some eight kilometres further on. Soon after the Regiment reached Monte Marrone, the Irish Regiment set out to finish cleaning up the division sector by capturing the village of Tomba di Pesaro (now named Tavullia), just below Point 253. 'C' Squadron supported the Irish attack by providing intensive high-explosive fire on the village as the infantry advanced, firing 165 rounds in seven and a half minutes. When the Irish got to Tomba di Pesaro, they found the village deserted; the Germans were long gone.

Tanks moving forward toward the Gothic Line (NAC PA204149)

The Gothic Line – Tomba di Pesaro. **Painting by Captain G. Tinning depicting the ground where the main German defences were positioned in the 5th Armoured Division sector of the Gothic Line. It vividly portrays the barren hills where the main battle was fought and the commanding view from German anti-tank emplacements such as the one in the foreground. (Canadian War Museum 13903)**

PURSUIT TO THE CONCA

No one was under any illusion the Germans were going to pull back very far. But if there were no more prepared lines of defence to the north, where would they make their next stand? Probably on a natural obstacle like a river; and there were a great many of them.

In many respects, 5th Armoured Division was not well suited to carry out a pursuit; its most battle-worthy units had already been 'used up' in the breakthrough battle and needed time to lick their wounds and replace casualties. The only fresh troops were two battalions of the new 12th Infantry Brigade – the Westminsters, which used to be the armoured brigade's motor battalion, and the brand-new Lanark and Renfrew Scottish (still going by the awkward temporary designation of 89th/109th Battalion). They would have to do the job, at least as far as the River Conca. The task given to the Horse Guards

was to push along the left flank and eventually seize a crossing over the Conca just west of San Giovanni in Marignano. En route the Regiment was to secure three dominant features, the last of which, a ridge south-west of San Gio-vanni, was codenamed Skeena. Perhaps reflecting the inexperience of 12th Brigade headquarters, there appears to have been very little prior coordination between the two battalions and the Regiment as to routes, timings and boundaries. This might be considered unusual, especially since some references, including the official history, state that one squadron was to be in support of each of the two battalions. It might also be said that there seems to have been little urgency in beginning the pursuit: it was not scheduled to get under way until the next morning.

The advance to the Conca began at first light on 2 September. 'C' Squadron led the Regiment, with 'B' Squadron close in behind, followed by Regimental Headquarters and then 'A' Squadron.

'C' Squadron encountered a variety of difficulties almost from the time it set out. Within a kilometre from the start point Lieutenant Pat Murphy, who was leading the column, took a wrong turn at a fork in the road, while the troop immediately behind was directed to follow the planned route. About two kilometres on, the troop sergeant's Stuart lost a track when it ran over a mine while trying to cross the River Tavollo, blocking the crossing site. The Germans were still resisting in this sector, and soon brought down a considerable weight of mortar fire, which made it very difficult to get the tank out of the crossing to repair the track. On the other fork of the trail, First Troop could not find a suitable crossing over the Tavollo for some time, so the entire advance came to a premature halt. Eventually both crossings were sorted out, the squadron was re-united and the column got on its way to the first objective, a high ridge about 2500 metres directly west of Tomba di Pesaro codenamed Crowmore.

'C' Squadron spent the better part of an hour on Crowmore, under heavy mortar fire for much of the time. Lieutenant Walt Lee's Sherman caught a direct hit on the gun, warping it sufficiently that the tank was put out of action. In his situation report over the radio, Lee is said to have reported the loss of some 90 cans of 'M&V' (the heartily disliked Compo ration meat and vegetables), which was cheered by everyone who heard the message! During this time First Troop moved to the west and knocked out an enemy SP gun that had been engaging elements of the 46th British Division, advancing on the left.

In the meanwhile, 'B' Squadron's Third Troop moved unhindered along the main Tomba di Pesaro-San Giovanni road. Just short of the intermediate objective, codenamed Carry Duff, the troop found the Westminster battalion headquarters. Their commander, Lieutenant Colonel Corbault, asked the troop not to advance onto the hill because they would draw fire on his men, so the 'B' Squadron vehicles stayed back. A second 'B' Squadron troop joined them at this time.

'C' Squadron encountered a whole series of misadventures which slowed its progress, but it finally got onto the Carry Duff feature at around 1400 hours. Major Burton met Colonel Corbault to arrange a joint attack on the final objective, Skeena, 2,000 metres to the north, and they agreed on a plan: the Westminster companies would put in their attack on the right, moving from bound to bound, while 'C' Squadron would advance quite separately along a spur some 800 metres to the left. This was pretty standard 1942 tank-infantry doctrine. Neither unit seems to have understood how tank-infantry cooperation tactics had changed to stress the use of a single axis, with tanks giving intimate support to infantry movement. These were the very close cooperation tactics that had been emphasized during 5th

Gothic Line
to the River Conca
2 – 3 September 1944

Armoured Brigade's intensive training after the Liri Valley battles, but being a divisional unit – armoured recce, not tank – the Horse Guards had not been involved.

Skeena was taken without opposition, and soon thereafter, 'C' Squadron was ordered to move down to the Conca to seize a river crossing 3,000 metres southwest of San Giovanni, the Westminsters being responsible for a crossing further to the right. However, before patrols could be sent forward new orders arrived: everyone was to remain at least 1,200 metres from the Conca so as to be outside the danger area when the Desert Air Force bombed the crossing sites to set off mines.

During the night, 'B' Squadron was sent on somewhat of a wild goose chase. The Regiment was directed to provide a squadron to race to the coastal highway to cut off the retreat of German paratroopers. Major Tim Hugman was given command of a motor company and a carrier platoon of the Westminsters, and just before midnight they passed through San Giovanni along the main road to the town of Cattolica. This foray was yet another example of very bad coordination within I Canadian Corps. These 5th Division troops were given a mission well inside 1st Division's sector, which all staff officers should have known was not acceptable, and in any case, a 1st Division force – the RCD and a Van Doo company – were already doing that very job. 'B' Squadron did not rejoin the rest of the Regiment until the next morning.

Fuel was the immediate concern on the morning of 3 September. The squadron 'A' echelons had not been able to get forward during the night, and most of the tanks were too low on fuel to go very far. The 'A' Squadron liaison officer, Lieutenant Ted Friend, was sent out in his Humber scout car to bring up the echelons. Sadly, he ran over a mine which blew off both his legs. He was quickly evacuated to a field ambulance but died that same evening.

THE APPROACH TO CORIANO

The general advance continued on 3 September amidst rumours that the Germans were conducting a widespread pull out. Some thought that the Italian campaign had entered a new, potentially decisive phase. From the Conca to the south end of the flat Po valley was but 20 kilometres, and if Eighth Army could get there before the heavy autumn rains, then perhaps the Germans could be forced back to the Alps. This was, of course, wishful thinking combined with very bad intelligence: much rough, defensible terrain still had to be taken before reaching the Po Valley, and then there was an endless succession of rivers and canals running at right angles to the advance.

The Canadian Corps' objective for the next phase of the campaign was the north bank of the Marecchia River which ran westward from Rimini. The first 'bound' was the capture of a ridge line two kilometres north of the Conca, and then it was on to the second, the River Marano, ten kilometres further on.

The Strathconas led the division attack, crossing over the Conca west of San Giovanni just after 0600 hours on 3 September. As the Strathconas moved beyond the river, the Westminsters crossed, and then the 8th Hussars. Very little opposition was encountered until the lead squadron of the Strathconas was just short of the village of Misano, where they set up a defensive perimeter while waiting for the Westmin-

sters to sweep up bypassed pockets of resistance. By noon it was clear there were still many German troops to the north and west of Misano, especially in the area of Monte Gallera, 1,500 metres to the west. Shortly afterward the 8th Hussars attempted to continue the advance south of Misano, but were brought to a halt by anti-tank guns in the vicinity of Monte Gallera and intensive shelling that had already been pounding the Strathconas for over an hour.

The Horse Guards were brought into the battle just after 1200 hours. 'A' Squadron, the first over the Conca, moved almost due west toward its immediate objective, Point 167 on Monte Annibolina, which overlooked the boundary between the Canadian and British Corps. The squadron had advanced only about 1,800 metres from the river when they were fired on by German infantry and machine guns. While taking out these positions, Trooper James Copeland was killed and Corporal Chuck Dobson, Troopers L.A. Hawkins and H. Stokoloff were wounded and had to be evacuated. The lead troop had only moved on by a few hundred metres when Sergeant Ron Humphries spotted an 88mm gun off to the left. Lieutenant Gordie Base saw it too, and hit the gun with two rounds of high explosive, which set it aflame. Minutes later three Mark IV Special tanks were seen on the main lateral road north of the river, but when fired on the enemy tanks "streaked up the road" and disappeared. The First Troop tanks continued toward Monte Annibolina, shooting up houses, haystacks and other likely targets. It had barely started to climb the southern slope when, coming around the corner of a house, it encountered two Tiger tanks only 25 metres away. Fortunately the German crew commanders were as surprised as our own and the Tiger guns were pointed in the opposite direction. (Because of the slow manual traverse system in the Tiger, the turret could not be swung around quickly.) Base's Sherman had a high-explosive round 'up the spout', which the gunner fired. Base then shouted an order to fire armour-piercing, but his gunner stepped on the machine-gun trigger pedal by mistake. It was probably just as well, since a Sherman was certain to come out second best in a duel with a Tiger. In any case, the Tiger commanders seemed in no mood to fight, for these formidable vehicles slowly lumbered away before Base got his other tanks in position to bring fire on them.

More German infantry were flushed out during the climb onto the wooded slope of Monte Annibolina, and one particularly brave man ran alongside a Sherman for nearly 50 metres – rifle at the ready and aimed in the general direction of the crew commander – before a burst of coax fire persuaded him to leave off. By 1500 hours First Troop was at Point 167 at the top of Annibolina, and the other 'A' Squadron troops adopted a defensive posture on the southern slope. The Germans did not seem to be especially happy with this arrangement, and the 'A' Squadron positions were mortared almost from the moment they arrived.

British infantry were seen moving up on the squadron's left, so Major Appleton, now commanding 'A' Squadron, sent a patrol from the Assault Troop to make contact and give the squadron's location. Corporal W.D. Johnson, the patrol commander, had just returned to make his report when a mortar bomb landed beside his scout car. Troopers James Hanley and Kenneth Morrison were killed instantly, and Troopers L. Levine and Gerry Major were wounded and had to be evacuated.

'A' Squadron remained in position on Monte Annibolina until just after 1900 hours, and their brief stay was anything but quiet. On three occasions mortar bombs set fire to Honey tanks, but in every case the crew was able to extinguish the flames, although always at great risk because of the likelihood of ammunition exploding, which did happen on one occasion. Then, a German SP gun on Monte Gallera came into action just before 1630 hours, threatening all the forward vehicles. Major Frank Classey brought his Sherman up, and as the wartime history recounts, "He fired four rounds of high explosive and three of armour piercing, scoring a hit, as the gun was seen to brew up and was later found abandoned and demolished when the squadron advanced." About then a troop of M10s tank destroyers from 82nd Anti Tank Battery moved in to give fire support, and only minutes later a British infantry company arrived with the intention of advancing to Point 130 – the top of Monte Gallera, about 1,800 metres due north. They were being held up by a machine gun in a barn 500 metres north of the squadron's location, so the forward tanks shelled the barn so the British advance could continue. (The British infantry never did get onto Monte Gallera, perhaps because someone recognized that it was in the Canadian Corps sector.) Later in the afternoon, British Churchill tanks belonging to the North Irish Horse arrived on the squadron's immediate left, but they were not especially interested in co-operative ventures. (The problem of close cooperation between units deployed right on a formation boundary persists to this day, to the extent that it is an operational principle: exploit the inherent weakness by attacking along a boundary whenever possible. While it was not known at the time, the 5th Division attack through the Gothic Line occurred on the boundary between two German divisions.)

'C' Squadron began moving forward late in the afternoon, arriving just short of Monte Annibolina at about 1930 hours,

![Safe conduct pass]

Safe conduct pass dropped over German lines in early September 1944 (Courtesy Bob Murray)

which allowed 'A' Squadron to carry their attack northward to Monte Gallera. The Horse Guards were not the only Canadian armour interested in Monte Gallera; the 8th Hussars were still being prevented from advancing westward from Misano by anti-tank guns on Gallera. The fighting was beginning to take on a much more intense character: the Germans had decided to make an all-out effort to stop the Canadian advance.

Before 'A' Squadron's lead troop got very far on the way to Monte Gallera, the troop sergeant's Honey was hit by an armour-piercing round which broke the track. The next instant, Lieutenant Gordie Base's Sherman was knocked out; one armour-piercing round throwing the driver's hatch over the turret and another penetrating the final drive right up to the ammunition bins. Watching what happened, Corporal Tom Ruff carefully eased his Sherman into a position where he could see the German 75mm gun.

Sergeant Thomas William Eric Ruff, MM. (GGHG Archives)

Corporal Ruff, with great skill and determination, manoeuvred his tank into a position from which he could engage the anti-tank gun with machine-gun fire. While his crew continued to engage the gun, Corporal Ruff dismounted under fire and working his way forward, took the gun crew prisoner. By his initiative, courage, and resourcefulness, this Non-Commissioned Officer ensured the continued advance of his squadron.

Thomas William Eric Ruff was awarded the Military Medal for his bravery that evening. The words above are from his citation.

It was getting dark by the time this sharp little battle was played out, and Major Appleton knew the squadron was well out in enemy territory. Rather than return to Monte Annibolina, which had been shelled all day, he decided to move on another thousand metres to a re-entrant on the southeast side of Monte Gallera which he had noted on his map. There the squadron would be out of sight and also get some degree of protection from shelling and direct fire. And, in a 'close laager' formation, the squadron could defend itself against whatever enemy might stumble onto the position.

Meanwhile, 'C' Squadron dug in on and around Monte Annibolina, while 'B' Squadron harboured on the north side of the Conca waiting a call to move to the front. In another example of difficulties coordinating operations on a formation boundary, this time tragic, 'C' Squadron's assault troop was attacked by a company of the Hampshire Regiment. The British unit was occupying a position to the left forward of the area assigned to the Assault Troop, and not knowing that other friendly units were in the vicinity they mistook the Horse Guards men as enemy. Unfortunately, Troopers Verdun Badgley and Llewellyn Eaton were killed before the British attack could be stopped.

The Canadians were to have no easy march to Rimini, or to the Marano River for that matter. While the Germans were making an enormous effort to thicken the defences along their Rimini Line, orders were given on 3 September to all German formations to hold the Canadians well south of Rimini. Ad hoc blocking groups were created out of the remnants of depleted units, and reinforcements were rushed in on 4 September. Most significant for the units of 5th Armoured Division, 29 Panzer Grenadier Division, although understrength, was deployed onto Coriano Ridge. While this six-kilometre-long feature was in the V British Corps sector, its garrison overlooked and dominated almost all the ground that would have to be crossed in the Canadian advance.

The next stage of the Canadian offensive began at first light on 4 September. The 8th Hussars passed through the Strathcona positions near Misano, intending to thrust to the River Marano, five kilometres distant, with their centre line generally along the feature known as Besanigo Ridge. The

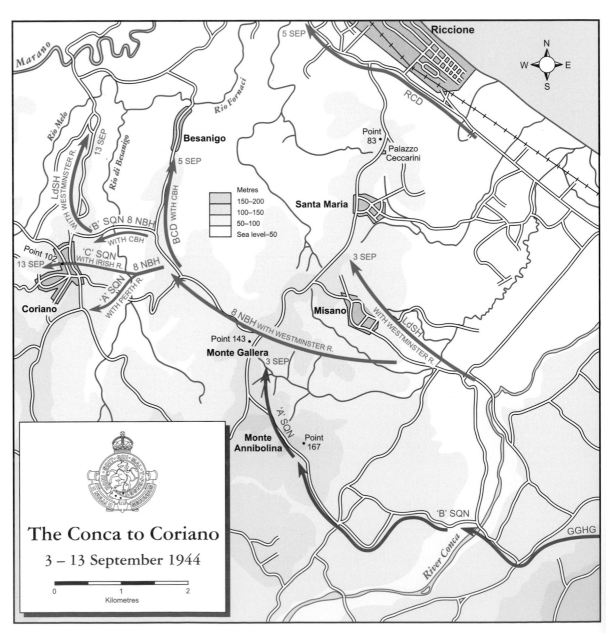

The Conca to Coriano
3 – 13 September 1944

Hussars first cleared the area of Monte Gallera, where 'A' Squadron held the southeastern slope, and they destroyed several anti-tank guns that had fired on all the Canadian units in the sector. Once the Hussars got onto Besanigo Ridge they ran into serious problems: their entire left flank was exposed to the Germans on Coriano Ridge just 2,000 metres away, and they began to lose one tank after another. Their push faltered and ground to a halt. The BCD were then brought up to push farther along the ridge, but they ran into the same sort of fanatical resistance. In fact, the entire Canadian offensive sputtered out until Coriano Ridge was taken in a well-orchestrated attack by 11th Brigade nine days later, on 13 September. The Germans had by then gained the delay they wanted, so there was little enemy resistance until the San Fortunato Ridge, west of Rimini.

After the battle for Coriano, 5th Armoured Division, many of its units badly mauled in the fighting from the Gothic Line to Coriano, was relieved and sent to the rear for rest. The division was to have just over a week, concentrated in harbours scattered in the countryside around San Giovanni, on the south side of the Conca, for rest and replenishment. In the meantime 1st Division fought on, capturing the vital San Fortunato Ridge west of Rimini, and establishing a lodgement on the north bank of the River Marecchia. On 23 September 5th Armoured Division was brought in to spearhead the long-expected "debouch" into the flatlands of the Po valley.

THE CROSSING OF THE USO AND SALTO RIVERS

5th Armoured Division was now given the grossly optimistic mission of advancing to Bologna. The first bound in this eighty kilometre thrust was to be the Fiumicino River, known in Roman history as the Rubicon. In the six kilometres between the Marecchia bridgehead and the Fiumicino ran two other lesser rivers, the Uso and the Salto. The first phase, the capture of a crossing over the Uso, was to be done on 23 September by 4 PLDG supported by a squadron of the Strathconas. This attack, however, was brought to a dead halt within an hour by stiff German resistance in the villages of Casale and Variano, not much more than a thou-

sand metres from the start line. In that short time, the Strathconas lost seven of their Shermans to anti-tank guns they never saw in the thick vineyards.

Over the course of the 23rd, 12th Brigade progressively brought up everything they had to try to break the stalemate; first the Westminsters were committed to a right flanking attack on the village of San Vito which stalled 1,500 metres due east of the village, then the Lanark and Renfrews were brought in on the Westminsters right, but they had no better luck. Finally, the Horse Guards were called forward.

At 0640 hours on 24 September, 'B' Squadron got orders to move through the Westminsters, who by then were holding a crossroad 1,500 metres east of San Vito. The squadron was then to swing west to the Uso and secure a crossing about a thousand metres north of San Vito.

One of the decidedly new aspects the Regiment encountered almost immediately after crossing the Marecchia was the Germans' prolific use of anti-tank mines: they seemed to have been laid everywhere. That morning 'C' Squadron had a Sherman completely disabled when it ran over a mine in the squadron harbour. Having been warned that the road serving as the brigade's right-hand axis was mined, Captain Bud Baker, who had temporarily replaced Major Hugman in command of 'B' Squadron, decided to move cross country through the vineyards and orchards to the area held by the

"A goose, sir??? – Not around here, sir!, 'At's Beanie he's got a bad cold, sir!"

Westminsters. While the ground was wet, it was still relatively firm, but things began to go wrong right from the outset. Almost immediately after leaving the main road just north of Variano, Sergeant Scotty Leith's Stuart went up on a mine. About a thousand metres further on Lieutenant George 'Chippy' Brown's Third Troop, in the lead, encountered a deep drainage ditch which anchored a dense belt of anti-tank mines. This obstacle delayed the squadron's advance by several hours, and there were a number of casualties in getting through. Trooper Charles Wilson was badly wounded and died the next day. One of the Shermans rolled over as it tried to negotiate the bank of the ditch, Fourth Troop had two

Stuarts disabled in the minefield, and one of its Shermans threw a track in the ditch. The other troops did not even try to get forward for the moment. It was mid-morning by the time Brown contacted the Westminster company commander to get a briefing on what was happening on this part of the front. Meanwhile, the Sherman that had rolled over rejoined the other troop vehicles just as the entire area came under heavy shelling. The tank received two direct hits, and three of the crew – Lance Corporal Charles Simmons, Trooper William Campbell and Trooper Charles Rumbles – were killed, while Trooper Thorolf Lade later died of his wounds.

The Second World War history describes the squadron's subsequent trials:

> By 1330 hours, 'B' Squadron had been reduced to a strength of six Shermans and six Stuarts and efforts to debog the casualties had not been successful. Two Sherman bulldozers attached to the Regiment had been sent forward to assist them, but … they refused to take them into the thick of the shellfire. After a great deal of work 1st Troop managed to make their own crossing of the two ditches blocking their advance by driving the tanks in and digging out their bows until they were clear.

The first tank to cross the second of the ditches was the one commanded by Cpl. Haggarty. It made contact at once with enemy infantry. The tank engaged them, killing at least six and forcing the remainder to flee to the nearby houses; but it was then faced with a Panther tank coming down the road at fifty yards range. Both tanks saw each other at the same time and the Panther backed in behind a farmhouse. The troop leader, Lieut. J.M. Murray, ordered a Stuart to proceed cautiously and attempt to locate the Panther…. Sgt. W.W. Gardiner of 1st Troop … spott[ed] two Panthers beside one of the houses and Lieut. Murray attempted to manoeuvre his Sherman into the best fire position. As they moved, Lieut.

"Not a total wreck, sir, the horn still works."

Murray's tank was knocked out, two shots penetrating the turret. Lieut. John Murray was killed, while Tprs W.H.B. (Wilf) Keen and N.A. Herimann were both seriously wounded.

The squadron dug and fought its way over a thousand metres beyond the Westminster Regiment's positions, crossing two substantial drainage ditches that were significant obstacles to tanks. But much depleted and with no immediate reserves, Captain Baker reported to the colonel that it would be useless to try to push on, and he pulled the forward tanks back by about 300 metres into a more defensible position. At last light a company of the Lanark and Renfrews came up to occupy the area, and the squadron withdrew.

In the rear area, Trooper Karl Abercrombie, driver of the 'A' Squadron kitchen truck, was killed when his vehicle ran over a mine while he was bringing up a hot meal for the men. The squadron later removed 142 Schuh mines from their daytime harbour area. In the evening 'A' Squadron moved to the front to be prepared for a further advance next morning, harbouring behind the Westminsters. Major Appleton's orders were to seize a crossing over the Uso at the point where a main road from San Mauro to the sea crossed the river. That night the squadron harbour was shelled with such intensity that it was impossible for the crews to dismount from the tanks.

On the morning of 25 September, Major Harry Appleton made contact with the commander of the Lanark and Renfrews to coordinate support for the next phase of the advance. The battalion had already planned a two-phased attack, but because the high rows of vines severely limited fields of view, the Horse Guards were asked to hold in their present position until called forward. Shortly before 1000 hours two recce troops and the assault troop moved north to assist the Lanarks in consolidating their objective. This move of about 1,700 metres took considerably longer than expected; because of the very real risk of mines in the fields the tanks had to keep to the road, which was cut by two large craters and yet another drainage ditch. But once having arrived at the Lanark and Renfrew position, it was obvious that the vehicles had passed through the belt of mines and could now get off the roads. 'A' Squadron then pressed on toward their main objective, the intended location of the main crossing of the Uso in this sector. While they ran into "a tangle of drainage ditches which were impassable to tanks", with a considerable amount of ingenuity and a little bit of luck, along with the skilled help of the assault troop, at about 1500 hours the squadron got almost up to the crossing site.

But the tanks were again blocked: a minefield covered all approaches to the river. To complicate matters, very accurate German shelling began to target the squadron and interfered with everything that needed to be done. Foot patrols were sent to the river bank, and they brought back very useful information: the bridge on the main road was indeed destroyed beyond repair, but there was a nearby ford which German tanks had recently used. Unfortunately, the patrols also found that the far bank of the Uso was defended by about two companies of enemy infantry, and they appeared to be well dug in. Trooper Earl Moulton was killed during this recce of the crossing site. 'A' Squadron could not take on a force of this size by themselves, so Colonel Jordan made arrangements that a company of the Westminsters would be sent forward. However, by the time this company came up, 12th Brigade had decided that the assault across the river would not be made until the next morning

During the night there was a drenching rain which turned the soil into heavy mud, and for a time there was serious concern that tank movement would be affected. At first light on 26 September, Major Appleton and the Westminster company commander went forward to look at an alternative crossing site that had been found about 1,500 metres to the south: it had good approaches, a firm gravel bottom, and there were no enemy on the far bank. But military bureaucracy is sometimes as unbending as other forms. Major Appleton was ordered to seize the originally intended crossing site, despite the mines and despite the enemy reported to be on the far bank!

The plan of attack was arranged accordingly. At noon, First and Fourth Troops moved up to positions on either side of the crossing site along lanes already cleared of mines, and a short time later a company of the Westminsters waded across the shallow river and took up positions on the far bank. Surprisingly, there was no immediate enemy reaction, but Tiger tanks were reported moving toward the crossing. First Troop then moved down in single file on a lane cleared of mines by the divisional assault troop. "As the leading Stuart moved up the far bank, it struck a mine, which blew off the right front sprocket, wounding the co-driver and completely blocking the crossing."

Quick action was essential, especially since the Germans were again bringing a heavy weight of mortar and artillery fire on the immediate area.. The squadron Assault Troop was detailed to cross to the far bank to give protection while the divisional assault troop cleared the a lane to re-open the crossing site. The Regimental history relates:

At 1345 hours the leading section was across and was being followed by the remaining two sections, when there suddenly occurred an explosion of terrible violence. To observers on the near side of the stream it appeared to lift the entire floor of the gully. Our assault troop was hopelessly trapped and sustained tragically high casualties with sixteen men killed and five wounded....

This was by far the Regiment's worst tragedy of the entire war. The loss of any member of the Regiment was sorely felt by his close buddies and comrades, but the death of sixteen men numbed the senses. The casualties in this action were Sergeant Arthur Rogers, Corporals Jesse Gilbert and Walter

A 5th Armoured Brigade tank making a difficult crossing of one of the diked rivers in the Po Valley. This scene is typical of conditions encountered by the Horse Guards in late September 1944. (NAC PA173521)

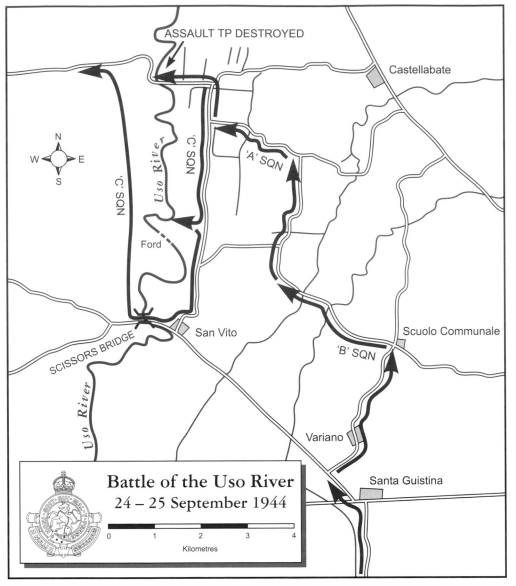

Battle of the Uso River
24 – 25 September 1944

0   1   2   3   4
Kilometres

use, Major Allan Burton got Colonel Jordan's permission to take his squadron south to where the Westminsters' 'B' Company had got across and which several hours back had been reported as suitable for tanks.

'C' Squadron's progress toward this southern site was slow because craters and mines prevented movement off the roadways. It was thus close to 1600 hours when the squadron got there, and it was immediately seen that the ford was not suitable because of mines and hopelessly boggy approaches to both banks. Burton had, however, become aware that the armoured brigade had set up a scissors bridge just north of San Vito, less that a kilometre away, and there he went. Thus by 1630 hours 'C' Squadron was across the Uso and heading northward to join the Westminster battle group. As the squadron moved it came under increasingly intense shelling and mortaring, and in this rain of steel Trooper Edmund Watson was killed by a piece of shrapnel.

During the night of 26/27 September the Cape Breton Highlanders relieved the Westminsters between the Uso and Salto rivers. For the Horse Guards squadrons at the front, it proved to be a day of confused waiting under continual shelling as preparations were made for an assault crossing over the Salto. Late in the afternoon 'C' Squadron pulled back to the east side of the Uso as there seemed no prospect that the operation would be attempted that day. In fact, the CBH did wade across late in the afternoon, but they were brought to a halt by enemy machine guns about midway between the Salto and the next river – the Fiumicino – the legendary Rubicon that Caesar crossed in an attack in the other direction in 49 BC.

There was enormous pressure at every level to establish a bridgehead on the far side of the Fiumicino, and the Horse Guards had their part to play in what turned out to be a tragedy. 'C' Squadron moved off at first light on 28 September, having been given the completely unrealistic task of passing through the infantry, seizing a crossing over the Fiumicino and then advancing to Bagnarola some 6,000 metres beyond

Johnston, Lance Corporal Hervé Deschenes and Troopers Allan Anderson, Robert Balfour, Samuel Hill, Kenneth Innes, Eric Kaulback, Victor Lane, Charles Lampman, Phillibert Robillard, George Snider, Frank Willett, Clarence Winterburn and Alexander Young. Each of them would, however, have known that the battle would not stop because of tragedy, and that the immediate problem of getting the better of the Germans there and then had to be confronted.

For the next several hours frantic efforts were made to repair the crossing by filling craters and double-checking for mines. In the meanwhile the entire Westminster Regiment waded across the Uso, one company using a second crossing site about 1,500 metres to the south. The infantry made good progress in pushing on toward the Salto, encountering only moderate opposition, but they needed tank support for the assault across the Salto. While 'A' Squadron was instructed to remain where it was, crossing when the site was put back into

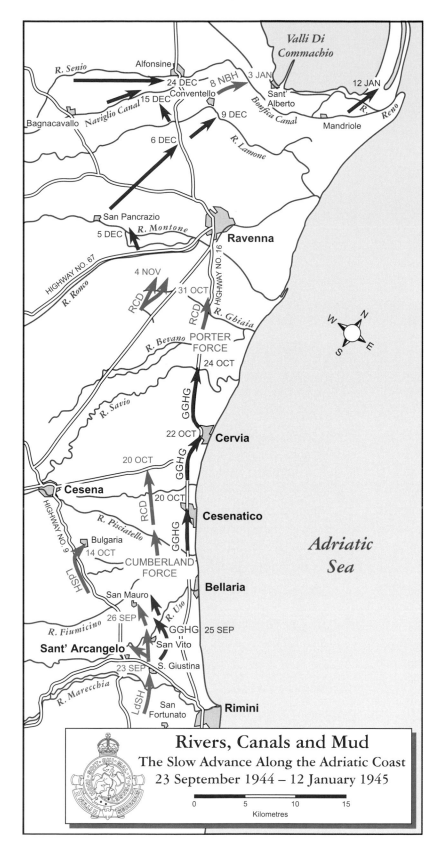

Rivers, Canals and Mud
The Slow Advance Along the Adriatic Coast
23 September 1944 – 12 January 1945

0   5   10   15
Kilometres

metre of the river before they simply could not move any farther. 'B' Squadron was also sent forward to fill a gap between the Irish Regiment and the CBH, but their push also stalled in the mud. In fact, the entire offensive – the grand debouch into the Po Valley – came to an abrupt, if not entirely unexpected halt at the Rubicon. This was the last major armoured offensive of the Italian campaign. There was a great deal of fighting still to be done, but the character of the war now changed very significantly.

The Regiment remained in position near the Uso until 4 October, when all squadrons moved to harbours in the rear near San Vito. But yet another member – Trooper Elmer Olney – was killed in action on 3 October before departing the battlefield. It rained continuously. The rivers and canals flooded over their banks, most bridges were washed away, and vehicle movement, even on the roads, became absolutely impossible. Armour just was not of any use in these conditions.

CUMBERLAND FORCE

At this time Eighth Army shifted the weight of the main thrust further inland where the ground was marginally better, so a greater part of the responsibility fell to V British Corps. The axis of the I Canadian Corps push at this time also shifted to the left – closer to Highway 9, and in the direction of Cesena. There was thus a pressing need for someone to take over an ever-increasing gap in the impassable coastal sector. With tanks all but grounded, 5th Armoured Brigade headquarters was not otherwise usefully employed, so an ad hoc group of units was put together as Cumberland Force, named for Brigadier Ian Cumberland, who was detailed as commander.

Cumberland Force was made up of an odd collection of troops – the 3rd Greek Mountain Brigade, soon to be sent home to newly liberated Greece; 'Wilder Force', two dismounted squadrons of 2nd New Zealand Divisional Cavalry, a dismounted anti-tank regiment and an assortment of other NZ units; the 27th (British) Lancers (dismounted); the Royal Canadian Dragoons (dismounted); and, after 16 October, the Governor General's Horse Guards, also dismounted.

The task assigned to Cumberland Force was to protect the

the river. The squadron never really got very far; the 'going' was very bad to begin with, and it got progressively worse as the heavy rain turned the soil into ever deeper and more liquid mud. To their credit, 'C' Squadron tanks got within a kilo-

right flank of I Canadian Corps as it advanced north to the River Savio. It was to maintain contact and exert such pressure as it could as the Germans withdrew in the face of Allied gains further to the west where the real battles were taking place. There was no intention of mounting large-scale attacks, but the units of Cumberland Force were told to follow up every rearward move by the Germans. It was to be a "slow deliberate process", as another regimental historian described the operation. Cumberland Force started functioning on 10 October when it formally took over responsibility for a six-kilometre sector along the Fiumicino River. There was, however, little real action until 16 October, when the Germans fell back to a major drainage canal known as the Scolo Rigossa.

At this time both the Greek brigade and 'Wilder Force' were withdrawn, with the Horse Guards coming in to replace the Greeks. On the night of 17/18 October 1944, the Regiment took over a 3,000-metre sector running inland from the coast. On the immediate left was the 27th Lancers, and beyond them the RCD.

Other than periodic sniper and mortar fire, the Horse Guards' sector was relatively quiet during the first two days. The Germans were, however, still firmly in possession of the far bank of the Fiumicino, with pillboxes covering extensive wire obstacles and minefields. The squadrons nonetheless patrolled actively on the enemy side of the river during hours of darkness, playing cat and mouse with German patrols. The situation began to change on the morning of 19 October when an attack by 2nd New Zealand Division, on the left flank of Cumberland Force, took the Germans by surprise and forced them to withdraw toward the Savio River, some 18 kilometres to the north.

While the Germans began to pull back in front of the RCD and 27th Lancers, rearguards held out opposite the Horse Guards throughout the day on 19 October. Anticipating that the Germans only wanted to impose a slight additional delay in the area of Highway 16, still the best avenue of advance, 'B' Squadron waded across the Fiumicino at 1700 hours under the cover of protective fire from 'C' Squadron tanks. By last light the squadron held a shallow bridgehead, but enemy machine guns prevented any significant advance. However, patrols sent out during the night found no enemy at all, and at first light on 20 October 'B' Squadron pushed forward nearly a thousand metres. The wartime history records subsequent developments:

> As the Germans seemed to have disappeared completely, the C.O. commandeered bicycles, and with [Second Lieutenant] Amadori [the Italian liaison officer] and [Captain

Frank Lalor], the battle captain, pedalled up the highway towards the town of Cesenatico. They passed the patrols and as they were greeted by all civilians with the cry of "Nienti Tedeschi" [no Germans], they entered the western part of the town, to find it almost deserted. The bridges across the canal that cuts across the northern outskirts were all demolished, but they rowed across with a couple of boatmen, and were met on the other side by an Italian nun of grandiloquent proportions....

Cesenatico was the first major town on the Adriatic to be liberated by the Horse Guards, and indeed the colonel himself rightly claimed that honour. Brigadier Cumberland's official report on his task force formally noted this accomplishment by a bicycle-borne component of "Canada's mechanized army!"

'A' Squadron was quickly brought forward, and by 1700 hours had positions on the north side of the town. 'C' Squadron attempted to move up with their vehicles just to the left of Highway 16, but had to harbour southwest of the town because road craters and blown bridges blocked their way. Because vehicles could not get to Cesenatico, resupply of the forward troops became a serious problem. Eventually, the technical adjutant, Captain Jack McKechan, overcame the problem by commandeering two DUKWs – American-built amphibious carriers – which could bypass the roadblocks and come ashore at the north end of Cesenatico.

The 'A' Squadron advance up Route 16 – the lead patrol on bicycles, the remainder of the squadron on foot – was continued on the morning of 21 October. As the wartime history noted,

> Extra supplies and ammunition were a problem; but not an insoluble one, for a weird collection of handcarts of all va-

'C' Squadron meal parade, autumn 1944. (GGHG Archives)

rieties was dragged and pushed up the highway. The resulting procession was certainly most unorthodox and a sight to shock the precisionist, but it served our purpose and everyone was enthusiastic. All we lacked were the dancing girls, the elephants and the band.

It was all very uneventful until German machine-gun positions, both on the main highway and on the secondary road 400 metres to the east, fired on the leading troops about five kilometres south of the town of Cervia. The enemy position east of the main road was taken out, twice it happened, by skilful flanking attacks by a dismounted patrol led by Lance Corporal Tom Leadbetter. Leadbetter received a well-deserved Military Medal for this and other instances of exceptionally bravery and competent leadership. His citation for the medal reads in part:

> Corporal Leadbetter was leading the forward section. At approximately 0930 hours the section was fired on and pinned by a Spandau machine gun at an important crossroads and the advance was halted. Corporal Leadbetter crawled forward to within a range of 75 yards and knocked out the enemy machine gun with a Bren gun. He was then ordered to return to his troop headquarters, and the next section continued the advance. In the meantime, the enemy had reoccupied the same position. Corporal Leadbetter again led his section forward and personally led an assault on the position, engaging it with hand grenades at very short range, capturing two Germans and killing another four, thus enabling the squadron to continue the advance....

The machine gun beside Highway 16 was surrounded by flat, open ground and there was no way to get at it in daylight without excessive risk.

For several days the Regiment had been employing a somewhat ragtag group of local men which some wag had dubbed 'The Italo-Canadian Amateur Sappers Incorporated', to fill in craters and rebuild damaged bridges, and the work they did, however slow, did help considerably to maintain some element of mobility in the Regiment. The afternoon of 21 October brought the unit into contact with another group of partisans from Cervia, who claimed to have a band of 200 men ready to assist in the capture of the town if only the Regiment would give them weapons and ammunition. The War Diary notes: "A frantic call was sent out for all the grenades, Tommy guns and Brens we could get. Under the personal instruction of the CO they had soon passed their TsOET [Tests on Elementary Training] and were ready for battle." Plans were then agreed: 'A' Squadron would take out the German machine-gun position by midnight, and the partisans were to attack the Germans from the rear at 0500 hours on the morning of 22 October.

The troublesome machine-gun post was removed during the night by a platoon-strength patrol led by Lieutenant Frank Clapp. "The success of this operation was largely due to the ingenuity and daring of Trooper J. Neuspiel who used his knowledge of German to lure the sentries away one by one, until he had bagged four. By calling them by name, having determined this from the preceding one, he lured them into the darkness where they were quite surprised to feel the muzzle of Neuspiel's Tommy gun in their backs." Trooper Neuspiel's exceptional devotion to duty was not recognized until after the end of the war when he was given a Mention in Despatches. Until close to the end of the war, Colonel Jordan refused to endorse most recommendations for awards sent forward by the squadron commanders; brave conduct, according to him, was no more than doing one's duty. The consequence of this policy was that the Horse Guards got proportionally fewer bravery decorations than other armoured regiments during the war.

The partisans never did carry out their intended attack on the morning of 22 October: it seems that the Germans were in greater strength than they had reported. However, that made little difference to the outcome. By 0630 hours, the lead troop, commanded by Lieutenant Bob Murray, had passed unopposed through Cervia and established a defensive perimeter 500 metres north of the town. German rearguards had, however, not entirely departed and in early afternoon a fighting patrol was sent into the north-

Members of 'A' Squadron with Italian partisans at their objective just north of Cervia, October 1944. (Courtesy of Bob Murray)

The Albergo Mare e Pineta, north of Cervia, occupied by Regimental Headquarters on 22 October 1944. (GGHG Archives)

ern suburbs. They succeeded in taking out five enemy machine guns, but in this fighting Lieutenant Frank Clapp was fatally wounded by a sniper. Active patrolling was also conducted west of the town, toward the extensive salt marshes. Here, Sergeant J.P. Ross was wounded while leading a patrol intending to take out a pillbox with a PIAT gun.

Meanwhile, during the morning 'C' Squadron carried the battle several thousand metres northwest of the town along Highway 16. At about 1030 hours one of Lieutenant Pat Murphy's Stuarts was knocked out by a *panzerfaust*. It took some time before another patrol was able to get forward, and they found Trooper William Beeswax mortally wounded, and he died soon afterward. Sergeant Bob Harding had multiple shrapnel wounds, and the other two members of the crew were shell-shocked to the point that they were incapable of moving.

In the early afternoon 'B' Squadron moved up. There were still isolated pockets of enemy troops holding out in Cervia, so the squadron was tasked to clear the built-up area. For the most part the house-to-house clearance was tedious but uneventful, but it was not without cost. A very promising, recently joined young officer, Lieutenant Lawrence 'Pete' McCormack, was killed by a sniper while directing his troops in the street clearance. Here was the unusual example of a reinforcement officer, all but unknown in the unit, whose innate leadership attributes had been immediately recognized by his men and by his peers.

By evening on 22 October the enemy had pulled well back from Cervia, and 'B' Squadron was able to advance nearly a thousand metres beyond positions previously held. Lieutenant Lorne Chesney had the good fortune to occupy the fashionable Albergo Mare e Pinetta on the beach, and the proprietor, in proper British style, graciously served tea and cakes to the whole troop (the tea, it was properly noted, was heavily laced with good-quality local brandy). This elegant establishment was soon to become the Regimental officers' mess.

The advance in the coastal sector continued on 23 October against somewhat dispirited enemy opposition – a few snipers and the occasional machine gun. By evening the leading elements of 'B' Squadron were at the canal immediately to the south of the Savio, and 'C' Squadron, attempting an outflanking movement off to the west, reached the junction of the Savio and the Canal del Duca without encountering any enemy. By this time a Bailey bridge had been built at Cesenatico, so the Regiment was able to move tanks up to Cervia, and when partisans made temporary repairs to a damaged bridge on the north side of Cervia tanks were sent up to the area of the beach occupied by 'B' Squadron's Third Troop.

In the meantime, Regimental headquarters had discovered the Albergo Mare e Pinetta:

> The proprietor had dug up his buried stock of wines and liquor, producing even Scotch whiskey and soda; and the whole atmosphere was so delightfully civilized that we determined to hang on to the hotel at all costs, leaving a rear party to hold it for the day we were relieved, defending it from the envious clutches of Div and Brigade headquarters.

At dawn on 24 October, 'B' Squadron continued its northward push. The Assault Troop, advancing astride Highway 16, made good progress until it came under fire from an enemy strongpoint 400 metres south of the Savio River. In the meanwhile, Third Troop, on the beach road, was stopped cold by a well-sited German machine gun while trying to cross a canal. In this attempt Sergeant Alexander Chambers was killed by enemy fire. Lieutenant Lorne Chesney then moved his tank to the bank of the canal to give cover to the men trying to get back, but almost immediately he too was killed by a sniper's bullet. At this point the Technical Adjutant, Captain Jack McKechan, went forward with two Shermans. They pounded the German position for nearly half and hour with high-explosive shells and machine guns, during which time the enemy troops lost their will to resist; twelve fled and at least six were killed. Nonetheless, no further attempt was made during the day to press onward, and just after nightfall 'A' Company of the Perth Regiment relieved 'B' Squadron.

The next day, the Perths discovered that the Germans had again withdrawn, and they pursued the enemy nearly to the Bevano River before being stopped by machine-gun and mortar fire. This was fighting at a very low tactical level, but it was relentless and frustrating; communications with troops at the front, for example, had become a nightmare. The infantry man-pack radios rarely if ever worked, so great reliance was put on line-connected field telephones. But these fragile wires were often cut by vehicles running over them by accident, by shellfire, or sometimes even by deliberate sabotage. Maintenance of the line communications became a vital element in the command and control of the Regiment, and one dedicated NCO was in large measure responsible for the success the Regiment enjoyed. Sergeant Raymond Johns, the regimental signals sergeant, was awarded a Military Medal for his dedication to duty and superb leadership. His citation reads in part:

> The complex system of line communications required for this role appeared impossible from the resources within the Regiment. Sergeant Johns immediately undertook to assemble the necessary equipment to provide signal coverage for this extremely difficult change-over. Working at high speed, Sergeant Johns and his detachment accomplished the task and when the Regiment went into action complete wireless and line communications were available. Throughout the long operation this outstanding Non-Commissioned Officer inspired his men to such a degree that maintenance and repair of signal cables were of the highest order. The initiative and devotion to duty displayed by Sergeant Johns have materially contributed to the brilliant success of the operation…..

Shortly after midnight on 26 October the Perth company waded across the Bevano River, and by first light it had a small bridgehead. It was intended that 'A' Squadron, mounted on bicycles, would take over the lead, but the Perth company commander sent word that they were pinned down by machine-gun and mortar fire, and that 'A' Squadron's push should be called off. It was just as well. Early in the afternoon the rain turned into a torrential downpour. The rivers, canals and ditches were already swollen almost to the top of their banks by the long stretch of wet weather. The wartime history recounts:

> During the afternoon the Savio rose at a rate that was most alarming, sweeping the floating bridge from its moorings

and beginning to batter the dykes. In the end the pressure was too great and between the highway and the branch road to the left, the northern dyke gave way. In a very short time the whole area was engulfed and 'A' Squadron retreated to the upper floors of their houses.

'A' Squadron and the Perth company were completely cut off by the flooding, and, as Murphy's Law would dictate, all forms of communication failed at the same time. Several efforts by engineers to get a cable across to the north bank of the Savio failed, so any thought of trying to build a Bailey bridge were also abandoned.

The floodwaters diminished over the next days. 'A' Squadron, freed from its second-storey refuges in abandoned farmhouses, crossed over the Bevano late on 28 October, and at least one patrol reached the Fosso Ghaiaia, nearly five kilometres north. By the time this happened, the Canadian Corps had been relieved and put into Army reserve. Cumberland Force was disbanded, its place taken by another ad hoc force, Porter Force, with the same holding role and this time directly under Eighth Army.

On this last day as part of Cumberland Force, Squadron Sergeant Major (Warrant Officer Class II) Alexander Russell led the squadron 'A' Echelon up to the front as he had on so many other nights during the campaign. All too often the enormous devotion to duty of the men serving in the administrative jobs can be forgotten in light of the 'real' action taking place at the front. Only rarely was their absolute necessity to the battle recognized at all, but this time it was noticed, and rewarded. Sergeant Major Russell was awarded a Military Medal for his repeated courage and inspired leadership. His citation reads in part:

The flooded Savio River, late October 1944. (Courtesy of Bob Murray)

The squadron supply line was an unbelievably difficult one, through the flooded three mile area between the rivers Savio and Bevano over the unbridged difficult crossing of the Bevano which was under constant heavy artillery and mortar fire, Sergeant-Major Russell worked for 48 hours without rest to supply the squadron over this hazardous route. He brought the supplies forward through the flooded areas by assault boats, when they were available, and by ingeniously conceived methods at other times he man-handled them across the Bevano and forward to the squadron. Through his gallant efforts the squadron was able to maintain its forward position.

Squadron Sergeant Major (WOII) Alexander Russell, MM. (GGHG Archives)

Sergeant-Major Russell has always proven himself more than willing to extend his work beyond the normal call of duty in order to supply his squadron. He has forced his way through unmarked mine fields and on several occasions when he came under direct enemy shelling and small arms fire has man-handled supplies to his men. … His standard of work and devotion to duty, in or out of action, has never been anything but exemplary and inspiring….

On the morning of 29 October the Royal Canadian Dragoons, now part of Porter Force, came forward to relieve 'A' and 'B' Squadrons at the front. There was heavy shelling during the handover, a reminder from the Germans that they had not yet given up the fight. As the troops moved back from the front, there was a certain perverse pride that the Regiment, dismounted, had advanced on foot about 25 kilometres over the course of twelve days. And the troops had given a very respectable account of themselves as infantrymen, albeit at a cost in friends' lives which everyone felt deeply.

The plain, unvarnished reality was that the Anglo-American offensive in Italy had petered out in the mud, well short of the objectives of Bologna and Ravenna. There would still be some costly tidying up of the battlefield over the course of the winter, but the Allied high command had already decided there would be no significant offensive until the spring of 1945. Another reality facing the formations and units in Italy was that North West Europe was now the key theatre of war. II Canadian Corps in Holland was at this time settling in for a winter of inactivity on the Maas River, waiting until spring to finish off an all-but-defeated Nazi Germany on its own soil. And the first tentative steps were being taken to arrange the transfer of I Canadian Corps from Italy to join First Canadian Army in Holland.

From the end of October until late November, the Horse Guards had a very pleasant period of rest and rehabilitation in extremely comfortable quarters in Cervia. Almost all the troops were billeted in resort hotels on or near the beach, not all of which were especially luxurious, but, after living in the rain and the mud during the past month, it seemed like sheer luxury. Every Horse Guard who served in Italy remembers this as another of "the best time[s] during the whole of the war". The men were able to swim in the Adriatic – even this late in the year the water was still considerably warmer than anywhere on the Great Lakes at the height of summer – and many also took advantage of seven-day passes to Rome or Florence where the Canadian Army had established leave centres. And for those remaining in Cervia, the training was seen to be useful given the likelihood that the Regiment was again going to be used as infantry. The Irish Regiment of Canada loaned a group of experienced corporals and sergeants who conducted a week-long course in section and platoon tactics, patrolling and street fighting. To the degree possible, tank skills were also kept current. Beginning on 18 November, for example, small groups of tanks – usually four Shermans at a time – were sent to the front to conduct indirect shoots onto enemy positions.

Sergeant Harold Finbow and Lance Corporal Gord Edwards checking stores, Cervia, autumn 1944. (GGHG Archives)

Regimental Memorial Parade, Cervia, 4 November 1944. (GGHG Archives)

THE LAST OFFENSIVE

The Regiment's idyllic existence in Cervia came to an end in the final week of November 1944. On 22 November, the Horse Guards was placed under command of Porter Force, which had been tasked to screen the concentration of 5th Armoured Division for a renewed offensive by Eighth Army intended to put the Allies into better positions to begin a major offensive in the spring. The first stage of this was to be an attack across the River Montone and the capture of Ravenna. On 26 November, 'C' Squadron deployed under command of the Westminster Regiment to defensive positions southwest of Ravenna. The sector allocated to the squadron was in dismal mud flats between the Ronco River and a wide drainage canal known as the Scolo Lama, which ran roughly 1,000 metres to the south of the River Montone. The squadron positions were centred on the village of Ghibullo, with troops about a kilometre apart. As the ground was in most places the consistency of thick, viscous molasses, individual troop positions were centred in and around farmhouses which were fortified as best could be done. For the next three days the widely separated positions played deadly games with the Germans at night and at other times when visibility was limited. Both sides sent out fighting patrols, which often came within metres of each other's listening posts. Both mounted small-scale attacks on each other's fortified houses and both sides mortared each other's positions, which were well known to everyone. The discomfort and general misery of the troops certainly came close to matching conditions in the First World War trenches in France and Flanders, and the operations conducted were nearly as futile and as deadly. Trooper Lorenzo Pelletier was killed on 29 November during one of the fighting patrols, but his body was not found until several days later.

'A' and 'B' Squadrons were brought forward into this same area on 30 November to reinforce the screen provided by the Westminster Regiment, and the Canadian units in Porter Force returned to their parent formations. The Regiment spent the next month supporting the Canadian Corps' last major offensive in Italy. The authors of the wartime history caught the *zeitgeist* of this messy, uncomfortable and inconclusive series of battles in the following passages:

During the offensives of December and January, the Regiment performed a variety of tasks that required great flexibility and a continual shifting of emphasis. The appalling spider web of Fosses, Fiumes, Scolos, Canales, Rios, Torrentes [Italian terms for the range of rivers, canals and other waterways], and just plain bloody ditches that covered the country, made the movement of armour extremely difficult and the brunt of the offensive was borne by the infantry.

The high dykes along both banks of the rivers, into which the Germans dug their defences, gave them excellent cover; and provided them with a never ending series of ready made alternative lines to which they could retire. Our attacks were opposed with grim determination, inflicting a high toll of casualties on the exhausted infantry, and progress was painfully slow.

The Germans retreated deliberately, in good order, sowing the area with their murderous wooden schuh mines, and counterattacking incessantly. In comparison with previous battles the allied forces were much smaller in number, and the frequent reliefs of the earlier period were consequently no longer possible. We never had that fresh brigade to exploit a bitterly won breach in the enemy defences. Each spasm ended with our troops exhausted and the enemy reorganized on the next water obstacle.

Operation "Chuckles", better known as the Battle of the Rivers, got under way on 2 December when units of both 1st and 5th Armoured Divisions attacked out of a shallow bridgehead on the Montone River at Casa Bentini. The spearhead of the 5th Division attack – 12th Brigade's unhorsed cavalrymen, the 4th Princess Louise Dragoon Guards – headed northwest with the objective of taking the village of San Pancrazio from the flank. The Dragoon Guards' attack was brought to an

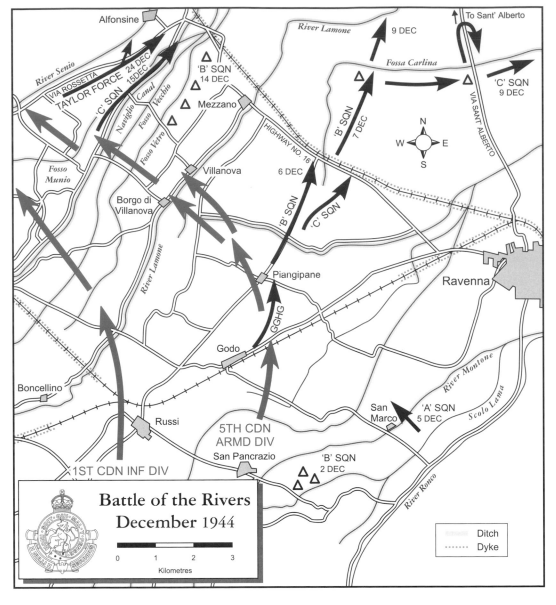

Battle of the Rivers
December 1944

Ditch
Dyke

0   1   2   3
Kilometres

front about mid-morning to engage enemy positions south and west of San Marco.

By nightfall on 2 December the Westminsters had their whole battalion across the Montone in San Pancrazio, leaving the Horse Guards responsible for the 5th Division sector south of the river. The outposts were incapable of dominating this large piece of ground, so aggressive patrolling became the major preoccupation of the forward squadrons for the next two days. As the Germans showed no inclination to pull back, patrols were not without their risk. Trooper John Moore was one of several casualties; he was killed on 3 December when a Recce Troop patrol was caught in the open during an attack on an enemy-held house. The rest of the patrol was pinned down for several hours until Trooper T. Allen, part of an 'A' Squadron section sent out to find the Recce Troop patrol, at considerable personal risk worked his

unexpected halt by strong German defences 2,000 metres west of the village, so the Westminster Regiment was ordered to make an assault crossing of the Montone on either side of San Pancrazio.

'B' Squadron, holding positions in relatively isolated farmhouses southeast of San Pancrazio, had an active morning before the Westminsters began to cross. The forward troop, about 500 metres east of the village, was concentrated around a house just below the high southern bank of the Montone, and twice this position was attacked by German fighting patrols that appeared out of the thick mist. Both attacks were beaten off without much difficulty, and the last time the Germans retreated behind the river bank under cover of two cows, one of which, the War Diary duly reports, became a casualty. The Germans still had a considerable number of troops south of the Montone, and 'A' Squadron tanks were brought to the

Bren gun into a flanking position where he could bring fire to bear on the enemy dugouts. Allen's bravery undoubtedly saved the patrol, but he got no official recognition other than a mention in the War Diary. There were other casualties that day: Troopers William Henderson and Arthur Perrott of 'B' Squadron were killed because of an accident with a grenade and nine other men in the troop were seriously wounded.

The divisional push toward Highway 16 made good progress over the next days. Ravenna was liberated on 4 December by the PLDG and a squadron of the BCD, who found that the enemy had already withdrawn. Other units penetrated to Highway 16 in the north and nearly to the River Lamone in the west. In the area east of San Pancrazio, the Germans continued to hold out on the north bank of the Montone, even though they were all but completely cut off. As a result, both 'B' and 'C' Squadrons were sent to cross the

'A' Squadron crewmen, autumn 1944. (GGHG Archives)

The Medical Officer and Regimental Aid Post staff with a de-turreted Stuart used as an ambulance, autumn 1944. (GGHG Archives)

Horse Guards was given a new task. Now under 5th Armoured Brigade, the Regiment was ordered to move immediately to positions on Highway 16 west of Ravenna to protect the division's right flank. Once the flank was secure, the Regiment was to be prepared to advance northward to Lake Comacchio, clearing an 8-kilometre swath on the west side of the Ravenna-Sant' Alberto road. By mid-evening on 6 December 'B' and 'C' Squadrons were in position astride Highway 16, while 'A' Squadron remained in Godo.

Having very little information about the enemy in this new sector, 'B' Squadron sent patrols north toward the Lamone River early on 7 December to determine where German troops were deployed and in what strength. The patrol met no opposition until across a broad drainage ditch known as the Fossa Carlina, when they were fired on by machine guns on the north bank of the Lamone. Working their way eastward along the near bank of the Fossa Carlina, the patrol eventually made contact with Major Popski, of Popski's Private Army fame, who with the 27th Lancers was holding the ground on the Regiment's right flank. Popski had already tried to cross the Lamone north of Ravenna, but his men had suffered heavy casualties. Major Baker, doing the rounds of the outposts just before last light, unfortunately was wounded when his scout car hit a mine, and Major A.H. 'Bing' Crosbie took over the squadron.

Montone in the 1st Division area further to the southeast, with the intention of swinging through Godo and attacking the remaining enemy from the rear. Before these squadrons completed this manoeuvre 'A' Squadron attacked across the Montone at San Marco on the morning of 5 December. When it got there the Germans had gone.

As the infantry brigades of 5th Division swung left into position to attack across the River Lamone between Villanova and Borgo Villanova, on the morning of 6 December the

The next day troop-strength outposts were established just to the south of the Fossa Carlina, one on the left near the southward bend in the canal, the other near the Via Sant' Alberto. The day after, even though the ground was too soft for cross-country movement, Shermans were brought forward into both locations. For the next week Horse Guards foot patrols played cat and mouse with German dugouts on the far bank of the Lamone, and Trooper Harold Cook was killed by a sniper on one of the forays near the Via Sant' Alberto. On 9 December,

'C' Squadron sent a troop of tanks to assist Major Popski in repulsing a German attack, and for a few days Lieutenant Bob Murray and Trooper D.J. Davies had a small standing patrol hidden on the enemy side. Continual rain had turned the Lamone into a "raging torrent" by 13 December, so there was little risk of serious enemy interference from this sector. Bob Murray's story was told in a column in the Toronto *Telegram:*

> It was while facing the Lamone that two G.G.H.G.'s crossed the river, entering enemy territory. With a radio they packed themselves into a small collapsable boat… In the dead of night they paddled across, landing between two German sentry posts. Their boat was then pulled back to the other side. … The radio refused to work, having received a splash or two in the river crossing.
>
> Next day they prowled around and found Hun locations, strength and gun positions. During the night, with the radio out, they again made the river dike, throwing a message across in a bottle. It was received. Another radio came, but it also got wet.
>
> The second night they occupied another house in which some Huns ate but this was discovered too late. They locked themselves in the attic. The Huns knocked and kicked at the door but didn't force an entrance. As they knocked at the door Murray and Davies stood in opposite corners of the room with their fingers on the triggers of their tommy guns. They sweated but were ready. The Huns went downstairs, had their meal and departed.

After several disastrous efforts in the 1st Division sector, units of both divisions succeeded in crossing the Lamone River on the night of 10/11 December, and, in the left part of the 5th Division front, the Irish Regiment penetrated further than any other unit that day – across both the Lamone and the Fosso Vetro to the near bank of the Fosso Vecchio. At this time the Regiment was moved closer to the division's main thrust, with 'B' Squadron taking up positions just south of Highway 16, overlooking the Fosso Vetro north-west of Villanova. The other squadrons were held near Villanova.

THE NAVIGLIO POCKET

In the meantime, the rest of the Canadian Corps was struggling to gain a foothold across the Naviglio Canal, a nearly dry waterway – because the Germans had dammed it upstream – but one with 14-metre banks.

'C' Squadron carried out a very special mission on 15 December. With all its tanks, the squadron crossed the Naviglio Canal in the 1st Division sector, and then, supported by a company of the Lanark and Renfrews, conducted a sweep along the length of the Via del Canale (on the north bank of the Naviglio) from Osteria to just south of Highway 16. At the time the Germans still had a significant number of troops dug in in the narrow strip of ground between the Naviglio and the Fosso Munio, and the intention of the sweep was to shoot up their positions in the high canal banks and in the buildings and thus hasten their withdrawal to the far side of the Munio (and allow our own troops to get across the Naviglio). This cavalry-style charge was remarkably successful, even though the squadron was subjected to very heavy shellfire from the moment it started out; eleven prisoners were taken, and 30 enemy soldiers killed. The squadron's only casualty was Corporal George Chalmers' Sherman, which was knocked out by an 88mm gun firing from north of the Fosso Munio. By late afternoon, 'C' Squadron and the Lanark company had set up an all-round defence at the junction of the Via del Canale and the Via Cocchi. The squadron remained in the general area for the next week, much of the time under mortar and shellfire which caused an ever-increasing toll of casualties. For example, Sergeant Charles Tompson and Trooper Lorne Graff were killed by a shell and five others were wounded by shrapnel on 18 December. Among the many individual acts of gallantry during this time under fire, one was eventually recognized. Sergeant Wallace Johnston was awarded a Military Medal at the end of the war in recognition of many instances of devoted leadership, courage and coolness under fire. Part of his citation reads:

> In Italy during the third week of December 1944, [Sergeant Johnston's] squadron was deployed on the right flank of the divisional bridgehead over the Naviglio Canal, in an area subjected to continuous and intense mortar and shell fire. As a result, the telephone lines were often cut and, without communications, the defensive operations would have been seriously prejudiced. In spite of the fact that the lines were laid within 200 yards of the enemy forward positions and the area was actively patrolled by the enemy, Sergeant Johnston repeatedly volunteered to go out to maintain communications both by day and by night. In every instance he remained until he had reestablished communications thus enabling his squadron to hold its position and to break up several enemy counter attacks….

Both Canadian divisions mounted attacks after dark on 19 December, and every infantry unit involved confronted a well organized defence in depth by countless small strongpoints manned by very resolute and determined German soldiers. Canadian casualties were extremely high in both divisions; some infantry companies were literally annihilated. In 5th Armoured Division, the situation was stabilized only when engineers bulldozed a crossing over the Munio for a squadron of Strathcona Shermans which reinforced the Perth Regiment at the Casa della Congregatione on the Via Chiara on 20 December. During the night of 20/21 December the Germans pulled the bulk of their forces back to the embankments on the River Senio, but many strong layback patrols remained to slow and harass the Canadian advance.

As the infantry closed up to the Senio, their axis was shifted to the southwest. The Horse Guards were then given responsibility for the security of the division's right flank between the Munio and the River Senio. During the morning of 21 December, 'A' and 'B' Squadrons moved into positions slightly south of the Via Rossetta, the main road running along the Senio, and both patrolled actively northeast from the Via Chiara. Lieutenant Bob Murray recalled his arrival:

'C' Squadron tank crews, 19 January 1945. (NAC PA168030)

'B' Squadron Assault Troop, January 1945. (NAC PA168028)

I was reporting that we had arrived safely at our destination when there was the scream of a German 88 and my tank was hit. It was something like sitting inside a bell when it was rung. I hollered "Driver reverse" and we backed to safety behind the house. I told my Bow Gunner to get out and check the damage. He motioned me to come down and have a look. There was a long gouge along the side of the tank. We missed having a major catastrophe by inches.

New orders came from Division headquarters on the morning of 22 December: the Horse Guards were now to strike northeast, clearing the flank between the Munio and Senio as far as the village of Alfonsine. 'B' Company of the Irish Regiment was attached to assist in clearing out enemy positions located in the nearly continuous line of houses along the Via Rossetta. At noon, 'A' Squadron's Second Troop, under Lieutenant Bob Murray, was sent to feel out the enemy. Moving cross country to the Via Bellaria, and then north to the Rosetta, Murray's tanks encountered fierce resistance from German machine guns in dugout positions on the banks of the Senio, so Colonel Jordan decided that a night attack would offer better prospects. To help soften up the enemy, that afternoon the German bunkers along the Via Rossetta were subjected to a new form of close air support – intensive low-level strafing of enemy positions in close proximity to our own troops. The terrifying effectiveness of this form of air attack was attested to by one of the forward troops which was 'nicked' when the fighters began firing a moment too soon.

At 2230 hours, 'B' Company of the Irish began the sweep along the Via Rossetta with their newly acquired Wasps, carrier-mounted flame throwers. The Wasps proved extremely effective in clearing the Germans from bunkers built into the dykes and stone houses converted into strongpoints, but many found the sight of screaming men burning to death in front of their eyes to be very distasteful. After clearing about 2,500 metres along the road, the carriers ran out of 'juice', and, as Lieutenant Bob Murray's supporting tanks were unable to give effective fire support to the infantry during darkness, the fighting died down until morning.

Just before first light on 23 December, 'A' Squadron moved cross country to the Via Bellaria, waiting for first light to move north toward the Via Rosetta. As this move was taking place, the forward Stuart of Murray's Second Troop was knocked out at close range by a *panzerfaust*. When the crew bailed out they were engaged by machine guns, and Troopers Norman Cameron and Howard Holmes were killed. "The Germans remained as determined and aggressive as ever." 'A' Squadron tanks fired on enemy positions for much of the day, but the fire became relatively ineffective when heavy snow reduced visibility to near zero.

A fresh attack opened at midnight. Taylor Force – a Regimental reserve of one tank troop from each of 'A' and 'B' Squadrons under Captain Eric Taylor – with two companies of the Irish, advanced cross-country and made good progress as far as the Via Utili, 1,000 metres beyond Via Bellaria, when Captain Taylor's tank struck a mine just south of the junction with Via Rossetta. The bow gunner, Trooper Gerald Class, was killed, having taken the full brunt of the exploding mine under the right track. Then two more tanks ran over mines while trying to get around the first casualty. As it was pitch dark and in the middle of a minefield, there was no point in trying to go on. Eric Taylor recalled:

With just dim moonlight and exploding shells providing the only light, apart from everything else going on, my heart suddenly was in my mouth as I discerned shadowy figures – perhaps six to ten – converging on my tank. Thinking they were Germans and fully expecting Bazooka-like attacks and to be over-run, it wasn't until they ran past that it dawned on me that they were Irish Regiment elements retreating to the protection of our tanks!

It was an uncomfortable night, but Taylor Force had no contact with the Germans.

Early on 24 December, 'A' Squadron, with 'B' Squadron's Assault Troop under command, advanced cross country toward the next objective, the Via Bastogi, a short road about 1,500 metres east of the position Captain Taylor had reached the previous night. At the same time, Taylor Force, having escaped from the minefield, attacked eastward along the Via Rossetta, while 'C' Squadron, still south of the Fosso Munio, gave fire support from their positions. 'A' Squadron came under very heavy shellfire when they reached the southern end of Via Bastogi. The 'B' Squadron Assault Troop, in open-topped White scout cars, suffered from the shelling far more severely than the tanks, so they made for cover behind the embankment of the Fosso Munio.

This area proved to be thickly strewn with schuh mines and the results were consequently disastrous. Tprs. Gordon Hayward and William McLean were killed, while Sgt. W.T. Kershaw and Tprs. J.L. Hudson and G.R. Rogers were wounded. ... The shelling continued, and Cpl. H.H. McCleverty and Tpr. G. Kolebara were wounded by enemy fire.

The fighting continued at an uneven pace for the remainder of the day, 'A' Squadron forming a firm base while Taylor Force and 'C' Company of the Irish continued house-to-house and bunker-to-bunker clearance along the Via Rossetta. By last light the area of the Via Bastogi was firmly held by two squadrons and two companies. During the night engineers put a bridge over the Munio at the southern end of Via Bastogi, so 'C' Squadron was again linked directly to the rest of the Regiment.

Christmas Day passed almost without incident, with both sides for the most part leaving the other alone. Unfortunately, two scout cars of 'A' Squadron's Assault Troop, driving along the Via Naviglio on the north side of the Munio, missed the turn at Via Bastogi and drove headlong into enemy-held territory. The lead vehicle struck a mine before going too far, and the crews had to dodge small-arms and mortar fire to get back to their own lines. During this action Trooper Clifford Craig was killed. To prevent the Germans from capturing the scout cars intact, with codes, radio frequencies and all, 'A' Squadron tanks shot them up.

The Regiment's last action in this slow but hard-fought operation took place on 27 December. 'A' Squadron sent an armoured sortie along the Via Rossetta toward Alfonsine to clear out some enemy who were still occupying houses on the near bank of the Senio. This move was covered by a spectacular attack by a squadron of Spitfires on enemy positions in Alfonsine, which kept anti-tank gunners in their holes. The tanks got to the outskirts of the town, but as it was still held by the Germans in considerable strength they returned to the main Regimental position on Via Bastogi. Trooper Walter Goodall was seriously wounded and succumbed to his injuries a week later. The next day 'A' and 'B' Squadrons withdrew to Piangipane, and thus ended the Regiment's longest continuous period in action during the war.

It was in Piangipane, on 31 December 1944, that the Regiment celebrated a combined Christmas and New Year's dinner in the traditional style where the officers served the men. Served out of doors at noon, it was a great success notwithstanding the chill in the air, but it was bright and sunny. To the members of Taylor Force, the great meal and the good time made up for the loss of a hot turkey dinner several days earlier.

Tanks Loading onto LSTs in Leghorn. **Painting by Orville Fisher depicting loading of tanks in Leghorn (Livorno) harbour prior to the departure for Marseilles. (Canadian War Museum 12606)**

THE LAST ACTION IN ITALY

When the Germans finally withdrew to the west bank of the Senio River at the end of December 1944, the Canadian Corps began to implement a plan to go over to the defensive for the remainder of the winter. But there was still some tidying up needed to shorten the defensive line: the Germans had to be cleared out of the area south of Lake Comacchio. On 2 January 1945, 5th Armoured Division launched a brilliant attack, taking advantage of frozen ground to restore the mobility of their tanks, with 11th Brigade first capturing Conventello, then exploiting to Sant' Alberto with 5th Armoured Brigade on 4 January.

The Horse Guards were brought forward on 7 January with the task of taking over the sector north of the Bonfica Canal, from Sant' Alberto all the way to the Adriatic coast. There were not

The Italy Star, awarded to all members with operational service in Italy. (GGHG Archives)

many Germans remaining south of Lake Comacchio, but there was a company-size enemy garrison holding out on a narrow spit of land separating the lake from the Adriatic (see map, page 225). 'C' Squadron deployed into the area west of the village of Mandriole, while 'B' Squadron focused on the Comacchio spit, establishing positions on the south bank of the Reno River. The Germans mounted small-scale attacks on 'B' Squadron's forward troop on 8 and 9 January, but they were beaten off without much difficulty. For the next several days 'B' Squadron patrolled actively on the north side of the Reno, including one absolute fiasco that involved a group of Italian partisans. While holding the line, Lance Corporal Thomas Hackett was wounded when he touched off a Schuh mine; he later died at the Regimental Aid Post.

Part of 'C' Squadron – the Assault Troop, dismounted, and a tank troop under Captain Bud Wass – was brought up on 12 January to clean out the German position on the Comacchio spit. Their adventure is told in the wartime history:

The force moved north through the woods, but the tanks swung out to the west before reaching the enemy position and it attacked from the flank, scoring a complete surprise. By one of those rare miracles, the first round of high explosive landed square on the commander's dugout, killing the company commander and his FOO, and at once destroying their whole system of control and communications. After that it was a field day. We killed a great number and captured forty-eight prisoners, the largest bag in any of the regiment's local engagements in the whole Italian campaign.

Major Alexander Crosbie, who had taken over the squadron from Major Burton, later received a DSO for his inspiring leadership in this action. An Italian battle group took over the sector on 13 January, and the Regiment once again moved back to Cervia. Sergeant Al Sellers recalls:

> When the Regiment withdrew from the area, Jack Guile, a wireless operator named Clark and I were left behind in the RHQ Tac Honey. We had two radios set up in different bands and we were all busy broadcasting messages to make the enemy believe the GGs were still there. Orders finally came to rejoin the Regiment. I recall it was raining like hell; it was cold and we were soaked, but we had a bonus. For some reason I had Lieutenant Howard Smith's troop ration of rum on board. The three of us managed to dispose of some of the contents. There was lots of water around, so we topped up the jug with some muddy water. I often wonder if Smittie ever noticed a difference in the proof of the stuff.

While no one could know it at the time, this was the Horse Guards' last action in Italy.

Cervia was a welcome relief after nearly a month and a half in the rain and mud, and the Regiment very easily slipped into a more relaxed, 'out of the line' routine. While some very serious training was carried out, everyone enjoyed the social amenities of messes, canteens, nightly films and, dare it be said, female companionship of one form or another. Troops were again allowed to take short periods of leave to Rome or Florence where it was warmer and not so wet, and it was a time of much-needed physical and mental rehabilitation.

Major A.H. Crosbie, DSO and Captain C.S. Wass, MC, January 1945. (NAC PA168027)

DEPARTURE FROM ITALY

At this time momentous decisions affecting all Canadian troops in Italy were being made. For many months, almost since Canadians had been sent to Italy in July 1943, First Canadian Army and the government had been lobbying the Allied high command to bring Canadian troops back to North West Europe. A decision on just this was finally made by the Combined Chiefs of Staff in a meeting in Malta at the end of January. The Canadians in Italy were to be moved through France to Holland, where 21st Army Group needed reinforcement for the final thrust to destroy Nazi Germany. Plans for this enormous troop transfer were drawn up in great haste, and I Canadian Corps was informed only on 4 February 1945. Colonel Jordan attended a division orders group on the morning of 6 February: the word was that the division was "to move a long way south to 'practice getting on and off boats.'" The first stages of Operation "Goldflake" had begun. It was all, of course, very hush-hush. Unit markings on vehicles were painted over, and everyone had to take divisional patches off their uniforms.

After a few days of careful loading of all manner of kit and equipment onto the tanks and trucks, the Regiment's wheeled vehicles departed Cervia as part of a 5th Armoured Brigade convoy early on 11 February. Travelling along the coastal highway through

Major Alec Boothe, Regimental Second-in-Command. (GGHG Archives)

Regimental Headquarters staff. (GGHG Archives)

Riccione to Porta Civitanova, the massive convoy turned inland to Foligno, Arezzo and Florence, and two days later finally reached its destination, Harrod's Camp 12 kilometres north of Livorno (Leghorn), the main Italian port on the Mediterranean coast north of Naples. The tanks, moving by train, arrived over the next three days. The commanding officer officially told the Regiment what everybody already seemed to know: the whole of I Canadian Corps was moving to join First Canadian Army in Holland.

The Regiment's departure from Italy was far from being a neat and tidy operation. Rather, it turned out to be, as the War Diary puts it, "a series of trickles". "The system seems to be steeped in mystery and no one seems able to predict when or what part of the regiment will move next." Twenty-nine vehicles on one ship, 12 on another, then 26, then 104 men, and so on. The first flotilla carrying part of the Horse Guards sailed at 0630 hours on 20 February, and others followed over the next few days.

The Horse Guards had gained its first modern-day experience of battle over 15 months in the searing sun and dust and rain and mud of Italy. And while no one spoke much about it, great lustre had been added to the Regiment's earlier laurels and every member was enormously proud of the unit's accomplishments. But, still, there was no great regret at leaving Italy. The wartime history puts what was probably the feeling of many members into apt words:

We have left many comrades in the ancient earth of Italia. Some of them were new hands, some of them old hands, but new or old, they are the deathless part of this Regiment, their sacrifice, its honour, its tradition for the future and its

pride. The campaign was hard and the enemy was resolute. For a large part of the time we had few advantages, in shells, in supplies, or manpower; and most of those we had were rendered useless by a terrain that was created for defence and difficult for tanks.

As fragments of the Regiment had been loaded on so many different ships, there is no single tale to tell of the Horse Guards arrival in the French port of Marseilles and the subsequent move through France. The first ship carrying part of the unit docked, after a 36 hour voyage, just before noon on 21 February, and other convoys arrived over the next two days. Almost as soon as vehicles were unloaded and marshalled, the wheeled vehicles began their long road journey through a series of staging camps, the first about 25 kilometres north of the port. The tanks, however, were moved by rail, with skeleton crews accompanying them in a primitive passenger car at the back of the train. The road journey to Belgium took six days of driving – through Lyon, Macon, Les Laumes, Monterlau (carefully and deliberately by-passing Paris with all its attractions) and Cambrai.

ISEGEM: REFURBISHING THE REGIMENT

Isegem, a pleasant Flemish town of about 20,000 people, located 80 kilometres west of Brussels, was to be home to the Horse Guards for a full month while the units of 5th Armoured Division were refurbished in structure and equipment to conform to policies and practice in 21st Army Group. The main body of the Regiment, both the tank trains and the wheeled convoys, arrived on 27 February 1945, and by 1 March the unit was complete.

Lieutenant Colonal Jordan and RSM Bentley inspecting a Saturday morning parade, Isegem, Belgium. (GGHG Archives)

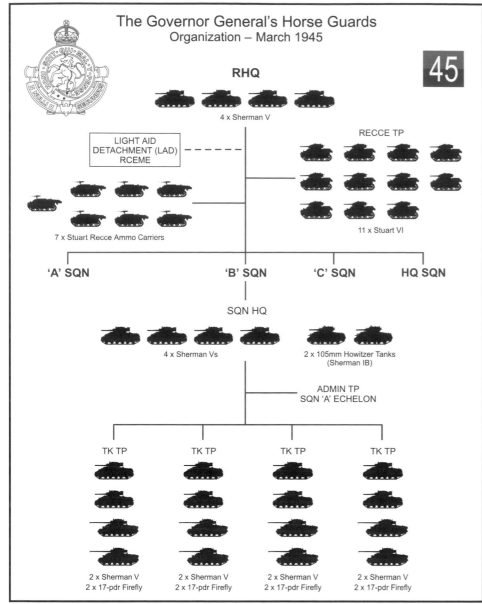

The Governor General's Horse Guards
Organization – March 1945

RHQ

4 x Sherman V

LIGHT AID
DETACHMENT (LAD)
RCEME

RECCE TP

7 x Stuart Recce Ammo Carriers

11 x Stuart VI

'A' SQN   'B' SQN   'C' SQN   HQ SQN

SQN HQ

4 x Sherman Vs   2 x 105mm Howitzer Tanks
(Sherman IB)

ADMIN TP
SQN 'A' ECHELON

TK TP   TK TP   TK TP   TK TP

2 x Sherman V   2 x Sherman V   2 x Sherman V   2 x Sherman V
2 x 17-pdr Firefly   2 x 17-pdr Firefly   2 x 17-pdr Firefly   2 x 17-pdr Firefly

45

Field Marshal Sir Bernard Montgomery visiting the Horse Guards, Isegem, 18 March 1945. (GGHG Archives)

squadrons were now to have four troops each of four Shermans – two Mark Vs and two 17-pounder-equipped Fireflys. Moreover, the squadron headquarters each got two Sherman 105mm howitzer tanks for indirect fire. The Regimental reconnaissance troop was re-equipped with eleven Stuarts with turrets, and seven de-turreted Stuarts were kept as ammunition carriers in 'A' Echelon.

The immediate consequence of the changed structure was that a lot of work had to be done, first to get the old Italian-issue Shermans cleaned and kitted for turn-in to Ordnance, and then to draw 33 Mark Vs with all their tools and equipment from 5th Armoured Brigade, plus 24 Fireflys from 'G' Squadron of the Elgin Regiment, the tank delivery squadron. The change in equipment made it necessary to re-train many of the men who had not served in Sherman crews, and, now that half of the unit's operational tanks were Fireflys, 17-pounder gunnery had to be taught quickly, and indeed 105mm gunnery was completely new as well.

A visit to the division by Field Marshal Sir Bernard Montgomery on 18 March provided a change of pace, and he was at his charismatic best. This was the first opportunity to see the commander-in-chief. The Regiment lined up along the Courtrai road, but instead of just the planned slow drive-past, Montgomery had his jeep stop in front of the Horse Guards. He stood up on the seat, waved to the troops to gather round,

Veterans remember the town as being as close to paradise as they had come in recent years. Everyone was billeted with a Belgian family, and the inhabitants were invariably friendly and kind. Most of the men were adopted into the family by their hosts, and, while meals were supposed to be taken in a Regimental mess hall, many an evening meal was eaten with the family. The town also boasted 428 bars and pubs, which were well patronized. And one of the biggest luxuries of all was that everyone was allowed a seven-day leave in England.

The first item of business was the reorganization of the Regiment. While the Horse Guards would still officially be the divisional reconnaissance regiment, it was ordered to adopt the organization of a standard armoured regiment so as to be able to provide full-time tank support to 11th Brigade. The

Arrival of the Regiment's Fireflys, March 1945. (GGHG Archives)

Beginning on 20 March the squadrons took their tanks and crews to a gunnery range on the French coast near Dunkirk (which was still held by the Germans) to zero the guns and learn new gunnery techniques. When the tanks returned to Isegem on 25 March the process of welding lengths of steel track to the turrets and hulls of the Shermans was begun. This was now accepted practice in 2nd Armoured Brigade (where it had begun) and in 4th Armoured Division, in that the track pads were believed to give added protection, especially against hollow charge ammunition such as the Germans used in their *panzerfausts.* This was slow work, for each length of track had to be lifted into place for welding by a crane on the recovery vehicle. In this same period the wonderful winter tank suits – never seen in Italy – were issued to the tank crews. These were marvellous weatherproof things, with zippers on the front that ran down both legs both for ventilation and allowed the suit to be turned into a sleeping bag!

and for about ten minutes kept everyone in what he called "my Canadian Horse Guards" enthralled by his wit and sense of purpose. Later in the day the officers heard him give a review of the campaign in North West Europe, at the end of which he predicted that the war would be over in two or three months. Many comments were heard hoping the war didn't end before the division had a chance to see action.

By the end of March it was clear that the Horse Guards had not arrived too late to see action. On the 'island' north of Nijmegen, Holland, a holding role had been assigned to 11th

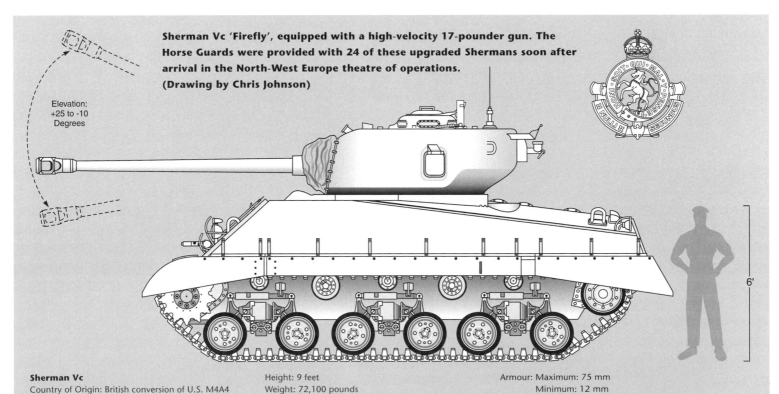

Sherman Vc 'Firefly', equipped with a high-velocity 17-pounder gun. The Horse Guards were provided with 24 of these upgraded Shermans soon after arrival in the North-West Europe theatre of operations. (Drawing by Chris Johnson)

Elevation: +25 to -10 Degrees

6'

Sherman Vc
Country of Origin: British conversion of U.S. M4A4
Crew: 4 (Commander, Gunner, Driver, Loader)
Length: 25 feet 9 inches
Width: 8 feet 7 inches

Height: 9 feet
Weight: 72,100 pounds
Engine: Chrysler A57 30 cylinder multibank, gasoline
Maximum Speed: 25 mph
Range: 100 miles

Armour: Maximum: 75 mm
Minimum: 12 mm
Armament: 17 pdr Gun Mk IV or VII in turret
.30 calibre MG M1919A4 co-axial to 75mm Gun
.50 calibre MG HB M2 in flexible mount on turret top

Horse Guards Shermans passing through Arnhem, 15 March 1945. Note the track extenders on both sides of the tank tracks. (NAC PA108014)

Brigade, between the Maas and the Lower Rhine rivers. Preparations for an assault on the city of Arnhem were now well underway, and as a preliminary it was necessary to clear the enemy out of the Nijmegen 'island', which was immediately south of Arnhem. 'B' Squadron, tasked to support 11th Brigade, moved to Nijmegen by rail on 28 March and next day relieved a squadron of the Ontario Regiment. The remainder of the Regiment arrived in Nijmegen before dawn on 31 March, and squadrons were to support each of the battalions of 11th Brigade in a night attack on 2 April intended to clear the sector as far as the Lower Rhine. By first light on 3 April all three battalions had captured their objectives. 'A' Squadron knocked out two enemy machine guns during the attack, but 'B' and 'C' Squadrons didn't get to fire a single round.

While waiting for further developments in the plan to attack toward the Ijsselmeer (Zuider Zee), the tank crews were busy attaching track extenders (some called them 'grousers'), which by widening the track by 10 cm lowered the ground pressure, and thus gave the tanks far better cross-country capability in soft, muddy ground.

OTTERLOO: THE LAST BATTLE

The assault on Arnhem got under way on 12 April 1945 when 49th British Division attacked the city from the east side. At the same time, 25 kilometres to the north, 1st Canadian Division was assaulting the city of Apeldoorn from the east, while the other divisions of First Canadian Army had begun a deep thrust into Northern Holland and Germany.

Once Arnhem was taken by the 49th Division, 5th Armoured Division was brought in to carry out a rapid thrust to the northwest – through Otterloo and Barneveld to Nijkerk on the Ijsselmeer (Zuider Zee) – to complete the clearance of the Germans between Arnhem and the Ijsselmeer up to an old north-south defensive line known as the Grebbe Line. A secondary purpose of this movement was to ensure that the large body of Germans still holding out in the hills east of Apeldoorn could not escape west into the part of Holland still occupied by the enemy. (As an aside, there was a tacit agreement with the German commander in Holland that he would not destroy the dykes and thus flood a large part of the country below sea level provided the Allies did not attack his forces in western Holland.)

Sergeant H.K. Robertson briefing his troops en route to the front, 15 April 1945. (NAC PA108015)

Operation "Cleanser" got under way early on 15 April when the 8th Hussars and the British Columbia Dragoons advanced on the villages of Deelen and Terlet, much of the way through heavy woods. That afternoon the Strathconas pressed on toward Otterloo, hampered by close country, halting at last light just east of the town. In the meantime 11th Brigade, supported by 'A' and 'B' Squadrons of the Horse Guards, was brought forward to clear out enemy which had been bypassed by the armoured brigade. Unfortunately, while passing through Arnhem Lieutenant John Clarke was crushed between two tanks and killed. "There was little work for the tanks", noted the wartime history, but that evening in Terlet a German 88mm SP gun fired on a 'B' Squadron tank, wounding Major Bud Baker, Lieutenant Ormord and three others.

Very early the next morning, 16 April, the Strathconas moved on to Otterloo. There were several short, sharp, pitched

One of the Regiment's Fireflys ditched near Otterloo, Holland, 16 April 1945. Note the tank track welded on the hull for extra protection against anti-tank weapons. (GGHG Archives)

battles before they got through the village, but once beyond they pushed on at top speed to Barneveld, where they encountered increasingly heavy resistance. On the right, the BCD got as far as the southern outskirts of Voorthuizen before being stopped. Meanwhile, 'C' Squadron moved to Otterloo with the Irish Regiment to carry out a thorough clearing of the town and the woods to the north east. In the early afternoon, 'A' Squadron, carrying a company of Perths on their back decks, cleared the high ground north-east of the village of Lunteren, 10 kilometres west of Otterloo. Later that day, 'B' Squadron advanced with the Cape Breton Highlanders to a feature east of Barneveld so as to be in position for an assault early the next morning. The entire operation appeared to be progressing much as expected, and during the day General Hoffmeister's 5th Division headquarters moved into Otterloo.

As with all rapid, narrow thrusts into enemy-held territory, pockets of enemy troops of varying size remained on all sides of the division. Three kilometres northeast of Otterloo, for example, it was known that there was still a sizeable German garrison in a barracks on the south side of a place known as Haarskamp. A patrol consisting of a platoon of the Irish and a troop of tanks had attempted to clear the town during the afternoon, but found it too strongly held. During that small action, a Mark IV tank fired on the Horse Guards tanks and hit one of them, but apparently because of the welded track no damage was done. The commanding officer of the Irish Regiment decided to mount a deliberate attack on this position early next morning, employing his 'C' Company and three tank troops, and he gave his orders at 2000 hours. An infantry platoon and Fourth Troop were sent to a wood on the north side of Otterloo as a standing patrol.

At 2330 hours, Major Crosbie gathered the 'C' Squadron officers at his headquarters, an old village church, to go over details of the plan for the morning attack. He was still giving orders when the proceedings were interrupted by loud shouting and bursts of small-arms fire just outside the church. It was soon determined that a strong enemy patrol had infiltrated into the town, and that even more Germans were on their way down the main road. Thus began a night of confusion and great gallantry. As the squadron officers were cut off in the church, the tank troops were led the whole night by sergeants and corporals, and they did a magnificent job.

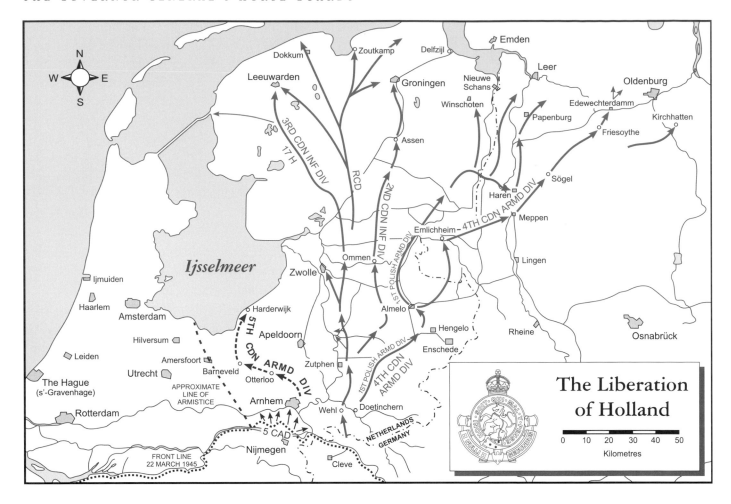

The Liberation of Holland

Somewhere between 600 and 900 Germans, remnants of a variety of units trying to escape from the Canadian attack on Apeldoorn, poured into Otterloo. It was a chaotic scene, Germans and Canadians mixed up in the dark. Fairly early on the Irish asked that a tank drive up and down the streets to intimidate the Germans. The wartime history relates:

> Sergeant Wood set out in a Squadron Headquarters tank, moving up the road to the east, from which direction the enemy was advancing. As the Irish and Germans were closely intermingled, the tank was ordered not to fire, but simply moved up and down, with Germans running beside it shouting "Canadians Surrender, Canadians Surrender".
>
> We were also requested to cover the road junction just east of Otterloo and First Troop was ordered to seize it. Sergeant Johnston led the troop to the position, discovering that it was then held by the enemy. He was at once engaged by bazookas, and although he was himself wounded in the head by a rifle bullet, none of the bazooka bombs scored and he continued controlling his troop.

Two members of First Troop received gallantry awards for their conduct that night. Corporal Herbert Dixon Stitt was awarded a Distinguished Conduct Medal, the only one won by a member of the Regiment during the war. His citation reads in part:

> Corporal Stitt was ordered to patrol up and down the main road … and to clear the enemy who by this time commanded the road. As his tank moved out on to the road it was immediately engaged by Spandau and bazooka fire. One bazooka bomb scored a direct hit on the turret ring and completely destroyed the traverse mechanism. Although the enemy were only ten yards away, Corporal Stitt immediately climbed out of his turret and traversed the gun onto the enemy by pulling it around by hand.
>
> During the ensuing three hours of darkness, Corporal Stitt continued to attack the enemy up and down the road, closing with them to point blank range. Throughout this period, he calmly remained on the outside of his tank, constantly exposed to enemy fire, pulling the tank guns onto the enemy by hand and engaging them with grenades and pistol.

Lance Corporal Donald Archibald Spence, a gunner in the troop leader's tank in First Troop, took command of his crew in the officer's absence and got the tank into action. Spence received an immediate award of a Military Medal. His bravery is described in the citation for the decoration:

Corporal Herbert Dixon Stitt, DCM. Corporal Stitt, the only member of the Horse Guards to be awarded a Distinguished Conduct Medal during the war, was killed in an accident on the morning of 17 April 1945. (GGHG Archives)

His tank was surrounded by enemy calling upon the crew to surrender. He replied with grenades and succeeded in driving the enemy off. For the next three hours he continued to attack the enemy wherever he could find them, always at ranges of from ten to fifteen yards. So keen was he to press home his attack that on several occasions he took his tank through heavy bazooka and machine gun fire right into the enemy, crushing them beneath his tracks. Although he had no previous experience as a crew commander, and had received no direct orders, Lance Corporal Spence's initiative and aggressiveness were responsible for preventing any further infiltration into the village from the eastern end. … His courageous leadership was an inspiration to those he commanded.

Squadron Sergeant Major William Cyril Clarkson also received the Military Medal, in part for his absolute devotion to duty under dangerous and difficult conditions throughout the campaign, but in part also for his conduct at Otterloo that night. An excerpt from his citation reads:

The enemy counter-attack had met with initial success and the situation was fast becoming critical. It became apparent that the existing supply of ammunition would be inadequate. Squadron Sergeant-Major Clarkson immediately volunteered to take a lorry back to replenish the supply. Having just arrived on his normal nightly trip, he was fully aware that the route to the rear had been cut by German infantry. He personally drove and ordered other personnel in the vehicle to fire into the dug-in positions on both sides of the road. He succeeded in reaching the regimental echelon and

returned with the badly needed ammunition, enabling the squadron to remain in action for the remainder of the night. But for the Sergeant-Major's determined action, the defensive operation would have been seriously prejudiced.

As an historical footnote to this battle, not far away from the fighting by the Irish Regiment and the 'C' Squadron tanks, the main headquarters of 5th Armoured Division also came under heavy attack, although it is very unlikely the Germans had any idea what was there. General Hoffmeister took part in the close-in fighting in the early stages of the enemy infiltration, but knowing that he had a responsibility to maintain command of the whole division, he locked himself inside his armoured command vehicle until the enemy had been driven off.

The situation had changed significantly by first light, in large measure because of the superb leadership of Major Crosbie during the counter-attack and the subsequent operation to clear the Germans from the village. The mopping up turned into an absolute rout for the Germans when the Irish brought in their Badger flame-throwers, fitted on a Ram chassis. Those Germans that were not burned to death fled in terror, only to be shot up by 'C' Squadron tanks. There were nearly a hundred German dead when it was over, and several hundred more wounded. For his inspired leadership, Major Crosbie was awarded the Distinguished Service Order.

The Regiment suffered a great tragedy that morning when Corporal Herb Stitt was unfortunately killed when he was run over by a truck while sleeping beside his tank. The Distinguished Conduct Medal he so greatly deserved had to be a posthumous award.

The wartime history notes, "The battle of Otterloo was the only real fight which the Regiment encountered in Holland, and the NCO's who had led the troops without officers had done an excellent job."

The next day the division continued its advance toward the Zuider Zee, first taking Putten and then late in the day capturing Harderwijk. The Horse Guards moved to Ermelo to form a defensive strong point. The wartime history notes: "This was our last real battle. Before we again made contact, the German army had surrendered. After Italy it seemed like an anti-climax."

The Distinguished Conduct Medal.

A pause for tea in the last days of the war, Holland, May 1945. (GGHG Archives)

(Right) "The Last Bag": a German anti-tank gun destroyed near Delfzijl, Holand, May 1945. (GGHG Archives)

VICTORY

The Regiment moved with the rest of 5th Division northward to the Frisian coast for the assault on the Delfzijl Pocket, but the unit's only involvement was in providing indirect fire in support of units of 11th Brigade. The German garrison in Delfzijl surrendered on 2 May, and 5th Division sent the order on 5 May, "Cancel all offensive ops forthwith and cease fire 0800 hrs 5 May. Further details later." The war was over!

Thus ended our operations in Europe. The rest was anti-climax, as it was patently only a matter of days till the victory should be final....

The collapse had been so piecemeal that it was difficult to arouse much enthusiasm. Nevertheless, there was a genuine gladness that it was over at last and that we could now be certain of ending our days in Canada. There were a few inebriated celebrations, a double issue of rum, and a couple of tanks found their way into canals; but the wild orgies that, for years, everyone had threatened, signally failed to materialize.

During the course of its battles the Regiment lost sixty-five all ranks killed, and two hundred and ten were wounded, but no one from the Horse Guards was ever taken prisoner or reported missing. This is a record that is almost unique, and of which we are justly proud.

There is something in the human condition, and perhaps especially in that of soldiers, which needs a ceremonial marking of great passages such as beginnings and endings. This was particularly so in the case of the end of the Second World War. Many in the Regiment had for the better part of five years been away from home and family and had experienced the fear and exhilaration of combat and the loss of friends who had become as close as brothers, and after all the struggle and striving the war had simply fizzled out. There was no sense of closure, of having finished the job properly, of having really won the war.

Everyone wanted to return to their families in Canada as soon as possible, but they also knew that the Regimental family they had come to cherish was about to be broken up. General Hoffmeister sensed this need for a formal ceremony, so a full-scale 5th Armoured Division victory parade was organized for 23 May on the grounds of Eelde airport, near Groningen.

Two days before the big parade, vehicles of every sort from every unit in the division began to congregate at the airport, where units were assigned tight positions marked off with white mine tape. A full day was taken up in cleaning and polishing, levelling the guns with clinometers, and then finally marshalling the vehicles into neat rows and columns. Having the whole division – over 2,000 vehicles and 15,000 men – in one place was an impressive display of armoured might, and it was a sight the troops had witnessed only once before. General Crerar drove up and down the ranks of this massive parade on the morning of 23 May, and after the troops ate a box lunch the division carried out what must have been the largest

mounted march past in history. Major General Bert Hoffmeister, respected and admired by every one of his men, led his 'Maroon Machine' on this grand finale for the division. Immediately behind the division headquarters came the Horse Guards, then the units of 5th Armoured Brigade, then 11th Brigade, and finally the divisional troops. It took three hours for the parade to pass the reviewing stand. The 5th Armoured Division – the first armoured division ever created in Canada – was sent off in fine cavalry style. To top the day, the colonel overheard General Crerar remark that the Horse Guards were the best looking unit on parade. But that was what the Regiment would have expected of itself.

The town of Assen, 25 kilometres south of Groningen in northern Holland, was to be home for the remainder of the Regiment's stay on the continent. If there had been any doubts the war was really over, they were soon put to rest. Over the next weeks, the Regiment's tanks and scout cars were stripped of all tools, radios, equipment, ammunition and 'buckshee'

Horse Guards tanks passing the reviewing stand at the final parade for 5th Armoured Division at Eelde airport, near Groningen, 23 May 1945. Note that the tank at front left is a Sherman IB mounting a 105mm howitzer. (GGHG Archives)

Regimental parade to say farewell to Major General Hoffmeister, Assen, Holland, May 1945. (GGHG Archives)

rations and kit the crews had managed to accumulate. Gradually the tanks and scout cars were turned in to Ordnance stores at Eelde airport, and by 3 July the last of them had gone. The Regiment was again as naked as it had been at mobilization in Toronto five years earlier.

REPATRIATION

Once the war was over, the primary problem for the Canadian Army was to get the men home as soon as possible. This, of course, was a very complex matter. The war in the Pacific – still a long way from being won – now took first priority. Then too, the limited number of available troopships meant that repatriating the hundreds of thousands of Canadian soldiers and airmen would take many months. To make the process of return as fair as possible a complex point system was set up, based in part on date of arrival overseas. As all three in-

fantry divisions had been sent to England first, the units of 5th Armoured Division had a fairly low priority, and at one point the Horse Guards were told that it would be Easter 1946 before the unit would get back to Toronto.

Some men volunteered to serve with the 6th Division being formed for service in the Pacific theatre and were sent home immediately, others were assigned to the Occupation Force in Germany, and the men with high points were selected a few at a time for individual repatriation drafts. There was thus a constant trickle of officers and men leaving the unit. For the most part the troops who remained accepted their lot with good grace, and the Regimental quarters in Assen were made as comfortable as possible. Once the tanks were gone there really was not much to do, so considerable efforts were made to keep the men occupied in the mornings learning skills that would be useful when they returned to Civvy Street. There was a heavy accent on sports in the afternoons, and passes were freely available to visit Amsterdam, London, Paris and other parts of Europe. But perhaps the main thing that made the long wait bearable was that the Dutch people were genuinely gracious and friendly, inviting men into their homes and gladly sharing what little they had.

The war in the Pacific came to an abrupt end after atomic bombs were dropped on Hiroshima and Nagasaki in early August, and the shipping situation eased considerably. The Regiment

MEDALS AWARDED TO MEMBERS OF THE REGIMENT AT THE CONCLUSION OF THE WAR

The France and Germany Star.

The 1939-45 Star.

The 1939-45 War Medal.

turned in the last of its vehicles and equipment in Holland on 25 November and moved to England to wait for a ship. The men spent much of December on leave, but finally, on 7 January 1946, the Horse Guards, along with the other units of 5th Division, boarded the *Queen Elizabeth* in Southampton harbour. Eight days later the Horse Guards were met on the quay in New York by Major Alex Boothe, and the rail journey to Toronto began shortly after midnight.

The train bearing the Horse Guards and the RCD pulled into a siding in the Exhibition Grounds, just behind the Coliseum, at 1900 hours on 16 January 1946. The Horse Guard families had all been alerted to be there. The last entry in the War Diary relates:

Our great moment came at 1930 hrs when the regiment, led by Lt Col Jordan, and headed by the band of the 2nd Regt playing "Men of Harlech", entered the Coliseum. The din was terrific as the thousands of relatives and friends who had come to witness the home-coming of the Horse Guards, fairly shook the rafters with cheer after cheer. The veterans of the regiment who had preceded us home had already entered the Coliseum and were drawn up in rear of the regiment under command of Brigadier Cumberland. … Both Mayor Saunders and Maj Gen Potts then spoke to the regiment, welcoming us home, but little could be heard above the uproar…. Lt Col Jordan … then stepped down

from the platform to fall out the officers. The regiment was dismissed by the RSM and then the mad scramble started, as soldiers and families sought each other out and the long-awaited reunions became a reality.

The war was over for the Horse Guards.

*   *   *   *

The wartime history closes with a passage that proved to be especially prescient:

The war has been fought on an island, suspended in time and space, that had little relation to the life we left or to which we were now returning. That, after all, is true of any war. Those who have taken part belong to a fraternity that is forever closed. Years from now, those who are left, no matter how ancient or decrepit, will still find pleasure in rehashing old times and laughing again at jokes that only those who "speak the language" will be able to understand.

It ends by saying, "It is hoped that this history, despite its limitations, will help keep the memory greener". With a bit of variation to accommodate the passing of nearly 50 years, today we can surely say, "It is hoped that this history, despite its limitations, will help a new generation of Horse Guards to know their past."

Regimental Sergeants and Warrant Officers, Holland 1945. (GGHG Archives)

CHAPTER SIX

COLD WAR TO BRAVE NEW WORLD

1946–2001

For The Governor General's Horse Guards, the formal end to the wartime era came on 31 January 1946, when the Active Service regiment was officially disbanded. The 3rd (Reserve) Armoured Regiment (The Governor General's Horse Guards), the wartime Reserve Regiment, simply continued to operate in the old quarters in the University Avenue Armouries under Lieutenant Colonel Alfred Bunting's leadership.

Despite the government's official disinterest in spending money on the armed forces, at the end of January 1946, the Minister of National Defence announced that Canada's peacetime army, at least for planning purposes, was to consist of 25,000 regulars and a Militia of 180,000 organized in six divisions and four independent armoured brigades. In late March, Brigadier Ian Cumberland was appointed commander of 19th Armoured Brigade, one of the independent brigades, made up of the Horse Guards, the 1st Hussars from London, the Fort Garry Horse from Winnipeg and the Ontario Regiment from Oshawa.

REBUILDING THE MILITIA REGIMENT

As soon as the veterans were reestablished in civilian life, Brigadier Cumberland gathered the Regiment's senior officers to make plans for rebuilding the peacetime unit. They decided to ask Lieuten-

Lieutenant Colonel G. deS. Wotherspoon, DSO, ED, Commanding Officer of the Horse Guards 1946 to 1948. (GGHG Archives)

ant Colonel Gordon 'Swatty' Wotherspoon – the dynamic pre-war Horse Guard who had commanded the South Alberta Regiment with great distinction throughout the North-West Europe campaign – to take command of the unit for a period of two years. Lieutenant Colonel Jack Eaton (who had commanded the 8th New Brunswick Hussars in Europe), stepping down a rank, was named second-in-command, with Majors Allan Burton and Charles Baker as squadron commanders and Warrant Officer Class I (WOI) Robert E. Thompson as Regimental Sergeant Major. The new command structure began to function in March 1946, but the reconstituted Militia regiment did not in fact become fully operational until September.

One of the Regiment's first important post-war activities was to play host to the new Governor General during his first official visit to Toronto. Field Marshal Viscount Alexander of Tunis, now the Honorary Colonel of the Horse Guards, made a brief visit to the unit on 23 May to meet the officers.

While there had been no plans made for summer camps for the Militia in 1946, at the last minute a number of units were allowed to send small detachments to Camp Borden for a ten-day camp in July. The Horse Guards was the only armoured unit in Ontario to participate, sending one tank troop for

The first post-war training. Horse Guards soldiers inspecting the suspension of a late-model Grizzly tank at the Royal Canadian Armoured Corps School in Camp Borden, summer 1946. (GGHG Archives)

driving and maintenance and gunnery refresher on Grizzly tanks belonging to the Corps School. The troop carried out a three-day shoot at the tank range in Meaford, the first serious tank training in the post-war era.

The post-war Militia Regiment opened for business on 10 September 1946. Captain Pat Grieve, who served during the war with the Canadian Grenadier Guards (later brigadier-gen-

The new Governor General, Field Marshal Lord Alexander of Tunis, inspecting a guard of honour commanded by Captain Reginald Wedge during one of his first visits to the Regiment as Honorary Colonel in 1946. (GGHG Archives)

eral and recognized as one of the great men of the post-war Armoured Corps), was the recruiting officer for the Regiment, enrolling the men who volunteered at this first parade.

Colonel Wotherspoon's first priority was to create a sound base for unit training, and the Regiment was fortunate that many of the wartime NCOs and officers chose to remain, giving a strong cadre of battle-experienced leaders and instructors. To provide substance to this orientation, the unit was organized into training wings rather than operational squadrons, and the pre-war practice of parading on Tuesday evenings and on one Sunday every month for theoretical training was reestablished, with occasional weekend schemes and weapons practice at the Long Branch range.

Warrant Officer Class I Robert E. Thompson, Regimental Sergeant Major 1946 to 1953, and from 1955 to 1958. (GGHG Archives)

On 10 November, a month after the reorganization parade, the Regiment marched to Timothy Eaton Memorial Church to reclaim the Regimental Standard that had been deposited just before the unit went overseas in the autumn of 1941. In time-honoured custom, the adjutant, Captain J. Chantler, rapped on the church door with the butt of his pistol and informed the minister, "I have been commanded by Lieutenant Colonel G.D. Wotherspoon, commanding the Governor General's Horse Guards, to inform authorities of this church he has repaired here to commemorate the fallen of this Regiment and to withdraw the Standard of our Regiment deposited with you for safekeeping." At the end of the memorial service the Standard was proudly paraded along St. Clair Avenue to mark its return to duty.

By the autumn of 1946, the Regiment boasted a strength of over 500, the majority from the overseas unit. This wealth of manpower came about because so many returned veterans were competing for the few available jobs on 'Civvy Street'. Many unemployed men with time on their hands stayed on with the unit in the company of their 'family' of wartime buddies.

This situation did not last: most overseas veterans really wanted little to do with a peacetime army. They had fought the good fight for King and country, and now it was time to move on, improve their education, find a career and start a family.

The Canadian economy grew quickly and opportunities for employment soon increased as industry converted to producing goods needed in peacetime, and, by law, veterans got preference in hiring for these new jobs. Another important factor which adversely affected the retention of men in the unit was the sheer lack of equipment for useful training. While the Regiment had been promised five Shermans and one Chaffee light tank, they never materialized. None of the Army's tanks or armoured fighting vehicles had been brought back from Europe, so there were very few for the Militia armoured regiments until the government bought new ones. Captain George Taylor, a corporal at the time, recalled, "Initially we had so many men and so little equipment that we had nothing for them to do. So most of them sat and socialized in the Mess during training time." Morale suffered, and by the end of 1946 the Regiment's numbers had dwindled to less than a hundred all ranks.

The manpower predicament experienced by the Horse Guards was reflective of the general attitude of the population toward things military at this time. The country itself obvi-

ously needed to be substantially re-built after ten years of economic depression in the 1930s and then six years of war that had severely depleted the treasury. The government's priorities just did not include anything to do with the armed forces, and it reverted to what had been standard pre-war defence policy: spend as little on defence as it could get away with politically. Despite the rather grandiose plans of early 1946, the Army was lucky to be able to retain about 8,000 regulars and 10,000 Militia.

The issue of a new Canadian Army uniform began shortly after the end of the war when the wartime closed-collared battle dress tunic was replaced with a new, more formal looking variant. Many of the veterans on returning home from Europe had their tunics 'customized' with an open collar that exposed a neatly pressed shirt and tie, giving the uniform a smart look for walking out and parades. As battledress was the only uniform issued to the men, it made sense to modify the tunic by adding lapels and removing the never-used field dressing pocket on the trousers. Cloth puttees were worn instead of canvas gaiters. This uniform remained in service for more

The Regiment's first post-war tanks, two Grizzlys, are shown at Stouffville in 1947. (GGHG Archives)

The Regiment's four 76mm gun Shermans during field training at Meaford in 1948. (GGHG Archives)

than twenty years with slight variations in insignia. Governor General's Horse Guards cloth titles were worn on both shoulders, and at some point a navy whistle lanyard was introduced. NCOs and men wore a black beret with this uniform, but officers and the RSM wore the Regimental navy forage cap with red hat band. Officers continued to wear pre-war service dress for parades and walking out.

There was some glimmer of better times in 1947. Perhaps the best news for Militia armoured soldiers was the purchase from the US Army of 294 M4A2 Shermans equipped with 76mm guns, and some 200 light tanks – Mark V Stuarts and Chaffees. After the two regular regiments were equipped, each Militia regiment was to get between four to six of the new tanks. The Horse Guards received its initial complement of one Grizzly and one Stuart from Camp Borden stocks in April 1947, and over the course of the next year four 76mm Shermans were taken on strength, along with another Grizzly, a Lynx scout car, two motorcycles and six trucks of various sizes. The vehicles were kept in a fenced parking lot behind the University Avenue Armouries.

The social life of the Regiment was regen-

Canadian Army post-war Battledress uniform. (GGHG Archives)

erated in this period, and among the popular activities was the Toronto Garrison Officers Indoor Baseball League which was, allegedly, the oldest organized baseball league in North America. Games were played on Saturday nights during the winter months at the University Avenue and Fort York Armouries, with great parties afterwards in the messes. As before the war, there was a spirited rivalry amongst all the participants – the Horse Guards, the 48th Highlanders, the Queen's Own Rifles, the Irish Regiment, the Toronto Scottish and the Service Corps – and the Horse Guards team won the championship many times.

An important development at this time was the creation of what was known as the 'A&T (Administration and Training) Staff' – the posting of experienced Regular Army officers and NCOs to Militia units to assist in planning and conducting training, unit administration and supervising the maintenance and control of vehicles and equipment. The first member of the Horse Guards A&T Staff was WO II Edward Douglas from the Royal Canadian Dragoons, and many members of that regiment would follow in years to come, creating a sound base for the formal regimental affiliation of later years.

In April 1947, there was a grand reunion of overseas veterans at the University Avenue Armouries with more than 500 in attendance. The event's success led to an even larger function in 1949 and the formation of The Governor General's Horse Guards Association. The first president was the wartime Regimental Sergeant Major, Arthur Finn. The association has been a thriving force within the Regimental family for more than 50 years, bringing together the fraternity of veterans for a variety of social events and for an annual memorial service to honour fallen comrades. It also serves to preserve close links between the wartime veterans and those serving in the Militia unit.

To oversee succession of command, as well as to ensure the perpetuation of the traditions and standards of the Regiment and to raise funds for unit activities not otherwise covered by the official DND funding, a group of officers led by Colonel Wotherspoon created a Regimental Board of Trustees in June 1947. Over the years the Trustees added former commanding officers and other prominent members of the broader community to their ranks, and have continued to look after and provide for the general well-being of the Regiment.

Regimental strength grew to 134 men in the spring of 1948, in part because of a cash bonus scheme devised to encourage members of the Regiment to bring in new recruits, and which was paid only after the new recruit had completed basic training. Militia service became more attractive to students when 'call outs' to serve with the Regular Army during the summer months became fairly widely available. The production of young officers for Militia units was also addressed by the re-creation of the Canadian Officers Training Corps in many universities. COTC cadets trained at their Corps school for ten weeks in the summer months, and after completing two summer phases they were granted a commission. Officer training was the main preoccupation of the Armoured Corps School every summer for the next two decades, and COTC was the source of many of the Regiment's officers for many years.

The Horse Guards' cavalry background was not forgotten in this period of intense work to create a peacetime

Two members of the Horse Guards Riding Club at the Three Gaits Stable. (GGHG Archives)

Lieutenant Colonel G. Allan Burton, DSO, ED, Commanding Officer 1948 to 1950. (GGHG Archives)

armoured regiment. The A&T Staff's WO II Edward Douglas, a pre-war member of the RCD Musical Ride, suggested that the Regiment form a cavalry riding club and offered to train the men in the art of military horsemanship. The idea got a rousing endorsement from the unit NCOs and work began in the spring of 1948. There would, of course, be no government funding, but The Governor General's Horse Guards Riding Club was formed by enthusiastic volunteers who paid for the training out of their own pockets. Horses were rented just as in pre-war days, initially from the Three Gaits Riding Stable at Warden and St. Clair Avenues, with members paying a dollar a ride and looking after the tack and the grooming of the mounts. In this early period of the club, members wore civilian riding breeches and battledress tunics that had been dyed dark blue, black berets and blue puttees. They rode every Thursday night, and as the organization grew training expanded to include Sundays and Mondays as well. Sergeant Major Douglas set a very high standard of training, and he was assisted by members of the Regiment who had served in the unit as cavalrymen before the war. While the club began as a purely recreational group, it laid the foundations for what would

Shermans and crews, Petawawa. Note the three different varieties of track on the tanks. (GGHG Archives)

become a significant part of the prestige and character of the Regiment, the modern-day Cavalry Squadron.

The Riding Club attracted many new recruits, and some of the officers who participated were from the local equestrian circuit that formed the Canadian Equestrian Jumping Team. Major Bud Baker and Second Lieutenant Tommy Gayford rode in competitions all over North America, winning many trophies and bringing honour to the Army and the Regiment in the same way that the Body Guard members of the Olympia team did in 1934.

The Regimental family also grew in an important way when a Horse Guards' cadet corps was formed in the spring of 1948, with an initial strength of 30 young men between the ages of 14 and 18. While using the cadet corps as a recruiting pool was officially frowned on, the cadets were indeed a significant source of new soldiers for many years.

Exercise "Plunder", the first collective training exercise conducted by 19th Armoured Brigade, took place at Camp Petawawa in July 1948, and the Horse Guards supplied the better part of a tank squadron's complement of men. Similar

numbers were sent by the 1st Hussars and the Ontario Regiment, but the Fort Garry Horse in Winnipeg was simply too far away to participate. The Horse Guards squadron had a magnificent time working progressively up from troop to squadron-level exercises using the RCD's new Shermans, and there was great pride in once more being a proper armoured unit.

As noted earlier in the book, back in February 1942, Lord Birdwood, Colonel of the Royal Horse Guards, remarked during a visit that The Governor General's Horse Guards ought to be brought more firmly into the family of the British Guards regiments, and he suggested that the Regiment adopt the badges of rank worn by officers of the Royal Horse Guards. One day in late November 1948, quite out of the blue, Colonel Burton received a letter from the commanding officer of The Household Cavalry informing him that "His Majesty The King as Colonel-in-Chief of the Royal Horse Guards, has approved of The Governor General's Horse Guards wearing the badges of the distinctive pattern authorised for officers of the Royal Horse Guards." Army authorities in Ottawa balked when this was presented to them, but no one dared question

Squadron Sergeant Major Grant Rook (far left) and 'C' Squadron Sherman crews during summer training at Petawawa, 1952. (GGHG Archives)

the King. Horse Guards officers wore the distinctive silver RHG crowns and garter cross stars on all uniforms until the 1970 issue of the dark green unification uniform with naval-style rank braid. But even now the RHG stars and crowns are still worn on Full Dress, Mess Dress and Patrol Dress uniforms.

The weight of tradition was felt in yet another area. As a result of some years of lobbying by the Royal Canadian Armoured Corps Association, the somewhat distasteful practice of numbering the regiments of the Corps was modified; while the numbering would remain, it would now be secondary to a unit's title. Accordingly, on 4 February 1949, the Regiment officially became The Governor General's Horse Guards (3rd Armoured Regiment).

The difficulty experienced in attracting a sufficient number of recruits in Toronto in the autumn of 1949 resulted in part of the Regiment returning to

Lieutenant Colonel Charles F. Baker, Commanding Officer 1950 to 1952. (GGHG Archives)

one of its places of origin. 'B' Squadron, initially commanded by Major Doug Crashley, was moved to Stouffville, near the area where John Button raised his original cavalry troop in 1810. The Squadron was based in the Legion Hall, and the unit's four Shermans were moved by flatbed to a fenced enclosure behind it. There the Regiment had access to a shed for maintenance and 30 hectares of fields where driver training and some limited tactical movement could be taught. Maintenance on these Shermans was conducted under the watchful eye of Sergeant Major Vern Slade, who knew these vehicles even better than anyone in the Regular Army. Major Eric Taylor took command of 'B' Squadron in 1950. This squadron, whose members were all from the surrounding area, remained in Stouffville for the next ten years.

ONSET OF THE COLD WAR

In the years immediately after the the war, the Canadian government's main military emphasis was on continental defence, in collaboration with the United States. Having to fight another major international conflict on the scale of the Second World War was at that time nearly unthinkable: the wartime Allies had founded the United Nations for the express purpose of preventing such a war. However, the international climate began to change significantly in 1947 and 1948. The United Nations did not function as had been expected because of the Soviet Union's use of its right of veto in the Security Council. The aggressive, expansionist drive of the Soviet Union was seen as increasingly threatening as one after another of the Central and Eastern European countries were taken over by Communist puppet regimes subject to Moscow's strict *diktat*. And, as important as anything, the massive Soviet Red Army in Eastern Europe was never demobilized, as were the armies in all western countries. There were well-founded concerns that the Soviet forces, always at high readiness, might one day march westward. Reinforcing the military threat, Communist parties had widespread popular support in Italy, France, Britain and Greece. Communism was also on the march in Asia; China fell to Mao Zhedong's Communist guerillas in 1949. But the year-long Soviet blockade of Berlin which began in June 1948 was the real catalyst for action by the democratic nations of North America and Western Europe. 'Containment' of Communist expansion became the central tenet of the grand strategy of Western nations in what soon came to be known as the Cold War. And the Cold War, always threatening to degenerate into all-out war, was to last for forty years!

It was obvious to leaders of the Western democracies that the freedom so recently won at such great cost could be pre-

Recruit being issued with boots and battledress at the Quartermaster Stores in the University Avenue Armouries. (GGHG Archives)

Stacking boxes of 76mm ammunition behind the firing point at Camp Petawawa. (GGHG Archives)

served only by a strong military alliance such as had existed during the war, and Canada was one of the first proponents of this important step. The North Atlantic Treaty Organization (NATO) was thus created in April 1949 for the express purpose of deterring a massive Soviet attack into western Europe. But even after the formation of NATO, the Canadian government still resisted any major increase in defence spending, arguing that the mere creation of the Alliance was sufficient to keep the peace in Europe. The act of aggression that altered the thinking of the Canadian government did not, however, occur on the centre stage of Europe – it came instead on an unlikely peninsula in the Far East.

On 25 June 1950, Communist North Korea launched a massive invasion into South Korea, at that time still a protectorate of the United States. Within days the United Nations Security Council called on all member nations to assist in repelling the attack and restoring peace by means of what was called a "collective police action". In early August, the government announced the creation of a Canadian Army Special Force brigade to serve in Korea as part of a Commonwealth division. Recruiting began almost at once in the same hasty and chaotic fashion that had characterized mobilization in 1914 and 1939.

The armoured component of the Special Force brigade was to be a tank squadron. A unit designated 'A' Squadron, 1st/2nd Armoured Regiment was formed in Camp Borden in August, with the majority of the men coming from the RCD and Strathconas. This squadron, later designated 'C' Squadron of

Lord Strathcona's Horse, trained in Fort Lewis in Washington state with the other units of 25 Infantry Brigade throughout the fall of 1950, and eventually arrived in Korea in April 1951. The fact that the country was once again at war, albeit in a limited way, brought with it a noticeable increase in interest in things military, and for the Horse Guards this had a very positive effect on recruiting new members.

The unit's place in the city's social order was also an important consideration in this period. The Regimental band, which had been resurrected immediately after the war, had by the autumn of 1950 regained its prominent place among the military institutions of Toronto. During the Royal Winter Fair that year, the band performed in the Coliseum every afternoon, and also periodically at Maple Leaf Gardens during the winter.

Unfortunately, at this same time membership in the Riding Club dropped considerably. Colonel Bud Baker, a champion horseman himself, took a personal interest in reinvigorating the organization, and he appointed Major Mac Burka to form a ceremonial Cavalry Squadron from the Riding Club, to be maintained and supported by the Regiment. The strength of the Cavalry Squadron grew quickly, and in 1951 it moved to the Eglinton Equestrian Club, where it began practising formation riding in earnest.

By the time the first Canadian brigade took its place in the line in Korea in April 1951, it was apparent that the war – now essentially confined to static defensive lines – would not be concluded quickly, and that a replacement tank squadron was going to be needed. At the same time 27 Infantry Bri-

Lieutenant Colonel J. Douglas Crashley, CD, Commanding Officer 1952 to 1954. (GGHG Archives)

Warrant Officer Class I Arthur C. Darnborough, Regimental Sergeant Major 1953 to 1955. (GGHG Archives)

gade was being prepared for service with NATO in Germany, and a tank squadron was also needed there. The solution to raising these squadrons was to have Militia regiments recruit entire troops, designated (for no particular reason) as 'Y' troops.

In June 1951, the Horse Guards, along with the Fort Garrys, the Calgary Regiment, the British Columbia Dragoons and the British Columbia Regiment, were requested to recruit a 'Y' Troop of 40 men for service in Korea. Within two hours of receiving the notification, two officers and 31 men had volunteered, and by the next day the full quota was reached. However, men continued to volunteer in droves over the next days, most civilians with no previous connection to the Regiment, and after cursory medical examinations and very hasty processing, 223 men were signed up, the largest number of volunteers provided by any Militia regiment for the Special Force. The large Horse Guards 'Y' Troop was sent by rail to Camp Wainwright, Alberta, under the temporary command of Lieutenant Tony Hawkins. Aboard the train, it became apparent that all too many of the hastily recruited troops were rowdy, undisciplined drunkards. During a stopover in Winnipeg, Hawkins spent much of the time marching the group up and down the streets to keep the men out of trouble, but after 'reading the riot act' he eventually let them loose on the town. Hours later, he was astounded when every one of them returned to the train station in time for departure. Once in Wainwright, they were joined by the other 'Y' troops in a tank squadron designated '2nd Armoured Squadron', which was to be trained by the Strathconas. For a variety of reasons, this squadron was never sent to Korea to replace the Strathcona's 'C' Squadron, but instead was absorbed into the Strathconas as 'D' Squadron. All 'Y' Troop members were required to put on Strathcona insignia, breaking a promise to the parent units that their men would be allowed to keep their own regimental badges. A few 'Y' Troop militiamen did eventually get to Korea as individual replacements.

Trooper (later Chief Warrant Officer and RSM of Lord Strathcona's Horse) Ron Francis from the Horse Guards 'Y' Troop was one of the first replacements sent to Korea. He arrived in the Strathcona squadron 'B' Echelon one dark night in late December 1951. Some years later he recalled this experience:

[After I had] jumped to the ground with all my kit, the truck immediately drove off into the dark evening, leaving me very much alone to ponder my existence. At this point someone started beating on a final drive sprocket ring with a track pin … the local fire alarm. From a myriad of small holes in the ground came dozens of troopers in a variety of dress, all running to the tank park. … An hour later, I finally found a van with an orderly officer inside. After taking my name and a few other rather significant details, the young officer led me to one of the holes in the ground, pulled back the poncho covering the entrance and quietly said to those inside, "This man's name is Francis and he will be staying with you until such time as we can figure out what the hell to do with him." Not a very inspiring welcome or introduction.

Trooper Francis went on to recount his introduction to the front line:

The war was nothing like I had envisioned it to be. The tank was dug in alongside the infantry trenches and bunkers, and our role appeared to be that of providing direct sniper fire support for the endless infantry night patrols. The nightly turret/radio watches were particularly nerve-wracking, although one would never admit to it. The noise of patrols going out or returning through the wire, the constant thumping of Vickers and .30 calibre [machine guns] firing on fixed lines, the frequent lighting of the sky by some nervous infantryman firing off flares, the shadows created by the searchlights providing artificial moonlight, and every shrub exposed by the flares appearing to move – all had the tendency to make one rather anxious.

One former member of the Horse Guards, 22-year-old Lance Corporal J.W. Kennedy, died of wounds suffered in a massive Chinese attack on 5 November 1951 while with 'D' Company of the 1st Battalion, Princess Patricia's Canadian Light Infantry. Another former member of 'A' Squadron, Corporal William Downs, served with the Medical Corps in Korea and earned the British Empire Medal for distinguished service.

By the summer of 1953, the unit had 242 officers and men, and attendance on parade night approached 100 percent. Lieutenant Colonel Peter Hunter, a subaltern in those days, recalled that: "The massive University Avenue Armouries parade square was full end to end when the Horse Guards formed up. Attendance was strong, and morale was very high".

The Coronation of Her Majesty Queen Elizabeth II was one

Marking maps before setting out on a 'trace', Camp Borden. (GGHG Archives)

of the most significant events of 1953, and the Toronto garrison held a mass parade on 2 June to mark the occasion. The Regiment had 146 men on parade that day, and the band, in full dress, made a marked contribution to the impressive ceremony. One member of the Regiment, Sergeant George Jeffrey, was part of the Canadian contingent sent to London to participate in the Coronation parade. He and RQMS Vern Slade were the only Horse Guards to receive the Queen's Coronation Medal.

Regular armoured units had a banner year in 1953, for both the RCD and Strathconas were reequipped with the new British-built Mark III Centurion tank, a much superior tank to even the very latest version of the Sherman. It carried a 20-pounder (83mm) gun firing a high-velocity armour-piercing round, every bit as good as the feared German 88 of the war years, and its armour was much heavier than the Sherman's. The new tank was greatly needed if Canadian tank regiments were to have to face hordes of Soviet tanks swarming into Germany. For the Militia units, the downside was that the operational equipment was no longer the same in Regular and Militia units, so borrowing tanks from the Regulars was no longer possible. And, having only obsolete vehicles, the Regulars started to look down on their shabbily equipped Militia cousins. Nonetheless, a significant number of Shermans were retained until the mid-1960s both at the Corps School in Camp Borden and at the Meaford Tank Range. They were used for training COTC officer cadets in the summer months, and those in Meaford were made available to Militia regiments for tactical training and exercises and for gunnery range practices.

Over the course of many years, the Regiment has always

taken a keen interest in preserving and recording its history, and one of Colonel Crashley's goals was to publish a narrative of the Horse Guards' wartime service. A committee of volunteer veterans worked throughout 1953 on a manuscript of the wartime history, based on the unit War Diaries and the recollections of the group of writers. *The Governor General's Horse Guards, 1939-1945*, a 243-page book, was the proud result. The new history was put on sale at a Regimental reunion in mid-May 1954 in the Horticultural Building on the Canadian National Exhibition grounds, and it was very well received by all veterans of the campaigns in Italy and Holland.

Winter indoctrination training, one of the imperatives according to the annual training directives of Central Command, was probably the sole aspect of training that was universally disliked in the Militia in the early 1950s. Clearly, if any country's army ought to be proficient in operating in the field in winter it should be the Canadians, and there was still some concern that the Soviets might just cause prob-

Lieutenant Colonel G.M. Brown, CD, Commanding Officer 1954 to 1956. (GGHG Archives)

lems in the Arctic islands. But if the Regular Army of the day was poorly equipped for cold weather operations, Militia units were totally unprepared. No proper winter clothing was available, but still winter training had to be done! So, soldiers outfitted in battle dress, greatcoats, garrison black gloves and parade boots, and frankly whatever else they could get on under their uniforms, went bravely out to try to function in sub-zero temperatures. Everyone was bitterly cold all the time and, as science has since told us, trying to keep warm occupied almost all of a soldier's time. Sleeping outside was the worst part of the experience: every soldier was issued with three grey wool blankets and a large safety pin called a blanket pin. He was expected to create an interlocking arrangement of three layers of blankets on the bottom, three on top. His rubber poncho was to be the 'insulation' between the bottom blankets and the frozen ground. All this was to be topped off with the man's greatcoat. It simply did not work, especially since the issue grey blankets were usually threadbare, so everyone was constantly chilled to the bone. It was better when the tanks were taken out, for then the men could sleep on the back deck and enjoy the benefit of the still-warm engine.

One of the most catastrophic national disasters of the century occurred on Friday 15 October 1954 when Hurricane 'Hazel' struck Toronto and the surrounding area, with extremely high winds and torrential rain lasting nearly a whole day. Water was soon metres over the banks of every river and creek in Toronto, and many bridges and hundreds of homes were suddenly washed away in the raging muddy floodwaters. A great many people went missing and the Toronto Militia units, including the Horse Guards, were called out in aid of the civil power.

Volunteers mustered at the University Avenue Armouries after the floodwaters had receded somewhat, and they deployed next morning. Two amphibious carriers were brought from Camp Borden to help with the search and rescue operations. Sergeant Jim Davis was a crewman on one of them, which was used on the Humber River in western Toronto to travel along the muddy banks looking for survivors and bodies of those who had drowned. Other members of the unit patrolled the banks on foot, prodding with long metal rods to

Horse Guards members searching for casualties along the bank of the Humber River after Hurricane Hazel, October 1954. (GGHG Archives)

THE 1954 PATTERN FULL DRESS UNIFORM

The Governor General's Horse Guards Full Dress uniform introduced in 1954 in most instances replicates a Full Dress uniform produced in 1938: a navy blue Dragoon-style tunic with red collars and cuffs and an Austrian knot on the cuff, in silver for officers and in white cord for other ranks. Trousers featured a 2½-inch-wide red Guards stripe down the side of the leg.

Other ranks wore a white leather cross belt which supported a black leather cartouche pouch at the small of the back. The belt was decorated with a red flask cord fastened along the centre by three leather loops, a practice adopted from the Royal Horse Guards. White cord aiguillettes were worn on the left shoulder fastened under a cord epaulette. The belt was in white cloth or plastic with a rectangular silver buckle on which a Regimental badge was mounted. Following an old Militia tradition, NCO rank was worn only on the right sleeve.

Officers wore a cross belt of metallic silver lace with silver hoof picks on the front, and a full aiguillette on the right shoulder, with rank badges on an epaulette. Headdress with this uniform could be either the silver dragoon helmet with red horsehair plume or the navy blue forage cap with red band. (Photo: GGHG Archives)

find bodies buried in the deep, soft mud. During their search, Sergeant George Taylor's patrol came across a hand sticking out of the mud; they had found one of seven fireman who had been swept away in the swift current the previous day. In all, over 80 people lost their lives in the storm. The Regiment was involved in the search operations only during the weekend, but they made an important contribution to the recovery of a badly damaged city.

By late 1954 two of the Regiment's 'orphan' vehicles – the Stuart and the Lynx scout car – were in such bad condition that they had to be taken out of service. Parts were no longer available, and these vehicles, which had seen several years of hard wartime service at the Corps School in Camp Borden before coming to the Horse Guards, were simply worn out. The two Grizzlies, the Canadian-made variant of the M4A1 Sherman, were also becoming increasingly difficult to keep on the road. The main problem was the limited life of the radial aircraft engines, and few parts for the Grizzly were common with the newer 76mm Shermans. Thus, when something broke down there was never any certainty that spare parts

would be available, and in late 1958 both Grizzlies, no longer serviceable, were returned to Ordnance.

One notable retirement took place in December 1954: Colonel R.Y. Eaton, the Honorary Lieutenant Colonel, whose son Captain Erskine Eaton had been killed during the Dieppe raid in August 1942, relinquished his appointment after 25 years of loyal service and great generosity to the Regiment. This was the sad termination of the Horse Guards' long association with the distinguished Eaton family.

One of Colonel Brown's objectives after taking command was to outfit all ranks in new dress uniforms so as to boost morale and improve recruiting. This was a costly project by any measure, but the Regiment succeeded magnificently: the entire unit was dressed in Full Dress just over a year later when the Horse Guards provided a 105-man dismounted guard of honour for a visit by Governor General Vincent Massey on 15 November 1955. Over the same period a concerted effort was made to outfit the Cavalry Squadron with full ceremonial trappings. The Regular Army A&T Staff, many pre-war cavalrymen, were especially helpful in gathering proper cavalry saddles and tack as they seemed to know where the old stocks had been hidden away at the start of the war. A number of old Body Guard silver dragoon-style helmets were found in storage in the Armoury. These were refurbished and new Horse Guards helmet plates were fitted. Some of the Regiment's 1908-pattern swords, which had been sold as scrap metal during the war, were located and purchased. And with the Regiment's many connections, the Cavalry Squadron was able to find suitable facilities for the horses and storage of its equipment. By dint of effort on the part of many, a uniformed squadron could be made available for ceremonial duties. The old cavalry stables at the University Avenue Armouries were on many occasions used as a staging area for ceremonial events.

The Cavalry Squadron's first call to duty came in the spring of 1956. Governor General The Right Honourable Vincent Massey, being the Honorary Colonel, knew about the Cavalry Squadron, and asked the Regiment directly to provide an escort from Union Station to the CNE Stadium on the occasion of the 48th Highlanders' trooping their colours. It seems someone in Army Headquarters got a bit miffed that the Governor General failed to go through proper channels in requesting the escort, but that was soon sorted out and no one ever again challenged the Governor General's right to communicate directly with his own Regiment. In mid-June the Squadron escorted His Excellency to the running of the Queen's Plate, a task that became an annual commitment. The Cavalry Squadron also expanded its horizons, providing mounted escorts, as in the distant past, to the Governor Gen-

Lieutenant Colonel Robert C. Rutherford, MBE, CD, Commanding Officer 1956 to 1961. (GGHG Archives)

eral for his annual visit to the Royal Agricultural Winter Fair, and to the Lieutenant Governor for the Opening of the Legislature at Queen's Park. These two commitments carried on for many years.

The Cavalry Squadron was far more versatile than just as a ceremonial escort to vice-royalty, for in the mid 1950s it learned to perform the intricate Musical Ride that had originated with the Royal Canadian Dragoons and had been copied and made popular by the RCMP. Resplendent in Regimental full-dress uniforms and shining silver cavalry helmets, the squadron carried newly acquired cavalry lances, which, with pennants flapping and lance tips reflecting the bright lights, added flair and colour to the ceremony. The Horse Guards, of course, had never carried lances, nor had any other Canadian cavalry unit. In fact, their only use by the Canadian cavalry was to mark the regimental headquarters during training camps, when a single lance flying a regimental pennon was planted outside the headquarters tent.

Another link to the cavalry past in the years immediately after the war was the retention of a few trumpeters in the Regiment's ranks, but the practice was soon banned by higher authorities. In their place, a trumpet band was formed in the early 1950s under the direction of the Signals Officer, Lieutenant Evan Herriott, eventually growing to some 50 members – 30 trumpeters, 10 snare drums, two tenor drums and a base drum along with glockenspiels and cymbals – under Drum Major George Taylor. The band became very popular, playing at prestigious events such as the Grey Cup and Santa Claus parades and Warriors Day. When on parade with the Regi-

The Cavalry Squadron, led by Captain A.M. Burka, marching past the reviewing stand at a parade for the Honorary Colonel, His Excellency The Right Honourable Vincent Massey, 2 June 1956. (GGHG Archives)

Regimental Shermans crossing a pontoon bridge during a bridging exercise at Petawawa. (GGHG Archives)

(Left) A Driving and Maintenance refresher course at the University Avenue Armouries, and, in the second photo, Two Horse Guards troopers getting instruction on the tank main armament on the Regiment's cut-away Sherman turret. (GGHG Archives)

ment, the trumpet band would be in the lead, with the brass band fitted between the squadrons. It was, however, disbanded in 1959 when the Regiment could no longer justify the expense of maintaining two bands

Training in the Corps trades – gunnery, driving and maintenance, and 'wireless' communications – was taken very seriously within the Regiment throughout most of the 1950s, and the standard was very high because of the skilled NCO veterans who did most of the instructing. Elementary gunnery training was carried out at the Armouries, where the unit had a 75mm Sherman turret as a training aid. Large parts of the armour on the sides and back of the turret wall had been cut away so a group of students could hear the instructor's fire orders and instructions and watch the student gunner carry out his practice shoot. 'Shooting' was done on a miniature range, where a high-powered light was aligned on the gun barrel to enable the instructor to check the gunner's accuracy – an early form of simulator training. The practical training of firing the real guns was done at the Regiment's annual gun camp,

His Excellency Major General The Right Honourable Georges P. Vanier, the Honorary Colonel, with Lieutenant Colonel Rutherford and a group of Regimental fanfare trumpeters. (GGHG Archives)

which was sometimes in Meaford and sometimes in Petawawa. Each gunner would fire 15 to 20 rounds of 76mm ammunition, a mix of armour-piercing and high-explosive, with the occasional smoke round if weather conditions were right. Safety standards were perhaps not quite up to modern peacetime requirements, in part because wartime expedients still held sway even if they might carry some considerable risk. Captain George Taylor, then an NCO, recalls being a loader during one practice shoot on a tank range:

> I loaded a round, but it jammed in the breech. The crew commander – a grizzled old veteran – asked over the intercom what the hell the problem was, and shouted at me to hurry up and get the gun loaded. I said the round was jammed. He told me to take another round and use it to hammer the jammed round into the chamber. I wasn't so sure about that, but he was wartime trained and experienced, so I did what I was told and hammered the round into the breech. It fired just fine.

Warrant Officer Class I Gordon K. Edwards, Regimental Sergeant Major 1958 to 1961. (GGHG Archives)

A TIME OF 'SNAKES AND LADDERS'

Throughout the 1950s, the threat of a Soviet attack into Western Europe appeared to increase with each passing year. The Russians had exploded their first nuclear warhead in 1949, and for a number of years there was broad acceptance that if war broke out in Europe it would involve the use of nuclear weapons. Both sides in those years produced low-yield nuclear warheads which could be used on the battlefield by being fired from artillery and surface-to-surface missiles or taking the form of highly destructive land mines. In this same period, the strategic nuclear threat to North America greatly increased with the advent of inter-continental ballistic missiles bolstering the already considerable threat from large fleets of Russian long-range bombers. Canadian cities were now considered at substantial risk of being hit by a nuclear strike. These immense changes in the strategic situation called for new thinking about defence and about the structure and roles of the armed forces.

In Europe, with the likelihood of all-out nuclear war after a brief battle of conventional forces, there seemed to be little point in relying on the mobilization of reserves for the decisive fight. What was needed were more standing conventional troops to serve as an even stronger deterrent to a Soviet attack, and, among many other things, Canada was asked to make good on its earlier commitment to provide a full division to the Central Front in Germany. This brought about the bolstering of the Regular Army by the creation of two new Regular armoured regiments – the 8th Hussars and the Fort Garry Horse – and the 'filling out' of two Canadian-based brigades which would be ready for quick deployment to Germany in time of tension.

If a 'come as you are' war was what was anticipated in Europe, plans for massive mobilization of the Militia to create two Army Corps seemed unnecessary and out of date. But for the first time in over a hundred years there was an enormous threat to the Canadian homeland: the threat of nuclear devastation. Here, it was thought, was a really important role for the Militia. If our cities were struck by large nuclear weapons, someone had to be able to determine the extent of the damage, someone had to be prepared to rescue survivors, someone had to be able to reestablish a rudimentary communications network and take charge until civil authority

Royal Escort provided for Her Majesty Queen Elizabeth II and His Royal Highness The Duke of Edinburgh during their visit to the 100th running of the Queen's Plate at New Woodbine Race Track, 30 June 1959. (GGHG Archives)

The Herald Trumpet, presented to the unit by the Allied Regiment, The Royal Horse Guards, for the playing of Royal Salutes during visits by the Sovereign. (GGHG Archives)

training. Then the other shoe dropped on 28 May 1959: overnight the role of the Militia was officially changed to 'National Survival'. The first major effect was that summer camps were immediately cancelled and authorized training days were cut from 60 to 40. Most armoured units had their tanks taken away, but the Horse Guards managed to hold onto their four Shermans for a few years. The small armoury in Stouffville was closed at this time, and 'B' Squadron re-located to Toronto. During the 'Snakes and Ladders' period, the tanks were kept at the Ontario Regiment's unofficial training area at Raglan mainly because the Ontarios, with their close ties to General Motors, were able to get spare parts specially made. However, after 1960 the Regiment's Shermans were used only for occasional unauthorized driving and maintenance training.

In the last heady days as a tank unit, the Regiment's proper and original name was restored. On 19 May 1958 all vestiges of the wartime system of numbering the regiments of the Armoured Corps were officially dropped. The Regimental name was once again The Governor General's Horse Guards. At this same time, nine Second World War battle honours were awarded to the Regiment, all selected to be emblazoned on the Standard at some time in the future: '**Liri Valley**', '**Melfa Crossing**', **Gothic Line**', **Lamone Crossing**', '**Misano Ridge**', '**Fosso Munio**', '**Italy 1944-1945**', '**Ijsselmeer**' and '**North-West Europe**, 1945'.

There was a very special ceremony in June 1959 when Her Majesty The Queen and the Duke of Edinburgh visited Toronto to attend the 100th running of the Queen's Plate at Woodbine racetrack. The Regiment provided a Royal Escort of 61 officers and men under the command of Major A. Macdonald Burka, a signal honour and national recognition of the capability and worth of the Cavalry Squadron. It was the first time in 20 years that the Horse Guards had provided a mounted guard for their sovereign, and the first occasion to do this for Queen Elizabeth II.

An interesting sidelight to the preparations for this grand event originated with Trumpet Major Art Galloway. The Trumpet Major held the view that he needed a very special type of trumpet known as a herald trumpet to give the Royal

was reestablished, and someone had to map radiation fallout so heavily contaminated areas could be avoided. National Survival was the 'in thing', and a lot of people took it very seriously. Across the country huge underground bunkers were dug and stocked with food, water and amenities so members of governments could survive and perhaps function until it was safe to emerge. Civil defence thus became a most important government priority.

The Militia first became aware of this impending sea change in 1957 and 1958, when Army training directives began to emphasize civil defence training for Militia units, but there was no effort to cut Corps-related trades or tactical

Communications training: a young trooper tunes the antenna of a No. 19 wireless set in a Sherman turret. (GGHG Archives)

– each carrying a 'National Survival box' filled with ropes, ladders, stretchers, shovels, axes, geiger counters, radiation plotters and a No. 42 radio set. The unit was to provide what was called a 'Mobile Survival Column' and a 'Mobile Survival Group Headquarters'. The garrison training consisted of first aid courses, truck driving, rope knotting, plotting and predicting nuclear fallout, radiation recce, along with communications and voice procedure, the only remaining armoured skill. Practical field training focused heavily on the evacuation of wounded people from damaged buildings using ladders and ropes, hence the derisory name given by the troops: Snakes and Ladders. It was dreadfully dull stuff. There was nothing military or challenging about this type of work, so morale suffered and parade attendance dropped significantly. The greatest loss was the large number of highly skilled NCOs who found the whole thing most unpalatable.

Warrant Officer Class I Frank Farris, CD, Regimental Sergeant Major 1961 to 1963. (GGHG Archives)

Salute in a tone befitting the pageantry of the occasion, but no herald trumpet could be found anywhere in Canada. Major Burka came up with an innovative solution: he sent a cable to the commanding officer of The Royal Horse Guards in England asking if a trumpet could be borrowed and sent over immediately. He then contacted the public relations officer for Trans Canada Airlines, asking if they would do a special delivery. Within 24 hours a herald trumpet was on its way across the Atlantic, and the Trumpet Major was able to play the Royal Salute properly as he knew he must. Later, The Royal Horse Guards, through the good offices of Sir Gerald Templar, Gold Stick of The Royal Horse Guards, very kindly presented the herald trumpet to the Regiment so this predicament would not recur in the future.

That same year, two of the three British allied regiments were amalgamated. The 1st King's Dragoon Guards and 2nd Queen's Bays, with whom the Mississauga Horse and the Body Guard had first forged links in the years between the wars, were combined to form the 1st The Queen's Dragoon Guards.

By the spring of 1960, the Regiment had been re-equipped with a variety of military-pattern trucks for their National Survival training – ¾ ton, 2½ ton and 3 ton

In this period of adversity the officers and NCOs made the most of the active social life provided by their messes. Lieutenant-Colonel John Burns recalls that when he first joined as a second lieutenant in 1960, all Regimental officers "dined in every Tuesday before parade – no excuses tolerated". The sergeants also maintained an active social life centred around their mess, even though Toronto had begun to discard its dour reputation as 'Toronto the Good' and nightlife in the bars and clubs was thriving. For many years, the sergeants in fact often held parties in marquee tents in the field, complete with carpets, white table cloths, candelabra and ceremonial lances

One might think that the government's true opinion about the place of the Militia in society was revealed by a variety of other actions. For example, in the summer of 1960 it was announced that the venerable University Avenue Armouries – two full blocks in the most prestigious part of the city core – was to be torn down to make room for a new

Lieutenant Colonel Harry T. Tye, CD, Commanding Officer 1961 to 1965. (GGHG Archives)

First Aid class typical of the training during the 'Snakes and Ladders' period. (GGHG Archives)

provincial court house. The Armouries, built between 1891 and 1894, was the largest in the country, and one of the very best examples of late Victorian architecture. The Defence Department promised three new ultra-modern armouries would be built to replace the old facilities – one in North York, one in Scarborough and one in Etobicoke. Only two were actually built over the next year, one on Dufferin Street just north of the 401 Highway, and another, named Moss Park, at Queen and Jarvis Streets in downtown Toronto.

The new armoury in Downsview, named Denison Armoury in honour of the long association of the Denison family with the Regiment and its antecedents, was to house the Horse Guards. The Regiment occupied its new home in the autumn of 1961. This move is not remembered with any pleasure or pride, in part because so many of the Regiment's possessions, acquired over the previous hundred and fifty years and proudly displayed in the offices and messes in the old armoury, went 'astray' during the move. The new armoury was modern, functional and cold, and some likened it to a sterile factory building – it simply had no character. But the

worst aspect of the new Regimental home was that space for offices, stores, classrooms and messes was exceedingly cramped because the unit was required to share the facilities with 5 Column, Royal Canadian Army Service Corps (later 25 Toronto Service Battalion), which had no home because the third of the promised armouries had not been built. Over the next 40 years the two units engaged in a constant struggle for space, but there could never be any satisfactory resolution: the armoury was simply too small for two units.

Colonel Harry Tye's time as commanding officer was surely one of the most difficult in the Regiment's history, for the first half of his tenure occurred after members of the unit had come to understand fully the negative aspects of the National Survival role. For well over a hundred years, in peace and in war, the Horse Guards and their antecedents had accepted assigned roles and tasks without question, soldiering on in spite of difficulties, poorly equipped, virtually unpaid and with little public recognition. The reluctance on the part of Militiamen to accept an assigned role was therefore an unusual situation. It proved almost impossible to generate any enthusiasm for the prescribed training, a widespread reaction within the whole of the Militia. Fortunately the Chief of the General Staff recognized the damage that had taken place to this venerable national institution, and in late 1963 he authorized a return to Corps-oriented training. But for Militia armoured units it was already too late: Sherman tanks had been withdrawn from most units and were about to be retired entirely from those units that still retained one or two. And there was the insurmountable problem that the talented NCO gunnery and D&M instructors were now also gone. The Army got a stark reminder of a lesson learned on many previous occasions: technical and tactical skills and capabilities disappear very quickly if they are not valued and continually nourished, and once gone they are not easily recovered. It seems that this lesson is repeated at least once every generation.

The Regiment's move to Downsview had many important repercussions. The first major impact was that many of the lower ranks simply dropped out, mainly because they could not easily get to the new armoury by bus, streetcar or subway train. The first impact produced the second: the character of

Warrant Officer Class I George Taylor, CD, Regimental Sergeant Major 1963 to 1966. (GGHG Archives)

Denison Armoury, home to The Governor General's Horse Guards from 1961 to 2002. (GGHG Archives)

Her Majesty Queen Elizabeth, the Queen Mother, arriving at Woodbine race track accompanied by the Royal Escort, June 1962.

the unit changed almost overnight: it ceased to be the bastion of old Anglo Upper Canada that it had been for more than a century. While it took some time to rebuild the unit strength, the new Regiment began to reflect the very changed demographics of Canada generally and North Toronto in particular in the 1960s. New recruits came from the ethnic communities of North York; first the Italians and the Jews, and later the Blacks, East Indians and Chinese. The happy thing about this change in the makeup of the unit's membership was that it was barely noticed while it was happening, and then it later became a source of considerable pride. The older, retired members – white, Anglo-Saxon protestants for the most part, and many from prominent families, the 'aristocracy' of Toronto – didn't bat an eye, and to their credit fostered the advancement of any and all. A Horse Guard was a Horse Guard!

Despite the difficulties common to all military units at this time, the Regiment continued to perform to the high standard its members had come to expect. In 1962 the Horse Guards were awarded the Cumberland Trophy for best armoured unit in Central Command.

The most loved member of the Royal family, Her Majesty Queen Elizabeth, The Queen Mother, came to Toronto for the running of the Queen's Plate at Woodbine on 26 June 1962. As had become traditional Regimental practice, the Horse Guards Cavalry Squadron provided a Royal Escort of 50 all ranks for Her Majesty. The Guard in fact included former commanding officers, officers and NCOs. At the end, always gracious,

Lieutenant Colonel Peter W. Hunter, CD, Commanding Officer 1965 to 1967. (GGHG Archives)

The Queen Mother made a point of coming to the Guard commander, Captain Peter Hunter, to compliment the guard for its appearance and performance and thank them for their care and concern.

In 1964, Canada's most famous race horse, 'Northern Dancer', won the Kentucky Derby and was advancing to the Preakness at Pimlico (in Baltimore, Maryland). Confident of a win in this second jewel in the legendary 'triple crown' of racing, the horse's owner, leading Canadian industrialist E.P. Taylor, contacted the Regiment and asked if the Cavalry Squadron could be on parade at Pimlico on the day of the race. In only a few days, Captain Peter Hunter organized a group of twenty-four riders and horses for the trip. The convoy, made up of two horse vans carrying a dozen horses each and a bus with the personnel, left Denison Armoury and arrived at the US border several hours later. The delay in getting past US Customs was interminable. After repeated inquiries about the wait, US officials explained that they were waiting for direction from Washington on how to deal with an alien army bearing arms (twenty-four lances and swords) invading

Jeeps in a laager during summer training in Meaford, ca. 1966-67. Note the radios in wooden boxes mounted over the left rear wheel well, remnants from National Survival kits. Machine gun mounts and angle-iron wire cutters had not yet been installed when this photo was taken. (GGHG Archives)

(Left) The Regiment's jeep were 'doctored' in 1967 for the reconnaissance role, including installation of a .30 calibre Browning machine gun on a pintle mount on the crew commander's side of the vehicle. (GGHG Archives)

the US, the first time since the war of 1812. The Horse Guards were flattered but not amused. Finally the bureaucratic nonsense was overcome and the unit moved on. Northern Dancer won the race. It was a proud occasion for the Regiment, and was the source of many 'war' stories for those who participated.

The most significant military event in Canada in 1964 was 'integration' of the armed forces. This far-reaching change was a necessary prelude to full 'unification' four years later, but integration in reality affected only the Regular Force, and even there it was felt mainly in the higher-level headquarters where bureaucratic and procedural aspects were torn to bits. But one thing did indeed affect the Militia that year, the report of the Suttie Commission, which ostensibly had been tasked to study the roles, tasks and organization of the Reserves. However, the real purpose of the Commission was to find ways for the government to cuts costs in the Militia so more funds could be directed to the Regulars. Among the Suttie recommendations were a reduction in Militia strength by 40 percent, to a maximum of 30,000 men. For a time, every regiment thought it was at risk of being disbanded – even the venerable Horse Guards felt it had to lobby politicians to ensure it would survive the purge. When the decisions were announced, the Armoured Corps had lost six illustrious regiments, all assigned to oblivion in the Supplementary Order of Battle, including the sister Guards regiment, 4th Princess Louise Dragoon Guards from Ottawa. Thenceforth, 'major' units were allowed a maximum of 300 men, 'minor' units, commanded by a major, 100 all ranks, and there was an inherent threat that any major unit without a consistent turnout of more than 100 men on parade would be reduced to minor unit status. While the Commission also recommended acquisition of tanks for Militia armoured units, this was ignored.

A RECONNAISSANCE REGIMENT ONCE AGAIN

In the spring of 1964, once the dust of Militia reorganization had settled, Colonel Tye held a briefing for the unit's other ranks. He had the adjutant, Lieutenant John Burns, write the word 'RECCE' on a blackboard and announced that this was now the unit's role. What exactly this meant was very uncertain. Was it 'sneak and peek' light recce such as had been done for some time by the Regular units' Ferret scout car squadrons, or was it the somewhat more robust 'armoured cavalry' light armour operations that the Regular regiments were just now getting into, and which was probably somewhat like the Horse Guards had done during the war. Militia armoured regiments were being equipped with wheeled vehicles capable only of light recce training. But the three Armoured Regiment Training Headquarters formed in 1966 to assist with the reconversion of the Militia units to war-fighting roles taught 'light armour' doctrine, and that was obviously to be the model even if the Regulars had difficulty understanding how it was meant to function. Thus in subsequent years Senior NCOs were sent on training applicable to the light armour role, such as the mortar platoon commanders'

Warrant Officer Class I A.James Davis, CD, Regimental Sergeant Major 1966 to 1970.
(GGHG Archives)

course and M113 armoured personnel carrier driving and maintenance courses, things irrelevant to the real state of the Militia.

In the Horse Guards, the changeover to the new role was fairly gradual. For the moment, the unit continued to train on Shermans in Borden and Meaford. Lieutenant Colonel Jeffrey Dorfman, then a driver, remembers firing the Sherman guns at Meaford, and getting a bit of a jolt when his tank crashed through the floor and into the basement of one of the abandoned farm houses still dotting the range.

The summer camp in late June 1965 was the first occasion when the Regiment conducted recce training, and Captain David Friesen commanded an ad hoc squadron, with Lieutenants Jamie Burton, Keith Marshman and Noel Bambrough as troop leaders of five-vehicle troops. The week of field training was challenging and great fun, and the main exercise was doubly worthwhile because there was a live enemy to pit wits against. But all was not quite as one may have wished: the mosquitoes were so bad that at least one officer had to be hospitalized because of an allergic reaction to their bites. And then a forest fire deep in the Petawawa woods forced an end to the exercise because everyone was needed to fight the fire.

On return from Petawawa to Denison Armoury, Colonel Hunter called his officers and the RSM together to discuss the circumstances in which the Regiment found itself and how to deal with the issues it faced. The Shermans were gone, the unit was still suffering the aftermath of 'snakes and ladders', there

A jeep section playing 'rat patrol' on a country road north of Toronto. The jeep in the foreground is 'covering' the movement of the vehicle in the distance as it moves to a new position of observation. (GGHG Archives)

was precious little equipment, and morale was starting to slip which would cause a retention problem.

For training in the recce role, it was decided to take the vehicles and 'doctor' them at the unit, at Regimental expense, to allow for aggressive training in tactics, driving, map reading, wireless, and, of course, maintenance. Further, an active programme of ceremonial and social events, including all parts of the Regimental family, would be undertaken to generate interest and build unit loyalty and *esprit de corps.*

In combination, these decisions produced a very busy, educational and satisfying programme for Horse Guards at all rank levels. Most important, a high standard of training and a revival in traditional Regimental matters were achieved.

In the fall of 1965, the last of the Horse Guards' Shermans was turned in by the Ontario Regiment, who had taken custody of them in 1960. There is a persistent rumour that at the turn-in the Ontarios had to admit that they had somehow 'lost' one of the tanks, a potentially fairly serious matter. Large things like tanks, especially when they had large guns, were really quite hard to lose. It turned out that the missing tank was later found – as a monument in Centennial Park on the lakeshore. In fact, two of the others soon found their way back to Toronto as monuments. One was placed in front of Denison Armoury, and the other sits in York Cemetery. To replace the tanks, the unit was issued four ¾-ton trucks and eight 1953-pattern jeeps. These vehicles, all hand-me-downs from the Regular force, were in desperate need of extensive maintenance. Fortunately, the jeeps and ¾-tonners were robust and simple in design and thus quite easy to maintain, and they were tough machines that could take a severe beating in cross-country driving. Several members who were civilian master mechanics did many unauthorized repairs over the next years to keep the fleet on the road.

Even though it was without armour protection, the jeep proved to be a fairly versatile reconnaissance training vehicle. It worked best with the windshield folded down: there was less glare and less height. The open front also allowed for the mounting of a .30 calibre machine gun on an ad-hoc pintle on the passenger side. But this configuration left the crew very vulnerable to low-lying wires, so to give some form of protection, a metre and a half-long piece of angle iron was welded vertically

Lieutenant Colonel Michael B.W. Davis, CD, Commanding Officer 1967 to 1970. (GGHG Archives)

onto the front bumper. Several deep notches were cut into the top end of this bar, serving as hooks to catch any low-lying lines and cut them before they could take off the heads of the crew members. And since the jeeps came without radios, 42 set radios were taken from National Survival kit boxes and placed in hand-made radio mounts welded to the left rear wheel well. All this work was done by unit members at the armoury. Within three years the Regiment had a complement of 16 jeeps, sufficient to form a three-troop recce squadron. Parts still had to be begged, borrowed or stolen, and it was not a totally uncommon event for the regimental transport sergeant to offer a bribe (usually a bottle of good whisky) to vehicle technicians at Base Toronto to get repair work done. Eventually a full-time vehicle technician was placed on permanent loan to the unit at Denison Armoury.

The jeep recce squadron was popular with the troops because the training was both interesting and fun. Interesting because what was taught in classrooms in the armoury during the week was practiced throughout southern Ontario almost every weekend. Fun because the modified vehicles were similar to those shown on the highly popular TV show 'Rat Patrol'. Indeed, the recce squadron became known as the Rat Patrol, and its vehicles and crews were frequently seen by the general population for miles in every direction from Denison Armoury.

In 1966, the officers hosted Governor General Georges Vanier at a Mess Dinner. At the same time, the Warrant Officers and Sergeants entertained Madame Vanier at a dinner where she was made an Honorary Sergeant – an honour and a tribute she always valued. This was to the dismay of the Royal 22e Regiment – the famous 'Van Doos' – which His Excellency had once commanded, and who also wanted to appoint Madame Vanier an honorary sergeant. She refused on the basis, "I'm already a Horse Guards sergeant!"

In 1967 the entire country celebrated the centennial of Confederation with great gusto. Every community, every organization embarked on some very special project to mark Centennial year. The main Horse Guards' Centennial celebration took the form of the presentation of a new Standard on 27 May 1967 by His Excellency The Right Honourable Roland Michener, the Governor General and

His Excellency The Right Honourable Roland Michener, Governor General and Honorary Colonel, presenting the Regiment's second Standard in Centennial Square, Toronto, on 27 May 1967. (GGHG Archives)

The second (1967) Standard of The Governor General's Horse Guards, on which the Second World War battle honours were emblazoned for the first time. (GGHG Archives)

Honorary Colonel of the Regiment. The new Standard had special significance for the veterans: the nine battle honours they had so gallantly won in the Second World War now took their place emblazoned alongside those awarded to the Regiment for battles in earlier wars. Their efforts, now ceremonially commemorated on consecrated Colours, would be honoured by the Horse Guards for all time. In an impressive traditional ceremony in Centennial Square across from the new Toronto City Hall, the Old Standard, presented in 1938, was first trooped though the ranks by a mounted Standard party. WO I G. Frank Farris had the honour of being the last bearer of the Old Standard. The New Standard, still in its case, was marched on by Regimental Quartermaster Sergeant (WO II) Robert Wise with an escort of two sergeants. After being uncased and laid on an altar of stacked drums, the new Standard was consecrated by the district chaplain, Lieutenant-Colonel The Rev. J.M. Anderson, the Regimental chaplain, Major The Rev. Canon M.P. Wilkinson and the 5th Armoured Bri-

gade's wartime chaplain, Captain The Rev. Percy Johnston. His Excellency then presented the Standard to RQMS Bob Wise and addressed the Regiment in the name of Her Majesty. The new Standard was then trooped through the ranks of the Regiment, who marched past with a troop of jeeps, the Cavalry Squadron, the Band, Cadets and three hundred Second War Horse Guards veterans.

The presentation of the Standard was surrounded by a series of social events including receptions, luncheons and a memorable Mess Dinner at which the Honorary Colonel, the Governor General, was guest of honour. His Excellency's heartwarming remarks that evening rekindled the love all in attendance had for their Regiment. He mentioned that he had no personal military experience, and that presenting the Standard was his first appearance in a military role – and that he had been terrified. Needless to say, the Honorary Colonel performed flawlessly, and for the rest of his life he remained very close to 'his' Regiment.

The new Standard corrected the errors made in the design of the original Standard, which had been based on a 1932 pattern created for the Body Guard. The unicorn, the central device on the Regimental badge, replaced the maple leaf in the annulus, and the facing colour behind the abbreviated Regimental title in the upper right and lower left corners, always a feature on cavalry colours, was changed from white to scarlet, the Regiment's proper facing colour.

The following day, the Old Standard was taken to Holy Trinity Church, and in time-honoured tradition was laid up to hang from the rafters of the church until such time as the fibres of the silk brocade crumble and decay and it exists no more except in the collective memory of the Regiment. But the Standard did not end its days there. In 1971, largely because the 'hippie' Holy Trinity congregation no longer made the Regiment welcome, the Standard was recovered and then laid up in St. James' Cathedral, the Regiment's original spiritual home, where, one hopes, it will remain until its days are done.

On 1 July 1967, The Governor General's Horse Guards turned out in large numbers and with great enthusiasm to celebrate the Centennial of Confederation. The weather was perfect, and the Toronto population was out in force. The entire Toronto garrison participated in a mammoth parade, replicating a similar event in 1867. The Horse Guards, Canada's senior Militia regiment, led the Army contingent in grand style: 24 members of the Cavalry Squadron, resplendent in full-dress uniforms and silver helmets, were first, followed by a squadron of 16 jeeps, then the band and the Regiment in 'Blues'. The cadets, in khaki uniforms, and Second World War veterans, smartly turned out in Regimental blazers, black berets and grey flannel trousers, were next. In total, there were more than 450 Horse Guards on parade.

In the autumn of 1967, the Regiment for the first time sent two men to serve for a few months with The Royal Canadian Dragoons in Germany as fly-over augmentation for the annual NATO Fall Exercise. Troopers Dave Mezzabotta and Terry Bannon both served as crewmen in tank troops, and had a magnificent experience. The fly-over to Germany became an annual event for the Horse Guards for the next two decades. Over a number of years Captain E.G. Brown accumulated a total of six

months service in Germany, and is the only member of the Regiment to qualify for the Special Service Medal with NATO bar.

In January 1968, following the death of Major General Frank Worthington, who had been Colonel Commandant of the Royal Canadian Armoured Corps since his retirement from the Regular Army in 1948, Brigadier Gordon (Swatty) Wotherspoon was appointed as Colonel Commandant of the Corps. It was, of course a great honour for Brigadier Wotherspoon, but equally the Horse Guards were enormously proud that one of their own had been selected to succeed the venerable Worthy as 'godfather' of the Corps.

Unification struck with a vengeance in 1968, and with it there was no more Canadian Army. Mobile Command, with its headquarters in the Montreal suburb of St. Hubert, became the Army in everything but name. But, the term 'Army' was banned: it was now the 'Land Force'. Over the next two years the unified dark green uniform gradually replaced the three service uniforms, and with that came the loss of all Regimental insignia except for the cap badge. For a time even black berets were banned, all ranks having to wear a nondescript green officer-style forage cap in garrison. When people took off their caps, neither their branch nor trade could be determined. Troopers were now officially privates, but in the Horse Guards this infantry rank was used only on official documents. The honourable rank of corporal became meaningless when everyone with 18 months of service was automatically promoted. Because there was a genuine need for 'real' corporals in the rank structure, the 'appointment' of master corporal was created. Officers rank badges were navy-style rings of gold-colour nylon braid.

All dressed in white and ready to go on winter indoctrination training. (CGHG Archives)

The Regimental Band (top) and the Trumpet Band. (GGHG Archives)

They recruited early in the Horse Guards! (GGHG Archives)

In truth, the Militia was far less affected by this drive to make everybody look alike than were the Regulars: the latter lost all their traditional uniforms except for scarlet Mess Kit. The Militia – probably more because of bold defiance than official sanction – kept Patrol Dress (Blues), Mess Dress and, in those units that had them, Full Dress. No one other than Paul Hellyer, the Defence Minister responsible for all this nonsense, liked what was happening, and little by little over the next years the nondescript unified uniform was 'done in'. First, unit collar badges were permitted, and then Regimental buttons, then the black beret was brought back, and then metal unit shoulder titles were issued. Many in the Armoured Corps made a big issue over the return of the black beret, but for the Horse Guards the beret never did have the significance others gave to it. It was not part of the traditional Regimental dress;

for much of the post-war era the black beret was worn only in the field. The Body Guard and the Horse Guards had for a great many years worn a forage cap in garrison, and there was not much support in 1976 when the black beret was decreed to be the only headdress for the Armoured Corps.

Unification, undertaken because there was a desperate need to reduce defence spending, could not solve the immediate budget problems, so defence spending everywhere was slashed, which had a very negative effect on the Militia. In

1968 annual summer training was cut to seven days and the Regiment sent only 71 all ranks to Mobile Command's first reserve concentration in Petawawa in July 1969. That December, the Horse Guards were informed that as of 1 April 1970 their authorized establishment would be reduced from 300 all ranks to 157, plus a 35-man brass band. At that time the actual unit strength was 143 all ranks.

In March 1969 the Allied Regiment, The Royal Horse Guards, was amalgamated with The Royal Dragoons to form The Blues and Royals, and a grand parade was held in Germany to mark the occasion. The commanding officer, Lieutenant Colonel Davis and RSM Davis represented the Regiment at the parade, and while in Germany took the opportunity to visit the other Allied Regiment, the 1st The Queen's Dragoon Guards.

The Trudeau era between 1968 and 1979 has been very aptly described in a few brief lines from the Granatstein and Bothwell book, *Pirouette:* "For the Canadian Armed Forces, the Trudeau years were a long, dark night of the spirit. Demoralized, embittered and frustrated, Canada's unified armed forces struggled to understand a government that treated them as an inescapable nuisance." While the Army had done an exceptional job in performing its duty as a

The Colonel Commandant of the Royal Canadian Armoured Corps, Major General Bruce MacDonald, DSO, CD, presenting the Worthington Trophy to Lieutenant Colonel Forbes, 1 October 1973. (GGHG Archives)

Her Excellency Madame Michener being made an Honorary Sergeant in The Governor General's Horse Guards by Regimental Sergeant Major Hans Busch. (GGHG Archives)

force of last resort during the separatist crisis of October 1970, it certainly did not gain any immediate political benefit. That same year the Armoured Corps was cut back when The Fort Garry Horse regulars were disbanded and the Grey and Simcoe Foresters reverted to infantry. The 1971 White Paper, *Defence in the 70s,* proclaimed a new high-mobility reconnaissance role for the Canadian brigade in Europe, and announced that the Centurion tank, "not compatible with Canadian-

Lieutenant Colonel Harold K. Forbes, CD, Commanding Officer 1970 to 1973. (GGHG Archives)

based forces", would be retired. In its place there was to be an air-portable "light tracked, direct-fire support vehicle". Many came to believe that the very existence of the Armoured Corps was at risk if there was to be no replacement for the Centurion. By this time, even the Regulars had given up all pretence of being 'light armoured' units: the Canadian-based regiments now each had two pure reconnaissance squadrons, one equipped with Ferret scout cars, the other with Lynx tracked recce vehicles, which had such different capabilities that they could barely function together. By 1972 the fiction that Militia recce regiments could somehow learn and practice light armour tactics had been abandoned, and all Militia armoured regiments were declared to be reconnaissance units. Meanwhile, the Corps hierarchy began to talk about 'tank trainers'. If there was to be no new tank, then perhaps the 'direct-fire support vehicles' (DFSVs) that the politicians insisted on foisting on the Army could be used to preserve some of the essential skills. There were to be many years of intrigue, and even as this book is being printed 30 years later there has been no resolution of the role or equipping of the Armoured Corps.

Chief Warrant Officer Hans G. Busch, CD, Regimental Sergeant Major 1970 to 1974. (GGHG Archives)

The arrival of Her Majesty The Queen and His Royal Highness The Duke of Edinburgh at New Woodbine Race Track on 27 June 1973. A part of the Regiment's Royal Escort, the Standard Party, is in the foreground. (Courtesy of Lieutenant Colonel Burns)

jor General Bruce MacDonald, presented both the Worthington Trophy (for the best Militia armoured unit in Canada) and the Cumberland Trophy (for best Militia armoured unit in Ontario) to Colonel Forbes. This was the first occasion the Regiment won the coveted Worthington Trophy. The high training standard was maintained through the following year, for in 1974 the Regiment was again awarded the Cumberland Trophy.

Throughout the early 1970s, the Regimental training and ceremonial programme followed much the same pattern each year. Trades courses, refresher training in basic military skills and weapons, tactics theory and recruit training occupied the winter months at Denison Armoury. Field training would begin in April with practical driver training and squadron recce exercises, and there would be more weekend exercises in May and June, with a summer concentration usually in August. The Cavalry Squadron would provide a mounted escort to the Lieutenant Governor for the Opening of the Legislature, and every November for the Governor General's arrival at the Royal Agricultural Winter Fair. In June 1975, a mounted escort was provided for the Duke and Duchess of Bedford at the running of the Queen's Plate.

During Colonel Friesen's period in command, training continued to show the same level of improvement as in the previous few years. More jeeps were received, and training advanced from sub-unit to formation-level exercises. Standard operating procedures were developed for jeeps in the reconnaissance role, and by 1975 Militia recce units across the country were following the same tactical doctrine.

In the summer of 1974, the concentration at Petawawa featured an exercise with two opposing brigades, one conducting an advance to contact, followed by a counter attack by the other. Colonel Friesen recalls:

The Regiment was again honoured to provide a Royal Escort for Her Majesty Queen Elizabeth II and His Royal Highness The Duke of Edinburgh on 27 June 1973, during their visit to Toronto to attend the Queen's Plate. Once again, the Cavalry Squadron, augmented with a host of temporary volunteers from among former commanding officers and other prominent Guardsmen, did a superlative job and brought great credit to the Regiment in doing duty to the Sovereign.

On 1 October 1973, the Governor General and Honorary Colonel, the Right Honourable Roland Michener, presided over the change of command from Lieutenant-Colonel Harold Forbes to Lieutenant-Colonel David Friesen at a Regimental parade in the Coliseum in Exhibition Park. Before the exchange of the command sword, the Colonel Commandant of the Royal Canadian Armoured Corps, Ma-

Lieutenant Colonel David E. Friesen, CD, Commanding Officer 1973 to 1977. (GGHG Archives)

The exercise was very challenging, and after several days it climaxed in a non-stop manoeuvre that lasted 36 hours. As commander of the recce regiment for one of the brigades, I was involved in an all night lights-out move that ended in near disaster for myself and my driver. Around three in the morning my driver drove off the road and our jeep rolled over several times down a slope. Although my driver was hospitalized, I escaped with cuts and bruises. The jeeps had no roll-bars or seat belts, and I credit the wire-cutter bar in front for minimizing the injuries.

Colonel Friesen brought about a change in the unit organization in the autumn of 1976 to give greater emphasis to the training so essential to the Regiment's well-being. 'A' Squadron became the general military training squadron, and 'B' Squadron became the crewman training squadron. That same year, the Regiment sent its first volunteer on a United Nations mission, and between 1976 and 1980 six members served on UN duty: Corporal D. Gobuty with UNFICYP in 1976, several with UNEF II in Egypt – Corporals C. Vondercrone (1976), D. Andrews and B. Macdonald (1978) and T. Francis (1979). Corporal D. Davidson served with UNDOF on the Golan Heights in 1980.

In 1976, the Horse Guards scored yet another 'first' in the Canadian Forces when the Regiment was formally affiliated with The Royal Canadian Dragoons. Earlier that year a policy had been introduced allowing the formal affiliation of units of the Canadian Forces, provided those units had historical or geographic ties. Soon afterward there were discussions between the commanding officers of the Horse Guards and The Royal Canadian Dragoons then serving in Lahr, Germany. The links between the regiments go back to the 1880s, when the Cavalry School Corps was based at Stanley Barracks in Toronto. A number of Body Guard members served with the RCD in the Boer War, and of course one, Captain H.Z.C. Cockburn, won the Victoria Cross while serving with the Dragoons. Both Regiments are allied with the Blues and Royals, and hold the distinction of being the senior armoured regiment in the Regular Force and the Militia respectively. The affiliation was commemorated in a ceremony attended by the RCD Association on 16 October.

There was renewed emphasis

Her Majesty Queen Elizabeth, The Queen Mother, taking the salute in front of the Royal Canadian Military Institute at a parade in her honour, July 1979. (GGHG Archives)

on training with the creation of the Regular Support Staff in 1978 – a modern-day version of the A&T staff – with a Regular Force captain, a warrant officer and a junior NCO attached to assist the unit in planning and preparing courses and field exercises. In time, members of the RSS played increasingly important roles within the Regiment, affecting both the training and administration of the unit. Captain Ed Carey and Chief Warrant Officer Harry Graham, the first of the RSS members assigned, made especially important contributions.

Chief Warrant Officer Jeffrey J. Dorfman, CD, Regimental Sergeant Major 1974 to 1979. (GGHG Archives)

The Horse Guards troop sent to serve with the RCD during the NATO fall exercise in 1981. (GGHG Archives)

Lieutenant Colonel John Burns, CD, Commanding Officer 1977 to 1981. (GGHG Archives)

Vehicles always played a vital role in an armoured unit, and duriing the 1970s the vehicle situation was the source of much concern. In 1973, the Regiment's 1953-pattern jeeps were replaced with a combination of 1956- and 1967-pattern vehicles, neither of which were nearly as robust as the jeeps they replaced. A few years later, some of the Regiment's trucks were replaccd with three 'militarized' General Motors 1¼-ton pickup trucks. Then, in 1979, some of the 56-pattern jeeps were replaced by 1974-pattern vehicles, the worst of the lot. The 74-pattern jeep had such a flimsy structure that roll-bars had to be fitted for safety. These thin-skinned vehicles were easily damaged in the field and consequently spent a lot of time in the body shop, and were no bargain for the Army at the end of the day.

The Militia Area concentration in the summer of 1979 provided some of the best training in years. The highlight was a major tactical exercise on the back roads of Southern Ontario from Meaford all the way to St. Thomas, and the Horse Guards provided a squadron of three five-car troops to serve as the enemy force. Moving tactically over such a long distance, and having real opponents to pit wits against, challenged the crews and their recce skills.

The Cougar – direct fire support vehicle cum tank trainer –

Chief Warrant Officer David C. Mezzabotta, CD, Regimental Sergeant Major 1979 to 1982. (GGHG Archives)

came into service in 1979, initially in the Militia Training Centre at CFB Borden. The importance of this for the Regiment can hardly be over emphasized, for the Cougar meant the return to training in traditional armoured skills. There was more and better training, and with the restoration of real armoured knowledge some members of the Regiment were afforded the opportunity for fly-over to the Regular regiment in Germany – the RCD – for major exercises. While this fly-over did not always work out as advertised – all too often plans were cancelled at the last minute – it

still gave some incentive to the junior ranks to remain engaged. A good indication of the quality of the training was the award of the Leonard Trophy for 1979, runner-up for best armoured unit in Central Area.

At the annual meeting of the Royal Canadian Armoured Corps Association in the autumn of 1979, the Director of Armour, Colonel Jack Dangerfield, gathered together the Militia commanding officers to tell them about the acquisition of the Cougar tank trainers. Lieutenant Colonel John Burns recalls:

At that meeting we had to decide the future of each of our regiments. My decision was to 'go Cougar' based on the undeniable fact that Recce was going to be a backwater, with all Corps qualifications being tank-oriented. In addition, the realization that the recruiting benefits would be better with Cougars than with the jeeps we had available sealed my decision. Thankfully Mike Davis, a senior member of the Trustees, was with me at the Conference and backed my decision…. As a result, two years later when I handed over to Lieutenant Colonel Bruce Palanik, we had two Cougars on parade, crewed by Regimental members.

Toronto Militia District organized a very innovative period of summer training during the last two weeks of August in 1980, when Exercise "Drum Con" was held at Camp Drum, New York. The Regiment took 87 officers and men to the concentration, and the recce troops were able to rove far and wide in the large US Army training reservation. That autumn, Colonel John Burns restructured the unit, making 'A' Squadron responsible for recruit and trades training, and 'B' Squadron became the operational 'sabre' squadron with two recce troops.

Lieutenant Colonel Bruce Palanik, CD, Commanding Officer 1981 to 1985. (GGHG Archives)

The continuing high standard of training in the Horse Guards was recognized by the Corps in October 1980 when it was announced at the Corps Conference that the Regiment had been awarded the Worthington Trophy for best Militia armoured unit in Canada, and the Cumberland Trophy for best regiment in Central Area. This was the second time the Regiment had won the coveted Worthington Trophy.

His Excellency The Right Honourable Edward Schreyer, Governor General and Honorary Colonel, at the Burns-Palanik change of command ceremony at Old Fort York, September 1981. (GGHG Archives)

"Eyes Right!" Guard of honour at the Burns-Palanik change of command. The two Cougars in the background, the first to appear at a Regimental parade, were borrowed from CFB Borden. (GGHG Archives)

In addition to the bragging rights, winning the Worthington Trophy allowed the unit to attach an entire recce troop to the 8th Hussars in Petawawa for over two months in the summer of 1981 for Mobile Command's Exercise "Rendezvous 81", and then flyover training with the RCD in Germany for two and a half months during the annual NATO Corps-level field exercise. This was truly a wonderful experience for Lieutenant L.M. Levak and his men, and they returned to the unit with a level of field skills that had not been seen for some years.

During this period the Regiment commissioned the first female officers. Lieutenant Colonel John Burns noted:

> Canadian social structure had matured in many ways. The realization by the Forces that women could and indeed deserved to be enrolled as combat officers allowed us the opportunity to promote the first woman from the ranks, Second Lieutenant Sylvia Straka. When she left the unit, we were fortunate in having two others join our ranks, Second Lieutenant (later Captain) Wendy Philips and Second Lieutenant (later Captain) Andrea Merrick. All proved worthy of wearing the Horse Guards badge.

Although these women were all combat arms-trained, their employment was limited to service support roles. It was not until the late 1980s that females could be employed in tank crews.

CONVERSION TO ARMOUR

The Horse Guards officially became an armoured regiment once again in 1981, equipped with the Cougar armoured vehicle general purpose (AVGP). The conversion from the reconnaissance role was, however, anything but rapid. Several NCOs attended Regular Force Cougar courses at Petawawa and Calgary during the summer, and the first D&M Trade Qualification level 1 (TQ 1) courses were conducted at Denison Armoury in the autumn. When the Regiment attended the Toronto Militia District concentration in Meaford in late August, it was, however, still functioning as a recce unit.

Chief Warrant Officer William L. Thomas, MMM, CD, Regimental Sergeant Major 1982 to 1985. (GGHG Archives)

The Regiment had been promised that at least one of its new Cougars would be delivered in September 1981, but as might have been predicted, it did not arrive. To draw the attention of higher headquarters to this failing, the recce exercises conducted in the fall of 1981 were named 'Missing Cougar'. Once again, the Regiment won the Leonard Trophy in 1981, the second time in three years.

The beginning of 1982 brought some substance to the Regiment's new armour role. In January, the 8th Hussars loaned a Cougar until the unit's own vehicles were delivered. Four Cougars finally arrived in May, one to

The Cavalry Squadron, led by Major Eric Constantinides, on parade at Old Fort York. (GGHG Archives)

squadron, while 'B' Squadron focused on Cougar conversion and armoured tactics. During the summer several senior NCOs and officers attended Cougar crew commander and troop leader courses in Wainwright, Alberta to learn the rudiments of armoured tactics which had not been practiced in the Regiment since 1958. All of the exercises in the spring and summer were joint recce/Cougar training, one squadron acting as enemy for the other. One of the major departures from the usual training cycle was the conduct of the Militia concentration at Camp Grayling, in Michigan, in late August. Here, half of the Regiment attended Cougar D&M and gunnery courses run by the 8th Hussars, with gunnery qualification shoots being done on the American ranges.

The first occasion when significant field operations training was conducted with the new Cougars came in August 1983 during a Militia Combined Operations Concentration held in CFB Borden and Meaford, where armour and mechanized infantry combat teams were the focus of the training. The Horse Guards, augmented with men and vehicles from the 8th Hussars, were paired with the Grey and Simcoe Foresters. Chief Warrant Officer Peter Crngarov recalls:

be kept at Denison Armoury and the other three in the Militia vehicle pool at CFB Borden for shared use by all armoured units in southern Ontario. As it would be some time before everyone in the Regiment could be cross-trained on the Cougar, 'A' Squadron was kept as a jeep-mounted recce

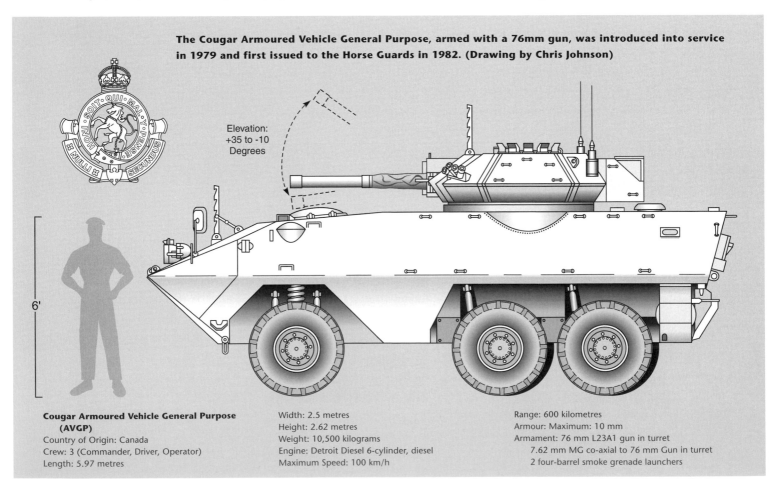

The Cougar Armoured Vehicle General Purpose, armed with a 76mm gun, was introduced into service in 1979 and first issued to the Horse Guards in 1982. (Drawing by Chris Johnson)

Elevation: +35 to -10 Degrees

6'

Cougar Armoured Vehicle General Purpose (AVGP)
Country of Origin: Canada
Crew: 3 (Commander, Driver, Operator)
Length: 5.97 metres

Width: 2.5 metres
Height: 2.62 metres
Weight: 10,500 kilograms
Engine: Detroit Diesel 6-cylinder, diesel
Maximum Speed: 100 km/h

Range: 600 kilometres
Armour: Maximum: 10 mm
Armament: 76 mm L23A1 gun in turret
7.62 mm MG co-axial to 76 mm Gun in turret
2 four-barrel smoke grenade launchers

When we arrived in Meaford and saw row upon row of Cougars and Grizzlys it was apparent that the Regiment had entered a new phase of its history: the Militia appeared to have the kit and equipment for very serious training. We were all so very impressed. We now believed we were truly armoured.

By the autumn of 1983, Cougar gunnery and D&M training were the main focus for both the Horse Guards and the Ontario Regiment, and the units shared the workload, the Ontarios conducting the driver training in Oshawa and the Horse Guards the gunnery course at Denison Armoury. Throughout the autumn these courses ran every weekend, an unusually busy arrangement for a Militia unit. At this time 'B' Squadron was made the Cougar squadron, with 'A' Squadron now being the training squadron. A Regimental Headquarters recce troop was a new feature of the organization, so the recce skills learned in previous years still proved to be of value.

The Regiment's long ties to the city of Toronto were brought to the fore in 1984 when the city celebrated the 150th anniversary of its incorporation. The Horse Guards were represented at

Her Excellency The Right Honourable Jeanne Sauvé, Governor General and Honorary Colonel, with a group of Regimental dignitaries during a visit to the Regiment in 1984. Front row: LCol Palanik, Her Excellency, LCol Tye. Rear row: LCol Friesen, LCol Crashley, Col Spence, LCol Rutherford, LCol Graham, LCol Forbes, Maj Burka, LCol Hunter and Maj Taylor. (GGHG Archives)

Horse Guards Cougars in the field during the 1985 Militia summer concentration in Meaford. (RCACA Archives, photo by Captain Chris Almey)

Sergeant Shawn Yearwood (right) and Corporal Pinto in the turret of a Cougar, with Corporal Mike Lipton in the driver's hatch. (GGHG Archives)

Lieutenant Colonel W. Allan Methven, CD, Commanding Officer 1985 to 1988. (GGHG Archives)

the grand ceremony by a colour party carrying the Standard, a 25-man guard in No. 1 Dress and a 32-piece band. Fifty years earlier, in 1934, the Regiment's mounted band had taken part in the city's 100th anniversary parade. During the summer, the Horse Guards and the Royal Regiment provided a combined changing of the guard ceremony at City Hall, and the last major ceremonial event of the year was the provision of a Royal Escort for The Queen during her visit to the Toronto Military Tattoo at the CNE.

While garrison training in the fall and winter every year concentrated primarily on essential aspects – basic training for recruits along with the Corps trades, communications, gunnery and driver courses – in most years in the 1970s and 1980s, usually in the depth of the arctic chill of February, the Regiment was required to conduct winter indoctrination training and the occasional winter weekend exercise. This was

never especially popular with the troops because they were always uncomfortably cold. At least now, though, proper winter clothing and equipment – parkas, tuques, layered gloves, thermal underwear, mukluks, sleeping bags and winter tents – could be drawn from a pool held in Base Supply, so the level of discomfort was substantially less than that experienced twenty years earlier. There is no doubt that most of the troops enjoyed the snowshoeing and cross-country skiing, even though they grumbled.

In 1985 the Cavalry Squadron lost the honour of providing mounted escorts for both the Queen's Plate and the Opening of the Legislature. It was a matter of funding: while the squadron had always received a small stipend for both duties – enough to cover the cost of renting and transporting the horses – the mounted division of the Metropolitan Toronto Police offered to do the duties at no cost. The Regiment simply could not compete with this, even though it meant the end of a tradition dating back 125

Chief Warrant Officer William G. Davidson, CD, Regimental Sergeant Major 1985 to 1989. (GGHG Archives)

284

years. The Regiment did, however, receive a noteworthy honour in May 1985, when Mayor Art Eggleton granted the Freedom of the City of Toronto to the Horse Guards at a parade at City Hall. This very old tradition allows the honoured unit to march through the streets of the city with colours flying, bayonets fixed and drums beating, all things that by ancient practice are usually forbidden. On Victoria Day that same month, a troop of Cougars fired a 20-round salute at CFB Trenton for the arrival of His Royal Highness Prince Andrew, a rare honour for a unit to provide a Royal Salute mounted in vehicles.

**Lieutenant Colonel Jeffrey J. Dorfman, OMM, CD, Commanding Officer 1988 to 1991)
(GGHG Archives)**

In 1985 the Board of Trustees created The Governor General's Horse Guards Foundation as an incorporated entity to undertake fundraising necessary to support the financial needs of the Regiment. Among the activities and projects needing monetary assistance were the Cavalry Squadron, special events such as Standards parades, production of the memorial window for St. James' Cathedral, the funding of this Regimental history and the maintenance and preservation of Regimental memorabilia and artefacts. A fund was also needed by the commanding officer for a variety of Regimental matters not paid by DND. The Trustees and the Foundation have thus become integral parts of the Regimental family, and are important contributors to the well being of Canada's senior Militia regiment.

The annual summer field training concentration for Central Militia Area in August 1986 was intended to be the last of its kind, as Militia field training was in future intended to be part of the Regular Forces' annual division-level "Rendezvous" exercises. While the 'Total Force' concept was not formally introduced until 1987, the stage was being set.

The Conservative government issued a new White Paper on Defence in the spring of 1987 which promised far-reaching changes throughout the military such as more money, more people and new equipment. Key among the ideas it presented was a renewed focus on mobilization of the Militia to be able to form a wartime Corps structure. Inherent in this notion was a significant improvement in the training standards of Militia units, and this brought with it the concept of 'Total Force'.

In theory, the idea behind Total Force was that there would no longer be any substantial difference between the soldier who worked part time and the soldier who worked full time. Training standards were intended to be harmonized, and Regulars and Reservists were to be integrated into the same units – some with 10 percent Regular and 90 percent Militia, other 'full-time' units with about 80 percent Regulars and 20 percent militiamen. How this was going to be made to work in practice was the great unknown. Militiamen were under no illusions about harmonized training standards: trades and professional advancement courses for members of the Militia had to be structured in two week-long blocks because that was all the average Militiaman could devote to the Army at any one time. But, many of the Regular Force courses, for very good reasons, lasted for eight or more weeks. Whose standards were going to change? If part-time soldiers really could do the same job as the full-time ones, why did the country bother to maintain a professional full-time Army?

The near-term impact on the Horse Guards was that all the unit's Cougars were pooled at CFB Borden, along with those of all other armoured units in Central Militia Area. The reasoning behind this was that an entire squadron complement could be made available to units on a rotating basis for gunnery, D&M or tactical exercises in Borden or Meaford. There were undoubtedly other reasons for pooling the Cougars (and the infantry's similar Grizzlys): spare parts were in desperately short supply, and even with centralized repair and maintenance carried out by Base Borden mechanics it was increasingly difficult to keep the vehicles running. Among the perpetual problems, there

**Chief Warrant Officer Eric G. Brown, MMM, CD, Regimental Sergeant Major 1989 to 1993.
(GGHG Archives)**

were high points that compensated, at least in part. For example, the old tank range at Meaford was formally reopened and plans were made to acquire an additional tract of land on the western side of the range and create Central Area Militia Training Support Centre, capable of providing the whole gamut of support for unit-level tactical exercises, range practices and trades training, including the provision

Queen's Crown badge of The Governor General's Horse Guards, taken into general use by the Regiment in 1989.

of serviceable vehicles that had been properly maintained, accommodation, food services, quartermaster stores, and repair and recovery. It was a worthy goal, but reality – finances – got in the way, and over the next year plans were significantly pared down.

Perhaps because of the uncertainty created by the White Paper, there was no Militia collective training in the summer of 1987. Militia concentrations once again took place in Meaford in the summer of 1988 and 1989, and the Horse Guards contributed two Cougar troops and elements of a squadron echelon to an ad hoc armoured regiment both years.

But even at the worst of times the Regiment was able to maintain a well-known sense of humour. Colonel Al Methven recalled one such incident where the commanding officer's leg was pulled:

At the annual gun camp, the COs of Horse Guards and Ontario Regiment agreed to a competition shoot. Warrant Officer Duane Waite was my crew commander, identifying

the targets and giving the fire orders. Each round was fired as ordered, but I could never see the fall of shot, so had to call out "not observed" after every round. WO Waite told me to be more diligent, and emphasized that the Ontario Regiment CO had already hit every target. I fired again, but once again saw only the flash. I was flabbergasted, and could not believe how bad a shot I was. On clearing guns I climbed out of the turret, embarrassed and disappointed, only to be told that blank rounds had been loaded. Everyone had a good laugh.

A singular honour accrued to the Regiment in 1988. On 13 August, the Canada Gazette published the following announcement:

Appointment
Her Excellency the Governor General has informed the Minister of National Defence that Her Majesty The Queen has graciously accepted the appointment of:
Colonel-in-Chief
The Governor General's Horse Guards

The whole Regiment was deeply honoured that The Queen had accepted this appointment, since it was never lightly undertaken by Her Majesty. It was seen as a token of the long and loyal service that the Horse Guards, and the Body Guard before, had given to the Crown for well over a century.

Matters of tradition and dress have always been of importance to Guards units, and the Regimental badge became an issue of some significance early in 1989. The Directorate of Ceremonial at NDHQ ordered the Regiment to cease wearing the 1936-pattern Tudor or King's Crown badge, used from the creation of the unit, and to use the authorized St. Edward's or Queen's Crown badge officially on issue since the early 1960s. For the NDHQ authorities, it was a matter of principle: the design of the badges of all Canadian units which included the Royal Crown had been changed after the coronation of Her Majesty in 1953, even though badges were not actually made available for general issue until into the 1960s.

Night firing on the range at Meaford. (GGHG Archives)

The Horse Guards did not like the appearance of the Ordnance-produced Queen's Crown badge; it was described as being shoddily produced and a decision was therefore made to simply continue using the wartime King's Crown badge which was still available in quantity. It was, after all, being worn with the 1954 full-dress uniforms, and it was widely believed that the Horse Guards had special permission to wear the badge brought into use at its creation in 1936. The Ordnance issue Queen's Crown badges were given to the cadet corps and all but forgotten. All was well on the Regimental badge front until about 1980, when the supply of wartime King's Crown

THE 1991 PATTERN FULL DRESS UNIFORM

The 1991-pattern Full Dress tunic of the Horse Guards is very similar to the 1954 Full Dress uniform, except that small details were modified to conform to the pattern of the Blues and Royals uniform and 1880 dress regulations. Shoulder cords were replaced by red epaulettes bordered in white cord (silver for officers), and the red collar was trimmed in white (silver for officers). Aiguillettes worn by junior ranks were simplified. All other accoutrements remained the same as for the 1954 uniform. (Photo: GGHG Archives)

Colonel The Honourable H.N.R. Jackman, Honorary Lieutenant Colonel 1988 to 1992, Honorary Colonel 1992 to 2002. (GGHG Archives)

badges was finally depleted. The Regiment then had a reproduction of the King's Crown badge cast privately, but it too was of very unsatisfactory quality and the troops went to great lengths to avoid wearing it. The issue Queen's Crown badge was thus belatedly introduced for general wear by all other ranks in 1989.

By the summer of 1989 the great hopes engendered by the 1987 White Paper had all but disappeared. The government's grand intentions of giving a major boost to the Armed Forces proved to be too costly, and instead a great retrenchment in both the Regular Force and the Militia was begun. Other highly important events contributed to the government's loss of interest in the military. In the autumn of 1989 one after another of the Communist regimes in Eastern Europe collapsed or was overthrown. The Cold War had in fact come to an end, but this momentous and long-hoped-for event caught the world very much by surprise, and it took some time to come to grips with the political and military implications of this enormous change in the global strategic situation. A full-scale war was fought against Iraq in early 1991, Germany was reunified, Soviet troops were pulled back into Ukraine and Russia, Yugoslavia erupted into civil war, and at the end of the year the Soviet Union dissolved into many separate countries. There was no longer any enemy in Central Europe. The government decided in early 1992 that keeping troops in Germany could no longer be justified, and by August 1993 the bases there had been abandoned.

For the moment, these great events had little effect on the day-to-day life of the Regiment, but once the full ramifications of the ending of the Cold War came to be recognized by the government, the Forces, and in particular the Army, suffered from the so-called 'peace dividend' being cashed in.

As always, the Regiment got on with the job at hand, soldiering on as it had throughout its existence. In May 1990, the Horse Guards accumulated yet another honour when the city of York granted the Freedom of the City to the unit. And the Regiment also had the honour of playing host for several weeks to the band of the 1st The Queen's Dragoon Guards, one of the Allied Regiments. That year Troopers R. Nevins and E.G. Pinto and Corporals R. Paquette, D. Serrao and S.D.A. Vanrooyen volunteered to serve with the RCD during a six-month tour with the UN Force in Cyprus. Then in 1992, Trooper L.S. Armstrong and Corporals R.E. Mathes and D. Serrao served in Cyprus with the Royal Canadian Horse Artillery, participating in the close-out of the Canadian contingent with UNFICYP.

The steps taken to revitalize the Militia-Regular Force relationship in the late 1980s, unconvincing as they may have been, reached a belated apex in 1990. The Reserve revitalization programme mandated by the 1987 White Paper generated a large-scale exercise for the Militia dubbed "On Guard" in 1990, with Militia Areas forming brigades filled out with Regular Force augmentation. This, however, did not long continue, and the exercise was much reduced in 1991 and then not held again. In fact, because of the Oka crisis near Montreal internal security training was given increased emphasis.

Ceremonial took an important part in the unit in

Lieutenant Colonel Klaus J. Bartels, CD, Commanding Officer 1991 to 1995. (GGHG Archives)

1990 and 1991. The role of escorting the Lieutenant Governor for the Opening of the Legislature – a task begun by the Body Guard in 1850 – had five years earlier been taken over by the Mounted Division of the Metropolitan Toronto Police. This traditional role came back to the Regiment in the fall of 1990, when the Cavalry Squadron once again took part in the ceremony. The Regiment had also redesigned its Ceremonial full-dress uniform, and with the generous support of the Honorary Lieutenant Colonel, over 100 full-dress uniforms were purchased in 1991. That same year the Honorary Lieutenant Colonel, Lieutenant Colonel H.N.R. Jackman, was appointed Lieutenant Governor of Ontario.

In the early 1990s the Regimental Band came under serious threat of being disbanded by the authorities in NDHQ, who appeared to think that military bands were now a luxury that the Forces could do without in a time of fiscal adversity. The band at this time was a mix of Militiamen and volunteers, all dedicated and highly skilled musicians. The Horse Guards brass band, of course, had one of the longest records of service in the Army, and while many fine bands were dissolved in this rather foolish cost-cutting venture, the Regimental Band was fortunately retained. Under the inspired direction of Captain Frank Merlo, the Band played an average of 35 separate engagements a year and contributed enormously to ceremonial events well beyond the Regiment throughout Toronto. The Horse Guards Band was an important Toronto institution, and the entire garrison took comfort in its retention. It has continued over all the years to contribute to the joy, the solemnity and the *gravitas* of military events in the city.

Armoured trades training was given renewed emphasis in the autumn of 1991, when a special effort was made to qualify a large group of new recruits as Cougar drivers and gunners, while the more experienced members learned to drive the eight-wheel Bison armoured personnel carriers recently brought into service at the Militia Training Centre in Borden. The hard training done by the Regiment was recognized by the Corps Association by the award of the Howard Trophy for the most improved Militia armoured

Chief Warrant Officer Scott M. Duncan, CD, Regimental Sergeant Major 1993 to 1995. (GGHG Archives)

regiment in Canada in 1991. By March of 1992, 'A' Squadron had three complete troops of qualified crewmen who began a period of intensive tactical training to prepare for the Central Area summer concentration. At this time a number of qualified female crewmen were fully integrated into the Cougar troops.

A concerted effort was also made to equip and train a full tank squadron 'A' Echelon. In past years, administrative and logistic support for field training had often consisted only of a vehicle for the sergeant major, which carried rations, and one or two 2½-ton trucks for fuel and a few spare parts. Squadron Sergeant Major Scott Duncan was, however, determined to train his 'A' Echelon to perform to the same operational standards as the Regular regiments. Putting a complete squadron echelon in the field was possible at this time in part because the Regiment had nearly a full slate of vehicle and weapons technicians and medical assistants to fill the Echelon's non-armour establishment slots, and the problem of insufficient vehicles was solved by borrowing them from other units. Thus, while the Cougar squadron was carrying out its tactical exercises, the Echelon was training in its own tactical and resupply skills both in garrison and on weekend schemes. Everything was done by the book. In the field, the echelon troops wore helmets and flak vests, and continually practised moving tactically from one harbour to the next. Whenever the squadron was resupplied at night, sentries were put out and anti-tank weapons deployed, and all work was done with no lights and minimum noise. The insistence on professionalism by members of the Echelon had a marked effect; morale soared as they recognized that the jobs they were doing were a vital part of the unit's operational capabilities. Sergeant Majors Joe Devogel and 'Tooner' Martin both maintained this substantial organization for another three years until resources and personnel dwindled.

Major changes in the Regiment's honorary appointments took place in the autumn of 1992, in cooperation with the other two Canadian guards regiments, the Governor General's Foot Guards and the Canadian Grenadier Guards. The Governor General, who for years had always served as Honorary Colonel of all three regiments was invited to accept the honorary appointment as 'Colonel of the Guards Regiments', a title thought to better reflect

the Governor General's status as de-facto head of state when the Sovereign is not present in Canada. Colonel The Right Honourable Ramon Hnatyshyn gave his approval to this change of appointment title. This allowed the Regiment to have Lieutenant Colonel The Honourable H.N.R. Jackman, now Lieutenant Governor of Ontario, promoted to the appointment of Honorary Colonel. At the same time, Lieutenant Colonel Peter W. Hunter was appointed Honorary Lieutenant Colonel.

Extensive budget cuts which took effect in the autumn of 1992, and a shortage of Cougars caused in part by the deployment of an RCD Cougar squadron to Somalia in January 1993, severely affected unit training throughout 1993. Initially both Tuesday training parades and Friday administration nights were cut back for lack of funds, and the spring gun camp was cancelled for the first time since the Regiment was equipped with Cougars. Only dismounted internal security training was conducted by the operational squadron during the spring and summer months. In the autumn, Friday administrative parades were cancelled entirely, and training was conducted only on two Tuesday evenings, one Saturday and one weekend each month. Regimental morale suffered severely.

The December 1993 reinforcement of the Canadian contingent in the UN Protection Force in Bosnia by a second Cougar squadron exacerbated the already serious training problems of Militia armoured units, as the Cougars for this additional squadron were taken from the already strapped Militia training centre pools. With their Cougars thus

Chief Warrant Officer James Martin, CD, Regimental Sergeant Major 1995. (GGHG Archives)

Chief Warrant Officer Joseph P. Devogel, CD, Regimental Sergeant Major 1996 to 1998. (GGHG Archives)

Lieutenant Colonel Duane R. Waite, CD, Commanding Officer 1995 to 1998. (GGHG Archives)

stripped away, Militia units simply could no longer carry out effective armour trades or field tactical training. In 1994, for example, the Horse Guards was able to provide only a five-car recce troop and a headquarters squadron for the Area summer concentration.

After the Liberal victory in the 1993 federal general election, there was no question that defence policy was floundering even more than it had in the last years of the Conservative administration. In early 1994 the new Chrétien government undertook a review of both foreign and defence policies, with a view to producing new White Papers in both departments. Public hearings were held across the country by parliamentary review bodies, and for a while defence issues seemed even to interest the general public. At the end of the process, the Special Joint Committee on Canada's Defence Policy strongly recommended the maintenance of effective general purpose combat-capable forces, but the government's underlying purpose was to trim defence spending, so it chose to ignore most of the Committee's important recommendations. The 1994 White Paper on Defence called, among other things, for a reduction of the Regular Forces to 60,000. The Primary Reserve, on the other hand, was to be increased from 14,500 to a total of 23,000 members. There was also to be a four-stage national mobilization plan which was to form the basis for reserve restructuring, but it should be noted this was quickly dismissed by NDHQ as being unnecessary since war was now seen as being "highly unlikely" and the plan has not yet been produced.

The Militia was especially hard hit in the aftermath of the White Paper. Instead of being the basis for rapid mobilization, the main role of the Militia was decreed to be "augmentation and sustainment" for the Regulars, in other words it was to be a pool of individual reinforcements. The White Paper went on to say that "a greater proportion of the Reserves' resources must go towards improving their operational capability and availability", adding that "many reserve units ... have diminished in size and effectiveness in recent years", and that this "will require a streamlining of reserve organizations and rank structure". The NDHQ hierarchy obviously believed there were too many Militia combat arms units and that some would have to go, and that there ought to be more service support units that could fill gaps in Regular Force capability. The essentially negative attitude toward the Militia expressed in the White Paper was a factor constantly underlying official policy regarding the Reserves over the next several years, and it was in large part responsible for the see-saw of good and bad years experienced by the Horse Guards in the latter part of the 1990s.

In spring 1994, after a very stiff competition for places, six members of the Regiment were chosen to serve with the RCD on a six-month tour of duty with the UN Protection Force in Bosnia. After several months of preparatory training, the RCD deployed to Bosnia in October. The whole of their tour was a time of ever-increasing tension and even hostilities, as the lightly equipped UN force repeatedly showed that it could not respond effectively to major violations by the Bosnian Serbs. One of the Horse Guards, Master Corporal S.M. Murphy, was one of 55 Canadians illegally held hostage for 16 days in December by the Serbs at Visoko, Bosnia. In that same group were Master Corporal P.M. Aviado, Corporals L.S. Armstrong, C.M. Massie and R.P. McCloskey and Corporal Dale Serrao who was on his third tour of UN duty.

With training activities so severely reduced, ceremonial events were of even greater importance. The presentation of Colours is always a major occasion for any regiment, and this was certainly the case for the Horse Guards on 1 October 1994, when the Governor General and Colonel of the Guards Regiments in Canada, His Excellency Colonel The Right Honourable Ramon Hnatyshyn presented the Regiment's third Standard. This Standard was in fact nearly identical to the one presented to the Horse Guards in 1967, but with continual use on parades in all sorts of weather, colours become torn and tattered, and for that reason regulations allow for their replacement every 25 years. That is what happened: two years earlier the Regiment had petitioned the Director of Ceremonial for a new Standard. Once the replacement was approved, the new Standard had to be manufactured. At that time, the Directorate of Ceremonial had decided that all new unit Colours were to be made of polyester rather than silk damask and metallic gold thread embroidery. This was not at all to the liking of the Regimental Trustees, so arrangements were made to have the new Standard properly produced in silk and gold thread according to time-honoured British specifications, with financial sup-

Corporal Dale M. Serrao, the only member of the Regiment to have served on four peacekeeping tours – twice in Cyprus, and in Bosnia and Kosovo. (GGHG Archives)

His Excellency The Right Honourable Ramon Hnatyshyn, Governor General and Colonel of the Guards Regiments, presenting the third Standard to Sergeant Major James F. Fisher, 1 October 1994. (GGHG Archives)

Regimental Sergeants and Warrant Officers, with the three trophies won by the Regiment in 1994 – the Worthington Trophy for best Militia armoured regiment in Canada, the Howard Trophy for most improved armoured unit in Canada, and the Cumberland Trophy for best armoured regiment in Land Forces Central Area. (GGHG Archives)

port from Barrick Gold Corporation arranged by Lieutenant David Gilmour, a former officer with the Regiment, then an executive at Barrick.

The new, third, Standard was ready in good time, and the very traditional consecration and presentation ceremony was planned. It would take place in Sunnybrook Park, a place with strong ties to the Mississauga Horse dating back some 60 years.

At the appointed time His Excellency, escorted by the Cavalry Squadron, arrived in a landau at the reviewing stand, and was met by the Honorary Colonel, The Honourable H.N.R. Jackman. It was, unfortunately, a dismal rainy day. The Old Standard, carried by Warrant Officer L. Walters, was trooped through the ranks by a mounted Standard party, allowing every member an opportunity to see it before it was marched off for the last time. The New Standard, still furled in its cylindrical leather case, was then marched on by Master Warrant Officer J.F. Fisher. It was uncased and laid on an altar of stacked drums. The consecration of the Standard, a liturgy going back several centuries, was then carried out by the Base chaplain, Major Yves Fournier, and the Regimental chaplain, Captain J.A. Thompson. The consecrated Standard was then given to the Governor General, who presented it on behalf of The Queen to the custody of Sergeant Major Fisher.

After the usual speeches, the new Standard was marched into position at the front of the Regiment, in accordance with a long-standing Regimental tradition that violates the ceremonial manual. The unit then marched past the reviewing stand, and, after the Governor General departed, was dismissed. That evening there was a gala Regimental Ball. And next day the Old Standard was laid up in St. James' Cathedral, joining the first Standard that had hung in the church since 1971.

At the annual conference of the Corps Association at the Armour School in Gagetown in October 1994, the Horse Guards took great pride in hearing that the unit had been awarded three of the most coveted trophies given by the Corps: the Worthington Trophy for best armoured regiment in Canada in 1994, the Howard Trophy for the most improved armoured unit in Canada and the Cumberland Trophy for the best armoured regiment in Land Forces Central Area (LFCA). This panoply of awards was indicative of the enormous pride and the quality of the officers and

A composite Cougar troop led by Lieutenant Mike Park at the dedication of the John Andrews Hangar in Meaford. (GGHG Archives)

men in the Horse Guards. Despite the training difficulties caused by the lack of armoured vehicles, that year the Regiment truly proved itself 'Second to None'. This was to be the last occasion for the Regiment to win the Worthington Trophy as the award was cancelled by the Armoured Corps after the 1995 competition; Land Forces Command judged that it was no longer a cost-worthy venture, the honour no longer worth the candle.

A shortage of vehicles and budget constraints continued to plague the unit, and throughout 1995 the Regiment of necessity focused on dismounted operations. Ham-handed, bureaucratic efforts by area headquarters to make significant changes while at the same time cutting costs had negative effects that ought to have been anticipated. Harsh operational evaluations were introduced, and disproportionate efforts had to be devoted to physical fitness conditioning for what was called Warrior training. Obtaining essential rank qualification became more difficult as all too often centralized courses were cancelled at the last minute for lack of funds. Recruiting,

which had been put in the hands of the Regular Force, became a nightmare of administrative deadlock and many potential recruits lost interest and dropped out while waiting to be enrolled. The sheer lack of interest by the Regulars in resolving Militia organization, equipment and funding problems led to the cudgel being taken up by a group called Reserves 2000, who over the next years mobilized the political force of informed Militia opinion throughout the country. The Minister of National Defence was forced to take notice, and he created a Special Commission on the Restructuring of the Reserves to make recommendations. Consultation was promised on the Land Force Reserve Restructure process.

There was a noticeable improvement in the quality of training in 1996: the Regiment's operational squadron deployed to Petawawa for three weekend exercises in the spring where they used Cougars belonging to the RCD, with one of the troops winning top honours in the Area evaluations, and the squadron performed well in the LFCA concentration in Petawawa in August. Then, in the spring of 1997 the annual

Hurry up and wait! 'A' Squadron troops waiting for a ride to the training area. (GGHG Archives)

Sergeant Major Yearwood gives orders to his 'A' Echelon soldiers during a field exercise. (GGHG Archives)

(Above) RHQ Recce Troop crew in an Iltis jeep, 1995. MCpl Mike Lipton (rear), Tpr Mark Cullen (foreground)

(Above) A Cougar crew being briefed before a training session on the computerized Cougar gunnery simulator. The crew's performance can be monitored on the computer screens on the right. (GGHG Archives)

Lucky crew members dig out their bogged Bison at Meaford. (GGHG Archives)

More scenes at Meaford gun camp. Corporal Stephen Sabaratnam loads practice rounds into the ready rack of a Cougar (far left) and Sergeant Don Anderson observes the fall of shot during firing. (Below) Cougars on the firing point. (GGHG Archives)

A Horse Guards Cougar in the field and (above) Corporal Kevin Brady in the driver's hatch during summer training in Meaford. (GGHG Archives)

gun camp and several successful exercises were conducted in Meaford, and a large number of soldiers served in Meaford as instructors with the Area armoured training squadron during the summer where 35 Horse Guards recruits completed basic training.

Her Majesty The Queen came to Canada on one of her periodic Royal Visits in June 1997. On 27 June, in her first engagement with The Governor General's Horse Guards since accepting the appointment as Colonel-in-Chief, The Queen honoured the Regiment by unveiling a memorial window in St. James' Cathedral. The large stained-glass window, given to the cathedral by the Regimental Trustees as a memorial to members of the Regiment who died in the service of Crown and Country, is located in the south-west porch, next to the main entrance to the cathedral. The dedication of the memorial window, a project organized by Lieutenant Colonel John Graham, former Honorary Lieutenant Colonel, further strengthened the ties between the Regiment and the cathedral, where two Standards have been laid up.

There was no summer training concentration in 1997 as the unit needed to conserve training funds for a period of intensive training in September and October to prepare for a new Combat Readiness Evaluation, a series of intensive tests intended to determine if a Militia unit was 'up to snuff' and should be retained as a major unit. This high pace of field activity proved its worth: during its test weekend in October the Regiment was rated as 'effective', which meant that it was not at risk of being disbanded or reduced to a major's command.

The structure of the Militia was again subjected to a major shuffle in early September 1997 in an attempt to make the Militia districts somewhat more operationally oriented, and in a half-hearted way to support the idea that the Army needed to have a mobilization plan to create at least a Corps in an international emergency. This restructuring grouped Militia units in ten territorial brigade group organizations, hardly a novel idea as Militia units had been grouped in brigades for much of the preceding hundred years. The Horse Guards were thus part of 32 Canadian Brigade Group, along with most of the other Toronto Militia units.

Her Majesty Queen Elizabeth II unveiling the Regimental Memorial Window in St. James' Cathedral, 27 June 1997. On The Queen's right are Colonel H.N.R. Jackman and Lieutenant Colonel D.R. Waite. (GGHG Archives)

The highlight of the autumn of 1997 was the deployment of 80 members of 'A' Squadron to the US Army Armor School in Fort Knox, Kentucky, as had first been done in 1991. There, for nearly a week in November the squadron took part in a simulated tactical exercise using the highly sophisticated M1 Abrams tank simulators. This was a wonderful experience for every member of the squadron, and the very realistic battlefield simulation was a most useful introduction to the study of offensive operations, which was the focus in LFCA throughout 1998 and 1999. The tactical simulator work at Fort Knox was so useful, and so well received by the troops, that this exercise was continued in each of the next two winters.

In January 1998, a massive ice storm pelted an area from Kingston to Ottawa to well north of Montreal. Hydro lines crashed down over much of this area, and over three million people were left without power, some for nearly a month.

Lieutenant Colonel John G.C. Spitieri, CD, Commanding Officer 1998 to 2001. (GGHG Archives)

Chief Warrant Officer Shawn M. Yearwood, CD, Regimental Sergeant Major 1998 to 2001. (GGHG Archives)

Downed trees and telephone poles blocked roads, and sheets of ice made walking almost impossible. Then the temperature dropped to below minus 30 degrees. Literally thousands of people were without heat and could not leave their homes, a situation which demanded that the bulk of the Army – Regular and Militia – be deployed to bring help. Roads had to be cleared. Temporary patches to the power grid were made, but many homes were without heat and light for several weeks. Soldiers literally went door-to-door and farm-to-farm in the rural areas, chopping wood for fireplaces and seeing if elderly or sick residents needed assistance. The Horse Guards contributed sixteen members to Operation "Recuperation", working mainly in Lanark County, south of Ottawa, until the operation was wound down in late January. This was one of the largest aid of the civil power deployments in many years.

Once again, in 1998 several members of the Regiment volunteered to serve overseas on peace support missions. Corporals D. Serrao and W. Hawkins, Trooper A. Melenovic, Master Corporal M. Snea and Lieutenant Ken Sproul served with 'Roto 2' in Bosnia with NATO's Stabilization Force, while Troopers G. Bowles and C. Powell and Master Corporal C. Gordon served with 'Roto 3'.

The Regiment spent much of March 1998 in Meaford, where the Horse Guards had been made responsible for the conduct of Exercise "Trillium Fist", the annual LFCA gun camp. Six armoured units conducted their annual Cougar range qualifications, and members of the Regiment gained a great deal of useful experience in the organization and administration of a major live-firing exercise. A side benefit was the qualification of ten new gunners for the Regiment, and gunnery skills were kept current for a further twenty Cougar crews. Despite further budget cuts the usual series of spring exercises were conducted in Meaford, and 60 soldiers participated in the summer camp at Petawawa.

'Buttons and bows' issues in a unit with very old traditions are never undertaken lightly, but in 1999 the wearing of a blue and maroon 'Guards patch' behind the Regimental badge was approved, conforming to the practice adopted in 1993 by the Governor General's Foot Guards and the Canadian Grenadier Guards. In that the Guards patch could not be worn with the officers' embroidered badge, a smaller Queen's Crown officers badge made of pewter was introduced, and the officers' embroidered badge taken out of use.

By 1999, no action had been taken by the Army to create a national mobilization plan and this blocked all progress on the promised Land Force Reserve Restruc-

Pewter officers' badge, taken into wear in 1999.

ture, which in turn prevented action on a planned increase in the overall strength of the Militia. Worse, all consultation between the Regular Army hierarchy and Reserve representatives about Militia roles and restructuring had broken down. Budgets and training continued to be cut. The causes of this conundrum no doubt included the Regular Army's confusion and uncertainty about its own future. A decision had already been taken that the Army would have to become more rapidly deployable and therefore 'lighter' and 'all wheeled', but would it be able to retain real combat capability or would it be organized and equipped only for 'constabulary' missions such as peace support operations? The so-called Revolution in Military Affairs was also beginning to affect thinking about how high-technology precision-delivered weapons and sophisticated battlefield command and control capabilities might require radical changes in the organization of combat units and future equipment acquisition. In these circumstances, revitalization of the Militia, which undoubtedly would make demands on the defence budget, did not rank high on the list of priorities, and in any case no one in the military chain of command was prepared to accept the political consequences of tampering with the existing Militia structure. As in the past, Militia units would have to soldier on as best they could.

The Regimental policy of encouraging members to volunteer for service with peacekeeping and peace enforcement operations continued. In February 2000, Corporals J. Kim and W. Hawkins

Lieutenant Colonel Robert A. Shaw, CD, Commanding Officer 2001 to the present. (GGHG

Chief Warrant Officer Peter Crngarov, CD, Regimental Sergeant Major 2001 to the present. (GGHG Archives)

deployed to Kosovo for ten months with the Canadian contingent on Operation "Kinetic", which was intended to restore some degree of normalcy to a province that had endured "ethnic cleansing" sadly reminiscent of the Nazi genocide of the Second World War. The following year, six members – Sergeant P. Aviado, Corporals M. Burrell, R. Crawford and C. Lewis and Trooper M. Menacola volunteered to serve with NATO's Stabilization Force (SFOR) in Bosnia. Then in the fall of 2001 Major P.R. Brunberg served with the UN force in Eritrea.

The question of equipment for Militia armoured regiments was the subject of heated debate throughout much of 2000. Cougars had by then been withdrawn from the three Regular regiments and the Regulars had decided to adopt a tactically senseless organization for reasons of political survivability – one squadron of the newly upgraded Leopard C2 tanks, one squadron of the new high-tech Coyote surveillance vehicles and one squadron of basic Coyotes without the sophisticated sensor suite which were used in a 'direct fire support vehicle' role. Would the Militia retain the by-now virtually worn-out Cougars, or would they be equipped with a Coyote minus its surveillance suite or some other vehicle based on the same eight-wheel chassis such as the LAV III? The dilemma centred around the fact that 100 Cougars had been sent for rebuild and were guaranteed to be available. On the other hand, there were no guarantees some new eight-wheel LAV III vehicles would be available any time soon, and, even if some were, they would have a 25mm chain gun, not a 'real' gun like the Cougar's 76mm. On the negative side, if Cougars were retained, they would be an 'orphan' fleet of vehicles and there could be no falling back on the Regular regiments for spare parts or training assistance. Then too, since Militia crewmen would no longer be

trained on the same vehicle as the Regulars, there would be fewer opportunities for attachments.

The matter was hotly discussed at the autumn 2000 meeting of the Armoured Corps Association, and at the end the consensus among the unit commanding officers was that the Militia should retain the Cougars. The following summer, 16 refitted and upgraded Cougars were delivered to the Training Centre in Meaford for the armoured units in LFCA, along with eight Grizzly APCs. It was a bare-bones fleet that could support, at most, one squadron at a time. There would be no more composite armoured regiments for summer concentrations! But at least the quite sophisticated Cougar gunnery simulators that had been installed in the armouries of Militia armoured units in late 1999 would get extended use.

The preservation of close ties with the Allied regiments in Britain has always been somewhat difficult if only because of distance, but a special effort in this regard was made in May 2001 when two officers and eight other ranks were sent to England for a week-long visit to the 1st The Queen's Dragoon Guards at their home station in Catterick Barracks, north of Leeds. The QDG were most hospitable, and the Horse Guards members thoroughly enjoyed their introduction to British Army equipment and training. A day trip to London allowed for a quick trip to the stables of the Household Cavalry, the senior of the two Allied regiments.

What would undoubtedly be the highlight of 2002 was the Regiment's move from Denison Armoury on Dufferin Street, home to the unit since 1961, to a new purpose-built super

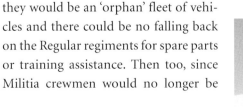

The new Lieutenant Colonel George Taylor Denison III Armoury in Downsview, the Regiment's home from July 2002. (GGHG Archives)

armoury located on the site of the former CFB Toronto at Sheppard Avenue and the Allen Expressway. While the new armoury was to be shared with the 2nd Field Engineer Regiment, 25 Toronto Service Battalion, 2 Intelligence Company and the area and brigade headquarters, the Regiment was allocated far more useable administrative and training space than ever before, and for the first time serious planning was underway to create a Regimental museum in one of the rooms. It was also of enormous satisfaction to the Horse Guards that the new armoury would bear the family name of the founders of the Governor General's Body Guard – Denison Armoury. The new Regimental home would provide the base from which The Governor General's Horse Guards could begin another century of dedicated service.

*   *   *   *

Her Excellency The Right Honourable Adrienne Clarkson, Governor General and Colonel of the Guards Regiments, inspecting the guard of honour at the Spitieri–Shaw change of command parade, September 2001. (GGHG Archives)

The story of The Governor General's Horse Guards must pause at this point, for the future defies all attempts to determine its course. That there will be a future is at the time of writing not at all in question. While the government has proven over the years to be predictably consistent in providing inadequate funding for its Reserve Army, the loyalty and dedication of its members has always been the consistent and dependable factor that now assures the lasting place of fine old Militia regiments such as The Governor General's Horse Guards. This Regiment has for nearly two centuries served through adversity in peacetime, through wars in which our Regimental brothers bled and sometimes died for our country, and through times when our fellow citizens seemed not to care whether or not we were ready to defend them if the need arose. This Regiment has also served through times when our members have stood tall and proud of their accomplishments, when we rejoiced in and with our comrades that together we could overcome insurmountable odds and make a real difference to the community and the world in which we live.

The Governor Generals' Horse Guards will continue to make that difference. There is a history and tradition that must be honoured, a sacred trust to be nurtured. This book has attempted to portray a small part of that proud legacy, a spirit that will be inspired as much in the future as throughout the past centuries by the motto *Nulli Secundus*, Second to None.

Marching to the future. (GGHG Archives)

Regimental Lineage

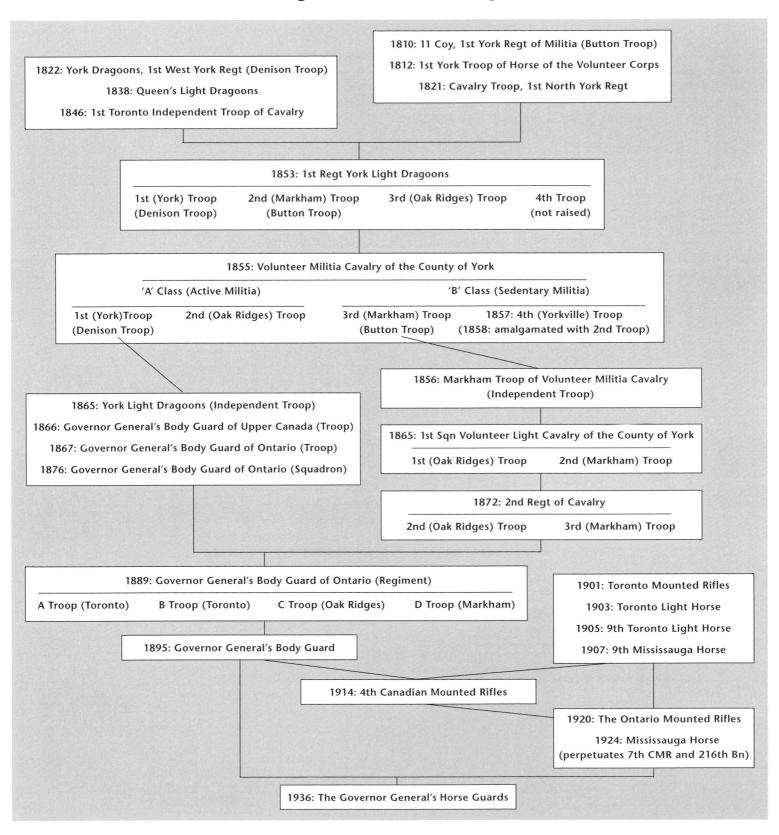

1810: 11 Coy, 1st York Regt of Militia (Button Troop)

1812: 1st York Troop of Horse of the Volunteer Corps

1821: Cavalry Troop, 1st North York Regt

1822: York Dragoons, 1st West York Regt (Denison Troop)

1838: Queen's Light Dragoons

1846: 1st Toronto Independent Troop of Cavalry

1853: 1st Regt York Light Dragoons

| 1st (York) Troop (Denison Troop) | 2nd (Markham) Troop (Button Troop) | 3rd (Oak Ridges) Troop | 4th Troop (not raised) |

1855: Volunteer Militia Cavalry of the County of York

'A' Class (Active Militia)

'B' Class (Sedentary Militia)

| 1st (York)Troop (Denison Troop) | 2nd (Oak Ridges) Troop | 3rd (Markham) Troop (Button Troop) | 1857: 4th (Yorkville) Troop (1858: amalgamated with 2nd Troop) |

1856: Markham Troop of Volunteer Militia Cavalry (Independent Troop)

1865: York Light Dragoons (Independent Troop)

1866: Governor General's Body Guard of Upper Canada (Troop)

1867: Governor General's Body Guard of Ontario (Troop)

1876: Governor General's Body Guard of Ontario (Squadron)

1865: 1st Sqn Volunteer Light Cavalry of the County of York

1st (Oak Ridges) Troop   2nd (Markham) Troop

1872: 2nd Regt of Cavalry

2nd (Oak Ridges) Troop   3rd (Markham) Troop

1889: Governor General's Body Guard of Ontario (Regiment)

A Troop (Toronto)   B Troop (Toronto)   C Troop (Oak Ridges)   D Troop (Markham)

1901: Toronto Mounted Rifles

1903: Toronto Light Horse

1905: 9th Toronto Light Horse

1907: 9th Mississauga Horse

1895: Governor General's Body Guard

1914: 4th Canadian Mounted Rifles

1920: The Ontario Mounted Rifles

1924: Mississauga Horse (perpetuates 7th CMR and 216th Bn)

1936: The Governor General's Horse Guards

Regimental Appointments

COLONEL-IN-CHIEF

Her Majesty Queen Elizabeth II, 1988–

COLONEL OF THE GUARDS REGIMENTS

The Governor General of Canada

The Right Honourable Ramon John Hnatyshyn, CC, CCM, CD, 1992–1995

The Right Honourable Romeo Leblanc, CC, CCM, CD, 1995–1999

The Right Honourable Adrienne Clarkson, CC, CCM, CD, 1999–

HONORARY COLONEL

The Governor General of Canada (to 1992)

Viscount Monck, GCMG, 1867–1868
Lord Lisgar, KP, KCB, GCMG, 1869–1872
The Earl of Dufferin, KP, GCB, GCSI, GCMG, GCIE, 1872–1878
The Marquess of Lorne, KT, GCMG, 1878–1883
The Marquess of Lansdowne, KG, GCSI, GCIE, 1883–1888
Lord Stanley, KG, GCVO, CB, 1888–1893
The Earl of Aberdeen, GCMG, GCVO, 1893–1898
The Earl of Minto, KG, GCSI, GCIE, GCMG 1898–1904
Earl Grey, GCB, GCMG, GCVO, 1904–1911
HRH The Duke of Connaught, KG, KT, KP, 1911–1916
The Duke of Devonshire, KG, GCVO, GCMG, 1916–1921
General Viscount Byng of Vimy, GCB, GCMG, MVO, 1921–1926
Viscount Willingdon, GCMG, GCSI, GCIE, GBE, 1926–1931
The Earl of Bessborough, GCMG, 1931–1935
Lord Tweedsmuir, CH, GCMG, GCVO, 1935–1940
The Earl of Athlone, KG, GCB, GCMG, GCVO, DSO, 1940–1946
Field Marshal Viscount Alexander of Tunis, KG, GCB, GCMG, CSI, DSO, MC, 1946–1952
The Right Honourable Vincent Massey, CH, 1952–1959
Major General The Right Honourable Georges-P. Vanier, DSO, MC, CD, 1959–1967
The Right Honourable Roland Michener, CC, CMM, CD, 1967–1974
The Right Honourable Jules Léger, CC, CMM, CD, 1974–1979
The Right Honourable Edward Schreyer, CC, CMM, CD, 1979–1984
The Right Honourable Jeanne Sauvé, CC, CMM, CD, 1984–1990
The Right Honourable Ramon John Hnatyshyn, CC, CMM, CD, 1990–1992
Colonel The Honourable H.N.R. Jackman, OC, CD, 1992–2002
Colonel Peter W. Hunter, CD, 2002–

HONORARY LIEUTENANT COLONEL

Lieutenant Colonel George Taylor Denison III, 1899–1925
Lieutenant Colonel Herbert C. Cox, (Mississauga Horse), 1911–1930
Colonel R.Y. Eaton, 1929–1954

Colonel W.C. Vaux Chadwick, (Mississauga Horse), 1930–1936
Lieutenant Colonel Clifford Sifton, DSO, CD, 1954–1962
Brigadier Ian H. Cumberland, DSO, OBE, ED, 1962–1964
Lieutenant Colonel G. Allan Burton, OC, DSO, ED, 1966–1970
Lieutenant Colonel John W. Graham, ED, 1970–1975
Lieutenant Colonel Robert C. Rutherford, MBE, CD, 1976–1980
Brigadier General W. Preston Gilbride, CBE, DSO, ED, 1980–1981
Lieutenant Colonel H.T. Tye, CD, 1983–1986
Lieutenant Colonel The Honourable H.N.R. Jackman, OC, CD, 1988–1992
Lieutenant Colonel Peter W. Hunter, CD, 1992–2002
Lieutenant Colonel The Honourable Margaret McCain, 2002–

COMMANDING OFFICER

THE BUTTON TROOP (MARKHAM)

Captain John Button, 1810–1831
Captain Francis Button, 1831–1856
Captain William Button, 1856–1872

THE DENISON TROOP

Captain George Taylor Denison I, 1822–1838
Captain R.L. Denison, 1838–1848
Captain George Taylor Denison II, 1848–1850
Captain R.B. Denison, 1850–1856
Captain George Taylor Denison III, 1856–1868
Captain E.P. Denison, 1868–1872
Captain Frederick C. Denison, CMG, 1872–1876

THE GOVERNOR GENERAL'S BODY GUARD

Lieutenant Colonel George Taylor Denison III, 1876–1898
Lieutenant Colonel C.A.K. Denison, 1898–1903
Lieutenant Colonel William Hamilton Merritt, 1903–1908
Lieutenant Colonel F.A. Fleming, 1908–1913
Lieutenant Colonel S.F. Smith, DSO ,1913–1921
Lieutenant Colonel W.W. Denison, DSO, 1921–1924
Lieutenant Colonel T.L. Kennedy, 1924–1927
Lieutenant Colonel J.E.L. Streight, MC, VD, 1927–1931
Lieutenant Colonel W.L. Rawlinson, MC, VD, 1931–1934
Lieutenant Colonel A.J. Everett, MC, VD, 1934–1936

THE MISSISSAUGA HORSE

Lieutenant Colonel G.A. Peters, 1901–1907
Lieutenant Colonel W.C.V. Chadwick ,1907–1913
Lieutenant Colonel H.D.L. Gordon, DSO, 1913–1921
Lieutenant Colonel J.F.H. Ussher, 1921–1924
Lieutenant Colonel W.T. Brown, VD, 1924–1927
Lieutenant Colonel W. A. Moore, VD, 1927–1931
Lieutenant Colonel N.K. Wilson, VD, 1931–1935
Lieutenant Colonel A.E. Nash, MC, VD, 1935–1936

4TH CANADIAN MOUNTED RIFLES

Lieutenant Colonel W.C. Vaux Chadwick, 1914–1915

Lieutenant Colonel Sanford Smith, DSO, 1915–1916

Lieutenant Colonel J.F.H. Ussher, March–June 1916

Lieutenant Colonel H.D. Lockhart Gordon, DSO, 1916–1917

Lieutenant Colonel W.R. Patterson, DSO, 1917–1919

THE GOVERNOR GENERAL'S HORSE GUARDS

Lieutenant Colonel A.J. Everett, MC, VD, 1936–1937

Lieutenant Colonel A.E. Nash, MC, VD, 1937–1939

Lieutenant Colonel R.P. Locke, ED, 1939–1941

Lieutenant Colonel H.M. Sharp, ED, 1941–1942

Lieutenant Colonel I.H. Cumberland, DSO, OBE, ED, 1942–1943

Lieutenant Colonel A.K. Jordan, DSO, ED, 1943–1946

3RD (RESERVE) ARMOURED REGIMENT (GOVERNOR GENERAL'S HORSE GUARDS)

Lieutenant Colonel W.L. Rawlinson, MC, VD, 1941–1943

Lieutenant Colonel G.D. Thomas, ED, 1943–1944

Lieutenant Colonel Alfred Bunting, ED, 1944–1946

THE GOVERNOR GENERAL'S HORSE GUARDS

Lieutenant Colonel G.D. de S. Wotherspoon, DSO, ED, 1946–1948

Lieutenant Colonel G.A. Burton, OC, DSO, ED, 1948–1950

Lieutenant Colonel C.F. Baker, CD, 1950–1952

Lieutenant Colonel J.D. Crashley, CD, ADC, 1952–1954

Lieutenant Colonel G.M. Brown, CD, 1954–1956

Lieutenant Colonel R.C. Rutherford, MBE, CD, ADC, 1956–1961

Lieutenant Colonel H.T. Tye, CD, ADC, 1961–1965

Lieutenant Colonel P.W. Hunter, CD, ADC, 1965–1967

Lieutenant Colonel M.B.W. Davis, CD, ADC, 1967–1970

Lieutenant Colonel H.K. Forbes, CD, ADC, 1970–1973

Lieutenant Colonel D.E. Friesen, CD, ADC, 1973–1977

Lieutenant Colonel J. Burns, CD, ADC, 1977–1981

Lieutenant Colonel B. Palanik, CD, ADC, 1981–1985

Lieutenant Colonel W.A. Methven, CD, ADC, 1985–1988

Lieutenant Colonel J.J. Dorfman, OMM, CD, ADC, 1988–1991

Lieutenant Colonel K.J. Bartels, CD, ADC, 1991–1995

Lieutenant Colonel D.R. Waite, CD, ADC, 1995–1998

Lieutenant Colonel J.G.C. Spitieri, CD, ADC, 1998–2001

Lieutenant Colonel R.A. Shaw, CD, ADC, 2001–

TROOP SERGEANT MAJOR

THE DENISON TROOP

John Watkins, 1837

Heyden, 1839

Wilby, 1853

Michael Power, 1856

Orlando Dunn, 1857

Stephen Scott, 1872

SQUADRON SERGEANT MAJOR

GOVERNOR GENERAL'S BODY GUARD

Robert Smith, 1876

George Watson, 1885

REGIMENTAL SERGEANT MAJOR

GOVERNOR GENERAL'S BODY GUARD

Charles Grainger, 1889

R.H. Bell, 1892

A.M. Stretton, 1892

E.W. Hodgins, 1903

George Smith, 1908

TORONTO LIGHT HORSE / MISSISSAUGA HORSE

H. Seddon, 1905

Edward Godfrey, 1908

S.A. Wynn, 1911

4TH CANADIAN MOUNTED RIFLES

WO1 R. Bumpstead, 1914

WO1 F.W. Tucker, 1916

WO1 A.W. Hawkey, DCM, 1917

WO1 G.L.M. Howard, DCM, 1917

WO1 C.A. Jordan, 1918

WO1 D.O. Smith, 1919

WO1 R. Bumpstead, 1920

GOVERNOR GENERAL'S BODY GUARD

WO1 Jack R. Honeycombe, 1918

WO1 Harry W. Clarke, 1923

WO1 Jack W. Finnimore, 1935

MISSISSAUGA HORSE

WO1 Bland, 1919

WO1 Lou Keats, 1920

WO1 Colson Hunt, 1923

WO1 W. Patterson, 1924

WO1 Gordon Gibb, MM, 1924

WO1 G. Quinn, 1927

WO1 Eldon Thompson, 1928

WO1 Fred Dewhurst, 1929

WO1 John Burry, 1935

THE GOVERNOR GENERAL'S HORSE GUARDS

WO1 Jack Finnimore, 1936

WO1 George Craven, 1940

WO1 William Huggett (Reserve Regiment), 1940

WO1 Arthur J. Finn, 1941

WO1 J.F. Keir (Reserve Regiment), 1942

WO1 George Bentley, 1942

WO1 Robert E. Thompson, 1946

WO1 Arthur C. Darnborough, 1953

WO1 Robert E. Thompson, CD, 1955

WO1 Gordon K. Edwards, CD, 1958

WO1 Frank Farris, CD, 1961

WO1 George Taylor, CD, 1963

WO 1 A.J.D. Davis, CD, 1966

CWO H.G. Busch, CD, 1970

CWO J.J. Dorfman, CD, 1974

CWO D.C. Mezzabotta, CD, 1979

CWO W.L. Thomas, MMM, CD, 1982

APPENDIX C

Decorations and Awards

EGYPT 1885

COMPANION, ORDER OF ST MICHAEL AND ST GEORGE

Lieutenant Colonel F.C. Denison

SOUTH AFRICA

VICTORIA CROSS

Captain H.Z.C. Cockburn (with RCD)

MENTION IN DEPATCHES

Lance Corporal J.C. Bond (with 2 CMR)
Sergeant E.W. Hodgins (with 2 CMR)
Private F.C. Page (with RCR)

THE FIRST WORLD WAR

VICTORIA CROSS

Acting Sergeant T.W. Holmes
Lieutenant G.T. Lyall (with 102nd Battalion)

COMMANDER, ORDER OF THE BRITISH EMPIRE

Lieutenant Colonel R.W. Stayner

DISTINGUISHED SERVICE ORDER

Lieutenant Colonel W.W. Denison
Lieutenant Colonel H.D.L. Gordon
Major C.H. McLean
Lieutenant Colonel W.R. Patterson
Major W.V. Sifton
Lieutenant Colonel S.F. Smith (with CLH)
Lieutenant Colonel R.W. Stayner
Lieutenant Colonel A.E. Taylor

MILITARY CROSS

Lieutenant A. Bean
Lieutenant A.H. Black
Captain H.A. Blake
Captain L.B. Bumstead (and bar)
Acting Major G. Clark
Lieutenant A. Clarke
Major W.E.L. Coleman
Major H.C. Davis, RCAMC (and bar)
Captain W.H. Davis, Chaplain
Lieutenant A.W. Deacon
Lieutenant T.W.E. Dixon
Lieutenant R.S. Dunlop
Captain A.J. Everett (and bar)

Acting Major M.M. Hart (and bar)
Lieutenant M.B. Hastings
Lieutenant G. Heightington
Lieutenant R.M. Hood (with Siberia Force)
Lieutenant P.N. Horton (with 58th Bn)
Captain C. Lea
Acting Major A.P. Menzies
Lieutenant R. Mitchell
Lieutenant E.V. McMillan
Lieutenant M.W. MacDowell
Lieutenant A.H. MacFarlane
Major A.A. MacKenzie
Lieutenant A.G. Moore (with 54th Bn)
Captain P.D. Poyser
Lieutenant F.W. Rous
Major W.H. Scott, RCAMC
Lieutenant Colonel R.W. Stayner
Lieutenant E.A. Steer
Lieutenant F.C. Thomson
Captain P.C. Tidy
Captain N.V. Waddell
Lieutenant R.H. Warne

DISTINGUISHED CONDUCT MEDAL

Lieutenant A.E. Griffin (as CSM)
Lieutenant C.K. Hoag
Lieutenant G.L.M. Howard (as RSM)
Lieutenant R.L. Layton
Lieutenant W. Nodwell
Private G.A. Bell
Sergeant G. Carr
Lance Corporal R.J. Clarke
Corporal S.T. Foster
Company Sergeant Major W.R. Goodchild (and bar)
Lance Corporal J.H. Hannah
Sergeant L. Harding
Regimental Sergeant Major A.W. Hawkey
Private H.E. Heggart, MM
Private D. Huyck
Sergeant D.W. Laycock
Company Sergeant Major R. McQuarrie
Company Sergeant Major J.B. Mitchell
Lance Corporal W.C. Mitchell
Sergeant N. Nicholas
Sergeant W. Older
Private J.A. Post
Sergeant G.F. Price
Sergeant C. Routledge
Company Sergeant Major L.O. Rule
Corporal C.R. Salsbury

Company Sergeant Major R.H. Sanders
Sergeant P.J. Seeley, MM
Sergeant E. Skellern
Sergeant E.E. Snelgar
Sergeant J.J. Spilsbury
Private J.W. Stewart
Private W. Todd
Sergeant P. Turner
Private R.W. Wilson
Company Sergeant Major E.C. Woodroof

MILITARY MEDAL

Lieutenant E. Davison
Lieutenant G.B. Dixon
Lieutenant T.W.E. Dixon
Lieutenant P.W. Drakes
Lieutenant A.E. Griffin
Lieutenant J.C. Hartley
Lieutenant N.E. McDonald
Lieutenant W. Nodwell
Sergeant F. Arbour (and bar)
Corporal E. Arlington
Private B. Arnold
Private R.G. Beasley
Private F.W. Boyd
Private L. Butler
Sergeant W.R. Carruthers
LSergeant H.J. Clarke
Sergeant B.C. Connelly
Private W.P. Coyne
CSM M. Crawford
Sergeant N.R. Crowe
Private J. Davison
Private C.J. Davis
Private A.W. Dore
Sergeant C.D. Dougherty (and bar)
Sergeant D. Duncan
Private T.D. Elson
Private J. Evans
Sergeant T.H. Fitchett
Sergeant A.L. Folliott
Corporal W.H. Fulford
Private J.R. Galbraith
Private G. Garbutt
Private G.M. Gibb
Sergeant C.A. Glass
Private J. Gordon
Sergeant W.E. Greenough
Sergeant E.C. Gurnett
Private H.E. Heggart (and bar)
Private H. Henderson

Private C.D. Hicks
Private J. Hocking
Lance Corporal R.R. Hodgkinson
Sergeant W. Houghton
Corporal W.H. Hunting
Corporal E. Ingleby (and bar)
Sergeant H.W. Izzard
Private C.A. Jones
Corporal H. Kee (and bar) (with Div Sigs)
Sergeant H.T. Kerr
Sergeant J.F. Lester
Private P. Lofthouse
CSM T.P. Martin
Private W.L. Masters
Private J.S. Matthews
Sergeant A.D. McCuskill
Lance Corporal H.C. McIntosh
Sergeant J. McKee
Lance Corporal F.J. McMullen
Lance Corporal K. Merriam
Sergeant R.D. Murphy
Private A. Napier
Private F.W. Oram (and bar)
Sergeant H.E. Page
Private B. Parker
Private C. Parker
Corporal O. Petit
Sergeant E.V. Pettie
Sergeant A.H. Plummer
Sergeant H.P. Poisson
Private J. Reed
Lance Corporal D.L. Reekie
Lance Corporal E.J.W. Richards
Private E. Robbins
Sergeant D.R. Robertson
Sergeant G.H. Rolphe
Sergeant F. Rose
Private D.E. Sale
Sergeant P.J. Seeley
Private W.. Sharman
Private C.E. Sheppard
Sergeant G. Sims
Private E. Stevens
Private J.E. Storey
Corporal W.J.R. Thompson
Lance Corporal J.M. Totten
Private A .Vhalik
Private J.H. Wainwright
Private H. Wall
Private W.K. Waters
Private J. Welsh
Private V.R. Whitehead

MENTION IN DESPATCHES

Company Sergeant Major A.J. Abbott
Lieutenant A.H. Black
Lieutenant H.A. Bostock
Private P. Butler

Major W.W. Denison
Lieutenant T.W.E. Dixon
Lieutenant D.S. Fleek
Lieutenant G.D. Fleming
Captain H. Franks
Lieutenant Colonel H.D.L. Gordon
Major A.S. Hamilton
Lieutenant G.L.M. Howard
Acting Major A.P. Menzies
Captain L.C. Mills
Lieutenant R. Mitchell
Major C.H. McLean
Lieutenant Colonel W.R. Patterson
Captain T.J. Rutherford
Major W.V. Sifton
Lieutenant Colonel S.F. Smith
Lieutenant Colonel R.W. Stayner
Captain A.E. Taylor
Captain P.C. Tidy
Captain J.R. Woods
Sergeant W.E.D. Cottrell
Sergeant M.H. Featherstonehaugh
Sergeant E.J. Flood
Private C. Gervais
RQMS A.C. Roberts

CROIX DE GUERRE

Lance Corporal C.N. Bilton
Captain H.H. Blake
Sergeant L.W. Cline
Private R.M. Hood
Private P. Lofthouse
Captain G.F. MacDuff
Lieutenant Colonel W.N. Moorehouse
Captain R.W. Warnica
Sergeant A.W. Yeates

POST FIRST WORLD WAR

KNIGHT OF THE ORDER OF THE BRITISH EMPIRE

Captain Sir Frederick Banting, MC

SECOND WORLD WAR

DISTINGUISHED SERVICE ORDER

Major G.A. Burton
Major A.H. Crosbie
Brigadier I.H. Cumberland
Lieutenant Colonel J.W. Eaton (with 8 PLNBH)
Lieutenant Colonel A.K. Jordan
Lieutenant Colonel G.D. de S. Wotherspoon
   (with SAR)

OFFICER, ORDER OF THE BRITISH EMPIRE

Lieutenant Colonel I.H. Cumberland

MILITARY CROSS

Lieutenant D.J. Chant
Lieutenant C.S. Wass

MEMBER, ORDER OF THE BRITISH EMPIRE

Major M.W. Rawlinson
Captain R.C. Rutherford (with 5 Armd Bde)

DISTINGUISHED CONDUCT MEDAL

Corporal H.D. Stitt

MILITARY MEDAL

WO2 W.C. Clarkson
Trooper T.E. Dickenson
Sergeant I.R. Johns, RC Sigs
Sergeant W.A. Johnston
Corporal T.A.M. Leadbetter
Lance Sergeant T.W. Ruff
WO2 A.H. Russell
Lance Corporal D.A. Spence

BRITISH EMPIRE MEDAL

Trooper R.A. Johnson

MENTION IN DESPATCH

Major C.F. Baker (two awards)
Captain F.O. Classey
Captain J.A. McKechan
Lieutenant J. Pallett
Sergeant K.J. Sewell
Warrant Officer II T.G. Neelands
Sergeant C.G. Thomson
Corporal Neil MacDonald
Trooper G. Nieuspiel

POST-SECOND WORLD WAR

OFFICER OF THE ORDER OF CANADA

Colonel G.A. Burton
Colonel the Honourable H.N.R. Jackman

MEMBER OF THE ORDER OF CANADA

Lieutenant Colonel J.D. Crashley
Lieutenant M.G. Sifton

OFFICER, ORDER OF MILITARY MERIT

Lieutenant Colonel J.J. Dorfman

MEMBER, ORDER OF MILITARY MERIT

Captain E.G. Brown
Major W. Thomas

BRITISH EMPIRE MEDAL

Corporal W. Downs (with RCAMC in Korea)

Honour Roll

THE BOER WAR
Trooper F.C. Page

THE FIRST WORLD WAR
Lieutenant E.A. Abbey
Private E.M. Abbey, MM
Private E.P. Adley
Private W. Ager
Private J. Aldcroft
Private G.T. Allan
Private L. Allen
Private F.J. Amos
Lance Corporal D. Anderson
Private F. Anderson
Private F.J. Anderson
Private M.R. Angel
Private J. Angus, 216th Battalion
Private V. Arbie
Private G.E. Archer
Private T.J. Armstong
Private A.I. Arnett
Private H.F. Arno
Private A.H. Ashdown
Lance Sergeant J.H. Ashworth
Private S. Asselstine
Private R.T. Aston
Private J.T. Astridge
Private C.H. Atchison
Private M.A. Attwood
Private J.B. Babineau
Private H.W. Bagnall
Private A.M. Bailey
Private K.G.F. Baldwin
Private C. Ball
Private G.H. Ball
Private J.L. Ball
Private J.F. Balmer
Private G.R. Balsden
Private H.E. Barker
Private D.N. Barnhardt
Sergeant L.W. Barnhart
Private J. Barry
Corporal F.C. Barter
Private H.E. Batch
Private P.G. Battin
Private J.T. Baxter, 7th Canadian
    Mounted Rifles
Private A. Beasley
Private R.J. Beaton

Corporal W.C. Beaven
Private T. Beck
Private I. Belaire
Private R.J. Bell
Private J. Bender
Private F. Bennett
Private G.E. Benson
Private C.J. Beyer
Company Sergeant Major A.G.
    Biggs
Private S.S. Biggs
Private W.G. Billington
Private R.E. Birch
Corporal W. Birse
Sergeant C. Bittle
Private A. Black
Private C. Blair, 216th Battalion
Lance Corporal J.F. Blake
Private L. Blake
Private R.W. Blaney
Private J.T. Blayney
Private T.H. Bocking
Private C. Bollingbroke
Sergeant H.F. Bonham
Private R.H. Boreham
Private A. Bossart
Lieutenant A.H. Bostock, MID
Private J.N. Bowman
Lance Sergeant H.W. Boyce
Private W.H. Boyce
Lieutenant M.B.H. Boyd
Private I. Bradley
Private G.B. Brake
Private C. Brash
Private M.H. Breakwell
Private M.W. Breen
Private W.B. Brett
Private C.B. Brewer
Private H. Brine
Private A.W. Brock
Private A.E. Bromfield
Private A.E. Brookman
Private T. Brooks
Private A.E. Brown
Lieutenant A.N. Brown
Private E. Brown
Private G.A. Brown
Private J.P. Brown
Private W.C. Brown
Private W.S. Brown

Private F.G. Bruce
Private G.W. Brunton
Private W.E. Bryant
Private J.R. Bryson
Private C.I. Buchanan
Private E.J. Buckby
Private C.A. Buckley
Sergeant H. Buie
Lance Sergeant J.A. Bull
Private W. Bullock
Private W.J. Burke
Lance Corporal E.E. Burns
Private J.J. Burrow
Private W. Burrows
Private G.E. Burt
Lieutenant W.G. Butson
Private A. Byers
Private J.J. Byers
Private W. Cade
Private F. Cain
Private G.W. Cain
Private G.C. Caldwell
Private W.A. Callow
Private C.J. Campbell
Lieutenant J.D. Campbell
Private W.F. Campbell
Private R.J. Canfor
Lance Corporal D.G. Cant
Private F. Carfrae
Private R. Carfrae
Private W.A. Carlyle
Private O.H. Carr
Acting Corporal W.J. Carr
Sergeant M.C. Carradus
Private A. Carroll
Sergeant C. Carruthers
Private J.F. Carten
Lance Corporal J.W. Carter
Private T. Carter
Private C.C.A. Carton
Private E. Cary
Lance Corporal R.C. Chamney
Private G. Chapman
Sergeant M.S. Chapman
Private A.H. Chisholm
Private L. Clanfield
Private C. Clark
Private G.S. Clark
Corporal S.O. Clark
Corporal W.T. Clark

Lance Sergeant H.J. Clarke, MM
Lieutenant L.E. Clarke
Private C.C. Clarke
Private J.S. Clayton
Private J. Clementson
Private G.H.E. Coates
Lieutenant H.W. Cockshutt
Private G. Coker
Private E.W. Cole
Sergeant A. Coleman
Private A.J. Collins
Sergeant J.B. Collins
Private R.H. Collins
Sergeant C.H. Collyer
Private J.E. Commodore
Private F. Conbeer
Private M.P. Conlan
Private B.C. Connelly, MM
Private S. Cook
Private W.H. Cook
Private C.A. Cooke
Private D.G. Cooke
Private G. Cooper
Private G.K. Cooper
Private W.J. Cooper
Private J.F. Corbett
Corporal W.J. Corr
Sergeant W.E.D. Cottrell, MID
Lance Corporal R.J. Courtney
Private A.E. Cousins
Private J. Couture
Private W. Cowler
Private H.J. Cox
Private N. Cox
Private T.H. Cox
Private R.A. Cragg
Private R.J. Craig
Private J.E. Crane
Private J.W. Crawford
Company Sergeant Major M.
    Crawford, MM
Private H. Crocker
Private C.E. Cromwell
Private D.L. Crowley
Private W. Cruickshank
Private T.L. Cuffe
Private A.J. Cuppage
Private J.W. Curran
Private E.J. Dadey

Private F.C. Daffin
Private A.R. Dafoe
Private W.A. Dafoe
Private W.H. Dainton
Private L.W. Dalton
Corporal A. Dalzell
Private R. Daniels
Private C. Dark
Private A.J. Davey
Private W.G. Davidson
Private J.G. Davies
Honorary Captain D.H. Davis, MC
Acting Sergeant G.J. Davis
Private P. Davis
Private W.C. Davis
Lieutenant E. Davison, MM
Private W.J. Davy
Private T. Dean
Private W.A. Defoe
Private H. Degrey
Private E. Dennington
Private L.G. Denyes
Private H.J. Devlin
Private G. Dixon
Private J.I. Dixon
Captain T.W.E. Dixon, MC, MM
Captain J.M. Dobie
Private J.F. Dolan
Private P. Donlan, 216th Battalion
Private W.S. Doran
Corporal B. Dornan
Private E. Douglas
Private G. Douglas
Private G.F. Douglas
Private W. Douglas
Private W.B. Downs
Private M.J. Dowsley
Private H. Drackley
Lieutenant P.W. Drakes, MM
Lance Corporal R. Dron
Lance Corporal E.C. Drury
Private J.A. Dubey
Private D. Dudgeon
Private R. Duke
Private R. Dundas
Company Sergeant Major A.H. Dunlop
Private J.H. Dunn
Private J.R. Dunn
Private A.D. Dunoon
Lieutenant L. Dunsford
Private H. Dunsmure
Private L. Dupuis
Private J. Easton
Private D.J. Eastwood
Corporal H.J. Eastwood
Lieutenant J. Eaton
Private R. Eccles

Lance Sergeant H.J. Edmunds
Private J. Edwards
Private A.E. Elford
Private C.G. Ellis
Private James Ellis
Private John Ellis
Private L.W. Embury
Private J.E. Emmott
Private A. Errett
Private R.F. Evans
Private H.A. Fairbairn
Private H.W. Fairway
Private E.W. Falls
Private H.L. Farrington
Private H.B. Ferris
Private H.T. Ferry
Private F. Filey
Private G.C. Findlay
Private S.J. Finn
Private W. Finnie
Private F.E. Flaherty
Private W.J.E. Flanagan
Private J.A. Flinn
Private W.C. Flint
Private C.R. Foames
Private M.J. Foran
Private W.G. Forbes
Corporal F. Forsdyke
Private G.E. Forsey
Private J.L. Fortier
Private C.R. Foster
Private R.W. Foster
Private G.M. Fountain
Private A. Fox
Private D. Freeman
Private M. Freeman
Private C.B. Frood
Private W.I. Fulford
Private G.W. Fulton
Private F. Funnell
Private F.E. Furry
Private C.W. Galbraith
Private R.C. Gale
Private F.L. Galvin
Private H.L. Gardner
Lieutenant J.U. Garrow
Private W. Geary
Private F.S. Gerry
Private A. Gibson
Private W.C. Giddye
Private G. Girvin
Private W.J. Glennie
Private C.R. Godfrey
Private T. Godin
Private D.H. Goodson
Private A. Gordon
Private A. Gordon, 216th Battalion
Private W.E. Gordon

Sergeant F.J. Gorman
Private J.A. Goudie
Private B. Gough
Private W.H. Gough
Private H.J. Gould
Private R.W. Gowdy
Private W.G. Gramson
Private D.B. Gray
Private E. Green
Private H.A. Green
Sergeant V. Green
Private E.J. Greengrass
Private E.T. Greenwood
Private C.A. Gregg
Private G.F. Griffin
Private W. Griffin
Company Quartermaster Sergeant H.M. Grimmer
Private T.H. Groves
Private A. Guay
Private A. Habick
Private J.W. Haddock
Private D. Haggerty
Private J.A.M. Haig
Private C. Haight
Private D. Hair
Private W.H. Hale
Corporal J.A. Hall
Private H. Hamill
Private E.W. Hanna
Lance Corporal J.H. Hannah, DCM
Private R. Hannah
Private K.A.C. Hansson
Sergeant L. Harding, DCM
Private F.G. Hardingham
Private F. Harford
Private G.O. Harkin
Corporal S.R. Harmon
Private H.T. Harper
Private T.F. Harris
Private G.S. Harrison
Private J. Hart
Private C. Hartin
Corporal F.J. Hartrick
Private J. Harwick
Private W.H. Haslam
Private J.E. Hatch
Private J. Hatheway
Private C.W. Havens
Private J.A. Haworth
Private V.A. Haydon
Private J.R. Heaps
Lieutenant G. Heighington, MC
Private G.S. Henderson
Private J.R. Henderson
Private G. Hennessy
Private M.G. Henry

Private J.F. Heron
Private C.E. Heslip
Private W.F. Hetherington
Private W. Hewitt
Private A.A. Hewson
Corporal W. Hickey
Private J. Hicks
Private S. Hicks
Private R.R. Hill
Private G.H. Hillier
Private D.J. Hiltz
Private R.R. Hobden
Lance Corporal H.B. Hodge
Private R.S. Hodge
Private J. Hogan
Private E. Hogg
Private W.J. Hollinger
Sergeant A. Holmes
Private W.H. Holt
Private E.D. Honeyford
Private W.J. Hopkins
Lieutenant A.M. Horner
Private J. Howard
Private T. Howard
Private E. Hriskewich
Private F. Huff
Private C.A. Hughes
Private E. Hughes
Private E.J. Hughes
Private F. Hughes
Corporal J. Hulland
Sergeant P. Hunt
Private S.E. Hunt
Private W.G. Hurley
Private W.M. Hurley
Private T. Hutton
Private W.G. Hyde
Private F. Ilcken
Private W.W. Ingram
Private H.J. Irwin
Private R. Irwin
Private R.I. Jackson
Private D. James
Private E.E. James
Private G. Jarvis
Private A. Jerome
Private A. Jocque
Private H. Johns
Private E.A. Johnson
Private H.H. Johnson
Private W.H. Johnson
Lieutenant L.C. Johnston
Private G. Johnstone
Private A. Jones
Private J.H. Jones, 109421
Private J.H. Jones, 637161
Private F.G. Jordan
Private H.A. Judd

Private R. Kallar
Private W.E. Keating
Private T.J. Keegan
Private P.C. Keith
Private J.B. Kellar
Private J. Kelly
Private J.P. Kelly
Corporal L.N. Kelsey
Sergeant E.H. Kemp
Private J.R. Kennedy
Private R.C. Kerr
Private W. Keyworth
Private G. Kimmett
Private A. Kimpston
Private A. Kish
Acting Sergeant G. Knowles
Private P.L. Krell
Private H. Kurtz
Lance Corporal J.F.B. Kyle
Private E.W. Lackey
Private P. Lacroix
Private F. Laflamme
Private J. Laird
Private C.D. Lake
Private J.W. Lambert
Private A.G. Lammon
Corporal J.W. Lamont
Private R.T. Lamont
Private J.X. Landry
Private W. Lang
Private W.A. Lang
Private J.A. Langdon
Lance Corporal W. Langridge
Private F. Lappin
Private W. Latham
Sergeant P.R. Lawson
Lieutenant F.P.H. Layton
Lieutenant C. Lea, MC
Private F. Leach
Corporal E. Lebas
Private J.M. Ledingham
Private G. Lee
Private J. Lee
Private J.B. Leemon
Private A. Lemelin, 7th Canadian
    Mounted Rifles
Private J. Lemon
Private P. Lemon
Private S. Lenton
Private R. Leppard
Private F. Lesperance
Private W. Lever
Private A. Lewis
Private E.P. Lewis
Private F.H. Lewis
Private A.H. Libby
Private A. Lineker
Private R.H. Linn

Private J.A. Livingstone
Corporal P.R. Lizmore
Private E.J. Lloyd
Private F.L. Logue
Private J.M. Loney
Private H.O. Long
Private L.G. Long
Lance Corporal S.H. Longmoor
Lance Corporal E.W. Lowrey
Lance Corporal T. Lowry
Private W.F. Lyle
Private T.R. Lyons
Private D.J. MacArthur
Lance Corporal A.D. MacDiarmid
Private A.T. MacDonald
Private C.W. Macdonald
Sergeant E.B. MacDonald
Private J.B. Macdonald
Private P.J. MacDonald
Captain D.R. MacKay
Company Quartermaster Sergeant
    R. Mackenzie
Private K.H. MacLeod
Private W.G. Maclurkin
Lance Corporal R.E. Macpherson
Private T.J. Mahy
Private C.S. Malcolm
Sergeant F.L. Manderson
Private H.G. Mansfield
Private W.P. Mansfield
Lance Corporal D. Manson
Private W.J. Markell
Private G.A. Marshall
Private W. Marshall
Private E. Martin
Private J.W. Martin
Private R.M. Martin
Private T.L. Mather
Private J.G. Mathias, 216th
    Battalion
Sergeant J.T. May
Private A. McAlpine
Private T. McAree
Acting Sergeant C.H. McAuley
Private J.C. McBride
Private C. McCabe
Lance Sergeant J.F. McCarthy
Private J.R. McCartney
Private C.M. McClure
Corporal W.S. McCluskey
Private W.H. McConnachie
Private H.F. McConnell
Private J.P. McCormick
Private R.W.J. McCormack
Acting Corporal W. McCullagh
Lieutenant A.D. McDonald
Private H.R. McDonald
Private H. McDonell

Private A.C. McDowall
Private P. McEdis
Private L. McFadden
Private E.A. McFarlane
Sergeant N.A. McGuire
Private H. McIntosh
Lance Corporal H.C. McIntosh,
    MM
Private G.C. McKean
Private A. McKenzie
Lance Corporal W.C. McKenzie
Private W.J. McKessock
Private J.W. McLachlan, 216th
    Battalion
Private W. McLarnon
Private C. McLean
Private J.L. McLellan
Private D. McLeod
Corporal J.A. McLeod
Private W.E. McMaster
Private D.T. McMillan
Corporal J.H. McMullon
Private W.C. McNair
Private D. McPhail
Private D.L. McPhee
Lance Corporal R.E. McPherson
Private F. McTaggart
Private J. McVittie
Private H. Mears
Private T. Meddings
Private C.A. Merkley
Private A.S. Merritt
Private H. Mesick
Private P.D. Metcalfe
Private E.J. Metherell
Private W. Middleton
Private C.J. Mildenhall
Private E. Miles
Private C.S. Miller
Private D. Miller
Private E.E. Miller
Private H. Mills
Lieutenant H.M. Mills
Private B.G. Minard
Private S.A. Mindle
Private J.S. Mitchell
Private H.A. Mombourquette
Private J.G. Monds
Lieutenant H.E. Moore
Private J. Moore
Sergeant F. Moorman
Private T.W.H. Morfitt
Private E.C. Morgan
Private A. Morris
Lieutenant G. Morrisey
Private A.A. Mort
Private D.W. Mossman
Private H. Mouck

Private E.J. Moylan
Captain W.R. Muirhead
Private J.T. Mullaly
Private B.P. Munns
Private W.F. Munro
Private W.C. Murison
Private M.J. Murphy
Private E.J. Murray
Lieutenant J.R. Myers
Private R.P. Myers
Corporal D.M. Neilson
Private J.J. Nellis
Private J.H. Nelson
Private H.H. Neville
Private W.H. Newell
Private A.S. Newton
Private R. Newton
Lieutenant C.L.W. Nicholson
Private M.S. Nicholson
Private C.F. Norman
Private A.A. Norris
Acting Sergeant H.L. Nown
Private C. Nutter
Private J. Nutter
Private J.T. O'Connell
Private D. O'Kane
Private F.J. Oldfield
Private H. Olliver
Private F. Openshaw
Private A.A. Orrett
Private J.H. Orser
Private C. Ouderkirk
Private V. Panacewich
Private E.W. Parkin
Private T.H. Parks
Private H. Parnell
Private T. Partington
Private G.H. Partridge
Private A. Paterson
Lance Sergeant W.J. Paterson
Private N. Paul
Private E. Payne
Private E.N. Peachey
Lieutenant C.H. Peaker
Corporal E.A. Pearce
Private H.N. Pearce
Private G.B. Pearson
Private J.W. Peet
Private F.W. Perry
Private T. Perry
Private T.L. Perry
Private N.B. Peters
Private S. Peters
Private O. Petit, MM
Corporal J. Pettigrew
Private E.W. Philips
Private G. Phillips
Lance Sergeant T.J. Phillips

Lieutenant H.V. Pickering
Lieutenant B.C. Pierce
Private O.W. Pingle
Private I.A. Pinkerton
Sergeant H.P. Poisson, MM
Private J.H. Polson
Private B.N. Post
Lance Corporal W. Post
Sergeant W.A.O. Potter
Private A. Potvin
Private W.E. Powell
Private H. Powers
Private W.J. Powers
Lance Corporal B.C. Powys
Sergeant F. Pratt, MM
Private R.V. Pratt
Lieutenant J.H. Prescott
Private A. Price
Company Sergeant Major L.D. Pridham
Private J. Pridmore
Private A. Priestley
Private C.C.D. Proud
Private R.J. Purdy
Private A.H. Rackliff
Private D. Rae
Private G. Rae
Private M. Rae
Private W. Rand
Private R.E. Ranger
Private C.L. Ratchford
Private G.A. Ratcliffe
Private W.D. Raybould
Private G.T. Raynor
Private W.H. Reddick
Private F.W. Redfern
Private C.B. Reid
Private G. Reid
Private H. Reid
Private G.A. Rennie
Sergeant W.J. Reynolds
Private J.A. Ricard
Lieutenant E.G. Richards
Private R. Riddell
Private G. Riddle
Lance Corporal W. Riddle
Corporal S.E. Rigby
Private W.S. Ritchie
Private S. Robb
Sergeant D.R. Robertson, MM
Private R.S. Robinson
Private R.W. Robinson
Private S. Robinson
Private A.R. Rodger
Private G.W. Rollings
Private T. Ross
Captain H.C. Rounds
Lieutenant F.W. Rous, MC

Private H.C. Roushorn
Sergeant C.F. Routledge, DCM
Private H.T.J. Rowe
Private J.A. Rudd
Lieutenant E. Rule
Lance Corporal P.D. Russell
Private W.T. Russell
Private G.H. Sadler
Private D. Sale, MM
Private F.J. Sammon
Private J.C. Sandercock
Private W.G. Sandercock
Private W.H. Sanders
Private J.M. Saunders
Private G.H.L. Schram
Private F. Schwardfager
Private A.W.G. Scott
Major H.A. Scott
Private W.E. Scully
Lance Sergeant G. Seabourne
Private R. Sears
Private J.R. Sedore
Sergeant G.E. Seehaver
Private D.L. Seguin
Sergeant R.J.I. Sewell
Private H. Shardlow
Private W.J. Sharp
Private J.P. Shaw
Private O. Shaw
Private J.W. Shearer
Private J.V. Sheffield
Private W. Shell
Lieutenant E.C. Shepperd
Corporal B. Sheridan
Private S. Shine
Private R. Shorey
Lieutenant D.C. Sims
Private M. Sinclair
Private W.J. Sinclair
Private J. Smit
Private A. Smith
Private A.D. Smith
Corporal A.J. Smith
Private E.C. Smith
Private F.A. Smith
Private G.E. Smith
Private H. Smith
Private James Smith
Private Joseph Smith
Private J.P. Smith
Private R.B. Smith
Private R.G. Smith
Private R.J. Smith
Private S. Smith
Private W.H.L. Smith
Private W.J. Smith
Private W. Smoker
Private J.J. Smollen

Lance Corporal C.W.R. Smyth
Private M. Smyth
Private S.R. Smyth
Private N.F. Somerville
Squadron Sergeant Major E. Southgate, 9th Mississauga Horse
Lance Corporal T. Speakman
Private G.E. Spencer
Private G.A. Spotten
Private H.I.J. Stamp
Private F. Stanley
Private W.C. Stark
Private T.R. Stead
Private L. Stewart
Corporal D.H. Still
Sergeant R.M. Stirling
Private J. Stoddard
Private A.J. Sumara
Private E.W. Sutton
Private G. Sutton
Lance Sergeant L.C. Sutton
Private A. Swan
Private H. Sweet
Captain J.H. Symons
Private R.W.H. Tait
Sergeant J.A. Tamblingson
Private G.E. Taylor
Private J.S. Taylor
Private L.R. Taylor
Private W.A. Taylor
Private W.H. Teal
Private W.F. Thomas
Private A.F. Thompson
Private E. Thompson
Private G. Thompson
Private H.J. Thompson
Private J. Thompson
Sergeant J. Thompson
Private R.A. Thompson, 216th Battalion
Corporal V. Thompson, 9th Mississauga Horse
Acting Sergeant V.D. Thompson
Corporal A.B. Thomson
Sergeant M. Tickner
Private S. Tink
Private W. Toms
Lance Corporal W.J. Toohmey
Private D.O.A. Townshend
Lance Corporal B. Tracey
Private S.J.B. Tracey
Private B.J. Traviss
Private G.R. Turner
Private H.W. Turner
Private R.S. Turner
Private T.A. Turpin
Lieutenant H.W. Uglow

Private W. Unger
Private R.J. Urquhart
Lance Corporal P.W. Vanduyse
Private F. Vassler
Private E.P. Vincent
Private M.A. Voccoro
Lance Corporal E. Wadham
Private R. Wailing
Private C.E. Wainman
Private H. Wakefield
Private C. Walker
Private F. Walker
Private F.D. Walker
Private W.H. Walker
Private R.D. Walton
Private D.J. Ward
Private J.E. Ward
Private P.W. Wardle
Private J.E. Warren
Private C.R. Watson
Sergeant J. Watt
Private J.B. Waugh
Private W.S. Weatherston
Private H.R. Weatherup
Private C. Webb
Private J. Webb
Sergeant F.W. Webber
Private G. Webber
Private R. Wells
Private M. Welsh
Private H. West
Private H.C. Westley
Private J.W. Wharrie
Lance Sergeant G. Wheeler
Private C. White
Private G.H. White
Private A.E. Whyte
Private J.I. Whyte
Private R. Wilcock
Private A. Wiley
Private W.L. Wilkinson
Private J. Williams
Corporal M. Williams
Private T. Williams
Private W.D. Williams
Private A. Williamson
Private H.A. Willis
Private F. Wilson
Private J. Wilson
Private N.F. Wilson
Private S. Wilson
Private W.J. Wilson
Private F.S. Wilton
Private J. Wiltshire
Private G.E. Wing
Private F. Wingate
Private J. Winnie
Private E. Wood, 144969

Private E. Wood, 835208
Private H.R. Wood
Lance Corporal J.M. Wood
Private R.C. Wood
Private N. Woodcox
Sergeant R. Wooding
Company Sergeant Major E.C.
    Woodroof, DCM
Private A.C. Woods
Private G. Woods
Private H.A. Woods
Captain J.R. Woods, MID
Private C.T. Woolley
Private H.N. Wright
Lieutenant P. Wright
Corporal J. Young
Private S. Young

THE SECOND WORLD WAR

Trooper K.L. Abercrombie
Trooper A.J. Anderson
Trooper C.L. Axtell
Trooper V.D. Badgley
Trooper R.E. Balfour

Trooper W.A. Beeswax
Lance Corporal G. Bohas
Trooper N.L. Cameron
Trooper W.H. Campbell
Acting Sergeant A.E. Chambers
Lieutenant J.L. Chesney
Lieutenant F.V. Clapp
Lieutenant J.F. Clarke
Trooper G.J. Class
Lieutenant F.J. Coleman
Trooper H. Conn
Trooper H.E. Cook
Trooper J.P. Copeland
Trooper C.H. Craig
Lance Corporal H.F. Deschenes
Trooper L.E. Eaton
Trooper C. Fairhead
Lieutenant E.D. Friend
Trooper J. Getty
Lieutenant G.D. Gibsone
Corporal J. Gilbert
Sergeant E. Gillam
Trooper W.H. Goodall
Trooper L.F. Graff

Lance Corporal T.M. Hackett
Corporal G. Hadley
Trooper J.E. Hanley
Trooper G.E. Hayward
Trooper W.A. Henderson
Lance Corporal C.B. Henry
Trooper S.W. Hill
Trooper H.R. Holmes
Trooper K.W. Innes
Corporal W.G. Johnston
Trooper E.R. Kaulback
Trooper T.N. Lade
Trooper C.M. Lampman
Trooper V.H. Lane
Lieutenant J.B. McBride
Lieutenant L.E. McCormack
Trooper W.S. McLean
Trooper J.S. Moore
Trooper K.P. Morrison
Trooper E.G. Moulton
Lieutenant J.M. Murray
Trooper J. O'Halloran
Trooper E.F. Oiney
Trooper L.C. Pelletier

Trooper A.E. Perrott
Trooper P.J. Robillard
Lieutenant E.A. Rodgman
Sergeant A.W. Rogers
Trooper C. Rumbles
Trooper T.R.W.B. Scollick
Lance Corporal C.H. Simmons
Trooper G. Snider
Corporal H.D. Stitt, DCM
Lance Corporal J.H. Strutt
Sergeant C.G. Tompson, MID
Trooper E. Watson
Trooper F.H. Willet
Trooper C.M. Wilson
Trooper C. Winterburn
Lieutenant G.C. Yavis
Trooper A.C. Young

KOREA

Lance Corporal J.W. Kennedy
Trooper J. Letkeman

Bibliography

Primary Sources

National Archives of Canada: War Diaries, Operational Reports and other files of, among others, the 4th Canadian Mounted Rifles 1915-1918, 3rd Canadian Armoured Reconnaissance Regiment (The Governor General's Horse Guards) 1941-1945, 5th Canadian Armoured Division 1943-1945 in Records Group 24. Annual Reports of the Inspector of Cavalry on the Governor General's Body Guard (1899-1935) and the Mississauga Horse (1905-1935) in Records Group 6.

Directorate of History and Heritage: Annual Historical Reports and other files.

Governor General's Horse Guards Regimental Archives: Operational Reports, Part I and Part II Orders, Personal Diaries, Scrapbooks of Newspaper Clippings 1885-1945, Regimental Albums, miscellaneous files.

Regimental Histories

Captain Frederick C. Denison, *Historical Record of the Governor-General's Body Guard and its Standing Orders,* Toronto: Hunter Rose & Co., 1876.

Lieutenant-Colonel George T. Denison (III), *Soldiering in Canada,* Toronto: Morang & Co., 1880.

Lieutenant-Colonel George T. Denison (III), *History of the Fenian Raid on Fort Erie: An Account of the Battle of Ridgeway,* Toronto: Rollo & Dunn, 1866.

Ernest J. Chambers, *The Governor-General's Body Guard,* Toronto: E.L. Ruddy, 1902.

Lieutenant-Colonel William H. Merritt, *Regimental Standing Orders of the Governor-General's Body Guard; with Prefatory Historical Summary,* Toronto: Hunter Rose & Co., 1910.

S.G. Bennett, *The 4th Canadian Mounted Rifles, 1914-1919,* Toronto: privately printed, 1926.

____, *The Governor General's Horse Guards, 1939-1945,* Toronto: Canadian Military Journal, 1954.

Other Published Sources

Daniel G. Dancocks, *The D-Day Dodgers: The Canadians in Italy 1943-1945,* Toronto: McClelland & Stewart, 1991.

George T. Denison (III), *Modern Cavalry,* London: Thomas Bosworth, 1868.

George T. Denison (III), *A History of Cavalry from the Earliest Times,* London: MacMillan and Co., 1877 (second edition 1913).

David Gagan, *The Denison Family of Toronto, 1792-1925,* Toronto: University of Toronto Press, 1973.

John Gardam, *Korea Volunteer,* Burnstown: General Store Publishing House, 1994.

Ernest Green, *History of the 2nd/10th Dragoons and Antecedent Corps, 1812-1946,* Unpublished manuscript (GGHG Archives)

Brereton Greenhous, *Dragoon, 1883-1983,* Ottawa, Guild of the Royal Canadian Dragoons, 1983.

J.C. Hopkins and Murat Halstead, *South Africa and the Boer-British War,* (two volumes) Toronto: J.L. Nichols & Co., 1909.

John Marteinson and Michael McNorgan, *The Royal Canadian Armoured Corps: An Illustrated History,* Toronto: Robin Brass Studio, 2000.

G.W.L. Nicholson, *The Canadian Expeditionary Forces 1914-1919,* Ottawa: Queen's Printer, 1962.

G.W.L. Nicholson, *The Canadians in Italy 1943-1945,* Ottawa: Queen's Printer, 1956.

Mark Zuehlke, *The Liri Valley: Canada's World War II Breakthrough to Rome,* Toronto: Stoddart, 2001.

Index